The Constructivist Metaphor

The Constructivist Metaphor

READING, WRITING,

AND THE MAKING OF MEANING

Nancy Nelson Spivey

Louisiana State University

Baton Rouge, Louisiana

ACADEMIC PRESS

San Diego   London   Boston   New York

Sydney   Tokyo   Toronto

This book is printed on acid-free paper. ∞

Academic Press, Inc.
525 B Street, Suite 1900, San Diego, California 92101-4495, USA
http://www.apnet.com

Academic Press Limited
24-28 Oval Road, London NW1 7DX, UK
http://www.hbuk.co.uk/ap/

Library of Congress Cataloging-in-Publication Data

Spivey, Nancy Nelson, date.
    The constructivist metaphor : reading, writing, and the making of
 meaning / by Nancy Nelson Spivey.
        p.   cm.
    Includes index.
    ISBN 0-12-657985-7 (alk. paper)
    1. Discourse analysis.   2. Constructivism (Philosophy)
 3. Structuralism.   4. Authorship.   I. Title.
 P302.S598   1996
 401'.41--dc20   96-26265
                                                       CIP

PRINTED IN THE UNITED STATES OF AMERICA
96   97   98   99   00   01   BC   9   8   7   6   5   4   3   2   1

. . . .

To Catherine, Craig, Hutton, Jennifer, Lindsey, and Wesley

Contents

Preface   xiii

Chapter I
. . . .
The Metaphor of Constructivism

A Metaphor and a Theory   2
Constructivism: An Overview   3
Historical Antecedents of Constructivism   5
    Three Conceptions   5
    Constructivist Themes and the Emerging Disciplines   9
Constructive Processes of Individuals and Groups   10
    Focus on Individuals as Agents   10
    Focus on Small Groups and Dyads as Agents   18
    Focus on Communities and Societies as Agents   19
The Shifting Lens of Constructivism   23
This Author's Perspective   26
Plan for the Book   28

Chapter II
. . . .
Remembering Bartlett

The Cambridge Milieu in Which Bartlett Worked   31
Bartlett's Work before *Remembering*   33
    Perception, Imagery, and Memory   34
    Cultural Forms   34

Cultural Change Processes   34

Remembering: Cognitive Processes   36

    Bartlett's Approach to a Study of Cognition   37

    "The War of the Ghosts" Study   38

    Transformations of Meaning   39

    Bartlett's Explanations   41

    Bartlett's Cognitive Positions Relative to Others' Positions   42

Remembering: Social Processes   44

    Social Constructs and Individuals' Responses   45

    Relations among Members of a Group   46

    Community Constructions: The Conventionalization Studies   46

    Transformations in Social Practices   47

    Bartlett's Social Positions   48

The Writing of *Remembering:* Bartlett's Composing Process   50

Bartlett's Work after *Remembering*   52

Reader's Memories of *Remembering:* Different Groups, Different Memories   53

Conclusion   54

Chapter III

Understanding as Construction

A Constructivist Tradition   57

    Bransford's Studies   57

    Some Classic Studies of Discourse Understanding   58

    Constructivist Themes   69

    The Constructivist Predicament   70

    Plan for the Remainder of the Chapter   71

The Reading of Expository Texts   71

    Conventions of Expository Discourse   72

    Readers' Constructions of Meaning for Expository Texts   75

The Reading of Stories   78

    Conventional Patterns of Stories   79

    Readers' Constructions of Meaning for Stories   81

    Affect in the Reading of Fiction   82

The Reading of Contexts and Intertexts   83

  The Sociocultural and Historical Context   83

  The More Immediate Situational Context   84

  Meaning Construction and the Intertext   86

Mental Products Constructed through Reading   88

Shifts in the Lens: Social Constructions   89

  Groups or Pairs as Agents   89

  Communities and Societies as Agents   92

Conclusion   93

A Post(modern)script   93

Chapter IV

Other Metaphors: Structuralism, Poststructuralism, and Deconstruction

Structuralism and Discourse Theory   97

  The Structuralist Movement   97

  Saussure's Structuralism   98

  Russian Formalism and Prague School Linguistics   101

  French Structuralism   103

  Structuralism and Semiotics   106

  Structuralism and Discourse Analysis   107

  The Structuralist Method   109

Poststructuralism and Discourse Theory   110

  The Development of Poststructuralism   110

  Deconstruction: A Form of Poststructuralism   113

Comparison of Constructivism with the Other Conceptions   115

  Comparison of Structuralism and Constructivism   115

  Comparison of Poststructuralism and Constructivism   118

Conclusion: Keeping Our Heads above Water   120

Chapter V

· · · · · · · · · · · · · · · · · · · ·

Composing as Construction

The Who, What, and How of Composing   123
The Author–Audience Dimension of Composing   125
    Development of the Ability to Write for Readers   126
    Nature of the Relationship between Author and Audience   128
    Effects of Audience on Writers' Constructions   129
    Writers, Readers, and the Explicitness of Texts   131
    Social and Cognitive Aspects of the Author–Audience Dimension   133
The Intertextual Dimension of Composing   133
    Writers and Their Intertextual Cues   134
    Writers and Textual Transformations   135
    Social and Cognitive Aspects of the Intertextual Dimension   137
The Co-Constructive Dimension of Composing   137
    Collaborative Writing   137
    Co-Authorship   139
    Response from Others   140
    Social and Cognitive Aspects of the Co-Constructive Dimension   144
Shifting Roles in Reading and Writing   144

Chapter VI

· ·

Discourse Synthesis: Four Studies

Discourse Synthesis: A First Study   149
    The Texts Used in Composing   149
    Transformations   154
    Quality of the Reports   161
    Summary of This Initial Study of Discourse Synthesis   162
A Developmental Study of Discourse Synthesis   163
    The Texts Used in Composing   163
    Transformations   165
    Quality of the Reports   168
    Summary of the Developmental Study   168

Discourse Synthesis and the Writing of Comparisons   169

    The Texts Used in Composing   169

    Transformations   171

    Quality of the Comparisons   176

    Summary of the Comparison Study   178

Discourse Synthesis and Disciplinary Tasks   179

    The Texts Used in Composing   180

    Overall Patterns of Organization   182

    Quality of the Syntheses   187

    Intertextual Connections   189

    Summary of the Task Study   191

Conclusion   191

Chapter VII

Textual Transformations in Written Discourse

Textual Transformations and Conventional Practices   193

Organizational Transformations   194

    Summarizing: Reducing *and* Adding   194

    Reporting on a Topic   196

    Proposing a Solution   198

    Critiquing: Commenting on a Topic   199

    Making a Causal Argument   201

Selective Transformations   202

    Criteria: Textual and Otherwise   202

    Selection and Generation   203

    Task Interpretations   204

    Form as Heuristic   206

Connective Transformations   207

    Topical Connections   207

    Whole-Text Connections   209

    Text, Intertext, and Hypertext   209

Conclusion: Readers as Writers   211

Chapter VIII

Authoring Identity

Changing Conceptions of Authorship over the Years   213
    The Medieval Author   213
    Authorship after the Printing Press   214
    The Romantic Conception   215
    Deemphasis of the Author   215
    The Rebirth of the Author   216
Authoring Identity as Construct   219
Development of Authoring Identity   223
    The Students and Their Course of Study   223
    Adoption of Disciplinary Genres and Conventions   224
    Creation of an Interrelated Body of Work   225
    Identities and Niches   233
Conclusion   234

Chapter IX

Constructive Criticism

Various Ways of Reading This Book   236
Response to Issues   237
    The Social and Cognitive Issue   238
    The Process and Product Issue   239
    The Originality and Conventionality Issue   241
Conclusion   242

References   244

Name Index   277

Subject Index   287

Preface

By studying metaphor, one discovers hidden features of one's culture and one's own thinking, as Lakoff and Turner (1988) pointed out in *More Than Cool Reason: A Field Guide to Poetic Metaphor*. This certainly has been true for me in my study of constructivism—a cultural metaphor that belongs to a large group of people interested in communication and also belongs to me as a member of that group. The metaphor of construction is deeply entrenched in current discourse theory, so deeply entrenched that one must make great effort to examine it as a figure: What is being built? Who is doing the building? What material is used in the building? What is the nature of the constructive process? This metaphor competes and contrasts, as one also discovers, with other theoretical metaphors describing communication processes, such as the machine metaphor of information theory, the organic plant metaphor of Romanticism, the related architectural metaphors of structuralism, poststructuralism, and deconstruction, and other diverse metaphors such as desire and language games.

A strength of this book, I believe, is its high level of integration. To accomplish this, I have pulled together related work from various disciplines, pointed out parallels in several bodies of research, and offered a unified framework for comprehending and composing. However, as the reader would expect and will see, I could not integrate all the discourse research in a single treatment. Even though much of what I say is relevant to oral uses of language and oral texts, my emphasis is on written communication. I will leave it to others to extend the discussion more thoroughly to oral communicative practices, to film and other media, and to other contexts. In this synthesis I have attempted to provide some means of sorting out the various constructivist orientations, which are often confusing: constructivism, constructionism, social constructivism, personal construct theory, and so on. My goal for the book is that even though it summarizes and organizes much of the prior work, it will be provocative, leading to new thinking and questioning.

Many people have contributed to this book, some indirectly and some directly. Particularly influential on my thought and my research through the years have been Steve Witte, David Kaufer, Diane Schallert, and Linda Flower, who have read and responded to various articles that preceded this synthetic piece. I am indebted to them intellectually and am grateful to them. I am also appreciative of the people with whom I have collaborated on studies reported here as well as related work and from whom I have learned a great deal: Maureen Mathison, James King, Maureen Goggin, Stuart Greene, Stuart Shapiro, William Smith, Victoria Stein, Cynthia Cochran, Barbara Sitko, Lorraine Higgins, David Bourne, Lois Fowler, and David Fowler.

For more specific contributions to the writing of this book, my gratitude goes to Peter Mosenthal and two anonymous reviewers, who read and commented on an earlier version of this manuscript; Martin Nystrand, who introduced me to the folks at Academic Press; Rosalind Horowitz, who received the prospectus and who has, on a number of occasions since then, reminded me of the potential value of this book; Alan Kennedy, William Pinar, and Peggy Rice, who read particular chapters; Larry Ventis, who read all the written versions, listened to many of the unwritten versions, and gave me much encouragement; Terry Whitehill, Terry Buchanan, and Betty Senger, whose interest in the issues often kept me writing; and Heather Villien and Kimberly Vannest, who provided much assistance in tracking down references. I am grateful to all members of my immediate and extended family for their support, but especially to my son, Craig Spivey, who produced the figures and heroically met all the deadlines, even when he had other competing deadlines of his own. I also thank the Academic Press editorial staff, particularly Scott Bentley, Beth Bloom, and Rebecca Orbegoso. All these people contributed, and this is a better book because of them.

Finally, I acknowledge the various funding sources that have supported my research: an Elva Knight Research Grant from the International Reading Association, faculty research grants from Texas Woman's University and the College of William and Mary, a Falk Fellowship for the Humanities at Carnegie Mellon University, and grants from the U.S. Office of Educational Research and Improvement/ Department of Education to the Center for the Study of Writing and Literacy at the University of California, Berkeley, and Carnegie Mellon University.

Credits

Illustrations and examples from other authors' work are credited where they are incorporated in the text. In addition to this use of others' prior work, I have used and adapted some of my own previously published writing and have been granted permission from publishers to include it as portions of chapters. I acknowledge the following sources:

Portions of Chapter V were adapted from "Written Discourse: A Constructivist Perspective," in *Constructivism in Education* (pp. 313–329), edited by L. P. Steffe and J. Gale, Hillsdale, NJ: Lawrence Erlbaum Associates, copyright © 1995 Lawrence Erlbaum Associates, and were reprinted with permission.

Portions of Chapter VI were adapted from the following publications and were reprinted with permission of the publishers:

Chapter I

. . . .

The Metaphor
of Constructivism

The best we can hope for is that we be aware of our own perspective and those of others when we make our claims of "rightness" and "wrongness." Put this way, constructivism hardly seems exotic at all.

—Jerome Bruner, *Acts of Meaning*

We humans are builders, shapers, and designers, creating our artifacts from containers to cathedrals to computers to be used, replaced, and sometimes left behind to be studied by others. We build these tangible, visible products by selecting materials, putting components together, and giving form to wholes that are greater than their parts. In addition to creating *things,* we also create mental products, *meanings,* which we call understandings, interpretations, responses, intentions, plans, memories, and so on. We construct these meanings in relation to various aspects of our lives when seeing patterns, making connections and comparisons, and inferring sequence and cause. It is this *constructiveness,* this characteristic building of meanings as well as artifacts, that is such an essential part of being human. Pribram (1971) put it this way: "To be human is to be incapable of stagnation; to be human is to productively reset, reorganize, recode, and thus to give additional meaning to what is" (p. 32).

Another important part of being human is the desire, as individuals and as societies, to communicate our meanings, to share them with others. In order to share meanings, we create texts, both oral and written, following established customs and conventions. We cannot put meanings in the texts, but we can use marks, sounds, gestures, expressions, and other kinds of signs and symbols to get those other people to construct their own meanings, which we hope will have some similarity to ours.

1

A Metaphor and a Theory

My treatment of discourse, which emphasizes this constructiveness, is undergirded with a metaphor that likens discourse processes to processes of building. This constructivist metaphor, which belongs not just to me but to an entire community, ties together some large bodies of work and runs through much of the theoretical literature about discourse. Metaphors, as we are now learning, are essential tools of thought, not simply literary devices, and by analyzing these metaphors, our own as well as others', we can better understand essential tenets and assumptions. In the academic world, individual scholars tend to sustain the same theoretical metaphors over time as they conduct their studies, and individuals belonging to the same group tend to share metaphors (Danzinger, 1990). Theoretical metaphors are explanatory in that they provide familiar frames for understanding complex, puzzling processes, but they can also be generative. Through metaphor, as two whole conceptual complexes are brought together, the attributes of one complex are projected upon the other and linguistic terminology becomes available for features of the topic of interest, including those newly discovered features that are not well understood (M. Black, 1979; Boyd, 1993).

In the constructivist conception, humans, either as individuals or as collectives, are portrayed as constructive agents, and their meanings and knowledge are portrayed as constructed products. According to Bruner and Feldman (1990), this metaphor of production, which portrays the mind as "creator, imposing its categories on what it encounters," has contrasted through the years with its major competing metaphor, that of reproduction, which portrays the mind as "order-preserving copying machine" (p. 231). When communication is likened to construction, certain aspects of discourse are highlighted, as, for instance, the active, generative nature of comprehending as well as composing discourse. The construction metaphor has been, and still is, as we shall see, a generative metaphor, guiding research of various types but also engendering debate because of certain differences in how the construction process is perceived, not only in respect to discourse but to other processes as well (cf. Phillips, 1995; Steffe & Gale, 1995). The debate can be healthy, as it leads to new thinking, particularly when the various forms of constructivism are examined relative to each other.

One of my purposes for this book is to organize these various constructivist conceptions, showing how they differ and what they have in common. As we will see throughout the book, one major issue raised by likening communication to the process of building is the issue of agency. Who should be seen as the constructive agent: the individual or the social group? I attempt to show how the differences among the various forms of constructivism often center on this issue of agency, since acts of literacy can be viewed with an individual as the agent or can be viewed with a social group, even an entire society, as the agent. Which agent is seen depends on one's focus. Whereas some constructivists favor one focus and other constructivists favor another, the foci that are not taken are not inherently "wrong." In fact, each can show us something that the others cannot. Similar themes run through all the constructivist work and thus these different perspectives can be considered complementary as well as oppositional.

Another purpose is to show how the understanding of texts and the composing of texts relate when both are seen as construction. To accomplish that, I look at theoretical work, including theories of authorship, and discuss some of my own studies of the textual transformations that people make as they compose new texts from the texts of others and create bodies of interrelated work. This is intended to be an integrative presentation, accomplished, in part, by bringing to conscious awareness the metaphor, which is often invisible. Although much attention in the name of constructivism has gone to reading and writing as separate processes, a constructivist conception highlights parallels and relations between composing and comprehending when both are seen as processes of building (cf. Kucer, 1985; Tierney & Pearson, 1983). It also highlights acts of literacy that involve *both* comprehending texts and composing texts. In such acts, meaning is being built for another writer's text even as it is being built for one's own new text. Texts are transformed to make new meanings, and issues of originality and identity are raised. Although constructivism is a position that has been taken by many, there is a need for an integrative conception of discourse that presents the cognitive work in relation to the work with a social orientation and that encompasses composing and comprehending.

Constructivism: An Overview

The metatheory known as *constructivism,* which has been developing over the years, has become particularly influential in the latter half of the twentieth century. What distinguishes constructivists from people with other orientations is an emphasis on the generative, organizational, and selective nature of human perception, understanding, and memory—the theoretical "building" metaphor guiding thought and inquiries. Constructivists view people as constructive agents and view the phenomenon of interest (meaning or knowledge) as built instead of passively "received" by people whose *ways* of knowing, seeing, understanding, and valuing influence what is known, seen, understood, and valued. Attention goes to how these *ways* are acquired and manifested. Constructivism takes different forms, which include cognitive-developmental constructism, personal construct theory, radical constructivism, social constructivism or constructionism, and forms that might be labeled cognitive constructivism and collaborative constructivism. These forms cut across various areas of inquiry: psychological studies (social psychology, cognitive psychology, clinical psychology, and developmental psychology), history, educational studies, rhetorical and literary studies, and sociocultural studies in anthropology and sociology.

This book is not a treatise on the metaphysical issue of the nature of reality, even though that issue is where many constructivists put much of their attention, as they consider the extent to which we humans can learn about and experience reality, or, put another way, the extent to which we create our realities. In general, constructivists point to the role of the observer in any observations that are made of the "world." Most would agree with statements like this one from M. Polanyi (1958):

> As human beings, we must inevitably see the universe from a centre lying within ourselves and speak about it in terms of a human language shaped by the exigencies of human intercourse. Any attempt rigorously to eliminate our human perspective from our picture of the world must lead to absurdity. (p. 3)

Although there is some general agreement, there are some important differences among various constructivists regarding the relation between what one *knows* and what is *real*. Some debating this issue take a stance that Mahoney (1991) called *critical constructivism*, which acknowledges an external reality composed of entities called objects but maintains that these objects can never be known directly, whereas others take the position called *radical constructivism*, articulated by von Glaserfeld (1984), which maintains that knowledge is "exclusively an order and organization of a world constituted by our experience" (p. 24; cf. Watzlawick, 1984) and is not a reflection of an objective ontological reality. Still others put the criteria for what is knowledge in social processes of negotiation in discourse communities, claiming that what are thought to be "facts" are instead social constructs (Gergen, 1985, 1995). Finally, there is the *radical relativist* position presented by N. Goodman (1951, 1978, 1984). His relativist perspective is radical in that, instead of realism or idealism, it is *irrealism,* a lack of concern with the metaphysical issue of realism versus idealism. To him both positions are "equally delightful and equally deplorable" (N. Goodman, 1978, p. 119), and the "rightness" of a particular claim is relative to the particular world—the theory—within which one is operating.

Instead of metaphysics, the major focus of this book is literate processes and practices through which people create meanings for and from texts. This is the focus of my work and the focus of many others who pursue studies under the label "constructivist." The constructivist position I present here locates meanings in people—authors and audiences, writers and readers, speakers and listeners. The construction metaphor undergirding this presentation contrasts dramatically with other metaphoric conceptions of communication. These would include various transmission–reception conceptions, particularly the pervasive "conduit metaphor," identified and described by Reddy (1979), in which one person puts thoughts into a text and transfers them by means of the text and another person extracts them from the text ("Put your thoughts on paper," "Did you find that idea in this text?"), and the telegraph metaphor of information theory (Shannon & Weaver, 1949), in which a transmitter encodes a message from its information source into a signal and sends it over a communication channel, and a receiver decodes the message from the signal for its information source. In contrast to transmission metaphors, the construction metaphor emphasizes the active and generative nature of communication and thus the similarities between composing and comprehending. It points to the importance of the relevant knowledge that people bring as their constructive material to acts of communication and to the limitations of what the text offers (marks or sounds, which are perceived as symbols). Moreover, it allows for different meanings for the same text because of differences in people, which might be in their relevant knowledge, their perspectives, or their purposes, and differences in the contexts in which they build their meanings.

The constructivist conception differs in certain important ways from some other current conceptions that are also based on an architectural metaphor: structuralism, poststructuralism, and deconstruction. A chapter will be devoted to these theoretical contrasts. The constructivist conception also contrasts, as we shall see, with the organic plant metaphor, which continues to be important in discourse theory (e.g., Abrams, 1953; Rohman & Wlecke, 1964; Rosenblatt, 1978).

Historical Antecedents of Constructivism

Although constructivism did not really become identifiable as a theoretical orientation until the 1920s or 1930s, constructivist positions have been taken through the years from classical times to the Enlightenment to our modern (and postmodern) age. Prior attention has gone to the means through which people make sense of, even construct, their own experience, both in terms of their providing order and in terms of their generating knowledge, instead of merely receiving it. And attention has also been directed to the varying ways of knowing, relative to the social group, that influence what is known.

Three Conceptions

To trace constructivist themes and issues, I would have to produce an intellectual history going back to the classical rhetoricians. Instead of taking on that huge task, I limit myself here to major theoretical claims made during the eighteenth and nineteenth centuries that are associated most closely with the work of Kant, Vico, and

Hegel. These provide a backdrop for the various forms of constructivism today, which are the major topic of this chapter.

Kantian Rationality

Constructivism today echoes Kantian themes from the eighteenth century. Kant (1781/1946) had argued in his *Critique of Pure Reason* that humans impose order on their sensory experience of the outside world, rather than discern order from the world, and that they create knowledge, rather than discover it. In his "categorical imperative" the German philosopher argued that the human mind is equipped with a rational structure that is composed of two forms of perception, space and time, and various Aristotelian-like categories for performing logical operations, which include cause–effect, community, negation, plurality, and necessity. Kant was describing a universal kind of "pure" rationality and a structure that was common across humans. By arguing for the rationality of human thought, Kant was attempting to rescue science from the skepticism of Hume (1739-1740/1907), who in his *Treatise* had dismissed scientific knowledge as mere opinion. To Hume, people do not and cannot have knowledge because the human mind deals only with what can be perceived through the senses and does not directly experience reality, and thus what seems to be knowledge is simply inferences about reality. For instance, the cause–effect relationship that one sees between two phenomena is an inference. It is not in nature, is not out there *in* what is observed. Kant agreed with Hume that the human mind has to *add* to what is perceived by making an inference but contended that, because the inferring is a rational process rather than an opinion, the result *is* knowledge. Knowledge is made—constructed—through synthesis, which is performed by applying the categories of pure understanding to what is perceived. Through its own structures, which Kant outlined, the mind achieves knowledge, and knowledge is this rational making sense of experience. Thus, in his treatment of scientific knowledge, Kant pointed to mental constructiveness, the cognitive contributions people make as they understand their world.

The influence of Kant's work has been profound, and various epistemologies, ranging from cognitivism to Romanticism, can be called Kantian or post-Kantian, in that they not only came after but also developed from Kant's conceptions. Constructivism, with its emphasis on the ordering of experience and the constructiveness of knowledge, can trace many of its assumptions to Kant (cf. Cunningham & Fitzgerald, 1996). This is particularly the case, as we shall see, for those versions of constructivism that emphasize the cognition of individuals, but those forms of constructivism that emphasize social knowledge have also built upon Kant's ideas.

Vichian Ingenium

Vico, whose work is now receiving much attention from constructivists, published some pieces before Kant, but neither he nor his ideas were well known until later. Nevertheless, in the early eighteenth century the Italian rhetorician had made his position on human constructiveness quite explicit in his *verum-factum* principle, which can be stated as either "the truth is the same as the made" or "we know it because we made it" (Vico, 1725/1968). The ancient Italians had used the two words *verum* and *factum* interchangeably, and Vico, who had studied the classical writings (as well as those of his favorite scholar, Francis Bacon), also identified truth, or knowledge, with the act of making. As he explained in his major work, *The New Science* (1725/1968), people create order because they bring the means of ordering to their experience, but the truth that can be achieved for the natural world differs from that that can be achieved for the human-made world because people made the latter and not the former. Humans see the world of nature through mental constructs, but, because they have not made the world of nature, they cannot truly understand it. However, humans *can* understand the human world—government, philosophy, history, law, religion, poetry, art, morality, and even mathematics—because they have made it. All these products of the human world illustrate people's constructiveness, which Vico attributed to their *ingenium* (inventive force). People make connections and create a "common sense" of things, which is wisdom.

Particularly important in Vico's theory is language, which he saw as binding together a society and serving as a means for its development. A similar conception of language appears today in much constructivist work, which will be discussed later, that focuses on societal groups. In Vico's treatment, myth and metaphor are the means through which people make sense of experience, myth representing the poetic logic of past times, and metaphor serving as a necessary tool for abstract thought. Only recently have theorists begun to consider some of the complex issues regarding metaphoric thought that were considered long ago by Vico and to examine the metaphoric nature of our theories (e.g., Edge, 1974; Levin, 1988; Ortony, 1979; Sternberg, 1990) and the important role of narrative in our understandings of diverse kinds of experiences (e.g., Bruner, 1985, 1990, 1992; Danesi, 1995).

Vico took a collectivist orientation, believing that people belonging to a particular society or nation share a psychological unity, "a common sense," which regulates their social life. Here in his work was the emphasis on the *ways* of a social group that is so important in constructivist work today. Vico incorporated this notion of psychological unity into his conception of history. He gave a psychological emphasis to history, which he portrayed as understanding the progressive mental states of a society going through a cyclical kind of development. He maintained that one has to try to enter the minds of people who lived at the time, which means finding rationality in what might appear to be irrational if one looks at that past period in terms of the current modes of thought. The Vichian position can be considered a form of *historicism* because of the movement from one's own perspective to see larger patterns and principles of continuity in history.

Thus Vico put his emphasis on societies as he considered their differing ways of knowing and their large socially constructed products, such as legal systems. This was in contrast to Kant, who had intended his notions about rational structures to apply across societies and who had explained constructiveness in terms of particular inferences. Today, Vico's work has most relevance to the forms of social constructivism that are often identified with the sociology of knowledge. These forms appear not only in sociology but also in anthropology, education, linguistics, history, psychology, philosophy, and rhetoric.

Hegelian Historicism

In the work of Hegel (1807/1931, 1812-1816/1929, 1827-1830/1894, 1843/ 1874), produced several decades after that of Vico and Kant, there is a strong focus on organizing principles, as this philosopher described a vast but orderly system in which mind, society, and universe all fit into a logical, rational, and unified whole. The historian's task, according to his version of historicism, is to discover the inner logic of past events and provide the structure for others to understand them. In the well-known statement "What is real is reasonable and what is reasonable real," Hegel summed up his position that mind and universe follow the same laws. He made the categories of thought a part of all reality—a move that was being attempted by other German philosophers—and he eliminated Vico's distinction between the human-made world and the natural world.

Hegel made claims about the relationship between cultural factors and psychological factors. In this respect, his work has some notable similarities to Vico's, and some Vichean scholars (e.g., Piovani, 1969) have complained that, because of the similarities, there have been excessive attempts to "Hegelize" Vico's work now that it is accessible. Despite placing value on the individual and on the questioning of conventions, Hegelianism has a collectivist orientation, in which individuals are constituted, to a great extent, by the communities to which they belong. Hegel pointed to a unity of spirit among the people who belong to a particular state and to differences between states as they develop historically. And he argued that each state must be understood in terms of its "idiosyncracy of spirit," which influences and connects such aspects of life as the political, religious, scientific, artistic, moral, and legal—those cultural products that differ in style, content, and reasoning from one society to another. So here, in the work of Hegel as in that of Vico, is an emphasis on the differing ways of different societal groups and also an emphasis on rationality as dynamic and relative, changing as society changes, without the stability and universality of Kant's conception.

Like some other nineteenth-century philosophers, Hegel thought that societies develop and history progresses in a dynamic, evolutionary fashion, which he explained in terms of his famous dialectic: thesis, antithesis, synthesis (which Marx was to transform into dialectical materialism). In its historical development a society is portrayed as going through phases with each phase having corresponding modes of understanding the world. The evolutionary notion of development was to gain much attention in the twentieth century and to be applied to both societal knowledge and individuals' knowledge. It can be seen in some studies of community that predated social constructivism and can also be seen in the work of Piaget (e.g., Piaget & Garcia, 1983/1989). Most work focused on social groups today does not have this same sense of an evolutionary development, but there is much interest among constructivists in diversity of knowledge among different social groups and changes in knowledge over time.

In addition to the attention on order and on the ways of different groups, a major Hegelian theme that I see as critical for constructivism and that I consider at several points in this book is the tension between different ways of seeing: looking at the general or looking at the particular. The two approaches are apparent, for example, in the tension and shifts between considering stories in general or a particular tale and in the tension and shifts between focusing on general patterns of history or on individual figures.

Constructivist Themes and the Emerging Disciplines

All three philosophers emphasized the constructiveness of human understanding and proposed a means through which people provide order to their experience, but there were differences among them regarding what knowledge people can build and what ordering principles they apply. For Kant, people could "know" the world of nature, even though that knowledge would be inferred. For Vico, people could know only the human-made world, comprised of their cultural products. And for Hegel, the boundaries between the knower and the known were broken. As to ordering principles, Kant saw knowledge created as a result of universal, unchanging categories, whereas Hegel spoke of different forms of reasoning associated with different societies and Vico portrayed such cultural forms as metaphor and myth as means of ordering. The latter two both pointed to the relativistic (or to use today's term, "situated") nature of knowledge.

Constructivist issues, which once belonged to philosophy, have been pursued in an interdisciplinary and cross-disciplinary fashion ever since the disciplinary boundaries were drawn toward the end of the nineteenth century. Much constructivist work has been conducted by researchers in psychology, which emerged as a scientific discipline for conducting studies of mental processes, as distinguished from philosophy, a discipline for theorizing about such topics as epistemology. However, in psychology constructivist questions about people's ordering of experience, which were being asked at the time of the disciplinary divisions, did not become of major interest again until the latter half of the twentieth century. This was because, at the turn of the century, the new discipline of psychology, with associationism as its undergirding theory, had taken the Kantian categories and put them back in the external world. It had placed most of its attention on external influences and observable behavior, where it was kept for decades. The pattern for educational research, which followed the model of psychology, was quite similar. Nevertheless, despite these general trends, there were some important exceptions in psychology, some notable studies of cognitive and social processes in the early decades of the twentieth century. This work, giving attention to ways of knowing of individuals and groups, has come to be known as constructivist. And as we will see later in this chapter and the next, this early work helped to shape constructivism as we know it today.

Much of the constructivist work focused on social groups has been conducted by researchers in disciplines other than psychology. In contrast to psychology, which claimed the individual as its unit, sociology and anthropology took the social group as their unit when established, and the major issues for study in these disciplines have included the characteristics of social groups and the differences between groups. During the first part of the century, studies of societies and cultures, undergirded to some extent with Hegelian and Kantian notions, examined the conventions and "psychologies" of different groups. These studies set the stage for those constructivist studies of social processes known as sociology of knowledge and social anthropology, which have more recently incorporated Vichian theory, as mentioned above. This work, too, will be considered later in this chapter and the next. In more recent times, there have been complementary studies in linguistics, rhetoric, and education focused on the ways of social groups and also in history, particularly that branch that has come to be known as *social history*. In my review I do not try to classify the constructivist work according to discipline.

Constructive Processes of Individuals and Groups

As we have seen, there were differences across three influential theorists—Kant, Vico, and Hegel—in regard to agency, although all emphasized the constructive nature of human understanding. Among constructivists today there are also many differences, and the differences still tend to center on conceptions of agency, as the following review demonstrates. Some focus on the individual, but others focus on groups. And among those who concentrate on groups as agents, some deal with small groups whose members interact, whereas others deal with large social groups, such as societies and communities, whose members do not all necessarily come into direct contact with, or even know, one other. The following review is organized according to these three conceptions of agency.

Focus on Individuals as Agents

In this review, let us first focus on individuals and consider the work that has portrayed individuals as constructive agents and that has given much attention to their cognitive processes. Individuals are thought to approach their experiences with ways of seeing, thinking, and knowing (frames, schemas, perspectives, filters, lenses, interests, or mental sets) that influence which aspects are most salient and that provide the means for ordering and interpreting their experience. Four major lines of this work include (a) one that can be called cognitive constructivism, beginning with the studies of Frederic Bartlett; (b) cognitive-developmental constructivism, beginning with the studies of Jean Piaget; (c) personal construct theory, associated with the ideas of George Kelly; and (d) worldmaking, associated with the philosophy of Nelson Goodman.

Cognitive Constructivism

The constructivist perspective on discourse that I present in this book is greatly influenced by the scholarly work of Bartlett, a psychologist in England who made his contributions during the first half of the twentieth century. The next chapter of this book provides more detail about his scholarship and that of his contemporaries, and subsequent chapters echo and elaborate observations he made. His major book, *Remembering: A Study in Experimental and Social Psychology,* published in 1932 and reissued in 1995, reports studies, some involving the reading of texts, that demonstrate the active—even proactive and generative—nature of perception, understanding, and remembering. Individuals in those studies built meanings and memories by relating new material to their prior knowledge, which Bartlett saw as organized by means of structures or patterns of more complexity than the categories Kant described. In Bartlett's conception these structures called *schemas* are the frames that influence what is understood, inferred, and remembered.[1] People's schemas for stories, for example, affect their constructions for the story-like texts they experience. Because such knowledge is developed through social experiences, there are commonalities among people who belong to the same social group and differences between people who belong to different groups.

Bartlett is well known today as a cognitivist, not as a person who studied social processes of groups. That is why I have put him here in this section and not in the other two. However, as I argue in the next chapter, he really should be known as a social theorist as well. In the 1932 book and the one published in 1923, Bartlett considered the two kinds of social constructiveness that are identified more closely with other bodies of work: a collaborative constructivism on the part of small groups, such as storytellers and their listeners, and also the building of conventions and customs on the part of large societal groups or communities. He was interested in conventionalization on the part of both individuals and groups—how material is transformed through selecting what fits and transforming what does not. And the psychological theory he used to explain individuals' performance was developed from an anthropological and sociological theory he had worked out to explain societal constructions. Even though he was a psychologist, in much of his work

---

[1] Actually, Bartlett (1932) used the Latinate plural *schemata* when speaking of more than one *schema*.

Bartlett relied heavily on work in anthropology and dealt with the issues being considered by sociologists and anthropologists.

As discussed in the next chapter, Bartlett's work focusing on cognition has had a strong impact on studies of cognitive processes in the understanding of texts since the 1970s, but his attempts to describe social processes and the creation of social institutions and conventions have only recently begun to receive much attention. The time seems right to bring them back together again. In the next chapter, "Remembering Bartlett," I discuss the differing foci of his work and thereby the scope of the constructivist enterprise.

A number of cognitive psychologists in the 1970s began to argue constructivist notions and, in doing so, they cited Bartlett. Some were saying that people, rather than texts, carry meaning, that linguistic inputs merely provide "cues" for readers to use their knowledge of the world to construct meaning (Bransford, Barclay, & Franks, 1972; Bransford & Franks, 1971; Kintsch, 1974), that understanding a text is an active, generative process (Frederiksen, 1972), not the passive, automatic parsing that was often assumed, and that in countless ways people go "beyond the information given" (Bruner, 1973; cf. review by Di Sibio, 1982). Attention was on inferences in a way that Kant would never have anticipated (e.g., Clark, 1977). Complementary work was being conducted by researchers in artificial intelligence, such as Minsky (1975) and Schank and Abelson (1977), who were also studying the knowledge of text structure and general knowledge of the world that seems to be required for discourse understanding. They, too, were asking what meaning is and what it takes to understand a text. In linguistics, as well, there were also developments important to a study of text understanding—developments resulting in new tools for examining the features of texts. Some linguists were beginning to consider whole texts as large linguistic units characterized by organization, staging, and connectivity (Grimes, 1975; van Dijk, 1972).

This was a time of change in reading education in the United States. Some educators were talking about the reader's active, strategic role in understanding a text and were portraying text comprehension, not as skills for "getting it right," but as bringing meaning to a text. K. S. Goodman (1967) argued that proficient reading was not accomplished by correctly identifying all linguistic elements but by selecting the fewest possible cues, and F. Smith (1971) explained that reading comprehension was a matter of relating prior knowledge to what one wants to know. A national Center for the Study of Reading was established in 1976 at the University of Illinois (with a major subcontract to Bolt, Beranek, and Newman). The Center had reading comprehension as the major research agenda, and its researchers, including the director, Richard Anderson, approached their studies with a constructivist orientation (cf. R. C. Anderson & Ortony, 1975).

A rather large body of work, which I have reviewed elsewhere (Spivey, 1987, 1990, 1994) and will discuss in more depth in subsequent chapters, has focused on the transformations that people make when they understand texts. They make these transformations on the basis of some kind of knowledge, which might be discourse knowledge, topic knowledge, or perhaps knowledge of the kind of performance that is expected. Studies have shown readers organizing and reorganizing, making selections, and generating inferences and elaborations as they use the cues of the text to make their meanings. In many of these studies a researcher has analyzed a text for some conventional feature (or some violation of convention), which might, for instance, be the marking of an organizational pattern, such as narrative or problem-solution, or some type of connections within the linguistic content, perhaps causal relations or repeated themes. Then the researcher attempts to gain insights into the meanings that readers construct with respect to the textual feature of interest. To study these meanings, analyses are made from some kind of response, such as a recall or a think-aloud protocol.

Within this research dealing with cognition, there has been much attention to social factors, particularly differences in meaning making associated with membership in particular groups, such as groups formed on the basis of age, occupation, disciplinary major, national origin, or expertise in a domain. These differences are often explained in terms of different knowledge built through social experiences. Thus, the social knowledge of interest to constructivists is viewed as *in* people, rather than as something external to them, as in other work to be discussed later. There has also been much attention to the relationship between particular features of the response and "quality" as judged by persons with authority in the group. Studies have demonstrated how meaning built for a text is not static but is dynamic, as readers adjust it so that it will be appropriate for the situation in which they recall the text or put the memories of the text to use for some other purpose (e.g., R. C. Anderson & Pichert, 1978). As I have discussed elsewhere and will discuss further in this book, most of the constructivist research in reading thus far has focused on reading to understand, but increasing attention is being directed to transformations when people read texts for other purposes such as writing their own texts. Most attention has focused on the reading of single texts, but attention is now being given to integration across multiple texts (e.g., Hartman, 1991).

Theorists have attempted to describe the nature of knowledge used in understanding a text as well as the nature of meaning constructed for the text. They give their attention to the constructive material and the constructed product, and thus return to epistemological issues considered by the philosophers discussed earlier. Some theorists, following Bartlett (1932), developed schematic conceptions for the organization of knowledge and used such labels for their structures as schemas (R. C. Anderson, Reynolds, Schallert, & Goetz, 1977; Rumelhart, 1980; Rumelhart & Ortony, 1977), frames (Minsky, 1975), and scripts (G. H. Bower, Black, & Turner, 1979; Schank & Abelson, 1977). Such hypothetical structures were incorporated into other theories, such as Kintsch's (1974; Kintsch & van Dijk, 1978) theory of propositional memory, in which meanings for texts have been conceived as sets of interrelated concepts organized with certain kinds of patterns. It is important to note, however, that constructivism is not tied to a particular conception of the organization of knowledge. Increasingly, network and connectionist conceptions are being used to guide research and interpret results of studies (cf. Kintsch, 1988; McClelland & Rumelhart, 1986; Rumelhart & McClelland, 1986). In such conceptions, organization is seen as emergent rather than established, as implicit rather than explicit. For example, in describing their connectionist conception, Rumelhart, Smolensky, McClelland, and Hinton (1986) explain that what seems to be organization is certain groups of smaller elements of knowledge that operate as "coalitions of tightly interconnected units" (pp. 20–21), acting in concert and activating one another. In this conception, meaning for a text would be explained in terms of activated units.

In the 1970s, when psychologists and reading educators began to study reading comprehension, researchers in English studies and in educational studies (English education and language arts) were becoming interested in the nature of the composing process. This interest was sparked by Emig's (1971) monograph on *The Composing Processes of Twelfth Graders,* which was followed by a set of related studies with people of various ages. This early work tended to be based on observation of process, and thus focused for the most part on external behaviors (e.g., drafting and rewriting) instead of the building of a cognitive product. However, the publication of the articles of Hayes and Flower (1980) and Flower and Hayes (1981) on the composing process (cf. Bruce, Collins, Rubin, & Gentner, 1978), which did describe the building of a mental product, opened up a line of inquiry in composing processes that has complemented, to some extent, the constructivist work being done in reading (e.g., Witte, 1985).

Unfortunately, the two bodies of work in composing and comprehending have not been well integrated, partly because, to a great extent, they are being developed by people in different fields who employ different vocabularies and methods and have different forums for presenting their studies. The work making the most explicit links has focused on acts of literacy that involve both reading and writing, acts that Bracewell, Frederiksen, and Frederiksen (1982) called "hybrid." These would include studies of summarizing (e.g., A. L. Brown & Day, 1983; P. N. Winograd, 1984) and writing to learn (e.g., Durst, 1987; Langer, 1984; Langer & Applebee, 1987; G. E. Newell, 1984) as well as the studies of synthesis and academic writing that some of us have been conducting since the mid 1980s (e.g., Ackerman, 1991; Greene, 1994; Mathison, 1993; J. Nelson, 1990; Spivey, 1984, 1991; Spivey & King, 1989, 1994). The latter include a number of studies conducted by researchers at the national Center for the Study of Writing, which was established in 1986 at the University of California, Berkeley, and at Carnegie Mellon University.

Cognitive-Developmental Constructivism

Another major line of scholarship in constructivism is that which began with the work of the psychologist Piaget and his colleagues, who initiated their studies in Switzerland at about the same time that Bartlett was conducting his in England. Although one of Piaget's major books, *The Language and Thought of the Child*, was translated from the French into English in 1932, others were not translated until the 1950s and 1960s, and some work from the latter part of his career has only recently been published (e.g., Piaget & Garcia, 1987/1991). Piaget, who focused his studies on children of different ages, is well known for his constructivist claim that the knowledge structures built by people at particular levels of development influence how they, at that point in their lives, construe their reality. In his view, the concepts of space, time, and causality are interdependent and are relative to the structure through which the person sees the world at that point in his or her life. Piaget is less well known for his sociological theories, which also focus on structural and structuring features (e.g., Chapman, 1986; Piaget & Garcia, 1983/1989).

Much of the work taking a Piagetian perspective has tended to focus on the developmental aspects—how structures change dynamically over time through *assimilation,* incorporating new elements into existing structures, and *accommodation,* modifying the structures because of new elements (cf. Paris & Lindauer, 1976). Although much of the work has supported Piaget's stages, some notable cross-cultural studies have shown different patterns for children in non-Western cultures (e.g., Cole & Scribner, 1974). There is growing acknowledgment of dialectical mechanisms in development (Pascual-Leone, 1987), and there is increasing interest in Piaget's theory of equilibration, the self-organization of knowledge through transformation, as when gaps in knowledge are noted and filled (Piaget, 1975/1985; cf. Chapman, 1992).

With the exception of his early work, Piaget did not give much attention to the role of language or social factors in cognitive development and thus he contrasted with others, such as Bruner (1986), who saw language as very important and considered it a mediating factor in cognitive development. For instance, whereas Piaget argued that the relation between language and success on tasks is correlational and not causal, Bruner maintained that language guides thought when a child first uses symbolic representations. Piaget and Bruner also differed regarding the role of social factors, with Bruner placing more emphasis on pedagogy and other social influences than did Piaget. Cognitive development, as Piaget presented it in much of his work, seemed relatively unaffected by social factors, even though in some early studies he gave attention to the role of social interaction in knowledge construction and to the nature of intersubjectivity (e.g., Piaget, 1923/1932, 1924/1928; cf. Youniss & Damon, 1992). And cognitive development also seemed unaffected by cultural factors. As Bruner (1992) noted, Piaget's conception of universal, invariant structures is at odds with current conceptions of knowledge as "cultural tool kits" that are domain specific and culture specific, as they are shared by people who belong to a particular societal group.

Most relevant to a constructivist conception of discourse is the cognitive-developmental scholarship dealing with the social and linguistic issues addressed by

Piaget in his early work, in particular the issue of perspective taking. This research examines one's ability to view a situation from a perspective other than one's own, and, when it concerns discourse, examines a speaker's (or writer's) ability to sense, and adapt to, the needs of an audience. Piaget (1923/1932) suggested that children have difficulty decentering and taking the listener's perspective and claimed that certain characteristics of young children's oral language, such as unclear referents of pronouns, reflect that inability to decenter. Much of the Piaget-inspired work in perspective taking has been conducted by Flavell and his colleagues (Flavell, 1966, 1992; Flavell, Botkin, Fry, Wright, & Jarvis, 1968), although Flavell has pointed out that decentering can sometimes be difficult for everyone, adults as well as children. Related work has examined developmental patterns in people's ability to produce writing that is appropriate for one's audience (e.g., Kroll, 1985). Of course, ego-centrism is not a sole determining factor in children's communication difficulties, and what often seems to be children's inability to decenter is instead a failure to understand what is expected of them (cf. Bruner, 1986; Donaldson, 1978).

Personal Construct Theory

When the term *constructivism* is used, some people, particularly clinical psychologists and psychotherapists, think not of Bartlett or Piaget but of Kelly, an American psychologist, and of the work associated with his personal construct theory. This theory, articulated in 1955 in two volumes, is directed mainly to therapists and is intended to help them understand the categories through which their clients perceive experiences and perceive other people. Kelly maintained that an individual creates categories as he or she makes distinctions and choices and interacts socially. A person's processes, including social, intersubjective processes, are "psychologically channelized" by these constructs that he or she has built and continues to build. Kelly spoke of cycles of conformity and extension: conformity, when one works within the present constraints of established categories, making clearer definitions, and extension, when one challenges those constraints to extend the limits.

Personal construct theory has undergirded some studies in discourse processes. For instance, Applebee (1978) traced children's developing concepts of stories in terms of Kelly's cyclical patterns and also applied the cycle notion to writing development in general. These two kinds of elaboration can be seen in various kinds of discourse learning, periods in which one repeatedly uses and develops a particular discourse concept and generates new knowledge about the applications of that concept, and periods in which one moves to a new concept. Also Hynds (1985) found an association between high school students' cognitive complexity, as measured by the number of different constructs they use in perceiving people with whom they interact, and the complexity of the construct system they employ in interpreting literary characters.

Within psychotherapy there has been much research, inspired by Kelly's emphasis on the constructive aspects of perception and understanding, that has studied people's construct systems. Therapists attempt to understand the categories that clients use to make sense of their life experiences as well as the categories that they themselves use in their own interpretations (reviewed by Neimeyer, 1993, 1995). This work focused on communication between therapists and clients will not be a major focus of this book, even though some of it parallels fairly closely the research in written discourse that I will discuss.

Worldmaking

Throughout his career N. Goodman (1951, 1978, 1980, 1984), the self-described irrealist whom I mentioned earlier, has focused on how people make the mental constructions that he called *worlds,* which are the constructions that some of us might call theories or perspectives or possibly world views. Goodman (1978) saw himself as belonging to that "mainstream of modern philosophy that began when Kant exchanged the structure of the world for the structure of the mind" (p. x), but saw himself as non-Kantian in his emphasis on multiplicity of worlds. Through his various writings, he argued that a person operates, not within a single world, but within a multiplicity of worlds, and deals with conflicting truths because what is "true" in one might not be in another. This shift from one world to another might be illustrated by a person operating with different kinds of truth when reading scientific reports and when listening to political candidates' positions. These worlds can be seen as theories belonging to individuals. But they can also be seen as social theories, perspectives, or ways of knowing that are shared by members of the same group or community.

In *Ways of Worldmaking,* Goodman (1978) discussed the mechanisms by which one world is created from another world or from other worlds—transformations such as weighting, ordering, and deleting—and provided illustrations of transformational processes in constructing "worlds," many of which come from the arts. For example, when representational art is transformed by recombining and reweighting some properties, we have abstract art, and when transformations are performed on abstract art, we have nondenotational music. But these transformations, from other worlds, which were described by Goodman, might be used to explain the development of such diverse worlds as the world of learning disabilities, the world of "whole language," the world of qualitative research, and the world of talk shows on television.

Goodman (1980) has also shown how the same transformational processes can change discourse from one pattern to another. He, like many other constructivists, was interested in the nature of narrative, and, when discussing his notions of worlds and transformations, he used this form of discourse as an illustration of a world. He portrayed a person reading or writing a narrative as operating within a narrative world, which is characterized, in part, by a chronological ordering, but he showed how various transformations could turn that narrative world into something else. Although narrative can remain narrative when the order in which events are told differs from the order in which they occurred, narrative stops being narrative under some transformations, particularly in weighting as well as in ordering. Goodman used as an example the transformations that Huxley (1937) performed on a narrative account of the life of the British painter, Benjamin Robert Haydon. Through a combination of transformations, which included ordering on the basis of aspects of character as well as giving weight to those aspects, Huxley turned the narrative into a character study.

Focus on Small Groups and Dyads as Agents

Now we move our attention to a collaborative pair or group operating as a single agent (a unit or a system) to produce a text or an interpretation of a text. For example, a group might produce a narrative, as in *talk story* (K. A. Watson, 1975), the collaborative telling of story that is a cultural practice in Hawaiian society. Or a pair of children in an American school setting might work together as co-authors in constructing meaning for, and in writing, a single text (Daiute, 1986). Or an entire school class might participate in collective remembering of a text that they have read (Middleton & Edwards, 1990). All three examples demonstrate how a group of individuals can be considered a single unit producing a single product. We sometimes hear predicates for individuals' mental functions (e.g., plan, decide) applied to such collaborative groups. For instance, a group can be said to be telling a story, remembering a story, or solving a problem. If asked who performed the act, the answer would be, "We did" (cf. Wertsch, 1991).

Much of the research by social constructivists emphasizing small groups as agents is influenced by the theory of the Soviet psychologist, Lev Vygotsky (1978, 1986; cf. Wertsch, 1985), who conducted psychological studies in the USSR in the 1920s and early 1930s. The *social* in these studies often referred to dyadic or other small-group processes instead of the constructive processes of such large social groups as societies, even though Vygotsky and his colleagues worked in a Marxist sociocultural framework. Of particular interest to Vygotsky were pairs composed of a child and an adult or a more advanced peer. When performing tasks collaboratively, a child can be more successful than when working alone because of the reciprocity of the relationship, the partner filling in what the child cannot provide. The child builds knowledge through the activity, and the knowledge is thus socially constructed, in a process that Leont'ev (1981), Vygotsky's colleague, characterized (in social terms) as *appropriation* in contrast to Piaget's explanation (in individual terms) of *assimilation*. Vygotsky traced the psychological development of individuals to such social processes and viewed intrapsychological functioning in the individual as derivative from interpsychological functioning in social participation (cf. Halliday, 1994).

An important component of Vygotskian theory, particularly as it contrasts with, and complements, Piagetian theory, is the role of cultural tools, both technical tools and symbolic tools such as language, which serve as mediators. Many have extended Vygotskian notions, among them Bruner (1990, 1992; Ninio & Bruner, 1978), mentioned earlier, who is well known for the notion of scaffolding in "partnerships" between a child and an adult and for his emphasis today on cultural factors.

Some of this work in collaboration has developed into what is known as *distributed cognition,* the idea that much cognition must be considered in terms of intellectual partnerships, or systems, comprising people and their cultural tools (e.g., J. S. Brown, Collins, & Duguid, 1989; Resnick, 1991; Salomon, 1993a). An example provided by Salomon (1993b) is a physician's developing a diagnosis in collaboration with colleagues and with an expert computer system. The product of such a partnership, in which cognition is distributed across individuals and tools, he argued, cannot be attributed to individual members but should be seen as a joint product. Some of those doing work in distributed cognition prefer to keep attention on the system itself and not give much attention to individual cognition (e.g., Pea, 1993). However, in much of the work focusing on collaboration, attention is given to the psychological processes and products of individuals who comprise the group or dyad, for instance, considering what a child learns through a collaboration or how individual memories differ in a collaborative session.

Focus on Communities and Societies as Agents

Finally we move our focus to the *macro* social constructivist work presenting a large, abstract societal group, such as community, society, and nation, as a single constructive agent. In contrast to those groups just discussed, people within these large groups do not necessarily know all of the other members, and they do not have direct interactions with them all. Yet they do identify with the whole group, adhere to its values, speak its language, and engage in its practices. The label *social constructionism,* or simply *constructionism,* is encouraged by Gergen (1985, 1995) to distinguish this work from constructivist scholarship that emphasizes the cognitive processes of individuals. However, constructionism, too, presents a problem because it is also being used for a particular position taken in the cognitive work on individuals' construction of inferences (Graesser, Bertus, & Magliano, 1995) as well as a particular position among historians that emphasizes the perspectives of individual historians (Goldstein, 1977; Nowell-Smith, 1977). I prefer to continue with the term *constructivism* across the various constructivist orientations, since I am attempting to create some connections among the lines of work. Social constructivist inquiry focused on large groups as agents is being conducted in a number of fields, including social psychology, sociology of knowledge, sociology of science, philosophy of science, social anthropology, social history, education, and rhetorical studies.

Early Emphasis on Community

At about the same time that Bartlett conducted his studies in England, Piaget conducted his in Switzerland, and Vygotsky conducted his in the Soviet Union, ideas were developing elsewhere that would later inform work in social constructivism. Some had to do with the social aspects of thought that had been discussed previously by Vico and Hegel. Also of particular importance to the later development of constructivism were the conceptions of society and social forces, to be discussed now, being developed in France by Durkheim and his colleagues, including Lévy-Bruhl, and the positions on social classes, being developed by Mannheim in Germany and later in England.

Durkheim (1893/1984, 1912/1968, 1898/1953; Durkheim & Mauss, 1901-1902/1963), like Hegel and Vico, gave attention to shared ways of thinking and knowing and even, like Hegel, spoke of commonalities in the (Kantian) categories of thought among people belonging to a particular society. These commonalities are there, according to Durkheim, because society, an entity above individuals, compels (in a psychological, not physical, sense) its members to think, believe, and act in *its* particular ways, which are *their* ways too. In his conception, which he developed with contributions from his numerous students and associates who contributed to the publication *L'Année Sociologique,* society is sometimes described with terms ordinarily applied to individuals' cognition. For instance, Durkheim is well known for his notions of the *collective conscience,* which refers to the shared norms of a society and sometimes translates to collective "consciousness," and the *collective representation,* which refers to the body of ideas, traditions, customs, and facts that constitute a culture. And Halbwachs (1925/1975, 1950/1980), one of Durkheim's colleagues and former students, developed a conception of *collective memory,* which he based on numerous studies into the shared memories of various groups. Integral to the Durkheimian social theory is an evolutionary portrayal of society's development, which, due in part to Darwin's theory as well as Hegel's (1807/1931), was a component of much conceptual work during the nineteenth and early twentieth century. Durkheim described change in terms of increasing differentiation: from homogeneity in patterns of life and thought in less developed societies to more differentiation of subgroups and of individuals in modern societies. In the former kind of society, social solidarity is based on uniformity of beliefs and practices, and in the latter, it is based on interdependence of societal units. These and other notions of social evolution motivated the research conducted then into the ways of thinking in so-called "primitive" societies. Some was conducted by an associate of Durkheim's, Lévy-Bruhl (1910/1926, 1922/1923), who spoke of *mentalités* as the collective representations of groups of people and who wrote about different *mentalités*—attitudes, assumptions, beliefs, categories—in less developed societies.

For Mannheim, who was influenced by Hegel and Marx, the social class was the group of interest. He, like Durkheim, pointed to a relationship between thought and social factors: "Even categories in which experiences are subsumed, collected, and ordered vary according to the social position of the observer" (Mannheim, 1929/1936, p. 130). But he did not take the same position that Durkheim had taken on social compulsion of thought and behavior. For him, the social domain was an integral part of the mental domain and vice versa. Mannheim (1952, 1956) rejected any notion of society as a "super-individual entity" and argued that it did not make sense to ask such questions as whether or not the mind is determined socially, which assumed that mind and society had separable substances. Even though most of his attention was on class memberships, he did not assume that class is always the major influence. Instead, he argued that, because people belong to multiple groups, it can be difficult to determine which affiliations are most influential.

Another early social theory with constructivist themes was developed by Fleck in Poland, but it would take some time for his work to reach social theorists and researchers in other countries. His book, *Genesis and Development of a Scientific Fact,* which was published in Poland in 1935, was not published in English until 1979, after attention had already been drawn to this sort of theorizing by M. Polanyi's (1958) description of science as guilds of knowers and apprentices, by Kuhn's (1962) influential consideration of social groups and their guiding paradigms, and by P. L. Berger and Luckmann's (1966) important summary of early work in the sociology of knowledge (cf. Merton, 1973). Fleck's major interest was in a scientific community, which might be an academic discipline or a subgroup in the discipline, and he used the term *thought collective* for such a group whose members work together to develop knowledge. The collective, he explained, has rules of behavior for its members and has its own forms of thought and discourse. Fleck used the term *thought style* for the shared perspective, or way of knowing, that guides, even exerts a compulsive force upon, members' thinking, although these people are not usually conscious of it. Although most of his attention went to this kind of group, a scientific research community, he spoke of other kinds of thought collectives to which a person in a research community would likely belong, such as a nation, race, social class, and a political party.

Studies of Discourse Communities.

The scholarship with this abstract kind of social-constructivist orientation, conducted for the most part since the 1950s, has focused on the activities, the practices, of societal groups. The group might be an "interpretive community" making meaning for literary works (Fish, 1980), or it might be an academic discipline building a particular kind of knowledge. Much attention has gone to the latter kind of group, the scholarly group that interested Fleck, particularly academic disciplines and subgroups within the disciplines. These are characterized as discourse communities (e.g., Bizzell, 1982; Porter, 1986) or even tribes with their own cultures, which include languages, conventions, forums, bodies of knowledge, leaders, and rites of passage (Becher, 1989). A discourse community, as Porter (1986) defined it, is composed of people who have common topics for their discourse and common conventions for their discourse practices. They share assumptions about what is appropriate for discussion and about how the validity of a particular claim might be demonstrated, and their discourse, which takes place through approved channels and in approved forums, is regulated by the group itself. The discourse knowledge that cognitivists see as belonging to individuals is portrayed as belonging to the group itself. The emphasis is put on what is shared.

Various terms have been used for the shared ways of knowing. Kuhn (1962) used the term *paradigm* for the guiding theories and assumptions that define what the relevant problems are, what approaches should be taken in conducting inquiry, and what criteria should be used for judging quality. The psychological similarity among people belonging to a particular community is what Vico called "common sense," Hegel called "idiosyncracy of spirit," and Fleck called "thought style." It is what Durkheim called "collective consciousness" and what Lévy-Bruhl called, and some present-day historians call, *mentalité* (cf. Burke, 1986). It is what some people have in mind when they say that members of a community share *ways,* "ways of being in the world" (Geertz, 1983), ways of "saying-(writing)-doing-being-valuing" (Gee, 1989, p. 178). N. Goodman might speak of a "world" in which members of the group operate, and Bartlett might refer to a social schema that members share.

Much attention in studies of discourse communities has been given to the forms and genres of written discourse, those same forms and genres that also interest constructivists studying individuals as agents. However, different sorts of questions are asked. One question asked about a discourse community might be: How did it develop a particular form over time? Some researchers have dealt with this question as they study the emergence and development over time of genres used by a partic-ular group and see how changes in discourse are tied to changes in the epistemology of the group. For example, Bazerman (1987) traced the development of the research report in psychology through its various codifications in the publication guidelines of the American Psychological Association. Another question might be: How do communities vary in what they value? A researcher dealing with this question was Becher (1989), who in his treatment of "academic tribes and territories," analyzed academic discourse to contrast the ways of different groups. This work suggested that criteria for appraising work are linked to the nature of knowledge in a field, for instance, historians' valuing of "good craftsmanship" and "masterly" treat-ment, mathematicians' valuing of "elegant," "economical," "productive," and "power-ful" solutions, and sociologists' valuing of "persuasive," "thought-provoking," and "stimulating" analyses (pp. 23–24). This kind of work illustrates how becoming a member of a discourse community entails learning its discourse as well as its knowl-edge, a process that is often viewed as enculturation or as going through rites of passage (e.g., Berkenkotter, Huckin, & Ackerman, 1988; J. S. Brown et al., 1989).

Much attention has also been given to the social aspects of authorship, which is at the center of the process of constructing knowledge socially. Members of a community produce their texts for an audience of community members, and they seek to make some texts public through various kinds of forums, which, in the case of academic disciplines, include journals, books, newsletters, and conference papers. For these forums, representatives of the community regulate the content and the form of the discourse through peer review, critiques, and other means (e.g., Myers, 1985a, 1985b). There are more immediate social relations, too. When producing texts, authors sometimes collaborate in pairs or teams, and they often consult with other colleagues on their work and on their texts, having these trusted peers read drafts and suggest modifications before submitting texts to be considered for publications (Reither & Vipond, 1989). Social constructivists see knowledge as the product of these various activities occurring over time. And some, such as Gergen (1985), see knowledge as *in* the texts or *as* the texts. The texts, according to Gergen, are "constituents of social practices" (p. 270). The process of authorship and knowledge construction is a dynamic process, and its development is studied over periods of time.

In this conception, meaning for a text is a consensus of members of the group. Such agreement is explained as resulting from processes of negotiation among community members (Fish, 1980) or from the particular ways of knowing of the group (Leenhardt, 1992). However, some social researchers have given attention to diversity among different individuals' interpretations. For instance, Gilbert and Mulkay (1984) metaphorically opened Pandora's box, pointing to the disagreements—the "divergent and conflicting voices" (p. 2)—that are often left out of accounts of social processes because the emphasis is on regularities. Fleck (1935/1979) pointed out that within a particular thought collective there are different understandings of texts because each individual in the collective belongs to more than one group and thus adheres to more than one thought style.

Although much of this social constructivist work has considered academic discourse, Schmidt (1982, 1992) has encouraged research into literary discourse that focuses on such large-scale social aspects as publication trends and readership trends, including varying interpretations associated with different times or places. In the third chapter we shall consider some of this work, which has been conducted for the most part by Europeans.

The Shifting Lens of Constructivism

As we have seen, several themes run through constructivism. These include an emphasis on active processes of construction, an attention to texts as a means of gaining insights into those processes, and an interest in the nature of knowledge and its variations, including the particular kinds of knowledge that are associated with membership in a particular group. But, as we have also seen, constructivism has a lens that shifts, allowing three foci: a focus on individuals engaged in social practices, a focus on a collaborative group, and a focus on a global community. When the lens focuses on one agent, certain questions are asked and answers are given, but, when the lens shifts, other questions are asked and other answers are given.

At this point I will use an example—the reading of this book—to illustrate differences in the three foci described above. The first focus that might be taken by a constructivist considering the reading of my book would be on the meanings built by individuals as agents. If this is the focus, attention would likely be directed to what the readers emphasize in their memories of the book, how they order the material, and what kinds of inferences and connections they make, including perhaps their inferences about the author. Despite viewing the individual as constructive agent, this constructivist would be cognizant of social factors, viewing readers as social beings with a great deal of knowledge acquired socially, which includes not only knowledge of the topic but also knowledge of social matters, such as the conventions of discourse. He or she might be interested in the relationship between readers' membership, in particular disciplinary or theoretical groups and the nature of meanings they construct. Also potentially interesting might be co-constructive activity, as, for instance, when readers' understandings of the text are influenced by what others have to say about it.

The second focus for a constructivist would be on a kind of collaborative, or shared, meaning that is built socially by a group composed of members who interact with one another. This kind of constructive process might be observed if a group of people, such as a graduate class, get together to discuss the book. If this is the focus, major interest would be in the shared aspects, which could be studied, for instance, through analysis of the negotiation process to see what statements about the book are agreed upon. This constructivist might or might not be interested in moving the focus afterward to the individual level to see if there are differences among the various individuals' meanings at that point or to study changes in individuals' understandings as a result of the discussion with others.

And, finally, the third focus would be on the constructions of a larger discourse community itself. These social constructions could be studied by analyzing reviews published in the community's journals or by studying citations of the book in articles and other books. In this way the constructivist would be able to make statements regarding the contribution that my "knowledge claim" makes to the communal knowledge.

Constructivists who have their lens focused in one way sometimes have difficulty seeing why someone else would see things in a different way, and the result is disagreements, some reminiscent of theoretical disagreements of previous times. (For discussions, see Bereiter [1994], Cobb [1994], and Phillips [1995], and the contributions to the collection edited by Steffe and Gale [1995].) Central to the debates are the issue of agency and the related issue of where to locate knowledge and meaning. People who focus on individuals tend to view knowledge as mental, locating it in the minds (or brains) of individuals, even though they readily point to social factors: that this mental knowledge has been built largely through social processes in which the learners have engaged, that it is used in social experiences, that it has social aspects, and so on. They also consider meaning to be a mental product. To their consternation, some socially oriented constructivists, particularly those who focus on large communities, seem to consider meaning and knowledge somewhere out there, *in* the texts or *in* the discourse practices of groups. Those who locate knowledge in the mind ask: "How can they *not* consider knowledge to be a cognitive product? A text is not knowledge. How can something that elicits different interpretations from individuals be considered consensual knowledge? A practice is not knowledge." A socially oriented constuctivist would wonder why the cognitivist chooses not to see the big picture, to see the larger patterns, which are where the real action is. To the constructivist interested in global social patterns, the research of the cognitivist focuses on the trivial.

It may seem that what we have here is a big-endian/little-endian difference like the one that Gulliver discovered among the Lilliputians, who argued about egg cracking (Swift, 1766). Some constructivists take a big-end position, envisioning large groups or societies as agents and seeing an abstract collectively constructed product as the result. Other constructivists take a little-end position, seeing individuals as agents and a mental product as the result. (The constructivists who focus their attention on collaborative groups are eventually situated at one end or the other. They either bring knowledge down to the level of the individuals in the group or leave it as an abstract collective product out there.) It may even seem that we have a demonstration of the difficulty that people have sometimes in taking the perspectives of others. I would argue, as I think N. Goodman (1978) would, that one is not necessarily the *right* view and the other the *wrong* view. Each can be right within a particular "world."

What I think we have is a rather predictable tension between alternative ways of viewing and describing the processes in which we are interested. One can focus on the individuals who are in social groups (their constructive processes, their choices and decisions, and the variability between them), or one can focus on the social groups themselves (their constructive processes, the abstract forces that seem to influence them, and larger patterns or systems in which all the variability among individuals might not be apparent). This was the tension addressed by Hegel. Years later Fleck (1935/1979) pointed to it, too: "The individual can be examined from the viewpoint of a collective just as well as conversely, the collective can be considered from that of the individual" (p. 45). Whichever major perspective we take, there is the opposing perspective that is possible. It is always there and we sometimes take it through upshifting or downshifting, but we cannot take both at the same time.

Even though socially oriented constructivists do not give major attention to the cognition of individuals, they assume that within the communities or systems are individuals who are cognizing beings, and they sometimes let that other perspective predominate. For example, Halbwachs, Durkheim's associate mentioned earlier, who gained some notoriety for his conception of collective memory as he described it in his 1925 book, spent some space in a later book (Halbwachs, 1950/1980) attributing remembering to the minds of individuals while pointing out that his major interest was in the common part of the memories of individuals who belong to a particular group. Cognitively oriented constructivists, who insist that knowledge is in the minds of individuals and not "out there" somewhere, speak of that socially constructed knowledge when they discuss such matters as conventional patterns for texts. And more than likely they tacitly consider a very abstract kind of social knowledge when providing a literature review of what is *known* about an issue or discussing a study's contribution to *knowledge* in the field.

When it comes right down to it, any account of discourse has to incorporate the individual and society. As Mannheim (1956) pointed out, "the group does not absorb the individual and the person does not completely assimilate and reflect his society" (p. 69). And as P. L. Berger and Luckmann (1966) argued, there are two "realities": one internal and one external. Our subjective meanings become externalized into social products, and our social products become internalized into our subjective meanings. The best approach for theory development is not to dismiss or ignore the other perspectives or become so eclectic that intellectual integrity is lost, but, cognizant of other ways of seeing, to give some attention to those factors that might be more apparent if we had the lens focused on the other kinds of agents. By being more aware of other perspectives, we can elaborate our own position and expand the kinds of issues we address and factors we consider.[2]

This Author's Perspective

For the most part, in my own studies of discourse processes I focus on individuals as constructive agents engaging in social activity, building meaning for texts, and producing texts intended to signal those meanings. I am interested in how people deal with the social forms and conventions constructed by their society and how their efforts are received by others in their society. The individual agent is a member of social groups, has a social identity, and employs socially acquired knowledge, including knowledge of social phenomena. He or she has experienced numerous

[2]Cicourel (1981) made a similar suggestion for dealing with the tension between micro- and macroresearch in sociology: "The challenge is to sustain one level while demonstrating that the other is an integral part of the discussion of the findings and theoretical perspective advanced" (p. 56).

texts written by other authors, and much of the knowledge used in literate practices has come from those kinds of social experiences. The individual works in a social context, both the large sociocultural and historical context and the more immediate situational context. And he or she is in social relationships with others, who would most likely include the potential audience for the piece, if the person is writing, or would be the author, if the person is reading. Sometimes these relationships are with other people, whom I call co-constructors, who can influence the nature of the meaning being built. For writing, they might take such roles as respondent, reviewer, or editor, or even collaborator, building their own meanings, which would have some features shared with the meaning constructed by the writer. For reading they are the people with whom one discusses a text. This focusing on individuals as constructive agents does not mean that a person, as writer and reader, is seen as holed up somewhere in a contextless vacuum without thoughts of others or interactions with others.

The kinds of transformations examined in my studies are those performed by writers (readers) rather directly on texts written by others. I am interested not only in commonalities among various people's performances of an act but also in the variability among them, and am interested in seeing which transformations are valued most by members of the social group to which they belong or aspire to belong. This interest in variability as well as commonality has motivated the kinds of studies that I conduct and that I discuss later in the book. This is not to say that I am uninterested in other transformations that occur in a less direct and immediate way, such as those that occur over long periods of time in the interpretations, knowledge, and conventions of social groups (e.g., van Rees, 1987) or the trans- formations that occur in some of the more abstract "worlds" described by N. Goodman (1978). It is simply to say that these transformations, though certainly relevant to a constructivist conception of discourse, have not received the major attention in my own studies of reading and writing processes. However, large-scale transformations and social constructions play an important role in my thinking, as evidenced in my writing of this book, which is a historical treatment of a body of knowledge and of the groups contributing to that knowledge.

Guiding my writing of this chapter and the rest of this book is a notion of authorship described briefly here but illustrated more fully in Chapter II and pre- sented in more detail later in Chapter VIII. As an act of composing, the writing of a text involves generating content, some of which is associated with reading done in the past and some with reading done specifically for that text. That is the case for my writing of this book: constructing meaning as a reader of texts written by others while constructing meaning as a writer of my own text. I have made various kinds of transformations as I read the texts of other authors: selecting, organizing and reorganizing, connecting, and elaborating to create a synthesis. Bakhtin (1929/ 1984, 1981, 1986) would point out the heteroglossic character of the writing and Kristeva (1967/1986, 1968) would point to its intertextuality.

The texts used in my writing have authors who include, to name just a few from this chapter, Vico, Kant, Hegel, Bartlett, Bransford, Piaget, Bruner, Kelly, N. Goodman, Salomon, Durkheim, Kristeva, Fleck, Becher, Schmidt, and Emig. These authors have names and also have authoring identities, which are based on identifiable themes and positions associated with their work and which are also based on their relations to other authors who have produced work with similar themes. A particular author's position would be supported and complemented by some authors and would be opposed by others. Even though work is attributed to a single author (or to a collaborative pair or team as co-authors), I assume that the author was engaging in the kinds of social processes described above, with other people, such as colleagues, and that the author had social connections with other authors who preceded him or her through reading their texts. Many of an author's claims could be traced to both kinds of social relationships. It is, of course, impossible to go into all the social relationships and all the different influences on a particular author.

There were people with those names who produced the texts I cite, but what I present reflects my construction of an author and his or her work—a construction created in a social fashion by reading relevant treatments by others as well as that person's work. The author's name is a sort of label for the construct, as Foucault (1969/1979) argued in the essay "What Is an Author?", the "author" serves as a means of classification and is a kind of projection of the various connections we make and the commonalities we see. So when an author is cited, that author's name functions as a tag for much more than that one individual person. When an author is cited, my own readers are cued to bring their own constructions of that author and that text to bear, even though I provide guidance for the sort of selections and inferences that they might make. In my historical treatments, as in this chapter, what I employ is not some kind of "great man and woman" approach but an approach based on this conception of author.

Plan for the Book

This chapter and the next are intended to situate a constructivist conception of discourse historically. In this chapter on "The Metaphor of Constructivism," a constructivist conception has been described in terms of its underlying metaphor in which agents can vary from individuals to small groups to large, abstract communities. The tension between opposing but complementary ways of conceptualizing agency has been reviewed and its importance to the development of constructivism has been noted. Chapter II, "Remembering Bartlett," is devoted to the influential work of Frederic Bartlett, who was able to see discourse processes from all three perspectives and who studied transformations of texts on the part of all three kinds of agents. This researcher, known for his cognitive work, attempted to account for social as well as cognitive aspects of discourse with similar explanations of constructive processes. I attempt to use Bartlett to illustrate the conception of authorship I described briefly above and to show how the various interpretations of Bartlett's *Remembering* are examples of the processes that he himself considered.

The next three chapters deal more specifically with reading and writing processes. Chapter III, "Understanding as Construction," moves into the large body of research guided by a sort of *zeitgeist* during the 1970s and 1980s. Attention in the chapter is on the reading of texts, contexts, and intertexts. And attention remains on reading in Chapter IV, "Comparison with Other Metaphors," as I plunge into what Fekete (1984) called a "maelstrom" of structuralist theories to compare constructivism to other conceptions based on a structural metaphor. These other metaphorical perspectives are structuralism, poststructuralism, and that often puzzling variant of poststructuralism known as deconstruction. Chapter V, "Composing as Construction," deals with social and cognitive processes of written composition. Although the book has separate chapters for the understanding and the composing of texts, some conventional distinctions between reading and writing are blurred.

The following three chapters are focused on reading–writing connections, and through them I present studies that my collaborators and I have conducted and relate them to studies conducted by others. Chapter VI, "Discourse Synthesis: Four Studies," presents my inquiries into acts of literacy that involve both reading and writing. In Chapter VII, "Textual Transformations in Written Discourse," these acts of synthesis are related to other literacy acts, such as critiquing and summarizing, that include both composing and comprehending. And in Chapter VIII, "Authoring Identity," attention goes to transformations individuals make over longer periods of time as they create identities through building their own interrelated bodies of work. My conception of authorship is contrasted with conceptions associated with other theories.

The concluding chapter, "Constructive Criticism," sums up many of these notions and relates the theoretical work and the research discussed in the preceding eight chapters to social and pedagogical issues that involve discourse.

Chapter II

· ·

Remembering Bartlett

Every book is a quotation; and every house is a quotation out of all forests and mines and stone quarries; and every man is a quotation from all his ancestors.
                    —Ralph Waldo Emerson, "Plato; or, the Philosophers"

If he were to come back today, Frederic Bartlett would, no doubt, be very surprised to see the interest that has been shown and is still being shown in his work. His reputation is international as well as interdisciplinary, and he maintains a citation rate that would impress anyone. And there on the cover of a 1995 reissue of his book *Remembering* is his picture.

This chapter focuses in more detail on Frederic Bartlett, not only his positions and his research but also the context in which he was working in the first decades of the twentieth century. I discuss Bartlett's theoretical and empirical work, particularly his well-known book *Remembering,* first published in 1932, and relate his positions to those of others. My rationale for devoting such attention to Bartlett is threefold: First, the influence of his work, both conceptual and methodological, has been profound since the 1970s and has been felt across many disciplines and fields that study human communication. It is an important link across much of the work discussed throughout this book, as many scholars today in various specialties are influenced by his work as they make their own contributions. Second, the issues with which Bartlett and his colleagues dealt are of great interest today and are the focus of current debates, particularly the question: In what ways is meaning making an individual process and in what ways is it a social process? When remembering and rereading Bartlett, one is struck by the relevance of his work to the issues with which we grapple today. My presentation is a revisionist portrayal of Bartlett, whose social theory has been missed in most summaries and discussions of his work. It seems to me that we are ready for it now. Third, his writing of his book and its interpretation (and remembering) by various other individuals and by groups of people are illustrations, I propose, of the very processes that Bartlett was trying to explain and that are the focus of my book.

As we will see, Bartlett's work and Bartlett himself illustrate the idea expressed by Emerson's (1903/1968) epigraph that introduces this chapter. Like any book, Bartlett's *Remembering* was a "quotation" in that it was a synthesis of ideas presented by prior texts, including some he authored and many other written texts and oral texts attributed to other people. And, like any person, Bartlett himself was a "quotation" in that he was a social being, influenced by people with whom he interacted directly and also by people from his own and from prior times whom he knew only through their writing. As we shall also see, the intertextuality of discourse was a question that interested Bartlett, too.

The Cambridge Milieu in Which Bartlett Worked

Bartlett was at Cambridge from 1909, the year he began studies there, to 1952, the year he retired after a long career as a faculty member. When he began that graduate work, psychology was emerging as an academic discipline with a method, a focus, and a body of work that were distinctive from those from the other disciplines that also dealt with human knowledge. An experimental methodology, particularly the psychophysical approach (varying physical stimuli and studying sensorial or perceptual reactions), helped to distinguish psychology from philosophy and give it affinities with physiology and other sciences. A focus on individuals helped make it distinctive from sociology and anthropology. However, disciplinary boundaries were not rigid for psychology or for other fields focused on human studies, such as anthropology and sociology, and scholars could cut fairly easily across disciplinary boundaries. The scientific turn was directed from Germany, but it was being taken in England and other countries. Cambridge was assuming the lead in making experimental psychology a branch of science in British universities, but Cambridge psychologists had interests that were strongly interdisciplinary.

Cambridge offered a complex interdisciplinary climate for pursuing studies in psychology, since scholars from different disciplines collaborated on projects and kept up with each other's work. Before entering Cambridge, Bartlett had become familiar with the work of W. H. R. Rivers on societal kinship patterns, which would be published later as the book *Kinship and Social Organisation* (1914/1968), had been intrigued by Rivers's ideas, and wanted to learn more about anthropology and psychology. Rivers, a rather remarkable man, had started his career at Cambridge as a lecturer in experimental psychology and physiology but was an anthropologist as well. He had been a member of the famous Cambridge expedition to the Torres Straits (New Guinea) in 1898 that was led and later described by the anthropologist A. C. Haddon (1901), who was also a biologist. In the late nineteenth and early twentieth century, with the impact of Darwin's evolutionary theory as well as Spencer's ideas, there was much interest in studying "primitive" cultures to learn about the genesis of the human mind (e.g., Durkheim, 1912/1968; Lévy-Bruhl, 1910/ 1926, 1922/1923), even though there was growing acknowledgment of social influences on factors previously considered to be cognitive and biological in nature. Others from Cambridge who went on the Torres Straits expedition and collected sensory-reponse data with Rivers were the psychologists C. S. Myers, who would in the future be a professor of Bartlett's and later his colleague, and William McDougall, who would join the faculty of Oxford and later go to the United States. Another member of the group was C. G. Seligman, who would become best known as an anthropologist, although he worked in medicine and psychology at the time of the expedition.

At Cambridge Bartlett did study with Rivers, who was his advisor and later his colleague. Rivers was known for his use of the psychophysical method in psychological studies, even in his field studies. But Rivers also was noted in anthropology for developing the geneological method, which he used for collecting and analyzing kinship terminology and other kinds of social data.[1] Following Morgan (1871), he studied the terms used by a particular society for relationships among kin and, from the analysis, made inferences about the level of the society's development. Although his early anthropological studies employing this method reflected an interest in the evolution of society, he became disenchanted with both the method and the evolutionary notion undergirding it and began to focus more on social processes to explain the similarities and differences among societies. He became interested in *diffusion,* the spread and modification of elements from one culture to another. In addition to his work in psychology and anthropology, Rivers also worked in physiology and collaborated with Sir Henry Head, a physiologist who specialized in neurology, on a study of nerve regeneration. In fact, for one study, Rivers had the nerves in his own arm severed so that he and Head could study the process of regeneration (Rivers & Head, 1908).

It was not only anthropology but also philosophy and psychology that interested Bartlett when he first went to Cambridge. He studied both of these interrelated disciplines under James Ward, Professor of Mental Philosophy, who was a major figure in British psychology. Ward, who was himself a product of Cambridge, had spent some time in Germany in the 1870s, where he studied with such notable scholars as Lotze in Göttingen and worked in Leipzig in the lab of Ludwig. While in Germany, Ward became immersed in the movement in the "new" experimental psychology. In the 1880s and 1890s he had taken a leading role in establishing experimental psychology as a discipline in England and in getting experimental psychology firmly established at Cambridge. He was author of the book *Psychological Principles* (1918), and was also known for his contribution to the 1886 edition of *Encyclopaedia Britannica,* in which he defined psychology as a discipline. His treatment of psychology in the latter piece was important—and authoritative—as Bartlett (1937a) later pointed out:

[1]This approach developed by Rivers would influence the work of Lévi-Strauss (1960/1969), who played a major role in developing French structuralism and whose work will be discussed in Chapter IV.

It was . . . a *system* of psychology, and it was based upon principles never intended to be within the reach of experimental verification or examination. But it was the first important discussion of psychology in England to pay attention to a mass of experimental work, then only recently performed. (p. 98)

Although Ward was supportive of the psychophysical method and had at the outset of his career conducted some physiological experiments himself, he did not want psychology to overemphasize method, become exclusively experimental and clinical work, and lose its analytic approach. Ward retired before Bartlett completed his graduate studies, and Bartlett was a student in the last class Ward taught.

Besides Rivers and Ward, the other faculty member working in psychology was Myers, mentioned earlier, who studied and worked with Rivers and had been a member of the Torres Straits expedition. Myers, who joined Ward and Rivers in establishing the *British Journal of Psychology* in 1904, became the first university lecturer to teach experimental psychology at Cambridge and was the author of a well-known textbook in psychology. It was Myers who got the funding in 1911 for the large-scale Cambridge Experimental Psychology Laboratory that Ward had wanted to establish before his retirement, and Myers became its director when it opened in 1913. Myers, who had a background in medicine, was known for his precise psychophysicial methods of measuring human perception and sensation.

Bartlett graduated with first-class honors in 1914, the year after the experimental laboratory opened. That year he became the interim director of the laboratory when the First World War began and Myers and Rivers went to war as doctors; his own health did not allow him to serve in the military. He was in an unusual position for someone at that stage of his career, holding a major leadership role at a major university. Two years later he completed his fellowship dissertation, which dealt with memory for shapes (Bartlett, 1916b). After Rivers and Myers returned from the war in 1918, Myers resumed his position as director, which he filled until 1922. That year—1922—was the year Myers left Cambridge and Bartlett became director, but it was also the same year that Rivers, Bartlett's good friend, died. In 1926 psychology was finally established at Cambridge in the way that Ward had envisioned it years before, as a science with the other sciences of physiology, biochemistry, and pathology. Bartlett was awarded the first chair in experimental psychology in 1931.

Bartlett's Work before *Remembering*

Bartlett published a number of pieces before *Remembering* was published in 1932. In fact, he published 40 or so articles before that book, most of them single-authored but a few written collaboratively (two on perception of faint sounds with E. M. Smith, who became his wife), and two books, one published in 1923 on *Psychology and Primitive Culture* and the other in 1927 on *Psychology and the Soldier.*

To appreciate *Remembering,* a reader needs to know something about Bartlett's prior writings, particularly the 1923 volume.

Perception, Imagery, and Memory

Even though he is best known for his studies with written texts, Bartlett used various kinds of semiotic materials in his studies: sketches of faces, picture writing, and other kinds of pictorial signs as well as texts. His early studies on perception and imagery, first reported in 1916 in the *British Journal of Psychology,* were closely related to those with texts. Bartlett noted processes of meaning making in his subjects' perception of pictorial material that were similar to the processes that he would also note in people's understanding of written discourse. His subjects tended to react to a design or pattern holistically as a single unit and to fit the pattern into some preformed scheme as they attempted to bring meaning to what they saw. Bartlett pointed out that perceiving, imaging, and remembering are all processes of making connections and that inferencing plays an important role in all. These were themes that he would repeat in *Remembering.*

Cultural Forms

One discourse form, the folk story, was of particular interest to Bartlett. He published two articles in 1920 on this subject and devoted a large part of his book *Psychology and Primitive Culture* (1923) to it. In the latter he explained that the folktale is a social product in two ways. First, it is a cultural artifact of the larger community, reflecting its history, values, and "tendencies." Second, it is a product that is socially shared in a storytelling group, told for listeners in a social setting within the community. Social factors within the larger community and within the immediate group account for such aspects of the form as repetition, sharp contrasts, metaphors, and conventionalized beginnings and endings. He attributed the elliptical quality of many of these tales to an unconscious reciprocity between storyteller and listeners, a kind of "comradeship," in which the listeners can fill in the gaps. In *Psychology and Primitive Culture* Bartlett used numerous examples from the anthropological work of Franz Boas (1909–1910) with the Tsimshian tribes along the northern Pacific Coast. Boas's (1901) collection of Kathlamet tales was the source of "The War of the Ghosts," the story that was to figure so prominently in the *Remembering* studies.

Cultural Change Processes

In *Psychology and Primitive Culture,* Bartlett (1923) also discussed the concept of cultural change, which would also be a major focus of *Remembering.* In this earlier treatment he discussed two processes, *contact* and *borrowing,* which were of much interest to anthropologists at that time. Contact occurs when a group migrates, taking its cultural forms to another group and the result is either blending or replacement, depending on the relationship between the two groups.[2] Bartlett's discussion of contact is supported with numerous examples from the work of Rivers (1914), who studied cultural change in Melanesia and elsewhere. An example from Rivers is the funeral practices in Melanesian societies that can be traced to the influence of multiple migrant groups. A recent disciplinary example, which I offer as an illustration, is the contact that has taken place in English studies as technical writing has become a subfield and "migrants" from other disciplines have brought in different cultural forms, knowledge, and values.

The other means of change is borrowing, the introduction of elements of culture by some important individuals or individuals who have been exposed to a different culture through travel or some other means. To illustrate borrowing, Bartlett used as an example the introduction of peyote culture into the Winnebago Indian society by John Rave. As the Winnebagos adopted peyote culture, it blended with their shamanistic practices. Even though certain elements were conserved, the blending of the new and the old resulted in unique elements. A disciplinary example today would be the introduction of protocol analysis by Flower and Hayes (1981) from cognitive psychology into the study of writing in English and language arts.

Both contact and borrowing are followed, according to Bartlett, by diffusion as the elements spread through the community and often persist. During diffusion they are subject to more modification. These notions of contact, borrowing, and diffusion were being discussed by many people at the time, not only Rivers (1913) and Bartlett, as an alternative to an evolutionary notion for explaining cultural changes.

Bartlett's major contribution with the 1923 book was his description of two processes—*conservation* and *constructiveness*—that account for the transformations that occur in contact, borrowing, and diffusion. These seem somewhat similar to Piaget's (1937/1954) concepts of change in individuals' cognitive structures, *assimilation* and *accommodation.* Bartlett's conservation is the culture's selecting what fits when there are points of similarity—the new fitted on the background of the old—and constructiveness is the culture's combining the new and the old into its own cultural patterns. Bartlett explained that in constructiveness "incoming new elements are inserted into the old cultural patterns, and the old is widened in fresh and often in striking ways" (pp. 160–161). In a brief article published in 1928, he again

---

[2]In similar terms Mulkay (1972) discussed the innovations in disciplinary knowledge that are often associated with migration. He spoke of such large-scale developments as the emergence of experimental psychology from the movement of physiologists into philosophy, and also discussed intellectual innovation from particular individuals who have moved into a different field.

discussed the eclectic nature of constructivity: that it can be seen in "the welding together of elements coming to a group from diverse sources and having historically very diverse significance" (p. 390). The conservation of what "fits" and the expansion of the old conventions would be seen in the funeral practices of the Melanesians and the peyote culture of Winnebago society and would also be seen in technical writing in English and protocol analysis in composition studies. Bartlett was interested in the psychological nature of these transformational processes when people experience, adopt, and modify forms that are new to them.

These kinds of social interests were echoed in *Psychology and the Soldier,* a collection of Bartlett's lectures for the public published in 1927. Bartlett described the modern army as a social organization, discussed the role of contact in building a social group, and applied his notion of borrowing to social progress that can come from cross-cultural placements.

Thus we have seen how Bartlett's work before *Remembering* dealt not only with the cognitive processes of perception and memory but also with the social processes of contact, borrowing, and diffusion. The latter processes, which involve both conservation and constructiveness, had been his major focus in *Psychology and Primitive Culture* and had been repeated in one chapter of *Psychology and the Soldier* and in two articles. These were important issues not only to Bartlett but also to his colleagues in the social sciences at Cambridge and elsewhere.

Remembering: Cognitive Processes

Remembering represented Bartlett's ambitious attempt to build, on the foundation of his body of work thus far, an integrative, unified conception of cognition that included consideration of perceiving and imaging as well as remembering. Moreover, it was also an attempt to build an integrative psychology that encompassed social processes, which had also been a long-time interest. For his studies of perceiving and imaging, conducted earlier, which had been reported in more detail in 1916, Bartlett used ink blots and pictures of faces. For his studies of individuals' remembering, he used written texts and picture writing. And for his studies of groups' remembering, he used written texts and pictorial material, including sketches of animals, objects, and human faces. Because my interest is in the relevance of his work to discourse, my discussion will center mainly on the memory studies with written texts, of which the study with "The War of the Ghosts" figures prominently. I should point out that Bartlett presented his studies as investigations into the remembering of texts, not the understanding of texts. But, as others, such as Gomulicki (1956), Kay (1955), and Spiro (1980), have pointed out, his studies can be considered studies of discourse understanding, too, because he was dealing with his subjects' initial meanings for those texts as well as transformations over time. Bartlett studied these transformations by analyzing recalls of the texts.

Bartlett's Approach to a Study of Cognition

In the first few decades of the 1900s, as psychology was being differentiated from philosophy, the methods of the "new" psychology were much discussed. Bartlett used the forum of his book *Remembering* to articulate his position. He began with a rather lengthy discussion of experiment as the method of psychology, maintaining that psychology should be *experimental* psychology but that "experimental" did not have to be defined as narrowly as it was being defined by some people in the discipline. Bartlett attributed the experimental method in psychology to influential psychologists who were also physiologists or physicists: Fechner, Weber, Helmholtz, and Wundt. It seemed inevitable to him that the first experimental studies would be psychophysical in nature, measuring individuals' responses as stimuli are varied, and he supported use of this methodology. However, he did not support the approach that Ebbinghaus (1895/1913) advocated for studying memory and complex processes: using nonsense syllables to try to equalize prior knowledge by making the stimuli meaningless and conducting studies in laboratory settings to try to neutralize effect of context. Bartlett devoted several pages of his book to arguing against that approach, which had become influential in the new scientific discipline of psychology. He pointed out that even nonsense syllables elicit associations and that artificial conditions change behavior into something that cannot generalize to natural situations. His position was that, in experiments examining complex mental processes, subjects should deal with naturalistic material and perform naturalistic tasks. He also maintained that researchers must take into account people's individual interests, attitudes, and goals as well as the culture in which they were operating. Those matters were the "stuff" of psychology, not simply conditions to be eliminated, and those were the matters he studied.

Actually Bartlett's position had some similarities to a position that Wundt (1863/1916) had taken earlier, even though Bartlett did not cite the German scholar to support his views. Wundt, considered one of the fathers of experimental psychology, maintained, as is well known, that basic psychological processes should be studied through laboratory experiments, but he also argued, as is less well known, that complex cognitive abilities should be studied through naturalistic inquiries and examinations of folklore. Complex acts, in which people use those basic processes, are inappropriate for study in a laboratory experiment, he thought, because it is impossible to establish adequate control. In fact, Wundt argued for creation of a subdiscipline, cultural psychology, to focus on such matters as language, myth, custom, law, and social structure, and he himself produced ten volumes that dealt with these kinds of cultural topics (Wundt, 1900–1920).

"The War of the Ghosts" Study

When remembered today, Bartlett is usually associated with his study reported in the 1932 book that employed a story titled "The War of the Ghosts." This Native American tale, a cultural artifact from the Kathlamets collected and translated by Boas (1901), was the major text that Bartlett used as he studied understanding and memory. Bartlett chose this story because it was "exceedingly different" from the stories of his British subjects' culture and thus had potential for eliciting the kinds of transformations that interested him. Folktales seem jerky, he explained, when they are out of their larger social community as well as out of the immediate storytelling group, where narrators can take it for granted that their audience will make the necessary connections. If the tales are removed from that context, the new audience must create their own connective links. In particular, he was curious about what his subjects would do with the events that seemed to have, as he put it, "no manifest interconnection" (p. 64).

This is the story he used:

The War of the Ghosts[3]

One night two young men from Egulac went down to the river to hunt seals, and while they were there it became foggy and calm. Then they heard war-cries, and they thought: "Maybe this is a war party." They escaped to the shore, and hid behind a log. Now canoes came up, and they heard the noise of paddles, and saw one canoe coming up to them. There were five men in the canoe, and they said:

"What do you think? We wish to take you along. We are going up the river to make war on the people."

One of the young men said: "I have no arrows."

"Arrows are in the canoe," they said.

"I will not go along. I might be killed. My relatives do not know where I have gone. But you," he said, turning to the other, "may go with them."

So one of the young men went, but the other returned home.

And the warriors went on up the river to a town on the other side of Kalama. The people came down to the water, and they began to fight, and many were killed. But presently the young man heard one of the warriors say: "Quick, let us go home: that Indian has been hit." Now he thought: "Oh, they are ghosts." He did not feel sick, but they said he had been shot.

So the canoes went back to Egulac, and the young man went ashore to his house, and made a fire. And he told everybody and said: "Behold I accompanied the ghosts, and we went to fight. Many of our fellows were killed, and many of those who attacked us were killed. They said I was hit, and I did not feel sick."

He told it all, and then he became quiet. When the sun rose he fell down. Something black came out of his mouth. His face became contorted. The people jumped up and cried.

He was dead. (Bartlett, 1932, p. 65)

[3]Reprinted with the permission of Cambridge University Press.

Bartlett had his 20 subjects, all of them English except for one person from India, read this story. Sketchy and disconnected, it requires a great deal of inferencing if a reader is to make sense of it. For example, what is the connection, if any, between the two reasons that the first young man gave for not going with the war party? Why did the other young man go? On what basis did that young man who went conclude that the men in the war party were ghosts? Why did he not feel sick if he had been shot? What was the "something black" that came out of his mouth?

Shortly after they had read it, he had his subjects write recalls of the text. Then, again, after longer periods of time, which might have been a matter of days or years, he had them produce recalls of what they had read. He studied these recalls, comparing the language of a recall with the language of the text, to see what was remembered. He analyzed them for deviations from the original material, taking note of what he saw as transformations. He was looking for patterns in the recalls of a particular individual as well as for patterns across the recalls of all the individuals. For his approach to studying memory, Bartlett gave credit to Philippe (1897), who had studied transformations in people's recall of common objects that had been presented to them tactually or visually.

Transformations of Meaning

Here, in the meaning-making processes of individuals, Bartlett saw the two processes that he had discussed previously in respect to cultural change: the tendency to conserve what fits and the tendency to appropriate the new and elaborate it so that it is more familiar. One obvious kind of transformation was reducing the content. After time had passed, Bartlett's subjects produced shorter recalls with fewer details and proper names. Whereas some elements were eliminated, others were "conserved," which Bartlett explained was done on the basis of subjects' determining tendencies. Other transformations were more constructive in that material was added. His subjects were, he said, rationalizing the material, making it more familiar and less puzzling. Subjects tended to make elements of the story conform to their own cultural experiences. For example, some recalled boats instead of canoes, and some remembered the Indians fishing instead of hunting for seals. But these readers also tended to make other constructions, additions, to fill in gaps. For example, some "remembered" the something black that came from the Indian's mouth was his breath as he was dying.

Moreover, most tended to supply connections, particularly causal connections. The following examples excerpted from the ghost story (on the left) and from one subject's written recall (on the right) illustrate some of the connections that the subjects made:

Then they heard war-cries, and they thought: "Maybe this is a war party." They escaped to the shore, and hid behind a log. Now canoes came up, and they heard the noise of paddles.

They (i.e., the young men) heard some canoes approaching them, *and so* hid.

One of the young men said: . . . "I will not go along. I might be killed. My relatives do not know where I have gone."

One said he would not go *as* his relatives did not know where he was.

He did not feel sick, but they said he had been shot.
  So the canoes went back to Egulac.

The young man did not feel sick (i.e., *wounded*), *but nevertheless* they proceeded home. (Bartlett, 1932, pp. 65, 86)

These excerpts show additions for connectivity. The first two examples show how causal connections (*and so* and *as*) are added to provide reasons for thoughts or behaviors. And the third example shows a change from a causal connection (*so*) to a contrastive kind of connection (*but nevertheless*), which in our cultural way of thinking seems a more logical way to connect the young man's not feeling sick and the group's returning home anyway.

Bartlett noted simplifications, regroupings, and modifications, some of which were elaborative rather than reductive, as he studied his subjects' written recalls for deviations from the original material. Through these kinds of changes, he saw the story being transformed to an "orderly narration" as his subjects deleted some content and added other content to fill the gaps. In making sense of the story, they were adding plausible material to make it conform more to their own knowledge of events and of human thought and behavior. Bartlett, like many others before him, including Kant, was acknowledging the important role of causal inferencing to satisfy humans' need to understand why something is done, why it happens.

Thus, the study reveals a process characterized by organization, selectivity, and connectivity, those three aspects of constructivity that are being studied today. Bartlett's subjects' recalls were organized, in that they suggested the chronological patterning of the narrative. However, in many cases these recalls seemed better organized—at least according to British standards—than the original text, conforming in certain ways to the story patterns with which these people were familiar. Their recalls were selective, in that certain elements were chosen for memory over others. Some selections seemed to be on the basis of individual factors, such as temperament and character, but others were on the basis of social factors, such as the conventions and values of a group The recalls were also connective, in that material was added and links were made to related experiences. Some material seemed to be invited by the text, and some was necessary to fill those noticeable gaps in the ghost story. But other material showed subjects' idiosyncratic connections to elements of their own experience.

Bartlett's Explanations

To explain these findings, Bartlett began with the concepts he had discussed previously with respect to social processes. He also introduced the schematic conception of memory for which he is well known today.

Construction

In discussing the findings from the ghost story study and other studies reported in *Remembering,* Bartlett proposed a constructivist explanation for the transformations people seemed to make—an explanation similar to the points that he had been making in his earlier work. He suggested that people do not take in something detail by detail, gradually building up a whole from the parts, but, because anticipation is a part of recognition, detect enough to develop a general impression and from that constitute the details. For example, in understanding or remembering a story, the identification of a text as a story influences how the parts are understood or remembered. In remembering, people construct or reconstruct the parts by generating the whole. He suggested that the changes an individual made were due to active, constructive processing that resulted from the "effort after meaning" to "connect something that is given with something other than itself" (p. 227).

Schemas

Bartlett explained that these constructive processes are possible because memory is composed of global knowledge structures, called schemas, by means of which people perceive, understand, and remember their experience. He defined a schema as "an active organisation of past reactions, or of past experiences," which has components, serially configured, that do not act serially but as a "unitary mass." He argued that memory is neither a "passive patchwork" nor "individual events somehow strung together and stored within the organism" but instead is composed of "living momentary settings belonging to the organism." These structures, which are interconnected and are tied to attitudes and interests, help explain the "determining tendencies" seen in perception, understanding, and recall. They are dynamic, "actively *doing* something all the time" (p. 201). People use them but change them through their use. He conceived of similarities in the structures of people of a particular group, or community, as well as individual differences between different people.

The term *schema* came from Head (1920, 1926; Head & Holmes, 1911–1912), the physiologist at Cambridge who had collaborated with Rivers. Bartlett credited Head with showing him how his "tangled mass of . . . experimental data revealed consistency and order in the human mind" (p. vii). Head had used *schema* for a person's holistic mental conception of his or her total body or posture, against which postural changes are related. This standard, built up by combining alterations in posture, is constantly changing but is still used even when a limb is amputated.

Bartlett employed various metaphors—"unitary mass," "living settings," not "passive patchwork," not events "strung together" (p. 201)—in his attempts to communicate his notion, which is still somewhat difficult to grasp.

These knowledge structures were Bartlett's answer to the whole–part question that had interested psychologically oriented philosophers and philosophically oriented psychologists through the years. Some, such as Leibniz (1704/1981) and the Gestaltists, emphasized the wholes, and some, such as the British empiricists of the past as well as the associationists of his time, emphasized the parts. Although Bartlett described a holistic process, he also conceived of parts, interconnected by associations.

Bartlett's Cognitive Positions Relative to Others' Positions

Before moving to the social studies of remembering also reported in the 1932 book, let us consider briefly how this British psychologist's explanations of cognitive processes contrasted with the explanations of some dominant camps within psychology at the time.

Contrast with Associationists

Bartlett believed that his findings—additions and transformations as well as omissions—argued against the claims of some associationists, particularly Ebbinghaus, who was so influential in psychology at that time. In contrast to these psychologists, Bartlett (1932) portrayed memory as an active, holistic process, and disagreed with those who portrayed memory as consisting of "innumerable fixed, lifeless, and fragmentary traces" (p. 213). In his attention to mental activity, he expressed ideas that were compatible with those of Ward (1918), who had been one of his Cambridge professors. Ward, influenced by Lotze (1852), emphasized unity of consciousness, activity of memory, and the role of interest in forming wholes. Bartlett also disagreed with the associationists' explanation of memory as merely a chain of associations: one small unit (e.g., an idea) being associated with another through a relation, such as contiguity or similarity, that unit being associated with another, and then that unit being associated with another, and so on, in an incremental fashion. He thought that the whole pattern could be generated before all the parts and that the whole could assist in remembering the parts, as in understanding or remembering a story.

Even though Bartlett put his emphasis on the whole as opposed to the parts, he did not dismiss the notion of associations, or relations (what Kant called categories). He explained that, when a recall is analyzed, one can see relations, such as coordination, superordination, subordination, contrast, cause-effect, chronology, and space, but that is not necessary to conclude that the structure is built up gradually simply because of those relations. Thus, Bartlett rejected some parts of associationism but accepted others. He did not consider associationism to be an adequate explanation of how understanding and memory work, but he thought that the associating principles were useful for describing the connections within a knowledge structure after it is built.

Contrast with Behaviorists

If he disagreed with the associationists, he also disagreed with the behaviorists, such as J. B. Watson (1916), who made the conditioned reflex their unit and linked stimuli and response rather than ideas. This is what he had to say about behaviorism:

> There is an active school in current psychological controversy which would banish all reference to consciousness. It is common to try to refute this school by asserting vigorously that of course we know we are conscious. But this is futile, for what they are really saying is that consciousness cannot effect anything that could not equally well be done without it. That is a position less easy to demolish. If I am right, however, they are wrong. (Bartlett, 1932, p. 214)

Contrast with Gestaltists

Some have considered Bartlett a Gestaltist. Certainly, there is some compatibility between his work and that of the psychologists known as Gestaltists who conducted their research and developed their theory in the early 1900s (Koffka, 1935; Köhler, 1929). Like Bartlett, these psychologists focused on form. They, too, were interested in how perception of parts is determined by the configuration of the whole and how gestalts result from organizational processes. Much of their work dealt with the kinds of transformations that are made in perceiving figures, such as simplifying, grouping, filling in missing parts, and seeing some parts as figure and other parts as ground. Figure 1 demonstrates the grouping transformation performed on the lines that are close to each other. Nevertheless, there were differences between Bartlett and the Gestaltists, particularly in regard to the nature of knowledge. The Gestaltists conceived of cognition as force fields (like electrical fields) that

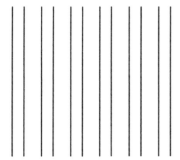

Figure 1. Gestalt demonstration of grouping.

create isomorphic facsimiles of the perceptual field, which are subjected to Gestalt principles such as leveling and sharpening to achieve symmetry, simplicity, and good form. Bartlett considered perception, imaging, or understanding to be proactive, resulting because people already had active schemas, not receptive, something laid down in the brain. His schemas, which differed across individuals and across social and cultural groups, were knowledge constructed about the world, not facsimiles of the world.

Contrast with Würzburgers

Bartlett's ideas also had some affinity with those of the Würzburg psychologists, who did their work under Külpe's leadership in the early 1900s. They, too, had found associationism inadequate to explain the purposeful nature of thinking and the order that people impose on their experience. These psychologists, who were known for their introspective methodology, also recognized the role of holistic processes in the solution of complex problems and placed an emphasis on motivation and attitudes. They had their subjects perform various kinds of tasks, which might be as simple as associating to words or as complex as solving Nietzsche's aphorisms. In particular, the concept of *Einstellung,* or mental set, developed by Watt (1905) and Betz (1910), seems similar to Bartlett's notion of attitude. In fact, Bartlett had cited Betz in his dissertation, which he completed in 1916, when he reported some of the same work that he reported in *Remembering.* Also apparently related was the work of Ach (1905), who spoke of the "determining tendency" (a term Bartlett used in his 1923 book). Despite what appear to be some similar ideas, Bartlett did not acknowledge any theoretical agreement with the Würzburgers. In fact, he indicated that he had not found their work relevant to what he was trying to do. In his final book, *Thinking,* published in 1958, he explained that, at one point in working on *Remembering,* he had taken some time to read the Würzburg research but decided it was a dead end for him.

Remembering: Social Processes

Remembering was more than Bartlett's attempt to explore the nature of mental processes. It was also his attempt to relate the cognitive processes of individuals to the social processes of groups and societies by considering the constructivity in both. Bartlett presented a portion of the book as studies in social psychology, which he defined in this book as "the systematic study of the modifications of individual experience and response due to membership of a group" (p. 239). This was a different definition from the one he had provided in 1923 in *Psychology and Primitive Culture.* There he had described it in quite different terms—group terms but not individual terms—as the study of "intimate knowledge of the group," which would include its "characteristic internal organization" and "its social relationship to the rest of the community" (p. 213). This shift in definition marked something of a shift in his perspective on constructive agent, as he began to give more attention to the individual as agent. He was seeing the individual as the major focus of psychology.

However, in *Remembering,* Bartlett still gave much emphasis to social factors, even when considering individual cognition:

> The group itself, as an organised unit, has to be treated as a veritable condition of human reaction. It means that, even if we said everything that theoretically could be said about experience and conduct from the point of view of its determination by external stimulation, or by individual factors of individual character and temperament, we should still leave wholly unexplained some—very likely a large number—of the most important human responses. (p. 241)

In words that had a Hegelian or Vichian ring, he discussed two types of groups: a physically contiguous group and a group that is tied together solely by such things as beliefs, customs, and institutions and is not physically contiguous. The latter would include what is today called a disciplinary discourse community, or what Fleck (1935/1979) would have called a "thought collective."

Social Constructs and Individuals' Responses

Some emphasis in the ghost story study, discussed above, was on the conventional knowledge, values, and beliefs that belong to individuals in the same group or society. In discussing this study as well as other cognitive studies, Bartlett pointed to the influence of social factors, saying that transformations resulted, in part, from social beliefs and conventions of the group to which the person belonged. As he put it, "What is initially outstanding and what is subsequently remembered are, at every age, in every group, and with nearly every variety of topic, largely the outcome of tendencies, interests and facts that have some value stamped on them by society" (p. 253). He claimed that a social group has a particular psychological tendency or group of tendencies, which makes for a sort of bias in its dealings (cf. Hegel, 1827–1830/1894, 1935/1979). That bias, which is manifested in interest, emotion, and excitement, he argued, influences what members of the group notice and how they remember their experiences. This term, "group difference tendencies," was one he had used in 1923 and attributed to Myers, but it had also been used by others.

Another basic concept he extended from the individual to the social was the schema notion. He explained that a group's preferred tendency is a "a persistent framework of institutions and customs" (Bartlett, 1932, p. 255), a kind of "lasting social 'schema' on the basis of which much constructive work in recall may take place" (p. 264). The ghost story illustrated a social schema, because the British subjects all seemed to have similar expectations for a story and similar difficulties with the one they read, which came from another culture.

But he also provided some illustrations from his observations in Africa in 1929. One came from the Swazi: A Swazi chief and some of his tribesmen visited London, and, when they returned to Swaziland, the British group there was interested in what they had noticed and remembered. The one thing they remembered best was a traffic policeman's holding up his hand to direct traffic. They were impressed with that particular act because the Swazi place great value on the lifting of one's hand, which they see as a friendly gesture. Thus, the policeman seemed friendly to them in this foreign land. The other illustration came from the Bantu, who were reputed to have excellent memories. Bartlett concluded from a little informal experiment he conducted that this remarkable ability to remember appeared only when the Bantu were operating within an area of interest. A Bantu man could give an amazingly accurate and detailed account of cattle transactions, but his memory did not seem at all exceptional when he was given the sort of task used in memory experiments.

Relations among Members of a Group

As in *Psychology and Primitive Culture,* Bartlett discussed the strong rapport that can be created when someone tells a story to people from his or her own group. The audience's social response, which he called its preferred tendencies, can elicit from the storyteller particular kinds of material, which might, for instance, be comic or pathetic. However, in *Remembering,* Bartlett was more interested in the effects of an audience on the form of a speaker's text, in particular, how speakers' delivery differs when the audience differs. Speakers modify their mode of presentation, he pointed out, when they are in different groups, and the narrator's position relative to that of the audience is an important factor in such shifts. He spoke of the power relations between speaker and audience, pointing out how a speaker asserts his or her dominance when the audience seems submissive and how the speaker can move into a recapitulatory mode when the audience seems superior. In this treatment Bartlett was giving more emphasis to the dynamic rhetorical relationship between speaker and audience and less emphasis to the group as a single, collective agent.

Community Constructions: The Conventionalization Studies

Bartlett had a long-term interest, mentioned previously, in social constructivist issues: how communities construct their institutions, how they transform customs, symbols, and materials from other groups or individuals to make them their own.

In *Psychology and Primitive Cultures* he had discussed the conservation and social constructiveness that occur during contact and borrowing and the diffusion that follows. But for *Remembering* he came up with an experiment to *see* these kinds of changes when a product is passed from one person to another. In the latter book he used the broader, more inclusive concept, *conventionalization,* which his former professor and colleague, Rivers (1914), had defined as "a process by which a form of artistic expression introduced into a new home becomes modified through the influences of the conventions and long-established technique of the people among whom the new notions are introduced" (p. 383).

Bartlett wanted to bring this abstract conventionalization process down to a concrete level so that he could study these socially influenced transformations in a rather direct fashion. He wanted to see how "elements of culture" or "cultural complexes," which might be a story but might also be a piece of art or a particular practice, change as they pass from person to person within a group or from group to group until they become part of the group's culture. His interest was in how such cultural artifacts are passed along and become conventionalized, much the way rumor works: what material remains, what is lost, what is added, and what is transformed in other ways. He would study a social process that parallels the individual process.

To study these social influences on textual transformations, he used a method of serial reproduction: having one person recall a story or informative text to another who recalled it to another who recalled it to another. This approach, he later disclosed, was suggested to him by Norbert Weiner, who asked him during a visit to Cambridge, "Couldn't you do something with 'Russian Scandal,' as we used to call it?" (Bartlett, 1958, p. 144). As an experimental psychologist, Bartlett was conducting an experiment—an experiment intended to simulate the natural cultural transformation processes that occur when a cultural artifact is introduced in a different group. People familiar with *Psychology and Primitive Culture* can see the relevance of this method to Bartlett's major issues, but people not familiar with that prior book might miss the relevance because Bartlett provided little rationale in *Remembering.*

Transformations in Social Practices

Bartlett described social processes in much the same terms as those he used to describe individual cognitive processes. In these social studies, the interpersonal process of passing along a story—"The War of the Ghosts," as well as others—revealed transformations that were selective, organizational, and connective and were similar to those in the ghost story study, which focused on individuals' processes. Proper names and other details dropped out as the stories were reduced to their essentials. This abbreviation occurred even as the stories were "rationalized" and made more coherent. However, in the one cross-cultural study, people from

India, who were given a story for serial reproduction, elaborated the text, making it more similar to stories from their own culture, and they even added a moral.

Bartlett's Social Positions

In his work, including *Remembering,* Bartlett articulated and organized a number of important concepts as he developed his integrative theory, but he was not developing these ideas in a social vacuum. He himself was involved in a process that was quite social. We have already seen how his positions on cognitive issues related to other positions that were being argued. The social issues with which Bartlett was dealing were the focus of formal as well as informal discussions, which took place through various forums at Cambridge as well as in the literature he and others were reading. For instance, Cambridge held a joint psychological and anthropological discussion in March of 1927, and the papers were subsequently published in the *British Journal of Psychology* in 1928. Bartlett's paper on social constructiveness, referred to earlier, was the first of four papers, and the others written in response to it were by the psychologists J. T. MacCurdy (1928) and W. E. Armstrong (1928) and the anthropologist A. C. Haddon (1928).

Conventionalization and Social Constructiveness

Particularly influential on Bartlett's thought was the work of his former teacher, Rivers, who had died the year before *Psychology and Primitive Culture* was published. Rivers, whose lectures had attracted Bartlett to Cambridge, had reported studies of contact between cultures and conventionalization in his *History of Melanesia,* mentioned earlier (which was work in progress when the two first met), and elsewhere, notably *Contact of Peoples* (1913). In *Instinct and the Unconscious* (1922) he mentioned constructiveness in regard to the group, a theme Bartlett was to develop. Rivers considered constructiveness to be a manifestation of the self-preservation of the group. Haddon (1894), too, focused much of his attention on conventionalization, particularly in regard to art and pictorial material in social groups, and he considered conservation the "sheet anchor of the ethnographer" (p. 179; cf. Haddon, 1901, 1920). Bartlett's major contributions were articulating such concepts as conventionalization and constructiveness in psychological terms as he developed his theory and showing how they were relevant to the cognitive processes of individuals as well as the social processes of groups. These were anthropological and sociological concepts as well as psychological ones, and they were Rivers's concepts and Haddon's and others' as well as Bartlett's.

Contrasts between Cultures

If people who belong to different societies differ in their ways of thinking, why is that so? This was a question that interested some psychologists but greatly inter-

ested many anthropologists and sociologists. Some, as mentioned earlier, were taking an evolutionary stance: that "primitive" societies were at a lower point on a
developmental continuum than more "civilized" societies. Others were taking the
sort of position that the American anthropologist Boas (1909–1910, 1910) took:
that different cultures, which are all adapted to their circumstances, have different
"designs for living" and cannot be ranked.

Much of the work on the issue of evolutionary patterns in society was associated with the French and influenced by Durkheim. Lévy-Bruhl (1910/1926, 1922/
1923), who, as mentioned earlier, took an evolutionary position, argued against
studying other cultures from one's own perspective: "Let us . . . endeavor to guard
against our own mental habits and try to discover, by analysing their collective
representations and the connections between these, what the primitive's way of
thinking would be" (Lévy-Bruhl, 1922/1923, p. 32). He thought that those who
study primitive cultures must try to understand the ways in which the people's ideas
are connected. His controversial thesis was that primitive people, who are in a
prelogical state, do not make the same kinds of connections that are made by people
from more developed cultures; in particular, they do not perform the same kind of
causal reasoning. He claimed that causal connections, "which to us are the very
framework of Nature, the basis of its reality and stability" (p. 37), are of little interest
to the primitive, who instead explains events in terms of mystical powers.

Bartlett had presented his response to these claims most directly in 1923 in
Psychology and Primitive Culture, and the position articulated there seems to guide
Remembering, too. Of course, he agreed that different groups have different perspectives. It was the point about connections with which Bartlett took issue: that more
primitive people make different *kinds* of connections. He claimed that differences
could be attributed, not to differences in type of reasoning or to differences in
cognitive capabilities, but to the aspects of life being considered and to the "determining tendencies," or sets, with which they approached events. (When he wrote
Psychology and Primitive Culture, he did not yet have the term "schemas.") Rivers
(1922) also critiqued Lévy-Bruhl's second point, arguing that what seemed illogical
to Lévy-Bruhl may instead be perfectly logical to those who understand the meaning of the ideas and practices.

Position on Issue of Collective Mentality

Another hotly debated issue was the notion of collective mentality influenced
by Durkheim's theory and being developed at that time. This notion, which was
undergirded with a biological analogy, also had an evolutionary focus: that units
combine to form higher units in ever-increasing sophistication. A few years before
Bartlett published *Remembering,* Halbwachs (1925/1975), mentioned earlier, who
had studied with Durkheim, published his book, *Les Cadres Sociaux de la Mémoire,*
which presented a concept of collective memory that was very much a Durkheimian notion. In *Remembering,* Bartlett responded to that notion, appreciating the
careful studies of families, religious groups, and social classes that Halbwachs used

to support his claims, but ultimately rejecting the metaphor. He could not accept the idea of a social memory that a group might have that would be separate from the memories of individuals within the group. He could speak of memory *in* the group but not memory *of* the group.

Bartlett had particular difficulties with a somewhat different notion of the collective, Jung's (1916) concept of collective unconscious, which was also being developed at that time. To him, Jung's collective unconscious presented the same difficulty as the associationists' concept of individual memory: Both seemed to view memory as a storehouse for traces of ideas, images, stories, and other material. Bartlett, who emphasized transformations, did not agree with this storehouse notion for individuals or for groups.

The conception of a collective mentality was much discussed then (as it still is now in some circles). For example, a few years before *Remembering* was published, Bartlett's colleague, the anthropologist Haddon (1928), discussed his responses to the conception of a collective mind, which were the responses that many people, especially the British, had to it. Although he, too, rejected it, Haddon could see how the idea developed through its biological analogy. He could see how seductive it was. As I mentioned in the previous chapter, Halbwachs (1950/1980) in a later book made it clear that he was not dismissing individual cognition and memory, as he described a sort of distributed memory in which different members of a group remember different parts to make a composite remembrance. This was, no doubt, an attempt to answer his critics as well as to provide a more complete presentation of his ideas.

Relation to Prior Work

Bartlett's prior work, particularly *Psychology and Primitive Culture,* provides the theoretical background for his social study in *Remembering.* It was really the large-scale cultural process that interested him: how products, including products from another culture, become conventionalized as they are passed from one person to another in a community. That process did not really fit within the parameters of the psychology of his time. So, for this book, he had come up with an experiment to study conventionalization. He devoted most space to discussing issues in psychology, but he did give some attention to controversial social issues discussed by sociologists and anthropologists.

He was trying to accomplish a great deal with this book. No wonder it was so difficult for him to write it.

The Writing of *Remembering*: Bartlett's Composing Process

As this review has shown, Bartlett was not a solitary scholar working alone in some ivory tower and creating his own unique theory. He conducted his studies and produced his texts in a complex social context that was not only interdisciplinary and international but was also intertextual. His Cambridge colleagues were his immediate community and were important throughout, as evidenced by the same names appearing in citations and acknowledgments: Rivers, Head, Myers, Haddon, Ward, and MacCurdy. Bartlett also credited his Cambridge colleagues with suggesting methods he could adapt from others. As I mentioned above, Ward had suggested Philippe's method for studying changes in memory over time, and a visitor to Cambridge and temporary colleague, Norbert Weiner, had suggested the "Russian Scandal" approach, the serial reproduction method.

In addition to that Cambridge community, Bartlett also showed his membership in a larger disciplinary community, that of the international community of psychology. As an "experimental psychologist" he showed respect for the fathers of his discipline, particularly those in Germany who developed the psychophysical method, and also showed his alignment or lack of alignment with particular groups or individuals within the discipline. He made clear his disagreement with behaviorists and with trace theorists, even though he largely ignored the Würzburgers and Gestaltists. In addition to the community of psychology, he placed himself within a larger community of interdisciplinary scholars interested in such issues as social evolution and the notion of collective mind that lay within the domains of more than one discipline—psychology, sociology, anthropology, and history, too—and that were being studied by continental and American scholars as well as those in England. But he distanced himself from certain evolutionary positions and from the stronger proponents of collectivism.

In his final book, *Thinking,* published in 1958, we have Bartlett's own retrospective account of his work on *Remembering,* which spanned more than a decade. He described the project as a struggle that took "twists and turns." And he used the metaphor of gap filling, which he had first used in his 1923 book, to describe his own thinking as he conducted his *Remembering* studies and wrote his book. He put it this way: "The whole process appeared as one in which gaps, progressively filled, opened up new gaps, and no final halting place was reached" (Bartlett, 1958, pp. 147–148).[4] As he explained, sometimes other people helped him fill gaps, for instance, Weiner, when he suggested the "Russian Scandal" method. Sometimes what Bartlett thought would fill a gap did not, for example, when he got sidetracked in the Würzburg studies. As a writer, he saw himself as an individual struggling to create coherence, making choices and decisions, discussing his work with other people, and getting ideas and responses from them.

Bartlett's portrayal of his own social process can be contrasted with the portrayal presented by the social anthropologist Douglas (1986). When she read *Psychology and Primitive Culture* and *Remembering,* Douglas noted a dramatic shift from an emphasis on social processes in the 1923 book to an emphasis on individuals in the

---

[4]Piaget (1975/1985), as noted earlier, also used the gap metaphor when he discussed constructive filling of gaps in knowledge.

1932 book. Because Bartlett had changed his emphasis to individuals, she saw him as a "self-referencing instance of the claim that psychologists are institutionally incapable of remembering that humans are social beings" (p. 81). She believed that psychology exerted its institutional force on him: His work had to conform—had to be coherent with—the method and prevailing political values of the discipline. Was she right? Certainly there were factors within his immediate situation as well as factors within the broader sociohistorical context that influenced his perspective and his persona as an experimental psychologist. He had become "the" experimental psychologist at Cambridge when Rivers and Myers went to war and he was responsible for running the lab and building the program. He was working in a discipline that emphasized collecting data from individuals, was working in a country that had a strong emphasis on individualism, and was working in a world that was becoming wary of collectivist notions.

So, were these changes in Bartlett the result of social influences, as Douglas argued? Or were they, as Bartlett explained them, the result of decisions that he himself made as he was becoming a different individual with different knowledge and interests? To both questions the answer is yes. It seems to me that we can see in Bartlett's own work the very processes that he was describing in his prior work in social processes. We see the conventionalization as Bartlett was becoming more a psychologist and less an anthropologist. The contrast between *Psychology and Primitive Culture* and *Remembering* is striking in the emphasis. We can also see constructiveness from contact of "cultures" as Bartlett brought together work from different disciplines: psychology, physiology, anthropology, and sociology. In the former work we can see sociology and anthropology, but in the latter we can see more *experimental* psychology and physiology. Rivers and Boas loom large in the former but not in the latter.

Bartlett's Work after *Remembering*

After the publication of *Remembering,* Bartlett continued his work in perception, memory, and social processes. He also extended his constructivist perspective to other issues. For example, he argued against the attempts being made at that time to achieve universal standardization for intelligence tests by testing people in various cultures (Bartlett, 1937b). To support his argument, he offered an observation that East African natives, who failed in their attempts to arrange colored pegs in an alternating sequence on a test, easily planted trees according to that principle in their everyday work. He made the point that forms of intelligence are culturally determined and culturally situated and that attempts to understand intelligence should be focused on *types* of intelligence (cf. Cole, 1985).

During the Second World War his work took something of a different turn as he worked on such applied problems as the effect of fatigue on pilots. After the war, when he was in his sixties, he taught a new generation of psychologists. From 1944 to 1953, when he was director of the Applied Psychology Unit, he received much recognition and many kudos, which included honorary doctorates from several universities and awards from various disciplinary organizations. He was knighted in 1948 and was given the Royal Medal in 1952, the year he retired. After retirement, he published the book *Thinking*, which he had been planning to do for some time.

Readers' Memories of *Remembering*: Different Groups, Different Memories

For the third memorial lecture at Cambridge honoring Bartlett, who died in 1969, Bartlett's contribution with *Remembering* was assessed by a former student, Zangwill (1972). Regarding its overall theoretical contribution, Zangwill's opinion was that the book would be of little interest, except perhaps to historians of psychology. He believed that, because few people would want to read it, it might as well be forgotten. In regard to the studies, he pointed to the informality of the methods, which "by modern standards leave much to be desired," and the qualitative, "highly selective" presentation of results (pp. 125–126). But his major problem was with Bartlett's explanations—the "shadowy operation" of the hypothetical structures and an overemphasis on constructivity in describing mental processes. Years before, Boring (1950) had given Bartlett an even harsher criticism, which took the form of omission. In his influential history, Boring gave *no* attention to Bartlett's scholarship, except in the most general terms, merely saying that Bartlett was a functionalist and an experimental psychologist. And this was the 1950 revised version, which had a "filled out and updated" chapter on British psychology, including a section on experimental psychology that had been completely revised from the earlier 1929 edition. Many others before Zangwill had commented on Bartlett's unconventional research methods, particularly those people who conducted replications and extensions (e.g., Gauld & Stephenson, 1967; Paul, 1959).

Unlike Boring and Zangwill, some other psychologists saw much potential value, particularly those who were examining the book for its relevance to the cognitive psychology that was becoming increasingly important in the late 1950s and early 1960s. For example, in an obituary for Bartlett, Broadbent (1970) was highly complimentary of Bartlett's theoretical efforts, particularly relative to the theories of the two major groups of psychologists of his time, the Gestaltists and Behaviorists:

> Neither party allowed for anything so complex as the mixed and hierarchical levels of processing which Bartlett was discussing; nor for the intimate links of social structure and individual psychology. They were confining themselves to facts about behavior which they had the theoretical apparatus to handle. Bartlett was pointing

onwards to facts which are certainly true of human nature, which he could grasp
in his own mind and for which a language needed to be created. (p. 5)

Bartlett did seem in *Remembering* to be struggling with words in a way he never did
in any of his previous work, particularly when, as mentioned above, he offered one
metaphor after another when talking about the schema notion. Before *Remembering*
was to be discovered by cognitivists and also before Zangwill gave his lecture,
Neisser (1967) offered an important consideration of the man he considered constructivism's "outstanding advocate." In his important book, *Cognitive Psychology,*
Neisser put new life into Bartlett's conceptions of cognition as he reinterpreted
them in light of the work that he himself was doing in perception. As he presented
his own constructivist view, he credited Bartlett, who "demonstrated long ago
that reorganization and change are the rule rather than the exception in memory"
(p. 279). Neisser discussed the role of the whole in recognition of the parts, which
he called "analysis by synthesis," and talked about importations and additions as a
normal part of perception. He pointed out that his approach was more similar to
Bartlett's than to any other contemporary psychologist's.

Conclusion

In the varying "readings" of *Remembering* and Bartlett's other texts, we have demonstrations of the process that interested Bartlett: people seeing the work from their
own perspectives (or schemas or tendencies or lenses), which also seems quite often
to be the perspective of a group to which they belong. We can contrast the readings
of people focusing on the norms of experimental psychology with those of people
interested in cognitive theory: Most of the attention thus far has been on the
cognitive studies and the cognitive theory. It is almost as if the social half of the
book is not even there. Shotter (1990) argued in an essay on "The Social Construction of Remembering and Forgetting" that Bartlett is an example of institutional-
ized forgetting, or a victim of what Jacoby (1975) called "social amnesia," because
his work in societal processes did not fit in the framework of psychology and was
thus forgotten.

    It was the 1970s that brought the widespread remembering of Bartlett among
researchers interested in cognitive processes, which will be the major topic of the
next chapter. But it is the 1990s that have finally brought some remembering of his
work in social processes of groups, as social constructivists have recently discovered
his work. In 1990 a volume edited by Middleton and Edwards, entitled *Collective
Remembering,* included several papers that used Bartlett's studies as a basis.

    In Bartlett's work we have an illustration of the constructiveness of writing that
comes from bringing together the ideas of different individuals and groups. Bartlett's

book *Remembering* is, as we have seen, a quotation of many other texts, not only his own prior work, such as *Psychology and Primitive Culture,* but also the work of others, including Rivers, Myers, Ward, Head, Haddon, Boas, Wundt, Ebbinghaus, Durkheim, Jung, and Lévy-Bruhl, and numerous others whose work is not explicitly cited. Bartlett (1958) speculated that what we consider originality is really a kind of synthesis: "Perhaps all original ideas come from contact of subject matter with different subject matter, of people with different people" (p. 147). And he added:

> The most important of all conditions of originality in experimental thinking is a capacity to detect overlap and agreement between groups of facts and fields of study which have not been effectively combined, and to bring these groups into experimental contact. (p. 161)

He was speaking of borrowing the schema notion from Head (and thus physiology) but he was doing this with other ideas, too.

What I think is the most strikingly *original* was his taking both a psychological perspective and a sociological-anthropological perspective on human constructiveness in order to see both the individual and the social group as constructive agent. But even this perspective shifting was not original with him, as others were doing it in their attempts to see parallels between cognitive development and development of society. Nor was the concept of constructiveness "original," because it had been discussed by Rivers and others. But what was original was the combination.

Chapter III

. . . .

Understanding as Construction

It has been said of Boehme that his books are like a picnic to which the author brings the words and the reader the meaning.
—Northrup Frye, *Fearful Symmetry*

The reading process . . . is an infinite process: it doesn't begin with the book we are reading and doesn't end with the last word of the book. It is always loaded with the memory of previous books and with personal experience.
—Jacques Leenhardt, "Does There Exist a European Reader?"

In the 1970s discourse researchers resurrected and summarized Bartlett's work as they began studying the organizational, selective, and connective nature of meaning making in discourse understanding. This was the beginnings of a constructivist tradition, which continues today, in which discourse analysis procedures are employed to gain insights into comprehension processes. Close attention is given to discourse conventions and to the effects that certain features and their variations have on readers, and, because the individuals are often studied in groups, established on the basis of some interest or ability, the research contributes to understandings of the *ways* of various groups. This chapter opens with some classic studies in the constructivist tradition and then reviews work on individuals as constructive agents reading the text and reading the context and intertext. After that, attention is given to the work often labeled "social constructivist," some coming from different traditions, that views social groups as constructive agents. This social constructivist research includes, first, the studies focused on groups or pairs of interacting members, such as discussion groups or classes of students and their teachers, and, second, the studies focused on macro social groups, such as communities and societies.

My review, which emphasizes the organizational, selective, and connective aspects of understanding, serves as a basis for, and complements, the more specific work to be discussed in subsequent chapters. Although I include some work of Europeans, particularly with respect to the understandings of literary texts with communities as agents, much of the research that I cite has been conducted in the United States, which saw the constructivist zeitgeist begin in the late 1970s and early 1980s.

A Constructivist Tradition

Bransford's Studies

One place to start this review is with the influential work of Bransford and his colleagues (Bransford et al., 1972; Bransford & Franks, 1971; Bransford & Johnson, 1972), who published some early studies dealing with the understanding of written materials. What these researchers demonstrated through their studies seems so obvious and so predictable now, given our current understandings of reading, but at that time different conceptions of reading comprehension predominated. Their findings challenged the accepted conception of reading, which gave little attention to the role of readers' knowledge in the understanding and remembering of texts. In a study conducted with pairs of sentences, Bransford et al. (1972) found that people had difficulty, after reading, in distinguishing sentences they had read from sentences that were "new" but were consistent with an interpretation of what they had read. The researchers explained:

> The constructivist approach argues against the tacit assumption that sentences "carry meaning." People carry meanings, and linguistic inputs merely act as cues which people can use to recreate and modify their previous knowledge of the world. What is comprehended and remembered depends on the individual's general knowledge of his [or her] environment. (p. 207)

They suggested that understanding a text involves constructing an interpretation of the situation described by the text.

Studies with brief texts, reported in Bransford and Johnson (1972), also provided rather dramatic demonstrations of the constructive nature of comprehension. The texts, which on the surface seemed easy to read, with fairly simple, straightforward syntax and no difficult vocabulary, were not easy to understand, after all, for participants in the study. The following is an example:

> The procedure is actually quite simple. First you arrange things into different groups. Of course, one pile may be sufficient depending on how much there is to do. If you have to go somewhere else due to lack of facilities that is the next step;

> otherwise you are pretty well set. It is important not to overdo things. That is, it is better to do too few things at once than too many. In the short run this may not seem important but complications can easily arise. A mistake can be expensive as well. At first the whole procedure will seem complicated. Soon, however, it will become just another facet of life. It is difficult to foresee any end to the necessity for this task in the immediate future, but then one never can tell. After the procedure is completed one arranges the materials into different groups again. Then they can be put in their appropriate places. Eventually they will be used once more and the whole cycle will then have to be repeated. However, this is part of life. (p. 722)

For a text like this, readers remembered very little of what was read. This was not because they struggled with the words of the text but because they did not know what the text was about (doing laundry) and did not have a particular kind of knowledge to which they could relate what they read. They did not have a context for understanding it. Like Bartlett, Bransford and Johnson showed that understanding a text required bringing knowledge to it and building an understanding on that basis, not simply taking material from it. Similar work was produced at the time by Dooling and Lachman (1971), and numerous other studies of comprehension followed shortly, so many that Spiro (1980) was later to call them a near avalanche. Also in the early 1970s, Freedle and Carroll (1972) published an edited volume on discourse processes. This is the publication that, according to van Dijk (1995), helped to establish discourse analysis as a new kind of approach to interdisciplinary research.

Some Classic Studies of Discourse Understanding

Researchers interested in discourse comprehension began to employ a method quite similar to Bartlett's: collecting recalls from people after they had read (or listened to) a text and analyzing those recalls for replications and transformations. In doing so, however, these researchers of the 1970s were more rigorous in their methodology than Bartlett had been, which meant, among other things, performing meticulous analyses of texts that were read as well as of the recalls that readers produced after reading them. This became a "traditional" approach established by some classic studies conducted by researchers in psychology and education, who were informed by movements in textlinguistics and artificial intelligence. These classics discussed here include studies by Kintsch (1974), Frederiksen (1975a, 1975b, cf. 1972), and Meyer (1975), each of whom developed an influential method of text analysis. They include a study conducted by researchers R. C. Anderson, Reynolds et al. (1977) of the newly established Center for the Study of Reading, who took a different kind of approach, creating an ambiguous text that could be read in different ways. They also include three studies with a story-grammar orientation, one by Thorndyke and another by Mandler and Johnson, which were published back to back in *Cognitive Psychology* in 1977, and yet another by Stein and Glenn that was not published until 1979.

Kintsch's (1974) Inquiries into Constructive Processes

Through his book, *The Representation of Meaning in Memory,* Kintsch (1974) began to lay out a theory of knowledge and memory and also reported some studies of text comprehension that supported the theory. In these studies he used textual passages, some from Boccaccio's *Decameron,* which he had parsed into semantic units. He did this in order to see how they were arranged and how they interrelated and to compare the configuration of the text with the configuration of the recall. The small units he studied, following Fillmore (1968), were propositions, composed of predicators (such as verbs, adjectives, and conjunctions) and the arguments (usually nouns) that stand in role relationships to those predicators. For instance, the sentence "Researchers use small units" would be composed of two units: (USE, RESEARCHER, UNIT) and (SMALL, UNIT). In the first, the verb is the predicator and the two nouns are its arguments, and in the second the adjective is the predicator with the noun as its argument. When parsing texts, Kintsch analyzed textual units for their *interconnectedness,* which he indexed through argument overlap from one unit to another. And he also analyzed the units for their *importance* relative to others, which he defined in terms of their embeddedness. The less embedded, the more important textually.

For example, Kintsch parsed the sentences "Two independent variables were investigated in this experiment. The two variables were combined factorially" into the following list of propositions:

(INVESTIGATE, EXPERIMENTER, VARIABLE)
 (INDEPENDENT, VARIABLE)
 (NUMBER, VARIABLE, TWO)
 (COMBINE, EXPERIMENTER, VARIABLE)
  (FACTORIAL, COMBINE) (p. 19)

These propositions are referentially connected in the redundancy of the items. There are three levels of importance represented here with (INVESTIGATE, EX-PERIMENTER, VARIABLE) positioned highest and (FACTORIAL, COM-BINE) positioned lowest. Kintsch provided the agent "experimenter" for the verbs "investigate" and "combine." This sort of addition would be considered an inference.

Kintsch theorized that, in understanding a text, a reader builds a mental representation of meaning that is propositional in nature. This he called a *text base.* In his conception the text base, too, was characterized by connectivity from one unit to another because a reader would discern or make connections between the interrelated propositions. The text base was also characterized by a hierarchy among the units, with some units more central to the meaning than others (and more likely to be remembered).

Understanding a text was thus described as a process that was both generative and selective. It was generative in that readers would generate some material not explicitly signaled by the text as well as material that was. Kintsch addressed the role of inferencing: "Meaning for a text is anything but verbatim" and involves "making use of inferences in complex ways" (p. 253). But he saw most inference generating as a means of achieving connectivity when texts did not provide connective cues. He also gave attention to selectivity. Some units would become part of the mental text base. They would be remembered, but some would not. Readers would tend to eliminate (and not remember) those units that are not connected and not high in the hierarchy. For example, for the sentences provided above, the last proposition would probably not be recalled as readily as the others. In these first studies Kintsch did not focus on the understanding of large texts, as he did in subsequent work. However, he did discuss the organizational patterns of such texts, saying that for texts like the research report in psychology, higher order units would have to be introduced. Through this book Kintsch was laying out, on the basis of some prior work, an agenda for theory and a methodology for his own studies in meaning construction, many of which he would conduct in collaboration with van Dijk (e.g., Kintsch, 1988; Kintsch & van Dijk, 1978; van Dijk & Kintsch, 1983) to create a model of the reading process that would be predictive as well as explanatory.

Meyer's (1975) Study of Selectivity

The next year after Kintsch's book was published, Meyer (1975) made an important contribution to the developing work in discourse comprehension through publication of her dissertation, *The Organization of Prose and Its Effects on Memory*. Despite the emphasis in the title on organization, her study can be seen as a study of selectivity because what received most attention was whether or not readers would select for memory what was prominent in the structure of a text. To Meyer, understanding and memory were characterized primarily by selectivity, not by transformations of other types, and Bartlett's (1932) finding of organizational transformations and additions was an artifact of the type of text that was used (cf. Gomulicki, 1956). In subsequent work she would examine the differential effects of different global organizational patterns (e. g., Meyer & Freedle, 1984), but in this first study she focused on the selectiveness of recall after someone reads a text. Her own prior work had suggested the importance of textual prominence (Meyer, 1971; Meyer & McConkie, 1973) and so had the work of others (R. Johnson, 1970), but for this study she could make a better demonstration because she had a better means of text analysis.

Like Kintsch, Meyer conducted propositional analyses of her texts, but, instead of using argument overlap for analyzing hierarchy, she used Grimes's (1975) rhetorical relations to place one unit relative to another. If a unit had a subordinating, or *hypotactic,* relation with another (e. g., if it was about some attribute of the topic in the previous unit), it was placed at a lower level. If it had an equal, or *paratactic,* relation, providing one part of a two-part pattern (e.g., if the content was a solution to a problem posed in the other unit), it was placed at an equal level. Thus, the propositional content could be parsed into many different levels of importance using the same sorts of patterns as causal, comparison, and problem solution that provide the overall organization for a text. If, as shown in Figure 1, the organization is conceived as a treelike structure, a unit placed high in the hierarchy would be near the organizing relation.

For her study of the effects of hierarchy on recall, Meyer used three expository texts, each on a different topic (schizophrenia, parakeets, and nuclear reactors), and identified a target paragraph in each. The whole paragraph would be her means of studying the influence of placement: Would the paragraph be remembered better if it were placed high in the text hierarchy than if it were placed low? Figure 1 illustrates such placement. The X represents content placed high because it is near the top-level organizing relation, the solution portion of the problem-solution pattern. If it were placed low, it would not be as near the organizing relation (would be lower in one of the chunks), even though it might come earlier in the text. For instance, for the text on schizophrenia, a paragraph about anti-s-proteins could be in a high or a low position. For the high version, Meyer placed the paragraph at a point where the protein seemed to present a possible solution to problems posed by the mental illness. For the low version, she placed the paragraph within a discussion of multiple treatments. Meyer prepared four versions of each text, for which she manipulated the placement of the content, high versus low. She also manipulated another variable she called *signaling,* which was rather explicit marking of organization and importance. This discourse feature, which some today (e.g., Crismore,

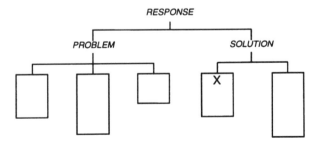

Figure 1. Placement of a unit (X) at a high level in text hierarchy.

1984, 1990; Vande Kopple, 1985) would call a kind of *metadiscourse,* indicates the author's perspective on particular content. This includes saying such things as "most importantly" and "the third point."

The college students participating in her study read and then immediately recalled the versions of the texts they were given and then a week later recalled the texts again. Meyer analyzed their recalls by scoring them against the propositional templates she had constructed for the various versions of the texts. The study confirmed her prediction that placement would influence recall because the target paragraph was better recalled when placed high. This was true for both immediate and delayed recalls. However, signaling, the explicit marking of structure, did not have much effect in that study with university-level students as readers. Meyer concluded that these skilled readers really did not need this explicit marking to discern what was important.

Frederiksen's (1975) Study of Task Effects

Frederiksen's (1975a, cf. 1972) focus was on context, as he wanted to see how a variation in context would affect the understanding of a text, particularly in regard to inferences and selectivity. This particular study, which did examine comprehension, was not actually a study of reading, since participants heard the text instead of reading it. To study context-induced transformations, Frederiksen gave groups different tasks for Dawes's (1966) "Circle Island" text, which was about a controversy on the island between ranchers and farmers over a canal, a controversy so serious that it could lead to civil war and economic collapse. Dawes, who took a constructivist position himself, had designed the text for his own study of transformations in set relations. Among the tasks that Frederiksen developed for his college-student subjects were a recounting task for one group, who heard the text several times and each time, after hearing it, had to retell what they remembered, and a problem-solving task for another group, who in addition to recounting the text had to constuct as many solutions as they could for the problem posed by the text. A third group worked only on the problem solving and did not have to recount the text until the fourth time.

To study their recalls relative to the text, Frederiksen analyzed the text into units and relations (cf. Frederiksen, 1975b). He identified word groups, which he called concepts, and also relational units, which were two concepts tied together with a relation. Figure 2 shows a portion of the template for the following excerpt, which is the third paragraph of the text:

> The island is run democratically. All issues are decided by a majority vote of the islanders. The actual governing body is a ten-man senate called the Federal Assembly whose job is to carry out the will of the majority. Since the most desirable trait in a senator is administrative ability, the Senate consists of the island's ten best proven administrators, the ten richest men. For years all senators have been ranchers. (Frederiksen, 1975a, p. 145)

Figure 2. A portion of the "Circle Island" text as analyzed by Frederiksen (1975a). Copyright © 1975 b; Academic Press.

The tasks elicited different meanings from readers in the different groups. Those who had been performing the problem-solving task included more derived material than those who had been recounting the text. Frederiksen suggested that these results were what would have been predicted from a constructive model, since, to construct meaning appropriate for that context, people had to "read" more into the text under the problem-solving condition.

Anderson, Reynolds, Schallert, and Goetz's (1977) Study of Perspective

With a research agenda focused on reading comprehension, the Center for the Study of Reading at the University of Illinois became an intellectual center for much constructivist work, and, as a national research center, it brought much attention to that work. Among the early contributions was the 1977 volume, *Schooling and the Acquisition of Knowledge,* edited by Center researchers Anderson and Spiro along with Montague from the Navy Research and Development Center. This book included Rumelhart and Ortony's, Spiro's, and Anderson's treatments of schema theory, in which they attempted to clarify and elaborate this conception of knowledge, as well as chapters by Meyer and by Bransford and some of his colleagues.

Also published the same year was one of the early Center studies, conducted by R. C. Anderson, Reynolds et al. (1977), examining the influence of readers' perspectives on their interpretation of a text. This study built on prior work with sentences that showed people adding material as they make interpretations (R. C. Anderson & Ortony, 1975; Bransford et al., 1972). To study perspective, these Center researchers created ambiguous texts that could be read in two different ways. Their texts were thus somewhat analogous to the Gestalt illustrations that can be seen two different ways, for instance, E. Rubin's (1921) famous goblet/faces drawing, shown in Figure 3. Instead of analyzing texts that were already written, these researchers composed their own (cf. Schallert, 1976).

This study can be seen as an examination of the "ways" of different social groups, following Bartlett's (1932) study. Bartlett, in studying "determining tendencies," had focused on perspectives associated with cultural group. These researchers focused on perspectives associated with disciplinary majors. The participants in the study were college students from two majors within education, physical education and music education. There were two texts, one that could be about friends playing cards or about people rehearsing music, and another that could be about a prisoner trying to escape from prison or about a wrestler trying to hold down an opponent. The following is the prison escape/wrestling text:

> Rocky slowly got up from the mat, planning his escape. He hesitated a moment and thought. Things were not going well. What bothered him most was being held, especially since the charge against him had been weak. He considered his present situation. The lock that held him was strong but he thought he could

Figure 3. Rubin's (1921) goblet/faces illusion.

break it. He knew, however, that his timing would have to be perfect. Rocky was aware that it was because of his early roughness that he had been penalized so severely—much too severely from his point of view. The situation was becoming frustrating: the pressure had been grinding on him for too long. He was being ridden unmercifully. Rocky was getting angry now. He felt he was ready to make his move. He knew that his success or failure would depend on what he did in the next few seconds. (p. 372)

Each of the texts, the prison escape/wrestling text and the card playing/music practice text, could be read from two perspectives, but one of those two perspectives was consistent with one of the two majors. In addition, one of the two perspectives had been established as the dominant perspective for other people who were not in that major. For one text it was an escape attempt, and for the other it was card playing.

On responses to multiple-choice questions and in written recalls after reading, the music education students showed that they took the rehearsal (nondominant) perspective for the first text, and the physical education students showed that they took the wrestling (nondominant) perspective on the second. In the other condition, when there was not a perspective that was particularly relevant to them, participants took the dominant one, as expected. The students generated inferences and made selections that were consistent with their perspective. The perspective taken was that of their disciplinary group, if that disciplinary perspective was relevant, or it was the dominant perspective of people in their society, if the disciplinary perspective was not relevant.

The Story Grammarians' Inquiries into Structure

Concurrent with the interest in comprehension in the 1970s was an interest in grammatical structures, which had been sparked to a great extent by Chomsky's (1957, 1965) transformational grammar. Grammars were being extended beyond the sentence to the text, and the text of interest to many text grammarians was the story. Attempts were being made by linguists to create grammars that specified the components of a story and the abstract, transformational rules guiding the production of stories. Much of this theoretical work on story grammars, which will be discussed in more detail in the next chapter, was being conducted in Europe (e.g., Barthes, 1975; Bremond, 1964, 1966; van Dijk, 1972), where it was influenced by prior analyses the Russian formalists conducted earlier in the century. Rumelhart (1975) is credited with introducing the story-grammar conception to cognitivists in psychology and education, when he proposed a connection between the grammar, which was the abstract, conventional rules belonging to society, and the schema, which was the cognitive structure for story. He cited Propp (1928/1968), a Russian formalist who several decades earlier had developed a grammar for Russian fairy tales, and Colby (1973), an American anthropologist who had done similar work more recently with Eskimo tales. Constructivists would check out this structural conception in studies of people actually reading, to see if it was psychologically valid, whereas the formalists and structuralists had discerned it from their own analyses of stories.

To see how this works, consider the procedure followed by Mandler and Johnson (1977), who first used a story that we all know well by now, "The War of the Ghosts," from Bartlett's (1932) study. They parsed the text into idea units, often at clausal boundaries, as follows:

The War of the Ghosts

(1) One night two young men from Egulac went down to the river to hunt seals, (2) and while they were there it became foggy and calm. (3) Then they heard war-cries, (4) and they thought: "Maybe this is a war party." (5) They escaped to the shore, (6) and hid behind a log. (7) Now canoes came up, (8) and they heard the noise of paddles, (9) and saw one canoe coming up to them. (10) There were five men in the canoe, (11) and they said:

"What do you think? We wish to take you along. (12) We are going up the river to make war on the people."

(13) One of the young men said: "I have no arrows."

(14) "Arrows are in the canoe," they said.

(15) "I will not go along. (16) I might be killed. (17) My relatives do not know where I have gone. (18) "But you," he said, turning to the other, "may go with them."

(19) So one of the young men went, (20) but the other returned home.

(21) And the warriors went on up the river to a town on the other side of Kalama. (22) The people came down to the water, (23) and they began to fight, (24) and many were killed. (25) But presently the young man heard one of the warriors say: "Quick, let us go home; that Indian has been hit." (26) Now he thought: "Oh, they are ghosts." (27) He did not feel sick, (28) but they said he had been shot.

(29) So the canoes went back to Egulac, (30) and the young man went ashore to his house, and made a fire. (31) And he told everybody and said: "Behold, I accompanied the ghosts, and we went to fight. (32) Many of our fellows were killed, (33) and many of those who attacked us were killed. (34) They said I was hit, (35) and I did not feel sick."

(36) He told it all, (37) and then he became quiet. (38) When the sun rose he fell down. (39) Something black came out of his mouth. (40) His face became contorted. (41) The people jumped up and cried.

(42) He was dead. (p. 136)

Then those units were identified as to their role in the grammar and placed in a framework, as shown in Figure 4, a hierarchical structure with components composed of subcomponents. Larger units, such as the setting, are composed of smaller units, such as location and time. The plot structure is composed of episodes, which are themselves composed of such units as goals, attempts, and outcomes. Holding together the various units are relations: In the case of this story they are the temporal relation *then,* and the logical relation *cause.* (The other relation Mandler and Johnson used in their analyses was the conjunctive [collection] relation *and.*) This analysis revealed problem areas where the ghost story violated conventions, particularly the fourth episode for units 26, 27, and 28, and after the fourth episode because little holds together the units (unless the reader can add what is needed). The boxes around items indicate violations of "rules" of the grammar, which became more numerous at these points. Particularly notable are the temporal relations where the grammar would specify causal relations. When reanalyzing protocols from six of Bartlett's subjects, Mandler and Johnson found that the data fit their predictions: problems at the points where they expected difficulties and better recall for causally related episodes than for temporally related episodes.

Although there were some minor differences, the grammars developed by Thorndyke (1977; cf. G. H. Bower, 1976) and by Mandler and Johnson had much in common, and the grammar by Stein and Glenn (1979), published two years later, was quite similar too. As a set, these three early story-grammar studies showed that

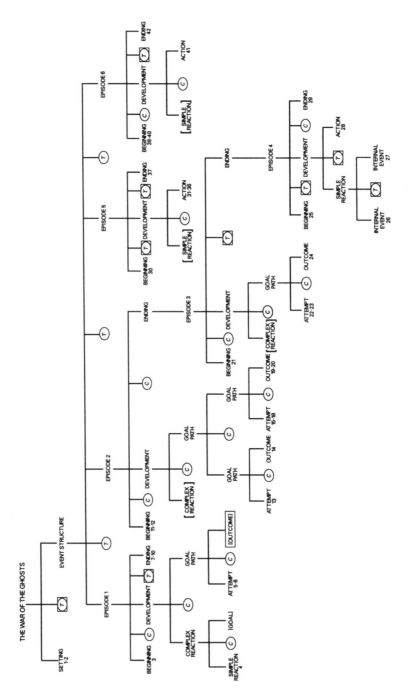

Figure 4. Mandler and Johnson's (1977) framework for "The War of the Ghosts" story. Copyright © 1977 by Academic Press.

recall for a story was better when chronological organization was followed in its telling; that particular components were remembered better than others (setting, initiating events, and outcomes); that readers often made inferences to fill in what was missing; that causal relations were particularly important for coherence; and that more mature readers produced more complete and more conventional recalls than young readers.

Constructivist Themes

We can see the constructivist themes in these early studies I have called "classics": the emphasis on organization of experience, on the generation rather than reception of meaning, on the selection of what is relevant to a particular perspective, and on the making of connections. Understanding a text was being portrayed as a transformational process in which social factors played a major role. Individuals generated meanings that were often quite compatible with understandings of others in their society or with those of a more specialized group within it. And they preferentially selected some content over other content in accordance with a perspective that was socially shared with others, either the larger society or a more specialized group within it. These studies provided only some initial insights into the process. There was much to learn—and there is still much to learn. The remainder of this chapter will consider major themes and issues in studies of discourse comprehension conducted, for the most part, during the two decades since this line of work began.

Detailed analyses are often still conducted, but the responses are increasingly likely to be something other than recalls. To study the online making of meaning, the products studied relative to the text might be think-aloud protocols, which would be subjected to their own text analysis with coding categories the researcher develops (e.g., Afflerbach, 1990; Olson, Duffy, & Mack, 1984; Pressley & Afflerbach, 1995). Or they might be responses to questions, asked of readers as they progress through the reading (e.g., Graesser, 1981). However, as we shall see, they might also be essays or other pieces of writing, which would be coded in some way (e.g., Spivey, 1991), or may be group-created products if one is studying social constructivist processes. The verbal product is analyzed for semantic content or relations with respect to the text that is read to see what seems to be transformed (added, emphasized, reordered or deleted). The analytic procedure, which is socially validated, is employed to stabilize what a text "offers" so that one can study transformations.

The assumption is that, through careful analyses and comparisons of textual products, which might be recalls, responses to questions, think-aloud protocols, transcribed conversations, summaries, or even essays, insights can be gained into cognitive products—the meanings that people have made of the texts.

The Constructivist Predicament

Before moving on to more recent studies, I will address a problem in discourse research that can be called the *constructivist predicament*. To study transformations, researchers need some stabilized representation of what the text offers. Thus, they often perform rather precise kinds of analyses like those just described. They read the text, interpret it, parse it, and even create templates. And that, of course, is the predicament: How can a constructivist who is a reader (a meaning maker engaged in constructive processes) say that his or her own reading is *the* reading against which other readings should be compared? How can a constructivist develop a constant, stabilized representation of a particular text, whether it is a written text or an oral conversation, particularly when so much of reading is inferential? Is that not claiming that his or her reading of a text is the correct one? Is that not the "self-excepting" fallacy" of which Mendelbaum (1982) spoke? How can the researcher's own particular reading be *objective* if reading by nature is *subjective*? Within Bartlett's work there was this kind of contradiction. Even though he took a constructivist stance as he made claims about his subjects' understandings, he did not apply these constructivist notions to himself. He seemed to have a "correct," conventional reading against which he studied readers' transformations and on the basis of which he drew his conclusions.

Two approaches, both involving social sanctioning, were taken by researchers in the 1970s and are taken today to ground text analyses for conducting such studies and to get one out of the predicament. One is the *consensus* approach; the other is the *authority* approach.

Consensus Approach

The consensus approach was established by R. Johnson (1970) in his study of selectivity in text recall. He had a large group of adults read the text, divide it into separate units of meaning, and rank those particular units for their importance to the overall thrust of the text. He then used these socially-determined units and rankings, purportedly representing a conventional reading, to prepare a template against which he could compare the memories of other readers for the same text. This approach was used also by R. C. Anderson, Reynolds et al., when they had a different group of readers determine what the dominant interpretation was before conducting the major study. Another kind of consensual justification is having a small number of people, who have some level of expert knowledge, perform the analyses and then establishing interrater reliability. For instance, Meyer reported interrater reliability, as did Mandler and Johnson.

Authority Approach

The authority approach, which is common in scholarship throughout the academic disciplines, is providing theoretical justification by citing authorities. Frawley

(1987) has described this as "establishing truth" citationally, which often leads to a kind of consensus, too. A researcher provides authorization for the particular method used for parsing a text into units, for ordering those units according to textual importance, or for describing organizational relations between groups of the units. For example, Kintsch and Meyer both cited Fillmore's (1968) case grammar for their units, and Meyer cited Grimes (1975) for her logical relations and noted Dawes's (1966) use of a set of relations. Frederiksen cited Grimes, and Frederiksen and Thorndyke both cited Dawes. In studies of narrative understandings, Thorndyke, Mandler and Johnson, and Stein and Glenn credited Rumelhart (1975) with the introduction of story grammar, which was being developed mainly by European textlinguists and literary analysts in the late 1960s, into psychology. They also credited those analysts he cited, Propp (1928/1968) and Colby (1973). Now that bodies of specialized work have been developed, more recent and more specifically relevant studies tend to be discussed instead. Fillmore's cases, Grimes's relations, and Rumelhart's story-grammar conception have become a part of the "shared" knowledge that is often presumed of people reading current studies.

Plan for the Remainder of the Chapter

We move now to other work with constructivist themes. The upcoming sections, The Reading of Expository Texts and Stories and The Reading of Contexts and Intertexts, show my emphasis at that particular part of the discussion, but texts, contexts, and intertexts should be seen as overlapping. In every literate act, a reader "reads" the context and builds an understanding that is consistent with his or her interpretation of the context as well as the text. And in every literate act, a reader "reads" the intertext, making connections with other texts that have been read in the past. I should note that researchers mentioned here vary in the extent to which they speak a constructivist sort of language and are self-conscious about their own stances. Some researchers have used phrases such as "contained in the text" that do not sound constructivist, but I take that as a shorthand way of speaking that reflects the pervasiveness of that powerful conduit metaphor in our culture (Reddy, 1979) and that is also an artifact of the methodology the researcher uses. When one assesses a response against a template of a text and notes repeated content, it does seem as if the replicated portion of the generated material was *in* the text.

The Reading of Expository Texts

As the constructivist research continues to show, reading is a process of organizing, selecting, and connecting content that is generated in response to various kinds of cues. Some cues are to organizational patterns, others are to the relative importance of particular material, and still others are to connections from one unit to another.

This portion of the chapter focuses on the reading of expository texts. *Expository* has become a rather general label for informational and persuasive discourse that sets forth, explains, and presents a topic through such means as definition, comparison, and causal analysis. First we will consider the conventions of expository discourse, and then we will consider the circumstances in which readers build meanings in conventional or unconventional ways.

Conventions of Expository Discourse

The conventions to be discussed are organizational patterns, textual importance, and interconnectedness of content.

Organizational Patterns

The first convention to be considered here is the overall organization of a text. There have been many attempts to label and classify the conventional patterns of discourse, to specify the kinds of order that people provide in their communications. Today many still find the organizational patterns described by Grimes (1975) and employed by Meyer (1975, 1985) useful for describing many texts. However, similar sets have been around for years in various versions of the Kantian categories, and other sets have been proposed by other discourse scholars (e.g., Beaugrande, 1980; Calfee & Chambliss, 1987; Mann & Thompson, 1988; Mosenthal, 1985). The set included here is based on Meyer's (1985) but modified slightly.

The illustration in Figure 5 begins with single sketches for three patterns: collection, chronology, and causal. A collection is seen as a loose kind of rhetorical relation, which might "hold together" various kinds of content. For instance, a topically focused report would present a discussion of the various aspects of one subtopic, then aspects of another and another, and so on, and the text that we think of as a description is usually organized as a collection of attributes, each of which is described in detail. A causal pattern might have effect first or cause first, but effect then cause is the order often used for causal arguments or other large pieces of written discourse. Chronology was not one of Meyer's separate patterns, as she presented chronology as a subtype of collection, but I have included it separately because of the temporal relation that characterizes it. Response, according to Grimes (1975), has some content from a first part that is repeated in a second part along with new material. Response can have within it units that relate to each other as problem–solution or question–answer, and I have added another major form that it sometimes takes: topic–comment, as for a critique, in which the text being critiqued is presented as a topic and commentary is offered in response to it (Mathison, 1993).

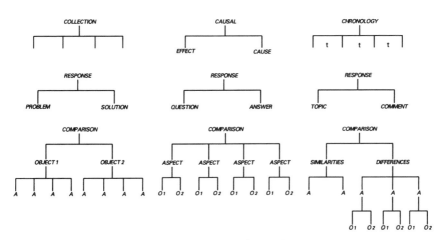

Figure 5. Organizational patterns illustrated as tree structures.

Another major pattern is comparison, which seems to have three major variants: (a) organizing according to the objects being compared and presenting aspects of one and then the other, (b) organizing according to aspect and discussing the aspect in terms of one object and then the other, and (c) organizing aspects in terms of similarities and differences and discussing the aspects for the objects within that subsuming relation (cf. Schnotz, 1982, 1984; Spivey, 1991). Although some texts seem to be organized at the most global level with only one of these patterns, many informational and persuasive texts cue some combination of these patterns.

Certain forms are predominant in certain social groups because of the recurring discourse practices of the group. For example, in the disciplinary community of psychology, a recurring form revolves around posing problems and providing solutions through studies (research reports). The constituents have changed, as mentioned earlier, with changes in the epistemology (Bazerman, 1987). The solution section today has particular kinds of semantic units: method (comprising such units as participants, materials, procedure), results, and discussion. In many elementary school settings, a book report presents a topic (a summary of the book that was read) and provides comments about it ("I liked/didn't like it because . . ."). Letters of reference, used in various contexts, suggest a causal pattern, presenting an effect (that the person would be hired) and then causes (reasons that the hiring should happen). These recurring combinations of patterns and particular kinds of content, which are accompanied by particular stylistic features, are what we know as genres, or types, of discourse (Berkenkotter & Huckin, 1993). Lemke (1988) considered comparisons, descriptions, definitions, and procedural instructions to be genres in science because they recur and are so important not only in its written discourse but also in its oral discourse. He described them as "elementary genres," which are mastered and used as separate forms but are also combined to create more advanced genres, which include research proposals and research reports.

The traditional tree structures of Figure 5 cannot do justice to the dynamic nature of such patterns, which are not static features of a text, but are recurring cognitive and social patterns by means of which we humans organize our thoughts and communications, as we write, read, and communicate orally, too (cf. Mann & Thompson, 1988). We consider a problem and attempt to come up with a solution, we consider some situation and infer causes for it, and we discuss a topic and make some kind of evaluative comment about it. These patterns work, as Meyer (1975) and Kintsch (1974) maintained, at a macro level to interrelate the "chunks" of the content we present, but they are also used at micro levels and other levels in between. They tie one sentence to another sentence, as well as one component of a proposition to another, one proposition to another proposition, and one clause to another clause.

They are also used in oral conversations and in written conversations, such as those on e-mail, with one person presenting one chunk of a pattern and another person presenting the other chunk. For example, one person might discuss a problem and another propose a solution for it, one person might discuss a situation and others suggest possible causes for it, and one person might discuss a topic and another make an evaluative comment about it (e.g., Bruce, 1993). At a more global (systems) level, we might even see the literature of a discourse community as composed of texts interrelated in such ways. One text becomes a topic for commentary made through other texts, one text treats a problem and another offers a solution, and so on.

Textual Importance

In addition to overall organizational pattern, a second major conventional feature of discourse is the hierarchical patterning of content, which was studied earlier by Meyer (1975) and Kintsch (1974). A discourse unit may be spoken of in terms of its *textual importance* or its *height* or *level,* its position relative to other units. Is it prominently placed near one of the major organizing relations, as in Meyer's (1975) conception? Or is it a detail? Or is it somewhere in between? This aspect may also be referred to as *staging,* which is thematic prominence. A particular thematic element can be staged in an entire text just as it might be staged in a sentence or a chunk, and being staged means that it receives emphasis within that unit, which might be the whole text but might be a part of it. As Grimes (1975) noted, staging decisions map onto the hierarchical structure, and both staging and hierarchy are concerned with what goes where.

Connectedness

A third major feature is the connectedness of one unit to the next. The linguists Halliday and Hasan (1976) explained that cohesion comes when the interpretation of one unit is dependent on the interpretation of another, or, put another way, when one unit presupposes another. Their book *Cohesion in English* provides a rather comprehensive treatment of the devices writers use to suggest links from one sentence to the previous ones. Their categories of "cohesive ties" include reference, substitution, ellipsis, lexical cohesion, and conjunction. The conjunction category includes the logical, or rhetorical, relations, discussed above, such as collection, comparison, chronological, and causal, when they are used to interrelate smaller units, although Halliday and Hasan would call them additive, adversative, temporal, and causal. These either are marked, through such words as *another, in addition, nevertheless, in contrast to, next, then,* and *in order to,* or are implied and readers are left to infer them through connective (or bridging) inferences (Clark, 1977). Different kinds of relations predominate for different kinds of texts (Beaugrande, 1980; J. B. Black, 1985; Mosenthal, 1985).

Connectedness is also suggested through topical continuity, when a writer comments about a topic already introduced. The topical aspect of connectedness was a subject that interested the Prague linguists (e.g., Mathesius, 1928/1964; cf. Daneš, 1974), whose general structuralist approach will be discussed more in the next chapter. They demonstrated in their studies of functional sentence perspective how a sentence can be viewed as a two-part unit: the *topic,* what is talked about, and the *comment,* what is said about it. The positioning of topic and comment throughout a text creates a kind of topical structure composed of topic–comment patterns, and it also makes for linkages among units. A whole text can be seen in terms of topic–comment patterns, with breaks coming when new topics are introduced unless there is a more inclusive hypertheme (Firbas, 1974). To facilitate connections, writers often help their readers, as Perfetti and Goldman (1975) showed, by positioning topical material so that it is prominent, in the subject part of the sentence, and by putting new information about it in the predicate position (cf. Chafe, 1977; Clark & Haviland, 1977).

Readers' Constructions of Meaning for Expository Texts

How do readers make use of these social conventions when they read expository texts? How do they organize, select, and connect content?

Organizing and Selecting

In many studies of text comprehension, as in Meyer's (1975), readers seem to use organizational patterns signaled by the text and they preferentially select textually prominent items as they build their own meanings (e.g., B. K. Britton, Glynn, Meyer, & Penland, 1982; Kintsch & Yarbrough, 1982; McGee, 1982). A relationship is often demonstrated between organizing and selecting because readers who replicate the pattern also tend to remember the units that are most related to the top-level pattern. This is what seems to happens when the readers are mature, are proficient in reading, are experienced with the discourse forms, and are participating in a study that does not invite some other kind of reading besides reading to understand and remember. Meyer, who reviewed this work in 1985, attributed readers' use of the author's organization to a *structure strategy*, and van Dijk (1979), who considered the research on selecting, attributed readers' selection of prominently placed content to use of a criterion based on *textual relevance*. Others have called this preferential selection of prominently positioned units a "levels effect" (e.g., Goetz & Armbruster, 1980).

A rather large body of developmental research in the 1980s showed that readers who are younger and less experienced do less well than mature readers in following writers' cues for organization and selection. Discerning and using a writer's cues for organization and textual importance are part of one's overall competence with discourse, and differences in organization and selection have been tied to age and grade level and to measures of general reading ability. In contrast to mature, proficient readers, younger and less skilled readers tend to make organizational transformations in reading informational texts when a conventional reading is expected, presumably because they do not have command of patterns and are not as sensitive to textual importance (e.g., McGee, 1982; Meyer, Brandt, & Bluth, 1980; Richgels, McGee, Lomax, & Sheard, 1987; B. M. Taylor, 1980). They do not have the same levels of discourse knowledge. Some instructional methods for unskilled readers emphasize the building of this knowledge and the learning of these conventions (e.g., R. C. Anderson, Hiebert, Scott, & Wilkinson, 1985; Armbruster, Anderson, & Ostertag, 1987).

Some researchers have tried various manipulations to see if changes in the text help readers organize material and select what is textually important. Meyer (1975) tried explicit marking in her dissertation study. We have already noted how the marking did not have much effect on the college readers in that study who did just as well without it, probably because through other more subtle cues they were able to discern patterns and relative importance of particular points. However, in a subsequent study with eighth graders, Meyer et al. (1980) found a facilitative effect for explicitness with students whose test scores suggested they were comprehension underachievers. And similar results have been found for other groups of readers, such as the elderly (Meyer & Rice, 1989). The conclusion about explicit marking seems to be that it can be helpful for readers who may not be as sensitive to other kinds of cues, such as the particular arrangement of material.

Other researchers have tried manipulating *interestingness* to see if, by adding some interesting details about authors' major points, they could get readers to give more attention to those major points and remember them better. However, this addition seems not to facilitate the retention of major points, even though the "seductive" details are well remembered (e.g., Garner, Gillingham, & White, 1989; Hidi & Baird, 1988; Hidi, Baird, & Hildyard, 1982; Wade & Adams, 1990).

Connecting

As they move through expository texts, readers determine connections between one unit and what came before through making various kinds of ties, including referential linkages (e.g., Kintsch & van Dijk, 1978). They also construct those logical relations, discussed previously. For example, a reader might relate one sentence to a previous one through the comparison relation if he or she sees it as providing some contrasting information to what came before, or might relate a pair of sentences through a causal relation if he or she sees that one presents an effect resulting from what was mentioned in another. Sometimes readers have guidance from the author through rather explicit marking of the relation, and sometimes they do not and they must generate the relation only on the basis of their relevant knowledge. It seems that, when relations are not marked, more cognitive effort is devoted to one's reading (B. K. Britton et al., 1982; Pearson, 1974), and unskilled readers can have difficulties in comprehension (Marshall & Glock, 1978–1979). However, some recent research suggests that the explicitness issue is rather complex and much may depend on the nature of materials and the purposes for reading as well as the reader's relevant knowledge. For instance, it seems that, for the reading of some brief scientific materials, people may remember more information when they have to generate the connectives themselves (Millis, Graesser, & Haberlandt, 1993). Also, much may depend on the type of relation. For example, understanding is facilitated by the explicit statement of the adversative (*however, but*), when that is appropriate, but explicit statement of the causal or additive relation is less necessary (J. D. Murray, 1995).

Topical continuity seems especially important in the reading of expository texts. Readers use topics to focus their understandings as they read (Kieras, 1980, 1981, 1985; R. F. Lorch, Jr., 1993), and, if the topic is changed, they slow down, but not as much if the new text topic relates to a preceding topic (E. P. Lorch, Lorch, Gretter, & Horn, 1987). Comprehension is improved when thematically related components are placed close to one another (B. K. Britton, van Dusen, Gulgoz, & Glynn, 1989; cf. Duffy et al., 1989), and recall is better for an expository text with high degrees of topical connection than for a text that is less connected topically (Vande Kopple, 1983). Texts characterized by topical connections between consecutive sentences are also preferred by readers rating texts for quality, as Witte (1983) found in a study of text revisions. Readers in that study preferred the versions in which a writer achieved topical continuity by staying with a particular topic and developing it with consecutive comments.

In understanding texts, readers make various kinds of inferences. In addition to those that seem necessary to establish connectivity from one unit to another, there are numerous other kinds of inferences, some adding more specific detail or some more general material (cf. Graesser & Kreuz, 1993; McNamara, Miller, & Bransford, 1991; Seifert, Robertson, & Black, 1985). Readers make these inferences—

these additions—on the basis of relevant knowledge that is cued in some way by their reading (e.g., Pearson, Hansen, & Gordon, 1979).

Some of this inferencing is global, making everything fit together as a unified whole. This is more than just being able to recount the text or produce a canonical kind of summary for it, as it involves inferring what the text is about, what its point is—the sort of thing that Bransford discussed (Bransford & Johnson, 1972; cf. Dooling & Lachman, 1971). It can involve making inferences about rhetorical factors, such as the author's persona and intentions (cf. Asch, 1952; Haas & Flower, 1988; Shanahan, 1993). And it can involve making inferences about how this author's text fits with other related texts by other authors in a particular domain of knowledge (Geisler, 1991; Haas, 1994; Wineburg, 1991, 1994). For example, in Wineburg's (1991) study, which compared historians and high school students, the historians discerned clues about authors' world views relative to those of other authors and thus made the parts of a text fit together as a coherent whole. However, the students did not, as they were reading the texts for the facts.

The Reading of Stories

The narrative is a particularly important form of discourse, as it is a means through which we humans organize much of our experience as well as much of our literature. The narrative mode, according to Bruner (1985), is a way of understanding that, instead of attempting to establish a foundational kind of truth, establishes "truth-likeness," or verisimilitude, in presenting human or "human-like" intentions and actions and their consequences. Stories, like other narratives, present human or human-like characters participating in goal-directed events in action sequences, but in stories, unlike some other narratives, the world created is a storyworld.

The story is a discourse form that cuts across cultures, although it has culture-specific features. As Bartlett (1932) and others (e.g., Kintsch & Greene, 1978) have shown, people can have difficulty with the conventions of stories from a culture other than their own. Brewer's (1985) analyses of oral and written stories indicate that the stories of oral literature have more cross-cultural commonalities than do written stories. Oral stories across cultures are characterized by such features as conventionalized openings and closings, characterization in terms of extremes, and repetitions of events. For written stories, some effects have to be achieved through structural devices that would be achieved through repetition in oral forms.

My treatment of stories considers, in rather abbreviated fashion, studies of the reading of folktale-like stories, which have been conducted mainly in the United States, and also studies of the reading of more complex forms of written stories, such as novels and short stories, which have been conducted by constructivists in Europe and the United States. Stories are of special importance in the constructivist conception because they are so central to human meaning making and play such a major role in various activities and practices. For this section, too, we consider first the features of texts and then the nature of the reading process.

Conventional Patterns of Stories

Let us briefly consider the conventions for stories in regard to organizational patterns, connectedness, and textual importance.

Organizational Patterns and Connectedness

With introduction of story-grammar notions in the 1970s, much attention went to the organizing patterns of rather simple, folktale-like stories. Subsequent studies have shown that, in the reading of these stories, there seems to be some psychological validity to the story-grammar units, as, for example, readers pause between episode boundaries (Mandler & Goodman, 1982). However, many reading researchers have come to think that what is really basic instead for a story is the relational patterns, particularly causal and temporal, that cue event sequences and causal connections among units (e.g., J. B. Black & Bern, 1981; J. B. Black & Bower, 1980). Much work today with folktale-like stories is undergirded with a causal conception, which was outlined by Schank (1975) and has been modeled by Trabasso and van den Broek and their colleagues (Trabasso, Secco, & van den Broek, 1984; Trabasso & Suh, 1993; Trabasso & van den Broek, 1985). This model is illustrated in Figure 6 from Trabasso et al. (1984), which shows how these researchers would characterize the causal relations for a brief story used previously in story-grammar research: the "Epaminondas" story employed by Stein and Glenn (1979).

(1) Once there was a little boy (2) who lived in a hot country. (3) One day his mother told him to take some cake to his grandmother. (4) She warned him to hold it carefully (5) so it wouldn't break into crumbs. (6) The little boy put the cake in a leaf under his arm (7) and carried it to his grandmother's. (8) When he got there (9) the cake had crumbled into tiny pieces. (10) His grandmother told him he was a silly boy (11) and that he should have carried the cake on top of his head (12) so it wouldn't break. (13) Then she gave him a pat of butter to take back to his mother's house. (14) The little boy wanted to be very careful with the butter (15) so he put it on top of his head (16) and carried it home. (17) The sun was shining hard (18) and when he got home (19) the butter had all melted. (20) His mother told him that he was a silly boy (21) and that he should have put the butter in a leaf (22) so that it would have gotten home safe and sound. (Stein & Glenn, 1979, p. 78)

First, as the figure shows, some units (clauses) of a story are interrelated by causal relations with other units, and, second, the story has a causal chain connecting

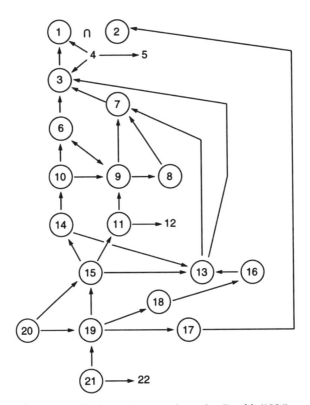

Figure 6. Illustration of Trabasso, Secco, and van den Broek's (1984) causal model. Copyright © 1984 by Erlbaum.

an opening event and final occurrence. Units are circled if they are on the causal chain, and unmarked if they are the dead ends. This model predicts that units are more likely to be remembered if they have causal relations with other units and are on the causal chain. The illustration here is for a brief story, but the model has also been applied to longer literary texts (van den Broek, Rohleder, & Narváez, 1996). I should point out that, even though the causal relations seem most important, temporality is involved too. The causal connections entail temporal connections, because in a plot a cause typically comes before an effect and that effect can become the cause of another effect.

Temporal relations have also received attention (e.g., Brewer, 1985; Brewer & Lichtenstein, 1982; Ohtsuka & Brewer, 1992), particularly in respect to what is called *temporal duality*. The Russian formalists (e.g., Tomashevsky, 1925/1965), whose work will be discussed further in the next chapter, had pointed to the two kinds of temporality that are involved in a story: the ordering of events in the fictional storyworld and the ordering of events in the telling of the story. Sometimes the two orderings match up, when chronology is the ordering principle, and sometimes they do not, when events are in some other order.

Textual Importance

As to textual importance, in the causal conception, the importance of a particular unit would be defined structurally in terms of its presence on the major causal chain and number of causal connections. However, storytellers may also indicate importance rhetorically in the evaluations they provide. This notion, developed for written texts by R. A. Hunt and Vipond (1986), comes from Labov (1972) who observed that, when telling oral stories, people communicate the value that they place on particular parts. He used the term *point* for a story's *raison d'être*, "why it was told, and what the narrator [was] getting at" (p. 366). "Pointless stories," he explained, "are met (in English) with the withering rejoinder, 'So what?'" (p. 366). To get their listeners to share their evaluations, storytellers use various rhetorical devices to communicate importance, which include such things as repetitions, delaying tactics, and metacomments. According to L. Polanyi (1985), storytellers orchestrate their evaluations so that their devices have "power" when the power is needed for their points. R. A. Hunt and Vipond built upon Labov and Polanyi's conceptions, applying the point notion to written literary stories. Their thesis is that authors of written fiction mark points by expressing something in a distinctive way, presenting unexpected happenings, and giving surprising "tellings." The devices for written stories differ from those for oral stories, they hypothesized, and include such things as rearranging elements of the plot.

Readers' Constructions of Meaning for Stories

How do readers organize, select, and connect content when building meanings for stories? In studies of story recall, certain story-grammar categories seem to be remembered better than others: settings, initiating events, and outcomes (e.g., Mandler & Johnson, 1977; Stein & Glenn, 1979). However, one limitation of the story-grammar conception was that it could not explain why particular units were selectively recalled. By reanalyzing Stein and Glenn's story-grammar data, Trabasso et al. (1984) found that causal relations seemed to account for the selective recall. A number of studies have provided support for the causal model and its two factors: the presence of a unit in a causal sequence and its number of causal connections. More memorable stories have larger proportions of events on the causal chain, and events on the chain are preferentially recalled (Trabasso et al., 1984). Also, a particular unit is better recalled if it has higher numbers of causal connections (Goldman & Varnhagen, 1986; Trabasso & van den Broek, 1985). The two causal components overlap, but each seems to make some unique contribution (Trabasso & van den

Broek, 1985). In addition to the causal connections, which seem particularly important, the reading of stories involves generating the other kinds of relations, too, which can predominate at particular points, such as the spatial relations in descriptions of a setting and attributive relations in descriptions of a character (Beaugrande, 1980).

Much of the research employing rather brief stories has focused on comprehension and recall. Readers seem to comprehend and recall a story better if relations are marked (e.g., Beck, McKeown, Omanson, & Pople, 1984; Paul, 1959; Segal, Duchan, & Scott, 1991), and if events are recounted in the order in which they are supposed to have happened in the storyworld (Ohtsuka & Brewer, 1992; Thorndyke, 1977). Some inferences seem rather necessary for connectivity as readers relate one unit to another, but other kinds of inferences, such as inferences about goals, emotions, or states, are made, too, as readers apply their knowledge of human events and actions. Graesser et al. (1995) have proposed what they call a *constructionist* hypothesis based on Bartlett's "effort after meaning" notion. The claim here is that readers make inferences when they are needed, and there are three circumstances in which they are needed: to construct an understanding that is connected (at both a local level, from one small unit to the one that preceded it, and a global level, for creation of higher order chunks), to meet their reading goals, and to explain why an author has mentioned particular things.

Regarding stories, too, there is also that global kind of connectivity that readers create to fit the story together as a coherent whole. For a literary text, the ideas tying it all together are what R. A. Hunt and Vipond (1986) would call its *point* and what many others would call *interpretation*. This would be a person's telling what a short story or a novel *means* instead of simply providing a brief summary of the plot. This sense making often has an intertextual character, in which the interpretation of one text is achieved by relating it to other texts by the same author or to other works of the same type. An interpretation can shift and change as the context of reading and recalling changes, and it is often associated with the ways of a particular group, as we shall see later. Schmidt (1981, 1982) has used the term *polyvalence,* or multiplicity of meanings, for such shifts and changes in meanings in literary reading.

Affect in the Reading of Fiction

Another important aspect of meaning making, particularly with respect to literature, is affect (feelings, emotions, and attitudes). Some reader-response theories, particularly Rosenblatt's (1978), have dealt with the aesthetic response in reading, and a number of studies labeled reader-response have put their attention there (reviewed by Beach & Hynds, 1991). In this section, I will focus on an important tension between the comprehensibility of a literary text and its affective potential. According to a number of theorists, a highly comprehensible "read" may not be a good "read" at least for mature readers. It seems that those features making a story more difficult can also make it more enjoyable. Kermode (1980) put it this way:

> In the kinds of narrative upon which we conventionally place a higher value, the case against propriety is much stronger; there is more material that is less manifestly under the control of authority, less easily subordinated to "clearness and effect," more palpably the enemy of order, of interpretive consensus, of message. (p. 83)

Much of the current theoretical work on affect suggests that, for literary texts, affective response can be greater when there is uncertainty and when more is required of the reader. For instance, Brewer and Lichtenstein's (1982) structural affect theory built on this sort of notion, particularly with respect to those nonchronological forms of organization, such as flashback and flashforward, that can lead, through defamiliarization, to such effects as curiosity, suspense, and surprise. Miall and Kuiken (1994) argued that, through experiencing such defamiliarization, readers can have "a felt engagement with the text that alters the interpretive possibilities" (p. 340). And van den Broek, Rohleder, and Narváez (1993) have pointed out that the reading of highly regarded novels can require much forward inferencing (which is rarely seen in studies with simple stories) as well as repeated backward inferencing as a reader works and reworks an interpretation.

For years now, Schmidt (1981, 1982) has spoken of the regulation of literary reading by the polyvalence convention and the aesthetic convention. A particularly interesting question to constructivists, it seems, is how the affective response is related to cognitive challenge, how aesthetic effects are associated with polyvalence.

The Reading of Contexts and Intertexts

Acts of literacy are performed in complex, multidimensional contexts. For a student reading a text in a Louisiana classroom the context would also include Western culture, American culture, regional and state cultures, the culture of the community, the culture of American education, an institutional culture, a school culture, a classroom culture, the culture of the content area or discipline, and so on. All have histories and their own conventional practices, including general and specialized conventions for discourse. And all have texts associated with them, some of which are highly privileged, even canonized, by people associated with that culture.

The Sociocultural and Historical Context

A sociocultural and historical context can be described as sets of systems, as sets of influences, or even as powerful forces. For instance, some people speak of ideology in an abstract but objectivist way as if it is *in* the context or, if it *is* the context, as if it has had a historical existence apart from people with ideological ideas and beliefs. But this sociocultural context can also be described in terms of sociocultural knowledge, either as collective knowledge of a social group or as the knowledge of individuals who belong to, or are being enculturated into, the group, and discourse knowledge would be a part of this larger kind of knowledge. Alexander, Schallert, and Hare (1991) used the term *sociocultural knowledge* for the filter through which experience is perceived. One's vision of the world, these authors explained, is filtered through the understanding, largely tacit, that he or she shares with others, who include family, community, ethnic group, national society, and so on (those elements that some consider context). This filter might be labeled *ways.*

That student in the Louisiana classroom would have some knowledge associated with each of the various cultures, which has been built by participating in the practices and experiencing some of the various texts of the community. Most of the studies discussed thus far in this chapter, with individuals as constructive agents, have focused on ways of people who belong to the large literate community of Western and of American culture (or, in the case of children, are beginning to gain entry into that community). But some studies, such as those by R. C. Anderson, Reynolds et al. (1977), have been more specialized, considering the knowledge of people in particular disciplinary communities.

The More Immediate Situational Context

In addition to this multidimensional sociocultural and historical context, which can be thought of as sociocultural knowledge, there is also a more immediate situational context. As Spiro (1980) argued, discourse is embedded in contexts, which influence "extra-textual" construction. The meaning constructed for a text is affected by other texts, written and spoken, that precede and follow it. Reading involves "reading" this context, which includes the time and place of the act and the nature of the task and also the other people who are involved. The situational context can, as van Dijk (1979) pointed out, override the textual influence: If a task is interpreted as requiring a particular kind of reading, a reader attempts to build meaning to accommodate that interpretation when reading the text and might not follow the writer's guidance to the extent that he or she might in other circumstances. The "effort after meaning" is an effort to make the meaning fit the contextual cues that are perceived as well as the textual cues (cf. Graesser et al., 1995; van Dijk, 1995). In Frederiksen's (1975a) study, the people given the problem-solving task were cued to generate a particular kind of product with an overarching pattern, problem–solution, that differed from the pattern cued by the text. It seems to me that these people had to shape the narrative of the "Circle Island" text into the problem portion and generate the solution portion. The task cued a form to be filled if the meaning they constructed was going to fit their context.

Some other experimental studies have also shown variability in generation and selection of content to be associated with variability in context. One such examination of context effects was Gauld and Stephenson's (1967) replication of Bartlett's ghost story study. This study indicated that readers have some control over the extent of their transformations and can adjust their understandings to fit the directions they are given. The researchers modified the instructions participants received for their recalls of "The War of the Ghosts." Some were told to write down the material as exactly as they could. Others were told that it was important not to add anything that was not in the original. Still others were told that it was important not to include anything not in the original and that, if they came to something they did not remember, to leave a blank, and, if they were not sure about something, to put brackets around it. The students given the first set of directions made many more transformations than the others. The researchers concluded that people would make such transformations in dealing with this kind of material unless given firm instructions to be accurate. As they put it, "Bartlett thought of human beings as active, organizing, striving, intending agents; and he may well be right" (p. 48). These inquiries are complemented by Rothkopf's (e.g., Rothkopf & Billington, 1979) studies of "mathemagenic" tasks leading to learning. Rothkopf demonstrated how readers' perceptions of their criterial tasks influenced what they remember and how they read (cf. R. E. Reynolds & Anderson, 1982).

A number of other inquiries have examined the effects of contextual variables, particularly the effects of an assigned perspective. Pichert and Anderson (1977) showed that people, when given the task of reading from a particular perspective, would "see" a text from that perspective. In that well-known study, which also used Gestalt-like figure/ground texts, participants who read a particular text from different assigned perspectives (homebuyer vs. burglar) remembered different items. Related findings were made more recently by Zwaan (1993), who also studied context effects through manipulating perspective. Some participants in his studies were told that they were reading a literary text, and others were told they were reading a newspaper article. The different perspectives resulted in different readings: For the literary reading there was better recall of form and longer reading time, and for the newspaper reading there was more inferencing of goals, reasons for actions, and causes. The newspaper reading presumably required such connections for sense making, whereas the literary reading did not require the same kind of understanding.

Reading the situational context often means "reading" other people. One must interpret what Freedle, Naus, and Schwartz (1977) called the "psychosocial context," which includes people for whom the act is performed. There is research suggesting, for example, that children adjust their understandings of texts in ways that correspond to the response registers they use when they converse with their teachers (Mosenthal & Na, 1980) and that some students, when reading texts for their teachers, can do quite well in predicting the content that teachers will emphasize in their discussions and quizzes—content that is not necessarily structurally important (Alexander, Jetton, Kulikowich, & Woehler, 1994). Reading the context can also mean "reading" the people with whom one discusses the text or people who comment about the text. Ruddell and Unrau (1994) examined this aspect of meaning construction in a study set in a high school English class in which students recorded their understandings in response logs. Analyses of these logs showed that students' understandings for texts were influenced by the teacher's comments as well as comments by other students in whole-class and group discussions. A person's understanding of a text was built in co-constructive fashion by hearing other people's interpretations, building meaning for them, and changing one's own meaning accordingly.

Context is a factor that many researchers have tried to control instead of study, thinking that, if context is controlled, then more general claims can be made about the reading process. So, instead of studying context and its effects, many reading researchers have tried to minimize it by conducting studies in laboratory-like settings. But in these situations, as in others, there are still context effects, as Spiro (1977, 1980) has argued. Participants in a study read in a fashion that is appropriate for the study, no doubt, as they interpret their task and infer what is expected. And they probably follow the author's guidance to a greater extent than they would in many other contexts and probably strive to retain what they read and to be able to demonstrate their retention. Others have attempted to study context effects on the understanding of a text, as we have seen. Some researchers have created enriched contexts for meaning construction, even multimedia macrocontexts (Sherwood, Kinzer, Hasselbring, & Bransford, 1987).

Later in the book in chapters on writing and reading, we return to the topic of task when considering writers transforming texts to create new texts. These sorts of tasks fit in a "reading for writing" category that R. F. Lorch, Jr., Klusewitz, and Lorch (1995) found to be one of the four major types of reading reported by college students.

Meaning Construction and the Intertext

The French poststructuralists, first Kristeva (1967/1986, 1968) and then others, used the term *intertextuality* for relations among texts. Although Kristeva coined the term about three decades ago, the concept had been around before then. For instance, Bakhtin (1929/1984), whose influence can be seen in Kristeva's work, had spoken of the multiple voices, which he called *heteroglossia,* in utterances. The poststructuralist conception, developed by Barthes (1971/1979) and Derrida (1967/1978), who built on Kristeva's ideas, is discussed in more detail in the next chapter. Suffice it to say here that, in the poststructural conception of intertextuality, human agency was downplayed, authors and readers were decentered, and the intertext was portrayed as operating rather autonomously from readers and writers. In contrast to this poststructural perspective on intertextual relations, my discussion maintains a constructivist emphasis on human agency and thus considers intertextuality in terms of intertextual cues made and discerned by people and in terms of intertextual knowledge used by people as individuals and as social groups (cf. Miller, 1985).

Intertextuality is implication on the part of authors and inference on the part of readers. As with other kinds of cues, some intertextual cues seem more explicit than others. Rather explicit guidance from authors often comes in the form of citations of, and quotations from, other specific texts. In dealing with such cues, readers who are familiar with the cited text should integrate relevant aspects of their meaning for that text in their understanding of the text being read. Citations, which are made with some awareness and intention on the part of authors, not only mention a text but also imply a certain kind of meaning for it (Small, 1978). What the reader generates in response to a citation would seem to depend on the kinds of additional cues that are perceived as well as what the reader knows about the text cited. Another kind of intertextual cue is allusion, which is less explicit. Some allusions are made consciously by authors, who intentionally use them to get their readers to think of another text. As Meltzer (1994) pointed out, "putting others' prose into a new context is the raison d'être of allusion, which . . . banks on the reader's memory" (p. 3). But other allusions are not made consciously by writers. As with other inferences, readers can perceive allusions when authors do not consciously intend them.

As Miller (1985) argued, some intertextual relations must be attributed only to the reader. Readers respond to some textual cues by making connections to other texts that were not cited or specifically alluded to by the author. Some connections, which involve using one's discourse knowledge, are to the general form or style of previously read texts. For example, a story relates to previously read stories and a research report in one's discipline relates in a rather general way regarding form and style to previously read (and written) reports. This is because readers use discourse knowledge abstracted from prior experiences with that genre. In addition, people sometimes make connections to more specific previously experienced texts, perhaps remembering specific stories or specific reports.

Some recent studies have focused on intertextual links associated with genre. Beach, Appleman, and Dorsey (1994) investigated the intertextual relations high school students created among texts read for an English class by interviewing the students. Most of the students reporting intertextual links made them among texts of the same genre, and these were often character traits (cf. Rogers, 1991), although some were thematic. In a study designed to elicit intertextual connections, Hartman (1991) had eight high school students think aloud as they read five short stories that he selected on the basis of thematic linkages he discerned. Three stories, which were set in the American Civil War, had common themes of motives, fighting, and dying in the war. The fourth story had similar themes, but was set in the Spanish Civil War. And the remaining story portrayed a man dying in the hospital but readers are not told why he is there. All readers made some rather general intertextual connections in understanding the texts as stories, and some of them made the sort of explicit linkages in their readings that Hartman had identified. Perhaps most interesting was that, even with such obvious thematic connections, some students did not seem to make them. Hartman explained that there were two ways in which the readers managed to keep their readings "discrete": One was to defer to the authority of the author and stay just with that one text that was being read, and the other was to exert their own authority by situating the interpretation in their own personal experience.

Intertextual connections are often topical. Readers make topical linkages to other texts on the basis of content knowledge that they have built through prior readings, and much of the reading that people do, as Spiro (1980) pointed out, is done to update knowledge. This updating of knowledge was the focus of Bazerman's (1985) study of physicists reading to keep up in their field. The researcher interviewed them and observed them when they read disciplinary journals. Not only were they highly selective in choosing the articles that they would read, but they were selective in what they attended to as they read particular articles. In their reading they looked for what was *new*, which meant new relative to what they had read previously. For instance, in reading much of the work, they skipped over most of the article (they could fill all that in through inferencing) and went right to the new technique or equation. One physicist put it this way:

> There are some things that go against what you expect, that trigger the attention: "Is this right?" If so, then something is missing [from our knowledge]. . . . From our theoretical knowledge and our basic understanding we know a great deal about how things are supposed to go. . . . Some other things are a little surprising. . . . Somebody should check that. (p. 11)

These physicists often read back and forth (attending mainly to introduction, conclusion, figures) or even worked their way from back to front. The only articles they read carefully were those that they saw as highly relevant to their own work.

At this point, too, I will refer to the writing studies to be discussed later. Writers use knowledge of other writers' texts when they produce their own texts (e.g., Cairney, 1990; Rowe, 1987). And usage of intertextual cues is also quite apparent when people use other writers' texts in literate acts that involve both reading and writing. Readers (writers) make inferences across texts as they make their selections and reorganizations. They restructure discourse as they read other writers' texts in the act of producing their own.

Mental Products Constructed through Reading

The nature of the constructed product has been the subject of much theorizing by those studying reading processes. Meaning is often conceptualized in terms of

Kintsch's text base: a propositional representation of the semantic content of the text (1974; Kintsch & van Dijk, 1978). The text base can often be a surface kind of understanding. However, another sort of product has also begun to gain prominence in the theorizing: a situation model, which is a "cognitive representation of the events, actions, persons, and in general the situation a text is about " (van Dijk & Kintsch, 1983, p. 11; cf. Johnson-Laird, 1983). This kind of product is more amenable to inferencing and to changes in meaning over time than is the linear kind of text base. As van Dijk (1995) explained, this model is "one specific interpretation of one specific text at a specific moment" (p. 394). Those who conceptualize meaning in terms of situation models retain the text base because it, too, is needed for the theory, and there is speculation that the two sorts of understandings can work together (cf. Schmalhofer & Glavanov, 1986; Zwaan, 1993).

If meaning for a text is thought of as a mental product, it has to be a dynamically changeable mental product. Also, it must be able to accommodate affective elements because feelings and attitudes are elicited during reading and are an integral part of the meaning that is built (Bartlett, 1932; Spiro, 1977, 1980; S. W. Tyler & Voss, 1982). Moreover, it must allow for imagery through some means because imagistic material is generated in the reading of many materials, particularly narrative and descriptive texts (Denis, 1984; Sadoski & Paivio, 1994; Sadoski & Quast, 1980).

Shifts in the Lens: Social Constructions

As we have seen, a great deal of research has been directed to individuals as constructive agents, building mental meanings as they read texts and contexts and intertexts while engaging in social practices. In addition to this kind of work, a growing number of researchers have begun giving attention to what is called the *social construction* of meaning. These people look at the meaning-making process with their lenses focused on social groups or systems as constructive agents and on products as something shared by members of the group.

Groups or Pairs as Agents

One line of social construction research conceives agency mainly in terms of groups or pairs with identifiable members, which might be, for instance, classes of students or persons connected through e-mail. Most of these studies are undergirded either by sociolinguistic conceptions, particularly the notion of communicative competence of community members (Hymes, 1974a, 1974b), or by the Soviet language and learning theories, particularly claims of the social genesis of knowledge (e.g., Bakhtin, 1981; Leont'ev; 1981; Vygotsky, 1978, 1986), or a combination of the two. In addition, some studies, such as Middleton and Edwards's (1990), are undergirded by Bartlett's (1923, 1932) notions of social processes of understanding and remembering, which might also be combined with the other social theories. In conducting this work, a researcher typically makes inferences about the social construction process by studying oral or written exchanges recorded on tape and in observational notes. This is done instead of examining recalls or some other products of individuals, as in the work described earlier. J. L. Green, Weade, and Graham (1988), who called this communal product the "social text," explained that it can be likened to a "group composition that is simultaneously being written, read, and revised" (p. 13). The text being read and understood would be embedded in this social text (cf. J. L. Green & Wallat, 1981). For instance, if a group of people are discussing a newly published book, the text of that book would be embedded in the oral-discussion text. Here, too, in this work on groups as agents, it seems to me, the constructive process is characterized by organization, by selectivity, and by connectivity.

Organization of this social product is often conceived in terms of participation structures, which are patterns of speaking and listening that are, to some extent, idiosyncratic to the immediate group (with rules collaboratively constructed by the group) but are also influenced by larger society. For instance, Mehan (1979) described the initiation-reply-evaluation (I-R-E) patterns of many classroom lessons, including those focused on reading and understanding texts. As illustrated in Figure 7, these I-R-E acts, jointly constructed by teacher (T) and students (S), make up directive, elicitative, and informative sequences. In the latter, evaluation is optional, EØ. These sequences, in turn, constitute the lesson (cf. Cazden, 1988). Other researchers (e.g., Almasi, 1995) have studied the participation patterns of smaller groups, which can be embedded within larger patterns, as, for example, discussion groups led by a teacher or another student. Some important analyses of participation structures have shown discontinuities, or mismatches, between patterns typically used in the schools and the patterns in the home communities of some students, such as Hawaiian American children in Hawaii (Au, 1980), Native American children on an Oregon reservation (Philips, 1983), and African American children in the Piedmont Carolinas (Heath, 1982).

The organizational patterns discussed previously in the chapter with respect to written texts also guide the oral constructions of groups. As mentioned previously, Lemke (1988) demonstrated the importance of such forms as comparisons and procedural instructions in the oral and written discourse of science classes. Also, some work has shown the narrative pattern guiding constructions of pairs or groups as well as individuals. For example, Middleton and Edwards (1990), who studied joint remembering of a story, found a group of students using a narrative frame to guide their collaborative recall, although this pattern had to compete with another pattern, that of topic comment, in which a student would speak of an interesting "bit" and comment about why it was interesting. In the narrative reconstruction,

Event	Lesson							
Phase	Opening		Instructional				Closing	
Type of sequence	Directive	Informative	Topical sets		Topical sets		Informative	Directive
			Elicit	Elicit	Elicit	Elicit		
Organization of sequences	I-R-E	$I\text{-}R(^E_\theta)$	I-R-E	I-R-E	I-R-E	I-R-E	$I\text{-}R(^E_\theta)$	I-R-E
Participants	T-S-T	T-S-T	T-S-T	T-S-T	T-S-T	T-S-T	T-S-T	T-S-T

(Left vertical axis: Hierarchical organization)

Sequential organization ⟶

Figure 7. Mehan's (1979) structure of classroom lessons. Reprinted by permission of the publisher from *Learning Lessons* by H. Mehan, Cambridge, MA: Harvard University Press. Copyright © 1979 by the President and Fellows of Harvard College.

connective words like *so,* of the sort discussed by Bartlett (1932) and others, were often used to establish consensus among group members rather than connectivity among the various contributions. Instead of implying "this happened because that happened," these connective words implied "this version should be accepted by everybody because . . ." (Middleton & Edwards, 1990, p. 31).

The importance of a particular contribution made by group member is often defined mainly in terms of its social consequences. For example, Bloome and Egan-Robertson (1993) studied the social consequences of proposals for intertextual links that were made in a first-grade classroom. These analyses showed that some of the teacher's proposals of intertextual links in the teacher–class interactions legitimized certain discourses, such as recitation, and some of the students' intertextual assertions in student–student interactions served to define the students as readers. In keeping with Soviet semiotic conceptions (e.g., Bakhtin, 1981; Voloshinov, 1929/ 1986), Bloome and Egan-Robertson defined intertextuality not in texts or in readers' minds but in the social interactions.

Connectivity among the various contributions is studied by analyzing the "social text" not only for linguistic ties, such as those that Halliday and Hasan (1976) described, but also for paralinguistic devices, such as intonation and gesture (Gumperz, Kaltman, & O'Connor, 1984). Through various means participants fill in ellipses, relate one contribution to another, and establish relevance to a given topic as they conduct their conversations about their reading. A recent study of the social construction of connectivity was conducted by Schallert et al. (1995), who analyzed conversations that members of a college class had about their assigned readings, which took place either in oral, face-to-face fashion or on a computer network. This analysis involved study of topic–comment patterns as one person would link up topically to a comment made by someone else. The two modalities, face-to-face and electronic, were characterized by different kinds of coherence: For the oral conversations coherence was achieved by the sorts of topic–comment patterns we have considered for the writing of a single text, except that in these conversations, it was created by one person relating topically to what another had said. For the written networked conversations, coherence was not constructed in turn-by-turn fashion, and it was not a single line of coherence. There were various topics running at the same time, and a person could comment about a topic that had come up earlier or even about more than one topic at the same time.

Even though a study might center around some activity involving reading, what is socially constructed might be coherence, intertextuality, or even social relationships, as we have seen. It is there in the interaction, although ultimately it may be brought to individuals' cognitions. Much of this work is based on Vygotskian notions of the social origins of thought and of the role of language and other cultural tools as mediators between past and present (Vygotsky, 1978, 1986).

Communities and Societies as Agents

The constructivist lens might focus instead in macroscopic fashion on a more abstract kind of process and on a large social group, such as a discipline, a nation, a society, or other large discourse community, as the constructive agent. The approach to study would likely be historical, primarily by studying written texts and other artifacts, but the socially constructed product could be most anything, such as a custom, a theory, an epistemology, a field of study, or a concept, such as those to do with academic disciplines (Fleck, 1935/1979; Kuhn, 1962). It can also be the social construction of the importance of a particular text or the social construction of an interpetation of a particular text, as with Bartlett's (1932) *Remembering,* which was discussed earlier.

Studies of literary works are conducted by some people looking through this lens. These literary scholars include Schmidt (1989, 1992; Meutsch & Schmidt, 1985) and others, mainly Europeans, who publish in *Poetics* and who call their approach a sociology of literature (cf. Ort, 1989; Verdaasdonk, 1985; Verdaasdonk & van Rees, 1992). Authors, editors, publishers, critics, and readers are in a dynamic social system, in which the roles are production, distribution, reception, and post-processing of literature. This system can be understood only in the context of other social systems (Schmidt, 1985, 1989).

Some work investigates the consensus-building process over years and even generations in which a literary text is attributed a particular status in a nation's literature through the collective effort of reviewers, academic scholars, and essayists (e.g., van Rees, 1983, 1987). For example, van Rees's (1987) study indicated that, over time, the variety of evaluations decreases as the critical community reaches agreement about the value of a particular work. However, Otter (1991) found some consistency through the years among critics belonging to a particular critical community (e.g., biographical, New Critical, poststructural).

Other work examines the differences among meanings constructed by different societies for the same text. One particularly important question now is: To what extent can people from different cultures understand each other's texts when social values, attitudes, and habits seem so different? This question, motivated by the unification of Eastern and Western Europe, has been tackled by some Europeans studying cross-cultural understandings of literature. For instance, Leenhardt (1992) reported a set of large-scale international studies comparing interpretations of novels made by readers in different European countries (cf. Halász, 1988). These studies were in a number of respects similar to Bartlett's work and the other studies discussed in the first part of the chapter into the ways of different social groups; however, the conclusions led to large claims about societal and national differences. In Leenhardt's study, readers' interpretations of the novel were similar for readers in the same country, and they seemed related to their shared life experiences as well as the kinds of literary texts with which they were familiar. The interpetations differed, however, across countries. For example, when reading a Hungarian novel, *The Notebook* by Agota Kristof (1986), French readers, who emphasized the psychology of characters, tended to see the conclusion as representing people's maturation, their growing up, but German readers saw the ending of the story in a more abstract fashion as representing the end of an epoch. In Fish's (1980) social constructivist terminology, these French and German readers would belong to different "interpretive communities."

Conclusion

We have seen in this chapter how, in constructing meaning, readers or groups of readers may organize and select content according to patterns that seem to be suggested by the text, or, in performing some tasks, they employ other patterns and principles associated with a particular perspective or with interpretations of the context and the intertext. And we have seen how readers, as individuals and as groups, provide connectivity through the making of inferences. They strive in this meaning-building process to create understandings that "fit"—the parts fit together and the meanings fit the textual, contextual, and intertextual cues that are perceived. Similarities in understandings, achieved when people with similar backgrounds, experience, and knowledge approach texts in similar contexts with similar purposes and perspectives, may be called "shared meanings."

A Post(modern)script

To a great extent, this chapter has been about discourse conventions and about conventional discourse, the reading of texts produced by writers using their social tool kits, and understood by readers using theirs. But what about contemporary texts that parody such conventions? I am thinking here about postmodern texts whose authors intentionally violate the norms to create what Barth (1967), a postmodern author himself, called "the literature of exhaustion." With postmodernism we seem to have both an ending and a beginning, the collapse of literature and the emergence of new rules, genres, and modes (cf. Cage, 1982). Consider, for example, Calvino's (1981) *If on a Winter's Night a Traveler,* which begins with ten first chapters of different novels, written in different languages and all rather banal, in which "you," the character looking for the missing parts, become involved with another reader, Ludmilla, and you have to deal with the author who keeps appearing. Consider Barth's (1968) own *Lost in the Funhouse,* whose narrator loses the narrative and gets lost in works of Aristotle, Joyce, and Dos Passos. Consider Sukenick's (1979) *Long Talking Bad Condition Blues,* which has a sentence that goes on for twelve pages, and J. Berger's (1972) *G,* which is a pastiche of fragments with no apparent connections. Consider novels that have double plots, one on the left page and one on the right, and a novel that comes as loose pages to be read in any sort of order.

The challenges presented by these texts require a reader to expend much cognitive effort, but, no matter how much is expended, matters are not resolved. Even so, readers do construct meaning, as Warrilow (1987) said when talking about Beckett's (1972) *The Lost Ones*: "There's something about the nature of the language, there's something about the clarity of the spirit of it, which makes it comprehensible" (pp. 95–96). The meanings constructed from reading such texts are supposed to have the kinds of gaps that would be considered problematic in some other kinds of reading. There is in postmodernism a struggle and also a playful quality—what Zurburgg (1993) called "*the groan of the text*" and "*the grin of the text*" (p. 27).

What is required of readers of these texts? Lyotard (1979/1984) maintained that such texts have no preestablished rules and that readers have to dispense with their knowledge of discourse conventions in reading them:

> They cannot be judged according to a determining judgment, by applying familiar categories to the text or to the work. These rules and categories are what the work of art itself is looking for. The artist and writer, then, are working without rules in order to formulate the rules of *what will have been done.* (p. 81)

Is he right? Do postmodern texts have no rules? It seems that some literary scholars can find conventions for these texts. The following characteristics have been listed by Lodge (1977): *contradiction,* which often takes the form of a passage canceling itself out as one clause contradicts another; *permutation,* which can mean multiple, alternative narrative lines; *discontinuity,* which is achieved by such shifts and breaks as changes in tone, blank spaces, addresses to the reader; *randomness,* which can result from pieces of the text or pieces of different texts put together in no discernible order; *excess,* which may be an overwhelming specificity of detail or an overkill of metaphorical devices (taking a metaphor, extending and extending and extending it, and thereby parodying it); *short circuit,* which is breaking the gap between the text world and *the* world through such means as exposing writing conventions, introducing oneself as the author, discussing authorship issues, combining fictional and factual modes.

Such writing, it seems, does not require readers to dispense with knowledge of conventions, such as organizational patterns, staging, and connective devices. They must know the conventions so that they know when they are broken. There would be no surprise, for example, from an author's discussing authorship issues in the midst of a tale if readers were not expecting the author to operate differently. Lodge put it this way:

> If postmodernism really succeeded in expelling the idea of order . . . from modern writing, then it would truly abolish itself, by destroying the norms against which we perceive its deviations. . . . It is essentially a rule-breaking kind of art, and unless people are still trying to keep the rules there is no point in breaking them, and no interest in seeing them broken. (p. 245)

What we seem to have here is "unconventional" discourse that is perhaps not so unconventional after all.

Chapter IV

Other Metaphors

STRUCTURALISM, POSTSTRUCTURALISM,
AND DECONSTRUCTION[1]

There is no structure apart from constructivism, either abstract or genetic.
—Jean Piaget, *Structuralism*

Question: What is the origin of what we loosely call Post-Structuralism?
M. Foucault: Indeed, why not this term?
—Michel Foucault, *Foucault Live*

What is at stake in the encounter with the structural "turn" is the Western mind itself.
—John Fekete, *The Structural Allegory*

When constructivism (with its building metaphor) was beginning to guide some discourse research in the 1970s, three other theoretical metaphors were also becoming influential in discourse theory: structuralism, poststructuralism, and deconstruction. Like constructivism, they have *struere* (to arrange, to build) as their root, and, like constructivism, they are employed in attempts to describe people's understandings of texts. Simply on the basis of labels, structuralism, a position privileging form in what is studied, would seem to have some affinity with constructivism, which, as we have seen, emphasizes organizational patterns and the ordering of experience. And poststructuralism, a development coming *from* and *after* structuralism, would seem to have some connection with structuralism but to differ from it in discounting the importance of structure or even dispensing with structure, and would probably

---

[1]This chapter is based on a paper, "Constructivism: Metaphor, Meaning, and Literacy," presented for the Special Interest Group on Constructivism at the annual meeting of the American Educational Research Association in New Orleans in April 1994.

96

not be as compatible with constructivism as structuralism is. On the basis of the labels, it is more difficult to place deconstruction in relation to the other two because of its inherent contradiction, both a building of structure and a tearing down of structure.

To understand constructivism, we must, I think, make some comparisons with these other orientations, must jump into what Fekete (1984) called a "maelstrom" of structuralist theories.

Structuralism and Discourse Theory

For this discussion, I go back to the status of structuralism a decade or two into the twentieth century, when constructivist research was initiated through the efforts of Bartlett, Piaget, and others. The disciplinary boundaries had been drawn before the end of the nineteenth century, but more and more boundaries were created in the years that followed, as lines were drawn between specializations and between sub-specializations within those disciplines. A countertrend to this fragmentation and specialization, as Gardner (1981) explained, was structuralism, the finding of structure in an object of study.

The Structuralist Movement

Structuralism, which cut across disciplines in the sciences, social sciences, humanities, and arts, emphasized generalizable patterns and systems. According to Piaget's (1970) account, structuralism as it emerged was undergirded by three major ideas regarding structure: wholeness (the whole is more than an aggregate of its parts), transformation (structures are *structuring* as well as *structured*), and self-regulation (structures maintain themselves autonomously against external disturbances). An emphasis on structure can be seen, for example, in the research of the Gestalt psychologists and in the interdisciplinary work known as cybernetics and information theory, and it is also apparent in the theoretical conceptions of knowledge configurations, such as scripts, plans, memory organization packets, schemas, and knowledge domains, developed in cognitive psychology and artificial intelligence in the 1970s and 1980s.

I shall begin here with the work of Saussure, whose concepts have been important in linguistics and have also helped to bind together some major bodies of structuralist work in discourse theory. I shall also consider the work of the Russian formalists, the Prague functionalists, and the French structuralists, as well as that related area of study known as semiotics. Special attention in my treatment is given to the structuralism undergirded with Saussurean concepts that developed mainly on the European continent before gaining a footing in the United States in the 1970s.[2] It is this position on discourse from which other positions known as poststructuralism and deconstruction (a stance within poststructuralism) developed, and it is this position to which many refer when they say "structuralism." In discussing structuralism, I also try to show that, even though structuralism has been given a *post,* which seems to mark its demise, the unprefixed structuralist enterprise seems to be thriving under other labels.

When considering poststructuralism, I give almost exclusive attention to the position developed in France by such people as Barthes (1968/1977, 1971/1979, 1973/1974), Kristeva (1967/1986, 1968, 1980), and Derrida (1967/1976, 1967/ 1978, 1970, 1995), a position that can be called *Tel Quel* poststructuralism, after the title of a journal this group published. I put my emphasis on this poststructuralism because these French theorists have been the most vocal in pronouncing the end of structuralism through their special kind of critique and revision. This is not the only kind of poststructuralism, but I find that I must establish limits when dealing with a *post,* because the *post* work is defined, not on its own terms, but only relative to something else. The *poststructuralism* label presents difficulties because a line must be constructed between what is structuralist and what comes *after* and *from* it and because the placement of that line is arbitrary. Almost any development in structuralism or semiotics can be, and probably has been, considered poststructuralist in that it is a critique of some other position. Some people even use the term so broadly that it encompasses reader-response theories, including those of Fish (1980), Bleich (1975, 1978), Iser (1978), and Holland (1968, 1975a, 1975b), that question the kinds of critical authority privileged in the past. Those theories developed concurrently with the work I discuss here, but they are not as much poststructuralist (in the sense of following, critiquing, and revising structuralism) as they are post-New Criticism.

My purpose for reviewing this structuralist and poststructuralist work is to present a more complete portrayal of constructivism, because a particular position can become clearer when one sees its similarities to and distinctions from other related positions. Comparisons are made in the concluding portion of the chapter: first a comparison of constructivism with structuralism and then a comparison of constructivism with poststructuralism, including deconstruction.

Saussure's Structuralism

A good starting point for considering structuralism is the work of Saussure, who taught linguistics at the University of Geneva from 1906 to 1911 and is considered

---

[2]This Saussurean structuralism differs from what became known as *structural linguistics* in the United States. The latter body of work is associated with L. Bloomfield (1933) and Z. S. Harris (1951).

the father of structuralism. His influential *Course in General Linguistics*, first published posthumously in 1916, was not, as one would think, a book that he had written himself. It was instead a synthesized work written by others on the basis of lectures that he delivered while at the university. Two colleagues, Bally and Sechehaye, wrote it after Saussure's death, starting with some sketchy notes he had made for his lectures but mainly using the notes eight students had taken from his lectures. After compiling the notes, Bally and Sechehaye, with the help of one of the students, ended up writing a "reconstruction," a "synthesis," a "recreation," which emphasized what to them were Saussure's major principles, "running through it like the warp of a well woven cloth of varied text" (Bally & Sechehaye, 1916/1983, p. xix [10]).[3]

Several of the Saussurean principles, outlined in the *Course,* have been particularly important in structuralist conceptions of discourse. One of the most central is that language structure is social, a system of signs that belongs to a language community. Individuals who are members of that language group would have some knowledge of the conventions of the language system, but each person's knowledge would be incomplete knowledge. Bally and Sechehaye, as translated by R. Harris, have Saussure (1916/1983) put it this way:

> If we could collect the totality of word patterns stored in all these individuals [who belong to a society], we should have the social bond which constitutes their language. It is a fund accumulated by the members of the community through the practice of speech. . . . The language is never complete in an individual, but exists perfectly only in the collectivity. (p. 13 [30])

There is a strong emphasis throughout Saussure's work on the social nature of linguistic knowledge, that larger abstract system, which can be studied through studying instances of language use. The major objective of language study should be, he maintained, to learn about that abstract social system, not the pragmatic use of language by a particular individual in a particular circumstance. Saussure distinguished between *langue* (language), the system belonging to the social group, and *parole,* the product that can be observed in a particular act of communication. Parole was to be studied, not to learn about pragmatic uses of language, but to make inferences about that abstract system, langue. For such study, he pointed out, the linguist has a choice of two different approaches: analyzing a language as it has changed over time, which he called a *diachronic* approach, or analyzing a language as a system at a particular point in time, which he called a *synchronic* approach. The

---

[3]Saussure's *Course in General Linguistics* has been through several editions and translations, but the standard pagination was established since the second edition in 1922. I have used a fairly recent edition, which was translated by R. Harris and published in 1983, and I indicate the standard page number in brackets after the page number for the Harris edition.

synchronic approach, examining language as structural relations frozen at a given point in time, was needed, he thought, if one is to understand how a language works, and for that reason he preferred it over studying changes diachronically, over time, which was the dominant approach of his day. It was not that he did not see value in historical study, only that he thought a synchronic treatment provided the means for gaining important knowledge about language that the other could not provide.

In addition to these statements about language and its study, Saussure also made his semiotic claim: that language is only one of many social systems. He saw language as only one of the sign systems that make up social life and suggested that a new area of study, *semiology*, be developed to study the nature of signs: "If one wishes to discover the true nature of language systems, one must first consider what they have in common with all other systems of the same kind" (p. 17 [35]). He thought that this area of inquiry belonged in social psychology.

Signs, the Saussurean units of meaning, are created mentally through the combination of a signifier (sound pattern) and a signified (concept). Thus, a sign can be denoted as Signifier/signified, or S/s. In conversation, when a series of sound waves is heard, a sound pattern (signifier) is perceived mentally from those waves, the sound pattern is associated with a concept (signified), and that connection between sound pattern and concept results in meaning (sign).[4] The mental connection between sound pattern and concept is *arbitrary* in the sense that it is not dictated in some way by the concept. The connection is instead determined according to the community's rules (which accounts for different languages having different sound patterns associated with the same concept). For instance, there is no obligatory connection between the sound *boi* and the concept "boy," but our language community has made a connection between the two. In Saussure's theory, the meaning of a sign—its identity—is determined by relations within the system, in particular, patterns of *difference*: These are differences from other items to which it is related through either association, called *paradigmatic* relations, or proximity, called *syntagmatic* relations. In language, where "there are only differences," sound patterns are recognized through distinctions from others, and concepts are understood only by their distinctions from others. These differences take the form of binary oppositions. For example, the sound pattern *boi* is known by its distinction from *ba* and *bou* and so on, and the concept "boy" is known by its distinction from "man" and "lad," as well as its binary oppositions with other concepts.

Thus, regarding the signification process, Saussure offered a cognitive explanation in which signifier and signified are bound together to create a psychological unit. The relationship between the two components is arbitrary, and meaning is

---

[4]"Sound pattern" is R. Harris's (1983) translation of *image acoustique*, which has often been translated as "sound image"—a term that seems confusing, given the current use of the word *image* for visual constructs.

achieved through difference, specifically binary oppositions. These components of his explanation—the unity of signifier and signified, the arbitrary nature of relationship, and the derivation of meaning through difference—were to play a major role in the development of poststructuralism, at least the French variety that would develop later and continues to undergird much work today. However, it should be clear, as I review this work in subsequent sections, that some other structuralists, intent on analyzing the structure of texts, did not deal with these microprocesses, although they applied other aspects of Saussure's theory.

In addition to these principles, Saussure also argued one more: that the oral form of language is preeminent over the written. The oral use of language takes precedence, he thought, over the written use (*écriture*) because the written form exists to represent the oral. However, the two are so closely related that written uses may be employed in a study of language structure. As we shall see, much of the structural attention to texts has gone to written forms.

Russian Formalism and Prague School Linguistics

Structural analyses of texts were being conducted early in the 1900s by the Russian formalists and the Prague School linguists. From 1915 to the late 1920s, the Russian group, centered mainly in Moscow and Petrograd, took an objectivist "morphological approach" to derive the structure of texts, particularly literary texts (e.g., Eichenbaum, 1926/1965). Although they may have been influenced to some extent by Saussure's theory, which was introduced to them by one of Saussure's former students, they had their own approach to the matter of structure, which often emphasized *device*. For example, Shklovsky (1917/1965a, 1921/1965b), one of the most prominent formalists, spoke of *defamiliarization,* which he saw as resulting from devices that fiction writers use to move the reader out of an automatic kind of reading. This is the notion, discussed in the preceding chapter, that has been resurrected by Brewer and his colleagues (Brewer, 1985; Brewer & Lichtenstein, 1982; Ohtsuka & Brewer, 1992) and others (Miall & Kuiken, 1994). According to Shklovsky, a writer can defamiliarize by doing such things as shifting perspectives from which the story is told but can also defamiliarize structurally by rearranging the plot, making events strange and thus more perceptible. A writer can also defamiliarize, Shklovsky (1921/1965b) pointed out, by doing what he called "laying bare the devices," which meant exaggerating or playing with conventions. This was one of the many means of defamiliarization used by Sterne (1779/1925) in *Tristram Shandy,* which Shklovsky admired and which seems "postmodern" and hypertextual today.

The formalists' studies, which dealt with a range of text features and devices, came to an abrupt end, largely because of Marxist disdain for their method and their emphasis, which to Marxists seemed to be overly "scientific" and to ignore context and social explanations for what was found. This point was also made by some of their fellow scholars, most notably Medvedev (1928/1978) in a piece rumored to have been written or perhaps co-authored by Bakhtin. According to Medvedev, literary texts, which are metasigns, are like utterances contributing to a dialogue. In this view language is not a system but is a process characterized by heterogeneity and by struggles between different ideologies. Bakhtin and his group were to have other criticisms of formalism and other kinds of structuralism, in particular, the artificial dualism between synchronic and diachronic and the presentation of language as an abstract object, separate from an individual (Voloshinov, 1929/1986).

However, the work of the Russian formalists has lived on in a rather remarkable way through the analyses that Propp, the formalist mentioned in the preceding chapter, conducted with Russian fairy tales, reports of which were published in Russian in 1928 and in English in 1958 and later in 1968. As mentioned earlier, Propp was one of the analysts Rumelhart cited when he introduced the story-grammar notion in American psychology in 1975. Propp was attempting to derive a master tale from his study of 100 tales. His major unit was the function, "an act of dramatic personae, which is defined from the point of its significance for the course of action of the tale as a whole" (p. 20). From his analyses he derived a finite number of functions, 31, performed by characters (e.g., member of family leaves home) and found that no tale could have all 31, but the functions, when present, always appeared in the same order. He derived 7 character roles, which were hero, false hero, princess (and her father), provider, villain, dispatcher, and helper, but noted that one character could play more than one role. The grammar he created—the abstract rules for deriving any and all stories—combined the functions and character roles.

The Prague School linguists, also pursuing such work in the early 1900s, saw themselves as part of the larger structuralist endeavor replacing atomism with systems and deriving universal principles (e.g., Trubetzkoy, 1933). In their descriptions of systems composed of dynamically interrelated parts, these structuralists are known for their attention to *function,* the uses of language. Function was the central concept undergirding their general conception of communication as well as of the linguistic structure of individual texts. These texts were viewed as functional systems in which elements are arranged in relations of mutual dependence, and, as we saw in the previous chapter, this functionalist approach carried over even to the sentence level in what is known as functional sentence perspective (Daneš, 1974; Mathesius, 1928/1964).

A major figure in this group was Jakobson, who had come to Prague after the suppression of formalist studies in Russia. One of his many contributions was extending Saussure's distinction between syntagmatic and paradigmatic relations to two polar modes of language, which distinguish between two kinds of aphasia and also distinguish between metaphor and metanonymy (Jakobson, 1956). He is well known for his model of communication, which seems on the surface to be a transmission conception much like Shannon and Weaver's (1949): A *message* in a *code* (speech, writing, numbers, etc.) referring to some *context* is sent by an *addresser* to an *addressee,* the two of whom have *contact.* However, his conception has a strong functional emphasis, in which a particular function, of the six functions he proposed, is tied to a particular constituent of the communicative act. The emotive function of a communication emphasizes addresser, the conative (directive or imperative) emphasizes addressee, the referential emphasizes context, the poetic emphasizes message, the phatic (seeing if communication is working) emphasizes contact, and the metalingual emphasizes code. In an act of communication a particular function and constitutent become dominant, and that dominance affects the nature of the discourse (cf. Kinneavy, 1971). However, Jakobson (1956/1971c) argued that dominants can shift because the elements are not in perfect balance. And, taking a diachronic perspective, he spoke of a "shifting" of dominants as forms used by a society change over time (Jakobson, 1935/1971a). He explained that, as canonical genres become less dominant, genres that had been subsidiary can become more dominant, and he thus described a process that sounded much like the transformations of "worlds" that N. Goodman (1978) has described.

French Structuralism

The structuralist enterprise has been international as well as interdisciplinary with a few major centers of productivity, including, as we have seen, Russian formalism in Moscow and Petrograd and functionalism in Prague. Another city that was to become a major structuralist center was Paris, for a time the adopted home of Jakobson, who moved there from Prague, and also of Greimas from Lithuania and of Todorov and Kristeva from Bulgaria. Paris became a kind of structuralist enclave for the radical, critical, and self-conscious structuralists who were known as the Tel Quel group and who were to move their version of structuralism to poststructuralism. Before any of them, however, the major French structuralist was the anthropologist Lévi-Strauss, whose name was almost synonymous with structuralism for some time.

Lévi-Strauss, who became acquainted with Saussurean notions when he was in the United States, devoted much of his attention to the structure of myths, which he had chosen for his analyses as far back as 1935. In one essay in the book *Structural Anthropology,* published in French in 1958 and in English in 1963, he explained that he chose myth because it "is both the same thing as language, and also something different from it" (p. 209). And later in the collection he equated language with humanity and society: "Whoever says 'Man' says 'Language,' and whoever says 'Language,' says 'Society'" (p. 389). Not only was the individual decentered but even society was decentered as attention went to language itself. By studying language through myth, he was studying society, or so his logic went. He was interested in that aspect of myth—its underlying structure—that is universal even as it is tied to a particular culture. In analyzing myths to derive this structure (the *langue*), which would encompass the variants (the *parole*), he employed a number of Saussure's concepts: units, relations, synchronicity. His larger units presupposed smaller units, each with a function or relation: "The true constituent units of a myth are . . . bundles of such relations, and it is only as bundles that those relations can be put to use and combined so as to produce a meaning" (p. 211). In these analyses Lévi-Strauss applied to myth a synchronic procedure similar to one he had used previously in analyzing how kinship terms are related within social groups, an approach that incorporated Saussurean concepts into systems. His work, as mentioned before, had some similarities to the analyses developed by Rivers, Bartlett's mentor and colleague, whom Lévi-Strauss credited. In his multivolumed *Mythologies,* Lévi-Strauss (e.g., 1964/1983, 1966/1973), a system builder, reported and discussed his analyses of hundreds of myths from North America and South America. He examined these myths not only for their *internal* structure but also for their *external* structure—where they fit in a kind of universe of related myths from their own culture and from others. The myths themselves became the units in that large system.

Although he employed many Saussurean concepts, Lévi-Strauss (1960/1969, 1962/1966) raised questions about some of them, particularly the distinctions between diachronic and synchronic and between individual and society, as he was noting the transhistorical and transpersonal.

Many other French structuralists, including Greimas, Todorov, Bremond, and Kristeva, focused on stories, as they attempted to improve upon Propp's method of analysis and to develop a more universal grammar. Greimas's (1966) grammar, based on the analogy of a story to a sentence, has actors filling six roles—sender, receiver, helper, opponent, subject, and object—that he saw as similar to Propp's. Each of Greimas's roles is played in relation to another. In a story an object, which is situated between a sender and a receiver, is desired by the subject, who has a helper and an opponent. Thus, there are three sets of binary oppositions: subject versus object (desire), sender versus receiver (communication), and helper versus opponent (participation). In the grammar these oppositions, which he called *actants,* are his structural units. Actors vary and the content of actions changes, but distribution of roles stays fixed. Todorov (1967, 1969), who was interested in analyzing large pieces of literature, used Greimas's basic approach with the binary oppositions to analyze Laclos's 1929 novel, *Dangerous Liaisons,* but, when analyzing the *Decameron,* he used propositions as his unit, each of which consisted of a character and either an action or an attribute (state, quality, or condition) as he attempted to develop a universal grammar to be used with large literary texts. Bremond's grammar (1964, 1966) focused on logical links by means of which one unit implied another unit even when separated, and Kristeva's (1969) focused on transformations and recursive combinations.

Although much of the French structuralist scholarship, including these studies of narrative, complemented analyses going on elsewhere, certain other French structuralists, in particular the Tel Quel theorists, were beginning to build a body of work that differed in stance and tone from other structuralist studies. Their work was, at the same time, both a structuralism and a critique of structuralism; moreover, it was also a critique of Western culture. A progression toward this kind of structuralism can be seen through the writings of Barthes, whose early work consisted of structuralist analyses of a French style of writing, published as *Writing Degree Zero* (1953/1968), and of myths produced by mass media, published as *Mythologies* (1957/1972). Barthes's critical and playful attitude toward such structuralist concepts and methods became very apparent in *On Racine* (1963/1964), a clever transformation of Racine's plays into a dramatically different form of discourse, whereby Barthes demonstrated the plurality of literature (cf. Barthes, 1964/1967).

It was quite clear by *S/Z* (1973/1974), written as an essay in 1968 and 1969, that Barthes had been pushing structuralism into another kind of *ism,* which some would call *poststructuralism.* This piece, a 200-page analysis of a 30-page story, *Sarrazine* by Balzac, opens with the following critique of the structuralist method:

> There are said to be certain Buddhists whose ascetic practices enable them to see a whole landscape in a bean. Precisely what the first analysts of narrative were attempting: to see all the world's stories (and there have been ever so many) within a single structure: we shall, they thought, extract from each tale its model, then out of these models we shall make a great narrative structure, which we shall reapply (for verification) to any one narrative: a task as exhausting (ninety-nine percent perspiration, as the saying goes) as it is ultimately undesirable, for the text thereby loses its difference. This difference is not, obviously, some complete, irreducible quality (according to a mythic view of literary creation), it is not what designates the individuality of each text, what names, signs, finishes off each work with a flourish; on the contrary it is a difference which does not stop and which is articulated upon the infinity of texts, of languages, of systems: a difference of which each text is the return. (p. 3)

Barthes's analysis, with almost 100 digressions, is accomplished by dividing the story into 561 chunks called *lexias,* analyzed in terms of five codes, or ways of speaking, which become threads, then voices, then both, "braided voices." In this work Barthes made his famous distinction between *readerly* and *writerly* texts and illustrated the distinction by transforming the Balzac story from readerly to writerly: A readerly text, attempting to achieve homogeneity, controls and constrains interpretation, as it moves the reader to *the* signified, that place where it originated with the "author–god." In contrast, a writerly text, attempting to achieve multiplicity and change, allows the reader to participate in the shifts and does not guide him or her to some predetermined signified. Other poststructuralist work would illustrate that for all texts—and for all language—there is no stability, no final signified.

Besides Barthes, there were a number of others who played major roles in the transition to poststructuralism. Kristeva (1967/1986, 1968, 1980), mentioned earlier, had a background in Marxist theory and also a familiarity with the positions of

Bakhtin and the methods of the Russian formalists when she arrived in Paris. Although she came to work with the French structuralists, she was already taking a strong critical stance regarding structuralism when she began her studies with Barthes. Three other Parisian theorists played major roles, too, even though they, even more than Kristeva, seemed not to have been structuralists before becoming poststructuralists: One was Derrida (1967/1976, 1967/1978, 1970), who was more of a phenomenological philosopher than a structuralist. Another was Foucault (1966/1970, 1969/1972), who never considered himself a structuralist, even though he gave his attention to the structure, or archeology, of knowledge, and defined *episteme* as "the total set of relations that unite, at a given point, the discursive practices that give rise to epistemological figures, sciences, and possibly formalized systems of knowledge" (Foucault, 1969/1972, p. 191). He worked rather independently of the others. And the other was Lacan (1966/1977, 1970), who connected Freud's psychoanalysis to structuralism and semiotics.

These people took structuralist concepts, pushed on them, and ended up with what Americans began calling *poststructuralism* in the 1970s. As will be discussed later, this group employed and reinvented such Saussurean notions as the social nature of language structure, the sign as a two-part psychological unit with an arbitrary relation between signifier and signified, the derivation of meaning through difference, the preeminence of oral over written language, and the status of language as only one of numerous kinds of social systems.

Structuralism and Semiotics

At this point we move to semiotics, a related area that overlaps with structuralism. Many of the people discussed above, from Saussure on, are known as both structuralists and semioticians, and members of the Tel Quel group are known as structuralists, poststructuralists, and semioticians. Semiotics, the study of signs, overlaps with this structuralist attention to analysis of texts and to the social meanings of texts but includes other kinds of signs, such as dress and food. Thus, much of the work I have mentioned in terms of structuralism, not simply the poststructural work, might be placed instead within semiotics, which has treated various kinds of signs but has emphasized linguistic signs, particularly texts, over other kinds. As Jakobson (1953/1971b) put it, "the basic, the primary, the most important semiotic system is language; language really is the foundation of culture" (p. 557). Hawkes (1977) also pointed to the language bias in semiotics as well as its overlap with structuralism:

> Its boundaries (if it has any) are coterminous with those of structuralism: the interests of the two spheres are not fundamentally separate and, in the long run, both ought properly to be included within the province of a third, embracing discipline called, simply, *communication*. (p. 124)

As noted earlier, Saussure called for a broader field dealing with various kinds of signs, including language. So did the American philosopher Peirce (1931–1958), whose conceptions of signification contrasted with Saussure's in several ways. One major difference regards the human subject, who is retained in Peirce's conception but decentered in Saussure's. Peirce spoke of different kinds of signs—icons and indexes in addition to symbols, which would be the type of sign for most language—and defined a sign as "something which stands to somebody for something in some respect or capacity":

> It addresses somebody, that is, creates in the mind of that person an equivalent sign, or perhaps a more developed sign. That sign which it creates I call the *interpretant* of the first sign. The sign stands for something, its object. It stands for that object, not in all respects, but in reference to a sort of idea, which I have sometimes called the *ground*. (II, p. 135)

Another major difference fom Saussure concerns the relation between signifier and signified. In contrast to Saussure's conception, in which a signifier relates to only one signified, in Peirce's theory a sign can refer to another sign, which can refer to another sign, and so on. This difference was to make Peirce's conception more compatible with poststructuralism than Saussure's conception was.

What exactly is this semiotics, this study of signs? It is difficult to define in any precise way because it has so many foci. Merrell (1992) commented on the limitless domain of semiotics: "The semiotician generates a theory of signs, and consequently a sign of signs, which ultimately embraces everything: the universe as a sign"; this can become a "cosmic circle," in which "signs sign signs, ad infinitum" (p. 187). Eco (1976), an Italian semiotician as well as a novelist, defined semiotics as "*in principle the discipline studying everything which can be used in order to lie*" (p. 7) because something cannot be said "to tell" (to signify) at all if it cannot be used to lie. He described the method of semiotics as separating an act, called a signifier, from its meaning, the signified, studying the visible part to make inferences about an invisible part (cf. Eco, 1984). His conception of the domain of semiotics included the following areas of study: natural languages, plot structures, text theory, aesthetic texts, mass communication, rhetoric, and medical semiotics, in addition to many others that do not involve language. We shall return to semiotics later.

Structuralism and Discourse Analysis

What is happening with structuralism now? As I said at the beginning of the chapter, it seems to me that structuralism is thriving but that it is going by names other than "structuralism." Here, I am talking about structuralism in a broad sense, not limiting my point to the particular variety associated with Saussure. Much that is today called discourse analysis, textlinguistics, rhetorical analysis, contrastive rhetoric, and even poststructuralism has structuralist underpinnings, as does that work called semiotics. I think that many people who do structuralist work today avoid the structuralist label because there are two problems with it. The first is the connotations of inflexibility and rigidity often associated with the term *structure,* which overpower the organic, functional, and dynamic senses of structure that are essential to systems theory. Many scholars today do not want to be associated with an epistemology that seems to ignore flexibility and variability in discourse patterns, especially now that knowledge itself is being conceived so flexibly in terms of connections that are emergent rather than preset. The second problem, I think, is the fact that the word *poststructuralism* is being used in more and more disciplinary and interdisciplinary contexts. Anyone hearing the word *poststructuralism* would think that structuralism is passé, out of fashion. When there is a poststructuralism, who wants to be a structuralist, particularly in academe, where it is so important to do what is new, what is cutting edge?

Yet, structuralism—the method and the major assumptions—persists and even thrives under those different names, thrives to such an extent that I cannot begin to do it justice here, given the constraints and purpose of this chapter. The work includes study of such pervasive forms as news discourse, represented by the analyses of van Dijk (1985), known for his structuralist as well as constructivist studies, whose graphic appears in Figure 1. In the following quotation, van Dijk (1985) presented the asssumptions under which he operated:

> We assume that there is a fixed, conventional schema, consisting of categories that are typical (at least in part) for news discourse. Each category must correspond to a specific sequence of propositions or sentences of the text. The order of categories, as it is specified by the rules, therefore also determines the overall ordering of the respective sequences or episodes.
>
> News schemata, due to their conventional nature, are at least implicitly known by their users in a given culture, that is by journalists and readers. (pp. 85–86)

He went on to discuss semantic restraints, such as restraints regarding the type of content to fit in each category, and then rules, some that are strict, such as Summary coming first and Comment almost always coming at the end if it is included, but others that are less strict, such as Previous Events and Context following Main Event.

Attention is being directed to a variety of discourse forms, including literary discourse, even the interactive fiction, as well as such everyday forms as classroom discourse, telephone messages and conversations, and such specialized forms of disciplinary and professional discourse as psychological assessment reports, doctor–patient interactions, and academic arguments. Also receiving attention are larger discourses between whole groups, such as professional associations. I could go on and on here, but will instead refer the reader to such journals as *Text, Discourse*

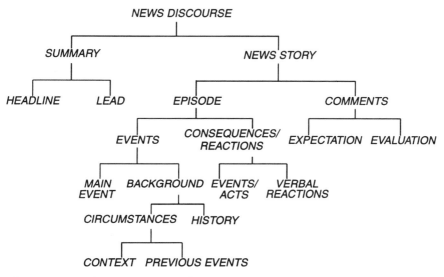

Figure 1. van Dijk's (1985) structure for news discourse. Copyright © 1985 by Walter de Gruyter & Co.

Processes, and *Poetics,* which publish structural analyses as well as other kinds of discourse studies.

The Structuralist Method

Structuralism, as it is manifested in analyses of texts and other signs, is a method, but it is also a set of beliefs, or assumptions. In general, its method tends to be synchronic, focused on how the parts of a particular kind of text (sometimes conceived broadly as an act or a practice) fit together at some point in time, not on how the composition of parts and whole has changed historically. It involves identifying not only the units of what is studied but also the relationships among those units and discovering, through such a parsing, an abstract kind of system which may be called a structure. In the case of texts, which have been the subject of most analyses and theorizing, an expert analyst, using his or her knowledge of how language works, does this parsing to see or to show how this type of text works. There is thus usually the interpretation of only this one person, but it is a person doing the work relative to what has been done before and attempting to be objective.

One assumption made in these analyses is similar to Saussure's: that a certain kind of conventional knowledge, which undergirds meaning for a text of that type, can be determined through the pattern of relationships, the conventional system that is discovered by the structuralist. And the other assumption is that those abstract, rule-governed structures belong to social, collective knowledge, so that, in analyzing a particular kind of text, one is learning about the community's discourse knowledge as well as the knowledge of people within that community (and not simply the knowledge of the particular person or persons who produced that particular text).

The method is both deductive and inductive, both top-down and bottom-up. The analyst approaches the process with an idea (even a theoretical position) regarding what will be found regarding the *langue,* checks that out through the analyses of *parole,* makes revision in the position if necessary, and so on. Even though there is the appearance of objectivity, which is a part of much scholarship of any kind, there is some reflexivity among structuralists and semioticians regarding their method. Eco (1976), for instance, has cautioned against the ideological fallacy that one's own approach is totally objective and neutral. As he put it, "all inquiry is 'motivated'" (p. 29).

Poststructuralism and Discourse Theory

It was 1966 when Derrida declared an end to structuralism at an international symposium in the United States, "The Languages of Criticism and the Sciences of Man," which was intended to promote structuralism and to demonstrate its relevance across various disciplines. In 1970 this poststructuralist statement, "Structure, Sign, and Play in the Discourse of the Human Sciences," was published in the proceedings along with the discussion that followed it. When asked during that discussion to define structure, Derrida had replied with a definition that seemed puzzling to some conference participants. He responded that structure should be centered but that the center could be a deficiency or could be something that makes "free play" possible. He was challenging the idea of structure by saying that structure, which many considered basic to knowledge, was not as stable as thought and was perhaps even missing. Instead of stability there was play, or wobble. He concluded his response with this understatement: "So, I think that what I have said can be understood as a criticism of structuralism certainly" (p. 269).

In this section I review the theoretical work tied to the French (Saussurean) structuralism that has come to be known as poststructuralist, which we will call Tel Quel poststructuralism, as well as that subset of French and American theory with Tel Quel ties that is called deconstructionist. This work addresses such structureless "structural" matters as deficiencies and free play.

The Development of Poststructuralism

By the early 1970s, as mentioned earlier, it was clear that some of the French structuralists, particularly those associated with Barthes and Tel Quel, were reinventing the structuralist conceptions to such an extent that "poststructuralism" was a more appropriate label. Barthes's work from *S/Z* on is often considered poststructuralist, as is much of the published work of Kristeva, Foucault, Lacan, and Derrida. The poststructural work called *deconstruction* was produced by Derrida as well as numerous others, most notably de Man, J. H. Miller, and G. Hartman, members of the faculty at Yale, where Derrida went as a visiting professor. In the United States the two lines of work—structuralism and poststructuralism—began at much the same time, in the 1970s, when constructivist research in discourse was also beginning.

Poststructuralism is sometimes portrayed as a reaction to structuralism, and in some ways it is. It rejects the scientific aspects of structuralism, the meticulous parsings. It also rejects the notion of a single meaning of a given text, maintaining that, instead of a single meaning, there is always polysemy, a multiplicity of "readings." Whereas structualists focus on text structures, or patterns, poststructuralists argue against the idea of a structure for a given text, pointing out that any such structure is collapsible, and argue against authority, including such notions as "the author," which, according to Barthes (1968/1977), "impose a limit on that text," "furnish it with a final signified," "close the writing" (p. 147). The following is what Culler (1975) has imagined that a poststructuralist would say to a structuralist:

> The ideology of our culture provides a particular way of reading literature, and instead of challenging it you make it absolute and translate it into a system of rules and operations which you treat as rationality and acceptability. . . . Texts can be read in many ways; each text contains within itself the possibility of an infinite set of structures, and to privilege some by setting up a system of rules to generate them is a blatantly prescriptive and ideological move. (p. 242)

Structuralism, with its emphasis on social rather than individual knowledge, had decentered the individual subject as the focal point in the reading of texts, as Culler also pointed out:

> Once the conscious subject is deprived of its role as a source of meaning—once meaning is explained in terms of conventional systems which may escape the grasp of the conscious subject—the self can no longer be identified with consciousness. It is "dissolved" or its functions are taken up by a variety of interpersonal systems that operate through it. (p. 28)

But this French poststructuralism did not reinstate the individual human subject in order to explain the instability and indeterminacy of meaning. The subject and the individual were targets of critique, considered to be products of the dominant ideology tied to Western rationality that poststructuralists wanted to expose and undermine. Instead, the instability and indeterminacy were explained mainly through the language itself. Neither the individual nor the social community has the central role; that goes to the text, to language, in a much more profound way than in structuralism.

Poststructuralism can be viewed as an *extension* of structuralism—structuralism in one of its developments—instead of simply a reaction to it. The Tel Quel post-structuralists and their fellows took and transformed a number of Saussurean concepts. It was this referring and returning to Saussure that, according to Angenot (1984), provided some self-regulation for this group's theorizing and that has made their work appear to have some coherence. For instance, they built on the Saussurean notion of the two-part nature of a sign, a signifier and a signified, and the claim that the relation between the two is arbitrary. In this conception, a signifier leads to what seems to be its signified but turns out instead to be a signifier itself because it leads to another, which leads to another, and so on. Instead of a *final* signified tied to something in the "real world," there is an infinite regress in the language itself (Barthes, 1971/1979), which was something that Peirce (1931–1958) had also claimed. Thus, in poststructuralism, there are no truths, everything is interpretations, and everything, it often seems, is language. Language thus has a much greater status than in the Saussurean semiotic conception, where it is simply one of various kinds of sign systems.

The infinite regress of signifier to signifier to signifier continues beyond what might appear to be text boundaries, as signifiers extend to what seem to be other texts. Therefore, texts do not exist as closed entities. As mentioned in the previous chapter, Kristeva (1967/1986, 1968) argued that, instead of discrete texts, there is intertext, which is always in flux. A text, she claimed, is a "permutation of texts, an intertextuality: in the space of a given text, several utterances, taken from other texts, intersect and neutralize one another" (Kristeva, 1967/1986, p. 36). She was influenced here by Bakhtin (1929/1984, 1981), who had spoken of the multiple voices—the heteroglossia—within the language one speaks, undermining the authority of one voice, but she expanded the notion to all texts and used it to critique the conventional conceptions of text, author, and reader.

It is the gap between signifiers and signifieds that interested Lacan and Foucault. Lacan (1966/1977) pointed to the line between S/s in Saussure's Signifier/signified, and spoke of that line as a barrier to signification. In Lacan's psychoanalytic conception that line is "the gap that constitutes the subject": The human subject, which "yearns to find itself" (but cannot because of that powerful bar), is "a fading thing that runs under the chain of signifiers" (p. 194) (cf. Lacan, 1968, 1970). Foucault's (1966/1970, 1969/1972) histories of epistemologies provide a different kind of treatment of gaps between signifiers and signified. Foucault described the gaps as the places in the discourse where ideology slips through and epistemic changes occur, as when, he argued, a gap in classical discourse provided the space where the discourse of the Enlightenment could come through.

Poststructuralists have also pushed on the Saussurean concept of *difference* to give a certain kind of preeminence to written language (*écriture*) over spoken language, using one of Saussure's claims, meaning through difference, to undermine another, the preeminence of oral over written language. Derrida (1967/1978, 1970) played with the words *différence* (difference) and *différance* (a word he coined to indicate *deferral* as well as *difference*) to argue this point, as he noted that the difference between these two words is apparent only in the written form because in French the two have the same pronunciation. With the written form there is more deferring back into the network of relations in the text—seemingly endless deferral. And it is this difference in terms of deferral that undercuts any Saussurean claim that the oral form is superior.

Deconstruction: A Form of Poststructuralism

The notion of *deconstruction* began with Derrida (1967/1976, 1967/1978), who presumably created the label from *construction* and *destruction* (the latter perhaps from Heidegger's *Destruktion*). However, through the years he expressed displeasure at being tied to that "entity," for example, saying at a conference on "Deconstruction Is/In America": "I have never claimed to identify myself with what may be designated by this name. It has always left me cold" (Derrida, 1995, p. 15). He saw no reason to define the term because, by attempting a definition, one would be missing the whole point of it. Nevertheless, B. Johnson (1987), a deconstructionist herself, attempted an explanation:

> The very word *deconstruction* is meant to undermine the either/or logic of the opposition "construction/destruction." Deconstruction is both, it is neither, and it reveals the way in which both construction and destruction are themselves not what they appear to be. Deconstruction both opposes and redefines; it both reverses an opposition and reworks the terms of that opposition so that what was formerly understood by them is no longer tenable. (pp. 12–13)

In deconstruction the instability of texts, described above, is demonstrated. They are said to deconstruct themselves (do themselves in) because they are complicitous with Western ideology. In deconstruction the collapsible structures of texts become ruptures, as ideology is revealed—including such "rooted ideologies" as "the concepts of causality, of the subject, of identity, of referential and revealed truths" and "most notably, of the autonomous power to will of the self" (de Man, 1979, pp. 136–137)—and the result might seem to be nothingness. Norris (1987) explained the process of deconstruction:

> Deconstruction is the vigilant seeking out of those "aporias," blind spots or moments of self-contradiction where a text betrays the tension between rhetoric and logic, between what it manifestly means to say and what it is nonetheless constrained to mean. To "deconstruct" a piece of writing is therefore to operate a kind

of strategic reversal, seizing on precisely those unguarded details (casual metaphors, footnotes, incidental turns of argument) which are always, and necessarily, passed over by a more orthodox persuasion. For it is here, in the margins of the text—the "margins," that is, as defined by a powerful normative consensus—that deconstruction discovers those same unsettling forces at work. (p. 19)

Let me illustrate with B. Johnson's (1987) deconstructive reading of Wordsworth's (1805/1974) "Preface to the *Lyrical Ballads.*" Johnson began with the theoretical claims made there: that the natural and passionate poetry of past times had been corrupted by mechanical devices of style, particularly personification, that poetry should once again become the "spontaneous overflow of powerful feeling," and that by recollecting emotion in tranquility the poet would develop "habits of mind" to be obeyed "blindly and mechanically." There was a contradiction here, Johnson noted, in that the good and the bad were both defined through the same figure of speech. However, this was not the basis of the deconstruction, since Johnson concluded that this contradiction demonstrated a key feature of the poetic process, the problem of balancing authenticity with convention.

Then she went on to do her deconstruction by demonstrating the "rhetorical slipperiness" of this theoretical text when related to one of the lyrical ballads, "Strange Fits of Passion." The poem not only illustrates the "neatness" of the theory but also undermines it. The contradiction Johnson found is the poet's dependence in the poem on personification—that very feature that was supposed to be avoided. This is, she said, "the revenge of personification, the return of a poetic principle that Wordsworth had attempted to exclude" (B. Johnson, 1987, p. 96).

The deconstruction of a text often involves two readings: The text is given a conventional interpretation (the conventional *and* ideological one), and that interpretation is undermined as a critical flaw or contradiction is exposed. In challenging the authority of the text, a critic engaging in deconstruction seems to be doing the deconstruction but is not necessarily committed to what he or she says. This tentativeness is suggested sometimes, in Heidegger's fashion, by putting words "under erasure" with slashes through them. The text (or intertext), which is autonomous and beyond any human power, is often portrayed as doing this to itself instead of having this done to it by a critic. The text even invents the reader: "The work . . . becomes an institution forming its own readers, giving them a competence which they did not possess before" (Derrida, 1992b, p. 74). The text is the constructive and destructive agent; it is the constructive and deconstructive material; and its deconstructed or dismantled self is the product.

Deconstruction is intent on breaking boundaries, conventional divisions, of various kinds. For example, Derrida (1980/1992a) deconstructed the concept of genre, which he saw as limiting:

As soon as the word genre is sounded, as soon as it is heard, as soon as one attempts to conceive it, a limit is established, norms and interdictions are not far behind.

"Do," "do not," says "genre," the word genre, the figure, the voice, or the law of genre. (p. 224)

He portrayed genre (who is a woman, because in French *genre* also refers to gender) destroying a comprehensive taxonomy and thus herself, not only eliminating boundaries within literature but between literature and other forms of discourse. Favorite targets are binary oppositions, which were so central to Saussure's structuralism, not only the terms that make up the label construction/destruction but also such pairs as philosophy/literature, understanding/misunderstanding, and central/marginal. Most anything can be deconstructed—*Macbeth,* Durkheim, the Kimbell, social psychology, and the theater—as some new book titles suggest.

Comparison of Constructivism with the Other Conceptions

After all this about structuralism and poststructuralism, we now return to our major topic, constructivism, to consider how constructivism relates to these other *isms* that are also based on some kind of building metaphor. What does constructivism have in common with them? What are the major differences? Are they compatible with constructivism?

Comparison of Structuralism and Constructivism

First, how does constructivism relate to structuralism? There are a number of connections, both theoretically and historically, between structuralism and the constructivist work described in the previous chapter. Constructivists interested in the understanding of texts have certain affinities with structuralists, often basing their methods of text analysis on the work of structuralists. There have been a number of "collaborations" across the years: the influence of structualist and formalist conceptions on story grammarians' research, the application of the formalists' literary conceptions to today's structural affect theory, and the relevance of Prague linguists' topic–comment patterning to studies of connectivity in comprehension. There is a natural kind of collaboration here between the two: the structuralist, whose interests and expertise center on the features of discourse, and the constructivist, whose interests and expertise center on processes of discourse. A notable example is the Kintsch–van Dijk (Kintsch & van Dijk, 1975, 1978; van Dijk & Kintsch, 1983) collaboration, which includes Kintsch, a constructivist theorist and researcher in cognitive psychology, known for his models of discourse understanding, and van Dijk, a linguistic theorist and analyst whose background is structuralist-semiotic and who has focused on macrostructures of discourse. In a recent *feitschrift* to Kintsch, van Dijk (1995) traced the development of their collaboration and described the context of the mid-1970s that fostered such a union of text linguistics and text processing. In addition to this collaborative work, there are, of course, individuals who put themselves in both groups. Most notably, Piaget (e.g., 1937/1954, 1970) was both a structuralist and a constructivist.

In the study of discourse, both constructivists and structuralists make the assumption that recurring patterns of discourse, including genres, are tied to social knowledge of discourse, knowledge that is shared, but not perfectly, by members of the same discourse community, and they make the assumption that something may be learned about that social knowledge through analyzing the texts of that community into constituent units and the relations among them. In fact, the line of research I have labeled the "constructivist tradition" has made extensive use of texts that fit in some type, or genre, in order to learn something about those conventions.

There are distinctions, nevertheless, to be made between constructivism and structuralism. The major distinction seems to center on what makes a constructivist a constructivist: an interest in constructive processes. Those constructivists who focus on individuals conduct studies of process, examining how people learn and use the conventional discourse patterns that might be studied by structuralists. These might, for example, be studies of the developmental process of learning particular text patterns, studies of inferences in the reading process, studies of task effects on discourse processes, or studies of co-constructive processes in understanding and composing discourse. These might be studies of the processes of meaning negotiation among members of small groups, or might be studies of the processes by means of which communities construct their cultural products over time. Many social constructivists are really historians of language, examining both diachronic and synchronic changes as a community constructs knowledge, conventions, and literature. Others attend to processes with a smaller scope, such as some aspect of enculturation into a particular discourse community.

Another distinction has to do with agency. In constructivist studies of cognition the individuals performing the literate acts are seen as active constructive agents (meaning is in them) making transformations, and in studies of social processes the group or community is seen as constructive agent making transformations. In structuralist inquiries the subject is decentered and the community is a distant agent, whose knowledge is implicit in the structures of that text. The "objective" analyst (the one really constructing the interpretation) makes inferences about the collective agent through its product.

The previous chapter showed the sorts of studies and analyses that constructivists, interested in variability as well as commonality, have conducted in order to learn more about the reading process on the part of individuals and groups. Some structuralist-semioticians, most notably Todorov and Eco, have also given attention to the process of reading, but in their descriptions the reader is not seen as an active constructive agent. In an essay with a familar sort of title, "Reading as Construction," first published in 1978, Todorov (1978/1990) asked a constructivist question: "How does a text lead us to the construction of an imaginary universe? What aspects of the text determine the construction we produce when we read, and in what way?" (p. 39). However, the approach he took and rationale he provided for that approach contrasts dramatically with the approach that would be taken by a constructivist:

> One of the difficulties of studying reading stems from the fact that reading is hard to observe: introspection is uncertain, and psychosocial interpretation is tedious. So it is with some relief that we discover the work of construction represented within fictional texts themselves—where it is much easier to study. (p. 46)

He went on to analyze the text for elements that would seem to lead a reader to create imagery, and, upon finding them, argued for particular kinds of effects they would have. It was a generalized societal writer–reader that concerned him, even though his objectivist and antisubjectivist way of talking seems to have the text doing it all. Eco, too, author of several theoretical treatments of the reading process, tended to take a similar stance, sometimes making it appear that the text is doing it all. For instance, in discussing the relationship between text and reader, he said that "every type of text explicitly selects a very general model of possible reader through the choice (i) of a certain linguistic code, (ii) of a certain literary style, and (iii) of specific specialization indices" (Eco, 1979, p. 7). These contrasting emphases in agency are related to the different kinds of studies that are conducted: The constructivists' studies, which might include text analyses, tend to provide reports of what a number of people know and do with respect to some aspect of reading, and the structuralists' studies often are characterized by text analyses and accounts of those analyses.

Now that I have considered some similarities and differences, I will point to a kind of convergence that seems to be developing, a constructivist kind of semiotics developing with more attention to process and human agency. Some current semiotic theory, considering relations between authors and audience, reinstates a conversational model, based on dialogic relations, that was introduced in semiotics by Peirce (1931–1958) and Bakhtin (1981). Consider the following quotation from Sless (1986) in a recent treatment of issues in semiotics:

> Any statement [the author] makes about readers must be a construction— imagined—and any notion of the readers which he uses either implicitly or explicitly to guide the constitution of his message must also be imagined. . . . The separation of author from reader is not an unusual occurrence but the normal condition for communication. But . . . the author always creates an image of a reader; similarly the reader creates an image of an author. (p. 35)

Even though some constructivists in cognitive psychology would disagree with the claim of an image always being formed, I think the parallels should be apparent between Sless's views and the constructivism dealing with social processes on the part of individuals. Leeds-Hurwitz (1993) has also pointed to a semiotics that incorporates constructivist concerns, and Witte (1992) has argued for a constructivist semiotics with a broader conception of text.

The parallels are particularly strong between social constructivists and sociosemioticians. They share an interest in the discourse of whole social groups, and they both see the group, usually the collective community, as agent. And some sociosemioticians focus on the communication and related signs of particular communities. For instance, Hodge and Kress (1988) have considered the signs that people use to mark their identities as group members, and the structuralist-semiotician Greimas (1987), using language that sounds much like the language of social constructivism, has spoken of "semiotic groups" whose members use a certain kind of discourse, assume "sociosemiotic roles," and help enculturate others who are apprentices. Sociosemioticians consider social practices of meaning making, as they develop their praxis-oriented theory (e.g., Thibault, 1991). There is much overlap between social constructivism and sociosemiotics today, and sometimes it seems that distinction lies only in the disciplinary affiliation one holds, the persons one cites, and the label one uses. Distinctions can perhaps be made in the *amount* of attention given to building processes, particularly transformational processes over time, and to human agency, particularly variability between different agents, both of which are the special emphases of constructivists.

I will sum this section up by saying that many constructivists are structuralists, too, as the previous chapter shows. They analyze texts in precise ways before they conduct their constructivist studies seeing what people do with those texts. And many constructivists are semioticians in that they consider the construction of meaning from various kinds of cues, textual and otherwise. It is possible, I suppose, to be a constructivist semiotician or a semiotic constructivist, although I doubt that anyone would want such a ponderous label. A constructivist kind of semiotics would emphasize agency and process, and a semiotic kind of constructivism would give attention to various kinds of signs in addition to language.

Comparison of Poststructuralism and Constructivism

So, now to a comparison of constructivism and poststructuralism, including deconstruction. It seems to me that constructivists would agree with the Tel Quel poststructuralists on some points: that texts do not have determinate meanings, that reading involves the making of intertextual connections, and that understanding is an ongoing process in which meaning changes. However, in respect to each of these apparent agreements, there would be major differences when one moves to explanations.

First, in respect to multiple meanings, constructivists who study cognitive processes would explain the polysemy by pointing to the people who read and understand the text, people who have different knowledge and different purposes and read in different contexts. Poststructuralists would be more likely to point to something going on in the text, signifiers referring to other signifiers and ever-shifting patterns of difference among texts. Holland (1992), who was annoyed by this anti-subjectivist orientation of those he called the "new cryptics," referred to the latter as an *active-text* notion. Whereas constructivists see meaning in people, poststructuralists see it constantly moving in the ever-changeable textual relations. To study multiplicity of meanings, some constructivists would elicit different readings from different individuals (or individuals in social groups), and others might study interpretations of the text in the community's literature. But poststructuralists, including deconstructionists, would be more likely to theorize about it, perhaps illustrating how a text could be read in another way through their own reading of it or how the conventional way of interpreting it is a function of ideology. Second, in respect to intertextual connections, many constructivists would attribute them to intertextual *knowledge* that people as individuals have built from their textual experiences and that people as social groups build through their practices. However, poststructuralists, who have decentered the subject and have made the (inter)text everything, would portray the intertext as existing autonomously, making its own connections. And third, with respect to changes in meanings over time, constructivists would explain them in terms of cognitive processes—memory processes, understanding processes, or processes of invention—and would consider how context can affect those processes. Poststructuralists would explain these changes, too, in terms of the text (or rather intertext), the endless chain of signifiers, revealing its aporias and ideologies, and perhaps allowing other discourses to slip through.

What we have here are epistemological differences tied to contrasting philosophical and disciplinary traditions. This difference is particularly profound because much constructivist work is based on traditional forms of rationality in Western culture, dating back to the Kantian categories, whereas poststructuralism is strongly influenced by the skepticism of Nietzsche and Heidegger. In constructivism, societal forms and categories are studied and are employed in research, though they are subject to critique and change, whereas in poststructuralism, any such ordering principles are viewed negatively as the products of ideology.

In addition to these overarching philosophical differences, there are also disciplinary differences in epistemology as well as in conventions of discourse. The constructivism focused on individuals has developed, for the most part, in cognitive psychology, education, artificial intelligence, and, to a lesser extent, in the rhetoric and composition components of a few English departments, from the model of knowledge making in the discipline of psychology. Knowledge is mainly built through the conducting and reporting of studies to support theories. The social constructivism focused on societal groups has developed for the most part in sociology and anthropology, disciplines that also emphasize the conduct of studies, and it has become increasingly important in education. Poststructuralism and the French structuralism that preceded it have developed primarily in linguistics and literary studies. In the linguistic model, knowledge is built through conducting analyses of samples and presenting conclusions in essay form with illustrations for major points. And, in the literary-studies model, knowledge is built through developing arguments and presenting them in essays.

Whereas constructivists conventionally speak of, as well as direct their attention to, human cognition, poststructuralists, and to a lesser extent structuralists, have a sanction against using the language of subjectivity and the language of human agency, even when they are talking about psychological matters. Some might argue that poststructuralists, instead of dismissing human cognition, simply do not speak of it, leaving it implicit in their discussions, because that is the way "they" *conventionally* talk. But I would make a Whorfian (and Vichean) kind of claim that beliefs, values, and language are intertwined and difficult, if not impossible, to separate.

Conclusion: Keeping Our Heads above Water

As we have seen, many constructivists and structuralists have some compatibility, and through the years there has been a natural kind of collaboration on some issues. But what about constructivism and poststructuralism? I shall start my response by acknowledging beneficial effects of the French poststructuralism on constructivist thought. The critical posture of poststructuralism has made us all more reflexive and has made us question our categories, our "ideologies," and our own writing. (Are there inconsistencies somewhere in the margins that make our argument fall apart?) It has made us question conventional boundaries, such as the boundary setting off one text from another, and conventional concepts, such as that of *the* author.

Constructivism puts its value, of course, on building: the building of meanings for texts, the building of knowledge, the building of conventions, and so on. These products, constructed by individuals and social groups, are dynamic, changeable products. Meanings change as texts are read by different people in different contexts, and means of ordering change because they, too, are constructs. To constructivists, transformation is integral to the constructive process. It might seem that, to post-structuralists, at least to those in the Tel Quel camp, the instability in meanings, which undermines meaning making and the possibility of communication, would lead to nihilism. And yet, it is that very instability that is productive, generative, and almost hopeful, at least in terms of language, as it leads to more text.

A major incompatibility, however, lies in different perceptions of society and its collective knowledge. Constructivists study the socially constructive process of building collective knowledge, beliefs, and literature, seeing how conventions and order change historically. A society's knowledge and beliefs, including some that poststructuralists consider ideological, are treated as products to be examined and interpreted, not necessarily critiqued. The Tel Quel poststructuralists, who take a stance that is political as well as epistemological, are inclined to see ideology, in its most negative sense, in almost any human product.

To conclude, I will return to Fekete's (1984) metaphor of a structuralist maelstrom mentioned at the beginning of the chapter. Even though this chapter is about the building-built-unbuilding metaphor, this other metaphor of a maelstrom seems appropriate for the theoretical mix I have been discussing. This is, in part, because of a contentiousness in the poststructuralist critique of structuralism and convention. But it is also because these epistemologies themselves are dynamic and changeable. They are constructs that are subject to transformation. I have devoted several pages to sorting them out, and some people would agree with my treatment, but others would provide a different kind of grouping, defining, and ordering.

A major difficulty in talking about poststructuralism, as I mentioned earlier, is that it is defined relative to something else. To show how much depends on definition, after swimming for a while in the maelstrom, I could fairly easily make a case that constructivism is poststructuralist in that it came after structuralism and it critiques structuralism for certain aspects of its position: decentering the subject, not attending to human agency (on the part of individuals or societal groups), and paying little attention to processes. I could point to Piaget, who was a structuralist but whose constructivist work was a kind of correction or critique of the structuralist position. He and other constructivists, like Bartlett, reinstated the subject and a sense of agency. And, after swimming much too long in the maelstrom, I could perhaps even make a case that in a strange kind of way constructivism might be considered post-poststructuralist. For the most part, constructivism developed after the French poststructuralists began their work, and it critiques poststructuralism not only for the same "faults" as structuralism, but also for its overly negative stance on issues of language and culture. The difficulty here would be showing that constructivism developed *from* poststructuralism, but even that could probably be managed. Lévi-Strauss could be categorized as a poststructuralist, constructivism (as a post-post) would begin the work of the 1970s, and such folks as Bartlett would become proto-constructivists. Constructivism in the 1970s critiqued the poststructuralist conception of a decentered subject and a dismissal of human agency.

Chapter V

. . . .

Composing as Construction[1]

> In one way or another, all writing and knowing, and all learning about writing and
> knowing, are processes we undertake not alone but with others.
> —James Reither and Douglas Vipond, "Writing as Collaboration"

Constructivism guided much research and theory development when applied to
reading. Even after two decades of extensive research, the metaphor, as applied to
reading, continues to be generative in considering the constructive *agent*, the *act* of
construction, the *setting*, and the *product*, even though it is now not novel to say that
reading is constructive. The construction metaphor may seem to have less generative
potential for a consideration of writing, since writing is so obviously a process of
constructing something because a text is created. I would maintain, however, that
constructivism (and its metaphor) has much potential for examining dimensions of
the composing process if we look more deeply into the cognitive and social aspects
of the process. There in the process, in its social and cognitive dimensions, are
important aspects of constructivity in writing. And there in the process is where
writing intersects with reading and where writer intersects with reader.

We begin this chapter by considering the agent and the product—the who and
the what—and then move to the nature of the building process—the how. The
process is considered in three social dimensions: the author–audience dimension,
the intertextual dimension, and the co-constructive dimension. As we shall see,
these social dimensions are cognitive dimensions as well.

[1]This chapter is a revised version of a paper that I presented in 1992 at a conference on Alternative
Epistemologies in Education at the University of Georgia. That paper, "Written Discourse: A Construc-
tivist Perspective," was published by Lawrence Erlbaum Associates in 1995 in a collection of papers,
Constructivism in Education (pp. 313–329), edited by L. P. Steffe and J. Gale.

The Who, What, and How of Composing

We start with a consideration of agency: Who is the constructive agent when a text is composed? The answer to this question is not as self-evident as it may seem because the answer depends on the perspective one takes. And that is why, as discussed earlier, the whole agency issue is so contentious sometimes.

Agents can be viewed, as I view them for this chapter, as *individuals* building meaning for texts and producing texts intended to signal those meanings. It may seem strange to say what I am going to say now: Attention to individuals as agents can highlight certain social aspects of discourse that might be missed when groups are seen as agents. Individuals belong to social groups, and they reveal and construct their social identities through their ways of speaking, thinking, and knowing. Individuals bring to their social acts of communication much knowledge, including discourse knowledge, topic knowledge, and world knowledge, that they have developed in prior social experiences. Individuals "read" the immediate social context from their own position within a larger socio-cultural-historical context, and they construe their audiences when they write. Moreover, individuals are in social relationships with others, who might take the role of co-constructor, perhaps as collaborator, respondent, or reviewer, and thus influence the nature of the meaning that is built. And they are also in social relationships with authors of relevant texts they have read previously and that they read as a part of their composing process. This perspective, focused on individuals as meaning makers, is the one that I take, for the most part, for this chapter, and most of the studies I cite also focus on individuals engaged in social practices of literacy.

But social groups—collaborative groups—may also be seen as constructive agents. A *group* of people working together can seem to operate as a single constructive agent, as a single system. These people in this partnership build meanings for the same potential text, and, even though there are surely some differences in those meanings among members of the group, the emphasis, when this perspective is taken, is on the joint product—a kind of shared meaning. Some obvious examples are a research team writing a grant proposal, a group of children planning and writing an oral history, or a committee preparing a report. However, even if there is only one named author, a group may also be seen as a collaborative writing team. Just about any book, for instance, may be considered the work of a group instead of an individual.

If the focus moves to a more abstract level with a broader scope, a *discourse community* can also be viewed as a constructive agent. The community can be seen as collective author and audience of extant texts and future texts as well as the current text, building a shared, or conventional, meaning while producing its literature, including the text currently being written (Porter, 1986). The text can be said to be written by the community through one or more of its members. (It is easier to take this perspective when we are talking about text production in the abstract or about a text that has someone else's name on it—not when it is our own.) Here, too, the points of agreement among community members would be the "shared" meanings, although there would be differences across individual members (Fleck, 1935/1979; Gilbert & Mulkay, 1984). This perspective has a macro social agent, as opposed to the micro social agent of the collaborative group.

These, then, are ways of looking at acts of composing. In almost any composing situation the agent can be seen as an individual or as individuals, as I view agency in this chapter, but also can be seen as a system whose components interact directly or as a larger discourse community. For instance, Bartlett's writing of *Remembering,* described in Chapter II, can be seen as the work of a single author, of a collaborative team at Cambridge, or of the larger community of psychology, going through epistemological changes as it separated from philosophy and distinguished itself from sociology and anthropology. Each of these three perspectives can also be taken on my writing of this book. It can be seen as the project of an individual agent interacting with others, a group project (a system in which my various collaborators and I are constituents), or a project of a discourse community to which I belong. One of these ways of looking is not the *correct* way, in some absolute sense of the word "correct," as N. Goodman (1978) might tell us, even though it may be considered the correct way in the eyes of a particular group, camp, or community.

Now I move to the product—the *what*—that an individual constructs in an act of composing. When agency is perceived in terms of individuals, there are two products to be considered, mental products and textual products, and it is important to distinguish between the two. Someone composing a text builds mental meaning and also produces a written text, which is usually intended to cue other people's mental meanings as well as one's own. In the case of writing, the mental product is built over the course of composing (cf. Flower & Hayes, 1984), which often begins long before a writer begins producing a written product and which can continue even after a final version is completed. During composing, semantic content is structured in some fashion, although the content and form may change considerably over time (Witte, 1985, 1987). The meaning being built may become more structured or may be structured differently. Some content may drop out, additional content may be generated, and, as a writer changes purposes or audiences, certain content may gain a prominence that it did not have previously.

Think-aloud studies have shown the recursiveness, the moving forwards and the going backs, the shifts and changes, of this process (e.g., Flower & Hayes, 1981; McGinley, 1992). The writer, actively building this mental meaning, is also producing a written product, using graphic marks to provide signals to that meaning for himself or herself and signals for readers to use in building their own meanings— signals to content and its relative importance, to organizational patterns, and to relations among units of content. There is much talk these days about *steps of the writing process,* as if totally different types of cognitive activity are brought to bear in different phases of text production. Some people, harking to Rohman and Wlecke's (1964) three-stage portrayal of composing, think that in prewriting a writer comes up with what he or she would like to say, then in writing puts it down in words, and finally in revising merely tidies up the text. The three-stage view may be fitting for a written text, which is "prewritten," "written," and revised," in some cases, but it is not a good description of what happens mentally.

The two products—mental and textual—connect in various ways in the composing process as reading relates to writing. The text produced by the writer is a set of cues to meaning, no matter what state it is in, whether it is a skeleton plan, fragments or phrases, or a completed version. Although the final set of cues is chosen by the writer to signal meaning to the reader, the text at all points can provide cues for the writer, who, when reading what he or she has written, organizes, selects, and connects material signaled by those cues and thus builds new meaning from those cues. The constructive process of reading one's own writing seems to be an important part of the constructive process of writing. A number of years ago J. Britton (1978) illllustrated just how important reading one's text can be. In his study people often could not maintain continuity in their writing when experimental conditions prevented them from reading what they had written. More recently, in Haas's (1989; Haas & Hayes, 1986) studies, people writing on the computer expressed a need to get a sense of the whole text if they were going to make changes in it that went beyond tidying up. To get that sense, they had to print copies of all they had written (more than what showed on the computer screen). When reading one's own text, a writer makes inferences from his or her own cues that lead to changes, which include development and elaboration. When reading, the writer constructs meaning from his or her text, as it is written so far, but may also construct meaning for a different text (which leads to making changes in what has been written).

In the remainder of this chapter, when considering three social dimensions of composing, I maintain this distinction between two products, but hope to blur, or at least complicate, another distinction that is often made in discussions of composing: the distinction between social and cognitive aspects of composing. In considering the constructive nature of the composing process, I focus on three dimensions that are social as well as cognitive. The first is the author–audience relationship between writer and readers, a relationship that has been a major concern of rhetorical theory since classical times. The second is the *intertextual* relationship between a writer and other writers, and the third is the *co-constructive* relationship between a writer and other people who assist in the composing. In all three of these relationships, people are engaged in cognitive processes that are social processes as well.

The Author–Audience Dimension of Composing

Acts of composing are situated in social contexts, in which writers produce texts to accomplish some purpose with their audience. They may write to inform their audience, to entertain them or evoke some aesthetic response, to persuade them, to express their feelings to them, or to have some combination of these effects (cf. Kinneavy, 1971). Or they may have some other purpose, which might even be, in the case of some authors of postmodern texts, as discussed previously, to puzzle them or present them with a challenge. An audience of readers, which may be one person or many (even a whole discourse community), may know much about the topic or may know little, may be present or absent, may be sympathetic or hostile, and so on, and there may be a great deal of diversity among those readers. Writers attempt through their graphic marks to provide cues, perceived as letters, words, and punctuation, that will lead their readers to build meanings they want them to build. In addition to these configurations, writers also use formatting features, such as amount of white space and type of print or manuscript, and sometimes illustrations to signal particular kinds of content, its relative importance, and patterns for organizing and interrelating it.

Development of the Ability to Write for Readers

As they mature, people develop their ability to write for their readers. This development includes learning social conventions for written discourse, which can be called discourse knowledge, and also learning to construe readers and anticipate their constructions, which can be called social cognition.

Discourse Knowledge

In order to write for an audience, writers must know something about the conventions of writing expected by that audience, which include conventions of written discourse as opposed to oral discourse (Horowitz & Samuels, 1987), conventions associated with particular registers (Gee, 1989), and conventions associated with particular types of texts (Meyer, 1975). There are conventional ways of signaling organizational patterns, staging content, and cuing readers to make certain kinds of inferences. This discourse knowledge is part of the social knowledge that people build over the course of a lifetime through informal experiences as well as formal instruction (e.g., Fitzgerald & Spiegel, 1983; Greenleaf & Freedman, 1993; Wells, 1986).

Through experiences as readers and listeners as well as producers of texts, people build discourse knowledge as well as content knowledge. They acquire knowledge of how texts are conventionally structured, what patterns are used in a particular kind of text, and so on, and this is knowledge that they use in both reading and writing. A genre that children begin to learn much about early on is, of course, the story. They listen to such stories as *The Gingerbread Man, The Little Engine That Could, The Cat in the Hat,* and *Where the Wild Things Are* and begin to read such stories, too. They acquire knowledge about the structure of a story (setting, goal, etc.) and its conventions ("Once upon a time . . .") (see review by Galda,

1984). Children's early reading often takes the form of pretend reading (Sulzby, 1985), which has parallels with early writing, particularly with respect to the protoform of writing, scribbling (Temple, Nathan, & Burris, 1982), and with respect to reliance on pictures (Dyson, 1986). Shanahan and Lomax (1986, 1988), who fit developmental data to competing theoretical models, concluded that writing knowledge develops in concert with reading knowledge, rather than following it.

Discourse knowledge continues to develop as people mature and as they participate in communication, entering new communicative contexts and experiencing new forms of discourse. Their writing becomes more complex syntactically (K. Hunt, 1965), more elaborated (Bereiter & Scardamalia, 1984), better organized (Englert & Hiebert, 1984; Richgels et al., 1987), and better connected for the reader (McCutchen, 1986; Rentel & King, 1983). Over time there are consistent relationships between reading and writing abilities (e.g., Loban, 1976; reviewed by Stotsky, 1983; Tierney & Shanahan, 1991). Discourse knowledge is often quite specialized, as it is tied to the practices of a particular group. Many college students, for example, learn the specialized features of disciplinary discourse as they pursue studies in their academic major and prepare themselves for their careers. A part of learning an academic discipline is learning its discursive ways, which include its ways of structuring discourse, making an argument, and supporting claims (Berkenkotter, Huckin, & Ackerman, 1988; Haas, 1994). Students begin to learn how to make their own texts conform, to some extent anyway, to the norms of the community (Charney & Carlson, 1995; Faigley & Hansen, 1985). And they learn that different disciplines have different practices, conventions, and notions of quality, and that what works in one class may not work in another.

Ability to "Read" Readers

Being able to write for readers is more than knowing and using conventions. It is also a matter of being able to anticipate readers' constructions, knowing how particular readers build their meanings from particular kinds of cues, and anticipating how they might respond to particular kinds of cues—the kinds of knowledge often labeled social cognition (D. L. Rubin, 1984). It involves becoming aware of, and making decisions about, a writer's options and their possible costs and benefits in terms of the readers. For instance, a person might know about different conventional ways to set up a comparison and decide on one because it would seem to work better for particular readers.

This ability to produce discourse for one's audience develops over the course of a lifetime as people participate in discourse practices. Developmental patterns in audience awareness and adaptation have been examined in a number of studies (e.g., Crowhurst & Piche, 1979; Kroll, 1985; W. L. Smith & Swan, 1978), all showing that older students are able to vary syntactic complexity for particular audiences. This is presumably because they have great command of syntax enabling them to make such manipulations and they are better able to tell when the manipulations might be needed for their readers. And it is also possibly because they have more awareness of the needs of their audiences. Some studies of audience awareness and adaptation have referred to the Piagetian notion of decentering, mentioned earlier: that people, as they mature, become better able to take the perspectives of others and are able to produce discourse that is more appropriate for them (e.g., Kroll, 1985; cf. Flavell, 1966).

Kroll's (1985) study of audience adaptation is notable in that it also examined semantic modifications as well as syntactic. Participants from the fifth, seventh, ninth, and eleventh grades, and college, rewrote a brief story so that it would be appropriate for young readers. These revisions, when analyzed for lexical complexity and syntactic complexity, showed linear patterns of development: The older a student was, the more successful he or she was in reducing complexity. And, when analyzed for content changes, the revisions also showed differences in how the moral was handled: All of the ninth graders, eleventh graders, and college students attempted to simplify it, whereas many of the younger students left it intact.

With maturity and experience, people develop different ways of approaching their writing, and they employ strategies involving more transformation of content. Kroll's study showed developmental differences in this respect as well as in the others. Older students tended to work with larger units, rewriting whole parts of the story, whereas the younger students tended to work more at the word level, copying or replacing one word at a time. Differences in approaches to writing have also been shown in think-aloud studies conducted by Bereiter and Scardamalia (1985). Young writers seem to approach their writing with a "knowledge telling" strategy, tending to plunge right into writing, without considering goals and audience, and turn a task into an invitation to tell what they know about the topic.

Nature of the Relationship between Author and Audience

What is the nature of the relationship between author and audience? This question posed here is, of course, a *rhetorical question* in more than one way. Through the years there have been various ways of conceiving the social relationship between speaker and listener and between writer and reader, sometimes seemingly in terms of a power struggle.[2] Some theorists, drawing from classical rhetoric, see potential power on the side of the writer who exerts persuasive force upon the reader—writer as rhetor using appeals to ethos, logos, and pathos to convince the audience of the truth of his or her claims (e.g., Corbett, 1971).

Other positions tend to empower the reader. For example, theorists in the hermeneutics tradition today tend to put their emphasis on the reader-interpreter,

[2]See Ede and Lunsford (1984) for a discussion of the long-standing debate among theorists as to whether audiences are real people who are addressed or are persons who are imagined or invoked.

who, in accordance with a set of canons, derives an interpretation from the text (does not impose it on the text), considering the text in terms of those for whom it was written as well as for people today. A major hermeneutic claim is that the reader (interpreter) can understand a text *better* than the author can (Gadamer, 1960/1975). In other conceptions, readers are seen as resisting the author's influence to create their own interpretations, for example, the "strong reading" described by McCormick (1987). And then there is the conception, mentioned earlier, in which the author is dismissed, as in Barthes's poststructuralist (1968/1977) pronouncement of the death of the author (and the end to any speculations about author's intended meanings): "the birth of the reader must be at the cost of the death of the Author" (p. 148), which was discussed in the previous chapter. Yet another way in which the relationship has been viewed is as a cooperative venture with both participants trying to fill their part of some tacit pact, such as Tierney and LaZansky's (1980) version of a Gricean contract with a set of responsibilities that writers and readers agree to assume (cf. Nystrand, 1986).

A constructivist position emphasizes variability in the author-audience relationship according to the particular situation. Writers interpret the context and they construe their audiences, anticipating the constructions their readers will build and how the signals of their texts might influence readers' constructive processes. As numerous think-aloud studies from Hayes and Flower (1980) have shown, writers tend to make assumptions about what readers will know, what they will want to gain from reading the text, and what will appeal to them. They construct meaning with respect to their audience, speculating about potential meanings to be built by readers when they use the textual cues. From a constructivist perspective, authors are in relationships with audiences whom they create themselves (some say create a "model" of the audience, cf. T. Winograd, 1977), even if they know their readers and even if they are interacting with them face-to-face. The writer must make many assumptions about readers—what readers might know, what they might expect, what might be relevant to their discourse goals, how particular material might make them feel, what sort of an authorial persona they would expect—assumptions that, in situations when there are multiple readers, may be more correct for some readers than for others.

Effects of Audience on Writers' Constructions

The social relationship with an audience affects writers' cognitive processes. One effect of thinking about one's audience is generative, or heuristic, with respect to the meaning being built, as Roth (1987) showed in a study to be discussed shortly, because a writer generates content and relations in respect to the audience—what they expect, what they need to know. When a writer anticipates different kinds of readers, the heuristic potential would seem to increase because the writer would have to anticipate those different expectations, biases, and knowledges, although, if there were too many to accommodate, there could also be a detrimental, overwhelming effect.

Another effect of thinking about audience is epistemic in that such thoughts about others can lead to knowledge. Writers must be authorities as well as authors, which means that they often have to learn what their audience already knows (and they do not know) that relates to their topic (cf. Cochran, 1993). They may have to become familiar with texts that members of their targeted audience have read or perhaps even texts that members of their audience have written. Put another way, writers must, to some extent anyway, know their readers' intertexts. As Kaufer and Geisler (1989) have argued, a writer must be aware of what is new and not new about his or her contribution. This is the case for academic authors writing their scholarly pieces or research reports, as Kaufer and Geisler explained, but it is also true for other people writing in other contexts, such as attorneys preparing briefs and business people preparing memos.

The audience, as conceived by a writer, can change over the course of composing a piece, and when a writer perceives an audience as changing, the meaning being built also changes. Those different readers would know and believe different things, would have read different texts, and would have different expectations. Roth (1987) studied audiences created by skilled writers in college producing essays over a period of several weeks. These essays would be included in a collection to be distributed in freshmen English classes. Over the course of composing, the three students participating in the study kept their notes, drafts, and revisions, and they met regularly with Roth for interviews, which were taped. Although one of them did not refer to an audience other than himself in these interviews, the other two, Laura and Johanna, did much talking about audience when they met with Roth, and they seemed to have done much thinking about audience as they wrote. Laura set out thinking of her audience as typical students at her college, whom she characterized as uninformed and apathetic, but over the course of composing, she eventually replaced them with a different audience that she thought would be more likely to agree with her point of view for the essay, a critique of American foreign policy: They were her "sisters," people who would be politically knowledgeable and liberal.

The other writer, Johanna, started out thinking of her audience as uninformed, unsophisticated freshmen but she added other audiences. One of these additions was people more knowledgeable, including a "superior reader," very knowledgeable and demanding, whom she described this way: "He's my nameless, faceless reader that is held up as a kind of a—. . . if I can get him, I can get anybody" (p. 49). She even began thinking of publishing the essay as an article, which would mean another form, another forum, and a larger, more diverse audience. In addition to these audiences, the other audience was herself, as she was trying to understand some of the things she took for granted.

What is most interesting about this study is that these writers seemed at times to use audience strategically. For instance, Laura manipulated audience to eliminate a writing block, which she experienced at the beginning when her position seemed too liberal for her audience. She was able to unblock by deciding to write what she wanted to write and by giving herself permission not to accommodate the readers she was envisioning at that point. Johanna used her audience to help her generate material for her piece. By setting up a contrasting viewpoint, she was able to come up with a more articulated version of her own. As she put it, she used audience to give herself something to "bump against" (p. 51).

Writers, Readers, and the Explicitness of Texts

Writers have options in terms of *explicitness,* how much guidance to give readers for generating content as well as for organizing, selecting, and connecting it. On one hand, they can attempt to be explicit, to provide much guidance. This would be through such means as specifying the details that might be left for readers to infer on the basis of their world knowledge or topic knowledge, marking relations between particular events or ideas, using metadiscourse to "say" what is important or what the organizational pattern is. Such explicitness, as discussed in the third chapter, has been shown to be beneficial for some readers and some texts. On the other hand, writers can choose not to provide this much guidance and can leave more for the reader to infer, such as the details, the connective relations, the relative importance of particular ideas, and the organizational patterns. But writers do not, and cannot, make texts fully explicit. They assume some knowledge on the part of their readers.

Writers can communicate a great deal with a single word if their readers make the inferences they intend. When a friend of mine, Peggy Knapp, who studies medieval literature, published a book in 1990 titled *Chaucer and the Social Contest,* I asked her why she called it *"the* social contest" instead of *"his* social contest." Her response, I think, shows how much meaning writers can want a single word to suggest. She explained that by using "the" she kept the focus balanced between the contest *inside* the Canterbury tales and *outside* the tales. Even though Chaucer's fiction is about a contest between social groups, the groups are in contest with the real world as well. The book *Chaucer and His Social Contest* would have been a different book, which could have been written but which she did not write. It would have privileged the storytelling contest inside the Canterbury tales. Shifts in words would have implications not only for the content but also for the theoretical positions of the author. She expected people who shared an interest and knowledge in medieval literature to understand the implications of *the,* or to be able to infer them as they read, and she did not need to say any of this explicitly.

Writers can also communicate a great deal through what they do not say— what they leave unsaid. S. A. Tyler (1978) has defined the *unsaid* as the "background

of unspoken presuppositions and implications" (p. 499) and has argued for the role
of the unsaid in suggesting meaning. As he put it:

> Every act of saying is a momentary intersection of the "said" and the "unsaid."
> Because it is surrounded by an aureola of the unsaid, an utterance speaks of more
> than it says, mediates between past and future, transcends the speaker's conscious
> thought, passes beyond [the speaker's] manipulative control. (p. 459)

Tyler's ideas can be extended to written discourse, although "saying" here has to do
with oral discourse. One can think of numerous illustrations of what the unsaid can
"say." By not defining unusual terms, writers can be *saying* that they assume their
readers know their meaning. By not going into detail on some matter, writers can
be *saying* that they assume their readers can supply those details or that they are not
relevant.

    G. M. Green (1989) also addressed this idea of the unsaid, suggesting that it is
a mistake to assume that spelling out what the connections are—making them more
explicit—will make text *better*. She used an example from Toole's (1980) *A Confederacy of Dunces* to illustrate:

> Suddenly Mrs. Reilly remembered the horrible night that she and Mr. Reilly had
> gone to the Prytania to see Clark Gable and Jean Harlow in *Red Dust*. In the heat
> and confusion that had followed their return home, nice Mr. Reilly had tried one
> of his indirect approaches, and Ignatius was conceived. Poor Mr. Reilly. He had
> never gone to another movie as long as he lived. (p. 79)

Green pointed to some of the inferences that a reader must make—and that most
adult readers make readily—when reading the novel:

> What, if anything, did Ignatius' being conceived have to do with the horribleness
> [of the night]? What did it have to do with Mr. Reilly approaching something?
> Who or what did he approach? Why should we feel sorry for Mr. Reilly? Why
> didn't he ever go to another movie? (Green, 1989, p. 105)

If all this were specified and the paragraph made more explicit, she argued, the text
would become more puzzling, not easier to understand. That is because, if the
connections were spelled out, Toole would direct a reader's attention to tangential
issues, and the reader would have to infer *why* the writer provided that level of
detail, *why* that information was noteworthy.

    As I have suggested before, a writer has a kind of cost–benefit trade-off in
respect to explicitness (Spivey, 1995). The writer may gain possible benefits from
leaving an idea rather implicit, since implications can be a means of showing respect
for the reader's knowledge ("that's something you know so it does not have to be

spelled out") and of showing that the writer is a member of the same group ("this is something that *we* know; it is part of our shared knowledge"). Texts that are a part of an ongoing conversation within a discourse community, as Cazden (1989) has argued, assume relevant knowledge on the part of the audience. By choosing implicitness, a writer avoids the dangers of being overly explicit for a particular reader, such as making the text tedious, discounting the reader's knowledge (implying that the reader does not have the required knowledge), or perhaps even depriving the reader of the challenge of inferring. But the writer may choose to go with explicitness because the risks of the reader's not understanding and not adding what the writer wants added seem greater than the likelihood of possible benefits.

Social and Cognitive Aspects of the Author–Audience Dimension

Here in the relationship between writers and readers, just discussed, is a dimension of composing that is very much a social aspect but a cognitive aspect as well. Writers think about their readers and their readers' cognition, they anticipate their readers' understandings, and they are engaged with their audience even if the audience is quite distant and quite abstract. When writing for their readers, people use knowledge built through prior experience in reading texts by others and producing texts of their own.

The Intertextual Dimension of Composing

The second social dimension of composing to be considered here is the relationship between a writer and people whom he or she often knows only through their texts. In the third chapter, we considered the inferences about the author that a reader can sometimes make during reading and that can influence his or her understandings of texts. Here we think about that reader now in the role of writer—a writer in social relationships with the writers of the texts read in the past or read currently. Some of what one gains through reading is abstracted into discourse knowledge and integrated into other kinds of knowledge, but some persists as more specific memories of those texts and the authors who wrote them. For instance, I know Vico only through translations of his books, mainly *The New Science* (1725/1968) and *On the Most Ancient Wisdom of the Italians* (1710/1988), and from what others have said, through written texts, about him and his books. But I am in a social relationship with him that is not totally unlike the relationships that I had with some of my professors. Some of the things that I say are related to things that Vico said, just as some of the things that I say are related to what I heard my teachers say.

In addition to these relationships associated with past reading, writers are also often in relationships with writers of the texts that they read *while* they are composing their own texts. In some literate acts they make meanings for other writers' texts as a part of the process of composing their own. For instance, in writing a particular chapter, I might locate a relevant article or book and read it, or portions of it, even as I am writing my own, making or renewing a relationship with that author. I have done that, for example, with Roth, Green, and Cazden in writing the pages immediately preceding this. Here we consider both kinds of relationships: relationships with writers previously read and with writers currently read.

Writers and Their Intertextual Cues

Links that writers make to other writers and their texts vary in terms of explicitness. Some rather explicit connections can be made through citations, which are cues to knowledgeable readers to relate those meanings for other texts to the meaning for the current text. For instance, I can cite Vico's *The New Science,* and those readers who are familiar with Vico and his positions can make connections. Citing is conventional in academic writing, which typically involves crediting and often summarizing others' work (Cronin, 1984; Gilbert, 1977). But the links may be less explicit. Instead of citing, writers can cue the connections more subtly through allusions, to which some readers may respond. For example, I can also talk about such things as metaphor as a way of knowing, poetry as a form of knowledge, and "truth" as construct, not even mentioning Vico, and some readers will make inferences about Vico under those circumstances, too. Citation is more explicit than allusion, but some readers will make inferences under both circumstances. The extent of their inferencing is influenced, I would think, not only by the explicitness of my reference but also by the extent of their knowledge of Vico and Vichian philosophy as well as such variables as their purposes for reading and the constraints under which they operate.

But the connections may be even less explicit, taking the form of broad thematic or content links (saying something similar about the same general topics). In the case of my writing, thematic links with other constructivists whose work I have not cited and possibly have not read would be inferred by some readers and not by others. Still other links are suggested through the form of the discourse, such as similarities in genre, syntactic patterns, or wording. In my studies of discourse synthesis, a relationship is implied with others who are not cited but whose writing has some similarities. For instance, by combining my results and discussion sections of my "Shaping" article (Spivey, 1991), I may suggest a relationship with a rather large group of people in English studies who use this modification of the research report form. One of my readers might see it as similar to some particular researcher's work and make a connection to that author, and other readers might connect it to different authors.

All this falls within the realm of what Kristeva (1967/1986, 1968) and other poststructuralists have labeled intertextuality. Texts are related to other texts to such an extent that some theorists argue that, instead of texts, there is intertext, which is the relations between texts. Although poststructuralists, such as Barthes (1971/1979) and Derrida (1967/1978) as well as Kristeva, who downplayed the role of human agency, portrayed the texts themselves (or rather the intertext itself) creating those interrelationships, the relations are achieved because of humans and their cognitive processes. Meaning for this book, for example, is achieved because of the intertextual relations that readers infer to other texts, which may be texts that I have written or texts written by others. These intertextual relations are inferences about similarities and differences—how particular positions or points are similar to or different from those of the other authors (and, if people have read my other work, how they are similar to or different from points I have made or positions I have taken previously).

When constructing meanings for their own texts, writers use their knowledge as the constructive material, and much of that knowledge has been developed from experiencing other texts by other writers. When a reader makes a connection to another text, it may be a connection that the author made, consciously or unconsciously, but it may not be. The perceived connection may be simply the reader's inference. I might, for instance, say something that makes a reader think of a piece written by someone else, even though it is not something that I have ever heard about, much less read. And many people reading Bartlett's *Remembering* today make intertextual connections to the work of such people as Bransford, Kintsch, Spiro, and R. C. Anderson, discussed in Chapter III, who produced their studies years after Bartlett produced his. As Miller (1985) pointed out, readers make different intertextual links for a text than were made by its writer, and some reading studies (e.g., Beach et al., 1994; Hartman, 1991), discussed earlier, have shown some of the links readers make when performing particular intertextual tasks. The major point I want to make here is that these intertextual implications and inferences work in the same way that other implications and inferences work. Some intertextual connections are made rather explicitly by the writer, and others are suggested in more implicit fashion. Some readers make intertextual inferences that an author did not intend to imply, and different intertextual connections are made by different readers when they read the same text.

Writers and Textual Transformations

Sometimes, in addition to relating to texts experienced previously, writers directly consult other writers' texts, read them, and transform them as they compose their own. They may read one text and write a summary or critique of it or write a response to it, or may read and transform multiple texts, performing acts of discourse synthesis. In the academic world writing based on other texts seems quite common, not only on the part of disciplinary scholars and researchers but also on the part of students. In secondary-school and college settings, students often read and build meaning from selected texts in order to produce their own texts, which may be formal papers or informal homework assignments (Applebee, 1984; Bridgeman & Carlson, 1984).

Because these kinds of acts will be treated in detail in subsequent chapters, I will not go into depth here. The main point to be made here is that in such acts, reading and writing processes tend to blend and a person is in two roles concurrently—the roles of reader, building meaning *from* a text, and of writer, building meaning *for* a text (cf. Bracewell et al., 1982). If one were to look only at behaviors in such acts, there may *seem* to be two phases, first a reading phase and then a writing phase, and researchers have often described the process in terms of these two phases (Flower et al., 1990; Geisler, 1991). A writer finds a relevant text, moves his or her eyes over the pages, and then puts pen to paper, sketches out a plan perhaps, and produces a text. However, if we think of reading as building meaning from a text and composing as building meaning for text and if we consider the constructive process rather than the behaviors, we cannot say that *this* is the building-meaning-from-a-text phase and *that* is the building-meaning-for-a-text phase—cannot say where construction from reading stops and construction for writing starts. A person can already begin mentally composing meaning for the *new* text when reading the source text, before putting pen to paper. When reading, the person would have some kind of perspective (directed toward the new text) guiding how he or she organizes content, selects it for relevance, and connects it with what is already known.

Creating the new meaning and new text can be a kind of appropriation and transformation of the other author's or authors' work, as the writer approaches the material from his or her own perspective and with his or her own purposes. This can involve transformations in organizing, selecting, and connecting. Writers often seem to "dismantle" the texts they read as they build meaning, attending mainly to the parts that are relevant to creation of the new text and that fit into the new organizational patterns they generate. They select some material as relevant to the new meaning being constructed in the new context and let other material become less prominent, and this relevance is often determined on bases other than the author's staging. They also make connections, which can include inferences about the author, regarding, for instance, the author's intentions and credibility and the relations that that author has to others (Geisler, 1991; Mathison, 1993). To form meaning that is internally coherent, the writer makes various kinds of connections—"efforts after meaning" to use Bartlett's (1932) phrase. These include connections between his or her previous knowledge of the topic and the new material suggested by the text or texts being read and, in the case of multiple texts, also links across texts. These connections are for understanding the texts that are read as well as for producing the new text.

A number of factors, no doubt, influence the extent to which writers make inferences about those authors who produced the texts they transform. Some of those are text factors, stylistic features discerned from the text, such as use of first person and metadiscourse (e.g., Beck, McKeown, & Worthy, 1995). And other factors are knowledge factors, such as the writer's rhetorical and disciplinary knowledge (e.g., Flower et al., 1990; Geisler, 1991). In Geisler's (1991) study, for example, writers inexperienced in the discipline of philosophy did not consider author's perspective when they were using others' texts as sources and did not make clear distinctions among the authors, whereas writers with expertise in the discourse tagged texts to authors and made inferences about those authors.

Social and Cognitive Aspects of the Intertextual Dimension

In summary, then, there is the second kind of social relationship that can also be described in terms of cognition. When writing, people sometimes make connections with other authors, remembering or reconstructing memories of their texts or using knowledge abstracted from their prior experiences with their texts. And in some literate acts, writers perform the cognitive process of reading those other writers' texts as they construct meaning for their own—making inferences about those writers and their meanings and making various kinds of transformations, such as reorganizing and making selections on bases other than the staging signals provided by the author.

The Co-Constructive Dimension of Composing

Now we move to a consideration of how meaning making can be *co-constructive*, how more than one person can build meanings for a single text as it is being written and how writers and their readers can shift roles. A writer can become a co-constructor's reader, and a co-constructor can assume the role of writer. Here, I still conceive agency in terms of individuals as I discuss two major forms of co-constructive activity: collaborative writing and response to writing.

Collaborative Writing

Collaborative writing is quite common in various kinds of settings—academe, research centers, businesses—but there is much variability in how pairs or teams are organized and how they manage their task. For instance, Ede and Lunsford (1990), when surveying across various professions and fields, found a number of different ways in which people organize their collaborative writing tasks:

1. Team or group plans and outlines. Each member drafts a part. Team or group compiles the parts and revises the whole.
2. Team or group plans and outlines. One member writes the entire draft. Team or group revises.
3. One member plans and writes draft. Group or team revises.
4. One person plans and writes draft. This draft is submitted to one or more persons who revise the draft without consulting the writer of the first draft.
5. Team or group plans and writes draft. This draft is submitted to one or more persons who revise the draft without consulting the writers of the first draft.
6. One member assigns writing tasks. Each member carries out individual tasks. One member compiles the parts and revises the whole.
7. One person dictates. Another person transcribes and revises. (pp. 63–64)

What is left out of these descriptions is the important role of comprehending—making meaning *from* texts—in the composing process as it is performed by collaborators. To see the role of reading in this social process of writing, one must consider what individuals do. For instance, in pattern one, for the activity summarized in the first sentence, "team or group plans and outlines," individual members of the group would, no doubt, begin to construct their own meanings for the text to be written and would probably attempt to communicate those meanings orally. Those oral texts would cue others to build meanings: to build meanings for those oral texts and also to build alternative or elaborated meanings for the text being written. Meaning for that to-be-written text would also be cued by reading the outline that was produced. Numerous texts (comments, suggestions, objections) about the text would be shared and understood, probably orally for the most part, as a plan is developed. Then, "each member drafts a part," which might or might not involve additional talking and possibly some reading as well. After parts are written—each person constructing meaning for a portion of the text and developing written cues—there would be the activity, "team or group compiles the parts and revises the whole," in which members of the team would read (and build meaning for) the parts as put together, construct alternative meanings, and suggest and make changes in the text. This collaborative writing is very much a process of *comprehending* (making meaning from texts) as well as *composing* (making meaning for texts).

From these surveys and from interviews with collaborators, Ede and Lunsford (1990), collaborators themselves, perceived two major modes of collaboration, called *hierarchical* and *dialogic,* established by the individuals who make up the group. The distinctions between the two modes are made on the basis of two parameters: degree of structure (in terms of rigidity of roles) and extent of dialogue (back and forth interaction among collaborators). One mode is high in structure and low in dialogue, and the other is low in structure and high in dialogue. Prominent features of the one they called hierarchical are the structure (and rigid roles) and the authority of one member:

> This form of collaboration is carefully, and often rigidly, structured, driven by highly specific goals, and carried out by people playing clearly defined and limited roles. These goals are most often designated by someone outside of and hierarchically superior to the immediate collaborative group or by a senior member or leader of the group. Because productivity and efficiency are of the essence in this mode of collaboration, the realities of multiple voices and shifting authority are seen as difficulties to be overcome or resolved. (p. 133)

The other mode, which they called dialogic, is characterized by a lack of rigid structure (roles shift and members have fairly equal authority) and by a high degree of dialogic interaction:

> This dialogic mode is loosely structured and the roles enacted within it are fluid: one person may occupy multiple and shifting roles as a project progresses. In this mode, the process of articulating goals is often as important as the goals themselves and sometimes even more important. Furthermore, those participating in dialogic collaboration generally value the creative tension inherent in multivoiced and multivalent ventures. What those involved in hierarchical collaboration see as a problem to be solved, these individuals view as a strength to capitalize on and to emphasize. (p. 133)

Co-Authorship

Collaborative writing and *co-authorship* do not overlap precisely, even though co-authors often write collaboratively and people who write collaboratively are often co-authors. Having one's name as co-author of a text does not necessarily mean that someone actually contributed directly to the drafting of the text, and participating actively in such drafting does not necessarily mean that someone will be named as co-author. Trimbur and Braun (1992) reviewed many studies describing academic research teams in which high status persons, such as laboratory directors, are named as author and relatively low status writers, such as graduate research assistants, are not named (even when, in some cases, they contribute substantially). And Stillinger (1991) has provided numerous examples of literary figures, from Joseph Conrad to Mark Twain to Jacqueline Susann, who were the single named author when the writing was collaborative. To use Stillinger's phrase, it "had other hands" in it. The other hands were often those of editors who went beyond what is typically considered editing, but they were also sometimes those of spouses or relatives or friends, including some people who were well known as authors of their own texts.

In such acts, team members or partners can be co-constructors of meaning. Co-constructors influence the meanings that others are building because they, too, have ideas about the text. They build alternative meanings for a potential text while the text is still being composed, before it is in final form, even as they are determining whether a text as written is acceptable for the purpose it is intended to serve. Their alternative meanings are meanings that the co-constructors think should be signaled. To communicate their ideas, they produce their own texts about the text—oral or written—in the form of questions or commentary, probably providing rationales for their opinion as to whether the draft in question is acceptable or is not acceptable (reasons that are based on their perceptions of the constraints of the task, such as the audience and the purpose, and so on). These texts about texts (questions or commentary) offer cues that can influence how the other person can reconfigure or develop meaning. People involved in this kind of co-constructive process shift between being "writer" (writer or speaker) and being "reader" (reader or listener). Since the goal is production of a text, it is conventional to see all this co-constructive activity as aspects of writing.

Response from Others

It is quite common for people when they are composing a text to get responses from other people who are not always called collaborators—people who are not writing the text and are not going to be named as co-author. Sometimes these people fill formal roles. For example, in the publishing process they might be an editor or reviewer, or in the educational process they might be a teacher or a response-group member (e.g., Sperling, 1990). But in other situations they are not in such specific roles but are merely friends or colleagues. These people read, and build meanings from, the text, and tend to provide their response through their own texts, which might be written or oral but might take such forms as facial expressions or body language.

Respondents are often seen as readers playing the role of the intended audience, but quite often they go beyond that, tending to assume a role that is much like that of the writer. They engage in a process of constructing meaning for a text as it *might* be written instead of as it is written—meaning *for* a text instead of simply *from* a text. Although respondents may be cued to some extent by writers' written or oral texts, they build alternative meanings for different texts. As a writer would, they interpret the situation and the audience, set discourse goals, and generate content and relations on the basis of their relevant knowledge.

Response can take various forms, ranging from a bull session about a piece that might be written to a formal review of a paper submitted for publication. Four major variables help to distinguish different forms of response: timing of response, mode of response, degree of interaction, and status of respondent. First, with regard to timing relative to a draft, people can respond before any sort of written text is produced, when the writer wants to try out his or her ideas on someone, or they can respond when some type of draft has been produced, or both. Second, with regard to mode, response can be oral but it can also be written, and it can be body language or facial expressions as well. Third, with regard to interaction, response can be monologic, with the respondent providing commentary in a one-way direction, or it can be dialogic, with the respondent and the writer engaged in back-and-forth discussion. And, fourth, with regard to status of the respondent relative to the writer, the respondent's status can be fairly equal to that of the writer (peer), or the respondent can have a greater degree of authority than the writer (cf. Ulichny & Watson-Gegeo, 1989). And perhaps in some situations, probably more rare, the respondent might have a lower status than the writer. A chat with a friend regarding preliminary ideas for a text would be before draft, oral, dialogic, and peer, and a critique of a manuscript by a reviewer for a journal would be after draft, written, monologic, and greater-authority.

An Illustration of Response

James Reither and Douglas Vipond (1989) have provided an account of the process that Vipond, a cognitive psychologist, and another co-author, Russell Hunt, a literary theorist, underwent when they wrote "Evaluations in Literary Reading," an article cited earlier. R. A. Hunt and Vipond's article, published in the journal *Text* in 1986, built upon their prior work in point-driven reading (Vipond & Hunt, 1984). For the "evaluations" piece, they developed an analogy between understanding of conversational stories and reading of literary stories, making the claim that evaluations mark the *points* (what the author is getting at) of literary stories for people who read them, just as evaluations mark the points of conversational stories for people who hear them. The case study of this collaboration is, I think, a good illustration of the nature of response, particularly in academic writing and publishing, as well as other social processes I have been discussing.

According to Reither and Vipond's account, when Hunt and Vipond began work on the article early in 1985, they targeted the journal *New Literary History* because the journal had recently invited submission of articles on what was "new" in the new literary history. The composing process of the two authors, described as "highly interactive," involved the two alternating as writer and reader (and reviser) as sections were drafted. Their collaboration would probably fit Ede and Lunsford's (1990) dialogic mode. One would produce a draft of a section on a disk and the other would read, reconceptualize, and revise (and mark changes) and return the disk. When the draft was near completion, the authors worked together at a single computer, reading what they had written and were writing, discussing options, and making further changes. They were, no doubt, thinking about the readers of this journal, as they attempted to situate their piece in the new literary theory of such concepts as poststructuralism, deconstruction, reader-response criticism, and they cited such literary theorists as Jonathan Culler and Terry Eagleton, who have published pieces on poststructural and other new theories of literary reading.

After they completed a draft, which took them five months, they gave copies to two colleagues at their university: Mason, on the anthropology faculty, and Reither, on the English faculty. They thus expanded the co-constructive nature of the process. Those two respondents produced written and oral comments, which were texts about the text. Largely because of these comments, Hunt and Vipond revised the article to make it appropriate for *Text* and thus for a different discourse community than that of *New Literary History*. The response at first was monologic and in written form, rather brief notes from Reither but seven typed pages from Mason, which had the title "Reading under the Microscope." Mason argued that the introduction, or the framing, of the text was misleading in focusing on "the concepts of literary theory, Culler, Eagleton, poststructuralist, deconstructionist, text, literary criticism, reader-response critics, the profession, nature of literature, literary experience, and literary reading," which put the article "in the lofty regions of capital L literary" when it really belonged "at the level of the foundations, the microcosm of the act of reading" (Reither & Vipond, 1989, p. 859). These two respondents also talked in dialogic fashion with the authors about the draft, emphasizing in particular the journal (and the community) for which it was aimed but also touching on such matters as organization and choice of metaphors.

These responses were texts for which Hunt and Vipond built their own meanings and which influenced the meaning for their own text. By means of their responses Mason and Reither helped the authors reach the decision to target *Text,* an interdisciplinary journal that publishes articles on discourse, including reports of linguistically oriented studies. When a revised draft was completed, these same two respondents provided comments on it (Mason's were two pages this time), and Hunt and Vipond asked for and received a response from another colleague, Parkhill, who was on the religious studies faculty. Reither and Vipond claim that these three respondents were acting as "surrogate editors" and "gatecrashers" and were helping the authors avoid an unsuccessful submission. However, I would suggest that they were doing what co-constructors (including respondents) do. They moved into the composing role, which entailed considering rhetorical considerations, building their own meanings for a different text, and producing their own texts to signal that different meaning and different text.

These co-constructors helped Hunt and Vipond conceive a different audience who would want and expect a somewhat different kind of text with citations of different authors from those cited in the previous version. The literary theorists, Eagleton and Culler, who had been prominently positioned in the *NLH* version, dropped out of the version for *Text*. In the *Text* version, the major authors to whom Hunt and Vipond related their work were two sociolinguists, Labov (1972) and L. Polanyi (1985), who had produced important prior work in conversational storytelling and evaluation. A note referred to Pratt (1977), a scholar whose speech–act theory of literature was related to this sociolinguist work. Instead of Culler and Eagleton, other literary theorists cited in the *Text* version were Riffaterre (1938/ 1983, 1979) for his analyses of style as devices for attracting attention, Rosenblatt (1938/1976, 1978) for her conceptualization of reading as a transaction, Weaver (1985) for a summary of transactional theory, Chatman (1978) for a distinction between story and discourse, that the authors borrowed, and Scholes (1985) for a note about the influences of ideology and history on reading of texts. In addition to these people, others credited included the rhetorician Phelps (1985) for a distinction between the online process of understanding a text and the process of contemplating a text that has been read, and the psychologist Gibson (1979) for the notion of "affords." Also noted was a historian of religion, J. Z. Smith (1982), for his metaphor of a "cultural fault," a break or inconsistency between what is said and what is done. This source had been suggested by the respondent Parkhill, also a scholar of religion, who was thanked for the suggestion in a footnote. The co-constructors helped the authors position their claims within an intertext more appropriate for an audience that would read *Text*.

Response and Authorship

Even when respondents contribute significantly to the nature of a writer's cognitive product, the textual product typically *belongs* only to the named author or authors. Except in the case of co-authoring, when people decide to be co-authors at the outset, respondents do not make claims to, or even want, authorship, which we may think of in terms of credit and responsibility. This means, for one thing, that, whether they are reviewers of academic journals or teachers of student authors, they do not expect credit for the text. The credit they receive, if any, is usually limited to an acknowledgment. R. A. Hunt and Vipond's (1986) footnote is a typical kind of acknowledgment: "We are grateful to our colleagues James A. Reither, Thom Parkhill, and especially Alan W. Mason for thoughtful critiques of previous drafts" (p. 68). Of course, not being given and not claiming authorship also means that respondents do not assume responsibility for the text. In fact, writers in their acknowledgments, after thanking particular people for their help, sometimes point out that these people are not responsible for any failings of the text.

Response and Pedagogy

Response has become an important component of writing pedagogy, and here, too, its various forms can be distinguished according to the four parameters mentioned earlier: timing, modality, interaction, and status of respondent. Today teachers are likely to respond to students' ideas and their texts in writing conferences (e.g., Freedman & Sperling, 1985; cf. Prior, 1991), where the response might be before or after draft, and would be oral, dialogic, authority. And students respond to other students' writing through written responses, which would likely be after draft, written, monologic, peer; and they also respond in writing groups or other kinds of sharing sessions, where the response would be either before or after draft, and would be oral, dialogic, peer (cf. Flower et al., 1989; Gere & Stevens, 1985; Nystrand, 1986). The traditional sort of response from teachers—written comments (Searle & Dillon, 1980)—would be after draft, written, monologic, and authority.

Social and Cognitive Aspects of the Co-Constructive Dimension

When there is talk of the social nature of composing, this last dimension is the one that is usually meant: writers working together collaboratively as co-authors or responding to each other's plans or drafts of texts. But these can be seen in terms of cognitive as well as social processes. People use knowledge of various types, including topic knowledge and discourse knowledge, as they make meanings from the cues of others, which might be oral, written, or nonverbal. In constructing their meanings, writers use the cues of their co-constructors' comments, just as the co-constructors use the cues of the writers.

Shifting Roles in Reading and Writing

Throughout this discussion, which is purportedly on the topic of writing, attention has also been given to the reading that is so much a part of composing. Reading one's own words as one composes is an important part of meaning construction for writing, since these written words can cue one's own constructive processes as well as those of others. A writer must shift to being a reader. But, in addition, the three social–cognitive dimensions of composing, discussed above, all involve role shifts, and all are dimensions of reading as well as writing. In the author–audience dimension, the writer is a "reader" of readers, using knowledge of various types (much of it built through reading) to prepare a text that will work for them and even shifting to others' perspectives. Thinking about readers and about their potential understandings of the text is conducive to the constructive process of composing. In the intertextual dimension, the writer is in the role of reader as well as writer, perhaps remembering a text that was read before and constructing meaning for it again or even actually reading a text when constructing meaning for one's own. When reading a text is a part of composing another text, it is impossible, I maintain, to differentiate the reading process from the composing process because meaning is being constructed *from* one text *for* another text. And, finally, in the co-constructive dimension, a writer becomes a reader, or a listener, constructing meaning from other people's written or oral comments, if they are collaborators or are responders, or, in the case of collaborators, from their drafts.

The importance of reading in the composing process has often been over-looked, as in Ede and Lunsford's (1990) description, because composing is defined in terms of text production. When writing is the topic, the spotlight is on the movement of the text to final form, and the aspects of the process that involve reading are in the background. A person is seen in the role of writer and not in all the shifts back and forth between roles of writer and reader. One must look rather closely at the process to discern the extent to which reading is a part of composing.

Chapter VI

. . . .

Discourse Synthesis

FOUR STUDIES

Let no one say that I have said nothing new. . . . I had as soon it [be] said that I
used words employed before. . . . Words differently arranged have a different meaning, and meanings differently arranged have different effects.

—Pascal, *Pensées*

Discourse synthesis is the term I use for the process in which writers are engaged
when they read multiple texts and produce their own related texts (Spivey, 1984).
Very often when writing, a person reads other texts, finds some material useful, and
performs various transformations to make that content work for his or her own
text. I limit the term to acts of literacy in which writers read texts for the purpose
of writing their own and in which they use the texts rather directly. And I do that
because, if not limited in this way, *discourse synthesis* would embrace virtually any act
of writing because of the intertextual nature of writing. The terms *discourse synthesis*
and *writing* would then be equivalent and there would be no need for a different
term. No piece of writing is discrete, unconnected from other texts, because writers
draw from their own experiences with other writers' texts when they write their
own, using knowledge they have built of discourse conventions and options, of
topic and domain, of contrasting views, and so on.

Understanding a text is an active process of constructing meaning from the
signals that a writer provides. And composing a text is an active process of constructing meaning for a text and using textual cues to signal meaning to readers. For more
than two decades, as described in previous chapters, researchers have studied the
nature of both processes, comprehending and composing, although the work on
one process has tended to develop independently of the other. Studies are most
often framed as either reading studies or writing studies.

Discourse synthesis is both comprehending and composing as a writer uses
cues from more than one text to construct meaning for the text being written.

146

Bartlett (1923, 1932) was interested in the constructivity that results from cultures coming together, but my interest is in the constructivity that results when people bring texts together. Even though the texts being read suggest possible methods of organizing, prioritizing, and linking content, the writer must supply new connections and possibly create a new organizational pattern to integrate the content for the synthesis. These transformations are motivated by rhetorical considerations, such as purpose and audience, and are achieved through strategies of composing and understanding. Because discourse synthesis includes both reading the source texts and writing the synthesis texts, it is a logical and necessary extension of both lines of inquiry and falls within the larger arena of meaning construction, which includes both production and comprehension.

Acts of discourse synthesis are social acts, performed in accordance with socially established conventions in various discourse communities. Writers employ knowledge they have built through social experience, including their knowledge of discourse conventions and their sociocognitive knowledge of possible effect on readers. In performing such acts, they engage in a process of communication that involves other people, in many cases the authors of texts that they are reading as well as the audience for the texts they are writing. They may also have co-constructors with whom they talk about their texts or who read and comment on them. Moreover, their act is situated in a social context, not only the immediate context (time, place, people) but the larger sociocultural and historical context.

For this chapter I consider transformations writers make in acts of synthesis, which have been the focus of much of my own work. The reader of the chapter will, no doubt, note commonalities across the four studies I discuss and will also perhaps detect a kind of progression. I began with an interest in what would be conventional performance in a very common kind of synthesis task in schooling: reading articles on a particular topic and writing a synthetic report that also provides information about it. I began with undergraduates. Then, to examine developmental patterns, James King and I conducted a similar study with elementary and secondary school students. In these two studies, in which writers read reports and were asked to produce reports, almost all writers produced texts of the same general type as the texts they read, as would be expected. However, analyses showed variability in specific aspects of organization as well as in other features and also indicated which text features were associated with text quality, as assessed by experts in that discourse form. The third study required writers to generate a different kind of pattern, comparison. Here, too, even though there was a commonality in the writers' general approach, individual writers exercised various options. In fact, there was more variability than might be expected for this type of text. These three studies all focused on presentation of topical information through a report, which is a common form of discourse in schooling at all levels.

The fourth study, conducted with Stuart Greene, examined students' attempts at disciplinary writing in a psychology class when they were given writing-to-learn assignments. Although report writing was still a focus of attention, this time writers were using full-length psychology articles, and the authors of those articles gained a prominence that authors did not have in the previous studies. However, in this study, reporting was contrasted with proposing to see how transformations might differ when writers were reading the same texts but performing different tasks. Chapter VIII on Authoring Identity discusses some work that relates to this last study but offers a different kind of perspective: a longitudinal perspective examining transformations over time as writers build their own bodies of work.

In all studies the focus was on general patterns in order to see what would be conventional performance for these groups of writers, but it was also on variability in order to see, within these general patterns, how individuals would differ in their performance. An important component of all four studies was evaluations of the students' writing by people who have expert knowledge of that type of text in order to gain some insights into what kind of performance is valued socially. Another commonality of all four studies was that all writers in a particular study were given the texts they would use in creating their new texts. This, no doubt, seems unnatural to some researchers, who would prefer studies in which writers choose their own topics and select their own texts. A more naturalistic approach with topic choice and text choice is certainly appropriate for pursuing answers to many questions, including the question that Maureen Mathison and I asked in the study discussed in Chapter VIII: How do writers begin to develop an authoring identity?

However, for gaining close insights into the textual transformations of interest and their relationship with text quality it was best to have some commonality in the readings and the task. It would be difficult to tie quality ratings to the specific transformational variables that interested me if everyone were writing on different topics and using different sources. The studies were much like studies of the reading process, conducted by researchers who try to learn what are the shared understandings of a particular text and what is the variability in those understandings. If every participant in a reading study were to read a different text, it would not be possible to answer those kinds of questions. One could probably, however, learn more about other matters, particularly regarding choice of topic and text. Nevertheless, I would argue that the tasks performed in these studies are not totally divorced from classroom practice. Students do write sometimes from the same texts, especially now that some teachers provide instruction in synthesis (Kaufer, Geisler, & Neuwirth, 1989) and now that hypertext facilitates development of multiple-text units of study (Dobson, Rada, Chen, Michailidis, & Ulloa, 1993; Kearsley, 1988).

In these studies my collaborators and I used discourse analysis methods similar to those used in many studies of reading focused on organization, selectivity, and connectivity. For the first three studies, we created templates by following the parsing procedures employed by many researchers in reading and adapting them to accommodate multiple texts. This kind of detailed analysis allowed comparisons of the linguistic material offered and the linguistic material generated, and it provided some stability in the material so that claims could be made about transformations. The methodology is a sensible one, I would argue, for studying the kinds of transformations of interest in these studies. This sort of analytic approach can be considered constructivist, in that it has been taken by many constructivists. However, taking such an approach is not an essential part of being a constructivist, as many take a more holistic approach and study other aspects of constructivity.

Discourse Synthesis: A First Study

I conducted my first synthesis study under the assumption of many researchers in reading before me: that I could gain some glimpses into the process that interested me through studying written products. This time, though, the focus would be on the writing as well. I wanted to "see" how people build their meanings when they are using other texts to compose their own texts. Here, I summarize the study, which is presented in more detail in Spivey (1984, 1992). Participants were 40 upper-level undergraduates at a private university in north-central Texas who were taking an educational-studies course on literacy instruction, which focused on such topics as instructional materials and strategies. The participants' task was to use three informational texts on a single topic to produce a single text, a synthesis, that would be appropriate for use in the schools and would present a comprehensive treatment for high school students. Thus, on this task, the writers' unique contributions would be the integrated presentation of material so that readers could learn about the topic by reading one text instead of three. The topic, "the armadillo," was my idea. I chose it because the mammal had attained an interesting status in Texas at the time, having recently become a state mascot.

The Texts Used in Composing

All three texts to be used by the writers belonged to the text type that Meyer (1975, 1985) called collection. They signaled topical clusters about such subtopics as size, species, habitat, and progenitors, although the ordering and nature of the content differed across texts. These texts from encyclopedias are provided below:

The *McGraw-Hill* text (Curtin, 1982), 373 words long and the shortest of the three, was as follows:

> ARMADILLO, The name for 21 species of mammals of the order Edentata, a group characterized by the lack of enamel on their teeth. They are indigenous to the New World, especially South America.

The nine-banded armadillo (*Dasypus novemcinctus*) is the best-known species and ranges from South America to the southwestern and southern United States. It is the only edentate which inhabits the United States. This species is adaptable, and has extended its range from the Rio Grande area to Oklahoma and eastward along the coast to Louisiana during the last century. It is of public health importance, since it is a reservoir host for *Trypanosoma cruzi,* the causative organism of Chagas' disease.

Armadillos range in size from the lesser pichiciego or fairy armadillo (*Chlamyphorus truncatus*), in which the adult is about 5 in. long, to the giant armadillo (*Priodontes giganteus*), which is about 4 ft. in length. The body is covered with horny dermal scales that replace the hair common to most mammals and overlay bony plates. These structures fuse to form rigid shields covering the anterior and posterior ends of the animal, whereas in the midregion they form jointed bands allowing a certain amount of flexibility. The number of bands varies for different species. The teeth, which are small, molariform, and peglike, lack roots and enamel. The giant armadillo has about 100 teeth, more than any other land mammal. The snout is long, and the tongue is cylindrical and viscous to assist in capturing food. The toes are clawed and are used by the animal to dig into ant and termite colonies for food, as well as for burrowing. When disturbed, many species roll into a ball or wedge themselves into a burrow opening. In both instances the dermal plates serve as a protection.

The nine-banded armadillo has been studied because of its unusual life cycle. Four young are born in a den or chamber at the end of the burrow. The young are always of the same sex and are identical quadruplets, all arising from the division of a single egg. This multiple-birth condition, or polyembryony, is natural for these animals and the exception in other mammals. The young are well developed at birth and are weaned at about 8 weeks of age.[1]

The *Encyclopedia Americana* text (Tate, 1982), 546 words and the longest of the three, presented some material that was redundant and some that was not:

ARMADILLO, är-mə-dil'o is any one of a group of mammals with few or no teeth. They are found in the south-central and southeastern United States and South and Central America. Armadillos are notable for their defensive armor. The armor consists of small roundish, bony plates, hardened within the skin. In most members of the group the plates are united to form solid shields, one over the shoulders, and one over the haunches. Between these shields are crosswise bands of movable plates that protect the body but leave freedom of motion to it. These plates are overlaid by a thin horny covering, and between them grow hairs varying in length and amount with the species, from almost none in some to a distinct coat hiding the shell in others. The unarmored undersurface is also hairy. The head has a shield entirely separate from that of the shoulders. In some species even the tail is protected

[1]"Armadillo" by C. B. Curtin, *McGraw-Hill Encyclopedia of Science and Technology,* 1982 (Vol. 1, pp. 705–706). Copyright © 1982 by McGraw-Hill, Inc. Reprinted with permission.

by concentrically overlapping rings of armor. In others (the soft-tailed armadillos) the tail contains only scattered plates that are not firmly united to each other.

The armadillo belongs to the family Dasypodidae; there are 9 genera and about 20 species. The various species of armadillos are distinguished largely by the number of movable thin bands of plates lying between the large fixed anterior and posterior shields, up to as many as a dozen in the cabassous (*Xenurus*). Those of the genus *Tolypeutes* increase the value of the armor by their ability to roll themselves up into a ball so that the tender underparts of the body are completely protected. This ability depends upon the number of bands in the central portion of the armor case.

Although true edentates (mammals lacking teeth), armadillos have numerous small, nearly useless teeth, without true roots. The tongue is covered with a sticky fluid like that secreted by the tongue of an anteater.

Armadillos are timid, nocturnal animals, living on insects, carrion, and vegetable matter. Their legs and claws are adapted to burrowing, and when pursued they usually bury themselves more quickly than the pursuer can follow them. One of the most interesting of them all is the pichiciago (*Chlamyphorus truncatus*) found in Argentina, which lives entirely underground like a mole, and exhibits many peculiar structures. The body has a truncated appearance, as if the rear part had been cut squarely off, instead of ending in curved lines. It is very small, only five to six inches (12½ to 15 cm) long. The giant armadillo (*Priodontes giganteus*) measures three feet, exclusive of the tail. Some of the armadillos range north and south as far as Texas and Argentina; among these is the nine-banded armadillo (*Tatusia novemcincta*). They are eaten by the South Americans and are considered to have a delicate taste.

Reproduction in *Dasypus novemcinctus,* a nine-banded form, is peculiar. The young, unless some mishap has taken place, are invariably quadruplets of the same sex. It is believed that the fertilized egg divides and redivides into four parts before each part becomes organized into a young armadillo.

Fossil armadillos have been found in both North and South America. One fossil species was six feet (1.8 meters) long. Another genus was *Eutatus,* which had a shield formed of 36 distinct bands, of which the last 12 were fused together.[2]

And like the other two texts, the *Collier's* text (Goodwin, 1983), 443 words long, offered some redundant and some unique information.

ARMADILLO, an insect-eating mammal of the order Edentata, having an armorlike shell encasing its back. The name armadillo, meaning "little armored thing," was given to the animal by the Spanish when they invaded the New World. Its original home is South America, but it is now also found in the southern United States.

The armadillo is not toothless as its order name, Edentata, implies; its teeth are simple, rootless pegs placed well back in the mouth. The shell covering of its back is made up of numerous bony plates with horny coverings that are often fused

[2]"Armadillo" by G. H. H. Tate, *Encyclopedia Americana*, 1982 (Vol. 2, pp. 328–329). Copyright © 1982 by Grolier Incorporated. Reprinted with permission.

together. Across the middle of the back, there is a hinge between the front and hind sections which permits the animal freedom of action. In some species, the face is shielded and the tail is encased in armor. The armor is a protection against flesh-eaters.

The breeding season of the armadillo begins in the latter part of July, but the young are not born until March or April of the following year. Although they resemble the parents at birth, their shells do not completely harden until they are full grown. There are up to four young in a litter. All are of the same sex, being derived from one egg, a phenomenon called polyembryony.

In prehistoric times huge armadillo–like animals, the glyptodonts, were as big as oxen. Some were armed with a formidable spiked club at the end of the tail which could be used as a weapon against such predators as the saber-toothed tiger. Today, there are many different kinds of armadillos. The common and best known species is the nine-banded armadillo, or peba, *Dasypus.* It is about the size of a house cat and has a long, sharply tapered tail. There is a three-banded armadillo, *Tolypeutes,* and also a six-banded armadillo, *Euphractus.* The nakedtailed armadillo, *Cabassores,* has eleven bands. The great armadillo, *Priodontes,* has an over-all length of 5 feet (150 cm). The third toe on its forefoot is armed with a great sicklelike claw used to tear rotten logs or to rip apart termite nests. The smallest armadillo is the fairy armadillo, *Chlamyphores,* a dainty creature that lives underground like a mole and is only 5 inches (13 cm) long. Others include the weasel-faced armadillo and the hairy, the greater, and the lesser peludo.

Armadillos are of benefit to mankind since they devour large quantities of termites and other injurious insects as well as scorpions. They also eat snakes, poultry, fruit, and eggs.

Such a strange creature as the armadillo could hardly escape folklore. The Mayan Indians, for instance, believed that the blackheaded vulture does not die of old age but changes into an armadillo.[3]

Through discourse analysis procedures, I parsed these three texts into propositions, as described more fully elsewhere (Spivey, 1984), following Kintsch's (1974; A. Turner & Greene, 1978; van Dijk & Kintsch, 1983) procedure. After this initial parsing, I used an informativity principle to determine the size of the units: I asked this question: Can this proposition stand, without having any other propositions embedded, as an informative sentence in one of the reports? If the answer was yes, it was considered a content unit and would be included in the composite template. For instance (BENEFIT, ARMADILLO, MANKIND) was considered a content unit because it could be informative. But some rather basic propositions would not be informative sentences to the audience for which the students were writing. For instance, the proposition (PART OF, ARMADILLO,

TONGUE) was not considered a content unit by itself, since it would not be informative for the audience to hear that an amadillo has a tongue. However, this proposition plus the proposition (CYLINDRICAL, TONGUE) to form (PART OF, ARMADILLO, (CYLINDRICAL, TONGUE)) would be a content unit because a writer could produce an informative sentence saying that an armadillo has a cylindrical tongue. Likewise, the complex proposition (PART OF, ARMADILLO, (VISCOUS, TONGUE)) was considered a content unit because a writer could produce an informative sentence saying that an armadillo has a viscous tongue. A writer could also produce one sentence saying that the armadillo has a tongue that is cylindrical and viscous, which would be considered two content units. According to my analyses, the three texts together offered 277 content units. Some units were associated with a single text, some with two texts, and some with all three. For example, all mention that *Dasypus* has nine bands, two say that that species is the best known of all the species of armadillo, and one says that it is eaten by humans. Roughly synonymous information signaled by two texts was considered a repetition. Table 1 provides more detail about the redundant and nonredundant material across texts as well as within texts.

These content units varied in their structural importance to a particular text—their staging—which was determined through another kind of discourse analysis procedure, a hierarchical analysis. I used Grimes's (1975) rhetorical relations, as summarized by Meyer (1975, 1985), to arrange the content units into hierarchical structures. Grimes's hypotactic relations—specification, evidence, attribution, equivalence, explanation, analogy, setting, manner, adversative, and identification—subordinated one unit to another. A content unit perceived as having one of the hypotactic relations with another unit was placed at a lower level in the text base. Take, for instance, the clause, "The tail is protected by concentrically overlapping rings of armor." Its constituent units would be arranged as follows:

Table 1
Content Units Associated with the Texts

	Text		
Content units	*McGraw-Hill*	*Americana*	*Collier's*
This text only	48	95	72
This text and one of the other texts	31	31	18
This text and both of the other texts	22	22	22
Repeated within this text	0	4	3
Total	101	152	115

. . . .

(PROTECT, (ON, ARMOR, TAIL), TAIL)
  (IN, (ON, ARMOR, TAIL), RING)
    (OVERLAP, (RING, (ON, ARMOR, TAIL)), (OTHER, RING))
      (CONCENTRICAL, (OVERLAP, (RING, (ON, ARMOR, TAIL)), (OTHER, RING)))

Each unit presents more detailed information about the one that precedes it.

Each content unit had an importance rating based on not only its position within the texts but also its repetition across texts. For the template, the units were grouped into five levels of *intertextual importance* based on position within a text and repetition across texts, which would be used in studying the effect of this variable on writers' selections.

A third procedure, which I would use to study organization, involved labeling content units for themes in a manner similar to that used by Paul (1959) in his replication of Bartlett's (1932) study. In this case they were: X, pronunciation; C, classification; H, habitat; N, name; E, folklore; A, armor; Ab, bands; Q, behavior trait; V, size; K, hair; T, teeth; M, mouth (snout and tongue); L, legs and claws; B, burrowing/digging; F, flexibility/protection; D, diet; I, impact on humans; R, reproduction; O, ancient armadillo(like) forms; S, species (including S1, fairy armadillo; S2, giant armadillo; S3, nine-banded armadillo; S4, other species and genera). A unit might have one or more than one of these themes. For instance, the content unit (TOOTHLESS, EDENTATA) would have C for classification and T for teeth.

Transformations

The transformations of interest were those studied by Bartlett (1932) and by any number of other reading researchers: organizing, selecting, and connecting. As mentioned earlier, I looked for overall patterns as well as variability among individuals.

Organizing

All 40 writers used patterning similar to that of the texts they read: The organizational pattern signaled was collection for their topically organized reports, as determined by text analyses. However, even though the general type of organization did not differ, there was much variability in the ordering and combining of content. All students' reports differed from all the texts read, and all differed from one another. I studied this organizational variability with a breadth/depth ratio of number of topical chunks to number of content units included, which was a means of quantifying organization for descriptive texts, which tend not to have a canonical order for content in their collection structure. This conception of organization was influenced by Longacre's (1979) notion of a text as constituted of large thematic units and Frederiksen's (1977) similar conception of a text as constituted of large thematic units, or "higher-order processing units."

When analyzing organization for a particular text, my co-raters and I created a vertical chain of those tags, mentioned earlier, for content units in the order in which the writer cued them. When we noted no overlapping content for two units, a boundary was tentatively identified. At that point we read the text to see if the writer had provided a link between chains by adding information to make a larger unit. If there was a link, the boundary was eliminated. When there was no overlapping content and when the writer did not supply a link, the boundary stood. The following student text serves as an illustration. In this example, words, phrases, and sentences that are underlined represent linguistic content that did not match up with the "source" content and was thus considered to be added by the writer.

The armadillo is a member of the *Edentata* family, which is a family of mammals characterized by a lack of teeth. The animal originally came from South America, has made its way north, and is now found all the way to Oklahoma. In the U.S. the armadillo has spread from the Rio Grande area to Oklahoma and as far east as Louisiana. There are about 20 species of armadillo, which are distinguishable by the number of thin, movable bands of plates along the back. The most common species is the nine-banded armadillo, or *Dasypus*. However, there are other species with 12, 11, 6, and 3 bands. They are called *Xenurus, Cabassores, Euphractus,* and *Tolypeutes,* respectively. Armadillo species range in size from the giant armadillo, or *Priodontes*, which measures five feet in length, to the *Chlamyphorus truncatus*, which only measures five to six inches in length.

Armadillos have been around since prehistoric times. Fossils have been found in both North and South America. It is thought that the present-day armadillo evolved from a huge "armadillo-like" animal the size of an ox.

Although true edentates lack teeth, armadillos have several small and practically useless teeth. The armadillo's soft body is protected by a hard shell. Its "armor" is made up of bony plates with sharp coverings and is hardened within the skin. The plates connect to form two shields; one covers the shoulders and the other covers the haunches. The two shields come together and hinge across the middle of the back to allow the animal to move freely. In some species, the tail also has an armor and the face is shielded. The three-banded species has the ability to roll into a ball, kind of like a turtle, so that all body parts can be protected by a shield. The shield is nature's way of protecting this animal from flesh-eaters, since it is harmless, feeding only on insects and vegetable matter.

The armadillo is a timid animal. To protect itself, it uses its legs and claws, which are adapted for burrowing, and digs itself into a hole.

This burrowing technique is also used when birth is about to take place. The young are born at the end of the burrow. Armadillo breeding season begins in late July, and the young are born in March or April of the following year. Baby armadillos are always born in quadruplets; the fertilized egg divides into four parts to form four babies, identical in every way. They are born with soft shells, which harden the following year.

The armadillo is an interesting animal. While we in Texas consider the armadillo our state's official animal, the South Americans eat certain species of them for their delicate taste and the Mayan Indians believe that blackheaded vultures turn into armadillos at their deaths.

Figure 1 is a graphic representation of the organization suggested by the preceding text. Figure 1A shows organization through topical chains and Figure 1B shows the same organization in a tree-structure format. The horizontal marks in the chains of Figure 1A represent boundaries between the chains—topical shifts— but the arrows represent links that overcome the boundaries. These were integrative inferences that affected structure. For example, in topical chain 6, after discussing armor, the writer generated a causal link: "The shield *is nature's way* of protecting this animal from flesh-eaters, *since it is harmless,* feeding only on insects and vegetable matter." (In these examples, italics indicate information that the writer added that was not offered by the source texts.) Thus, she integrated diet into the discussion of armor and protection. In chain 7, after linking the animal's timidity with its using its legs to burrow underground for protection, she added information that related

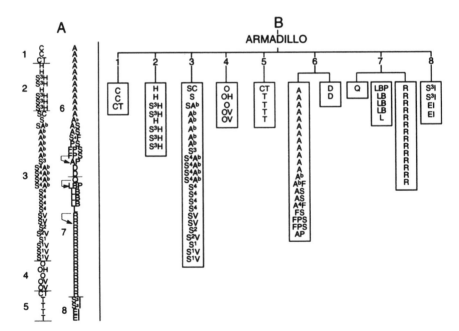

Figure 1. Thematic chaining (A) and thematic chunking suggested by a student's text.

burrowing ability to reproduction: "*This burrowing technique is also used when birth is about to take place.*" These links were of the following types: contrastive, similarity, causal, instrumental, temporal, and attribute-possessor.

Figure 1B illustrates this patterning through chunks instead of chains. When two topical chunks were connected with a link, the larger unit created was considered a single topical unit. The global units 6 and 7 in the figure illustrate combined chunks in the organization of the same student's text. The student who produced this text seems to have organized it into eight content clusters.

When analyzed in this fashion, students' texts varied in the size of the chunks developed, ranging from 3 to 20 chunks per 100 content units, but averaging 10. There were two ways in which writers created the larger chunks. One method was to stay with a particular topic and develop it before moving on to another (cf. Witte, 1983). Consider the following discussion of armor, introduced at the end of one paragraph and continued in the next:

> Its name comes from a Spanish term meaning "little armored thing" in reference to its defensive armor.
>
> The hard shell encasing the armadillo serves to protect it from flesheaters. Other animals would have a hard time getting through the roundish bony plates which form shields hardened within the skin over the shoulders and haunches. Freedom of motion is allowed by crosswise movable plates. It is the number of thin bands of plates which distinguish the various types of armadillos. These bands allow the mammal to roll itself into a ball, thus protecting its tender underparts.

The preceding treatment can be contrasted with that of another writer, who moves from topic to topic and back to a previous topic without focusing on any of them for very long:

> The armadillo is best characterized by the number of bands on its armor. They range in size from five inches to five feet, although there was a fossil found indicating one as large as six feet in length. This armor is made of horny, dermal scales, unlike most mammals that are covered by hair.

The latter synthesis continued on in much the same way, offering little for its reader in regard to focus or development. The difficulties such texts give readers have been discussed. Collins and Gentner (1980) spoke of texts with flat structures that give readers too many parallel elements to remember (cf. Nold & Davis, 1980).

The other method that writers used to create larger thematic chunks was to provide linkages to tie together two or more small chunks. Writers made inferences that integrated content. For instance, one writer connected a chunk about the armadillo's name with a chunk about species and sizes:

The name armadillo means "little armored thing." However, some armadillos are not little.
The largest armadillo is the *Priodontes giganteus*.

Then the writer went on to discuss the sizes of various armadillo species.

As in studies of summarizing, some writers constructed broad subsuming statements that have been called *macropropositions* (van Dijk, 1977). For example, one student who had the following topics on a formal outline for the final section of his paper,

III. Specific Armadillos
    A) Fairy Armadillo
    B) Banded
        3, 6, 9
    C) Giant
    D) Prehistoric

produced a well-integrated discussion of ancient armadillo-like forms and current species. The writer added a subsuming link (contrastive and temporal) that held together the content and also reordered the content from his original plan as he meshed together the information from the different texts. He produced an integrated treatment by inferring relations among the units and signaling them for a reader:

> The armadillo is an animal that has survived for many years in different forms. The glyptodonts were large prehistoric animals that had bony armor and a spiked tail. Many fossils of armadillos have been found. Today the largest armadillo is about four to five feet in length (*Priodontes giganteus*). The smallest armadillo is the fairy armadillo (*Chlamyphorus truncatus*), which is a mole-like creature only about five inches long. There are many different species of armadillos. They are best distinguished by the number of bands that they possess. The best known forms of armadillos have from three to nine bands.

In integrating the material for this topical chunk, the writer added a comparison-temporal link and reordered it from what he had on the outline.

This study also showed a connection between reading ability (as measured by a standardized reading test) and writing ability, especially with regard to text organization. When contrasted with less accomplished readers, better readers produced texts with tighter structures. That is, they had larger topical clusters in their collection structures because they developed their discussions of the topics they introduced and provided more links between units of content.

Selecting

In this act of discourse synthesis, meaning construction was a selective process, as it had been in the single-text reading studied by Bartlett (1932) and many other reading researchers. The writers were selective in including content, averaging only 88 of the 277 units suggested by the texts. How did they select content? I tested for linear trends to see if they were making selections on the basis of intertextual staging (repetition across texts as well as position within particular texts), and there was strong evidence that writers were making selections on this basis. The writers were more likely to include, for instance, a unit cued by all three texts but playing a moderately imporant role structurally in each, than a unit staged very prominently in the hierarchy of a single text. The levels effect, which was well supported by previous research with recall of single texts (e.g., Goetz & Armbruster, 1980), as discussed in Chapter III, was also demonstrated intertextually in discourse synthesis on a multi-text task when the texts were actually present.

As students read and reread these texts, most underlined particular content, but some students used other marks as well, such as asterisks, stars, and brackets. Some students apparently bracketed passages of content that they selected for inclusion in their syntheses and then scratched through the passages after the information was incorporated. These marked copies also give evidence of the relation between organization and selection. When reading the sources, many of the students wrote labels for recurring topics, such as *habitat, species, food, armor*, in the margins, as shown in Figure 2. As they marked and labeled, they seemed to be identifying sets of topics that would become the constituents of the collection patterns they would use to organize their texts.

Connecting

In composing their synthesis texts, writers had to produce new connected discourse by creating chunks of thematically related material, but they also had to provide for the kind of connective flow that a reader needs in moving through a text clause by clause and sentence by sentence. To investigate this feature, connectivity, I used a reader-based measure. Three raters independently read all 40 of the synthesis texts, and marked each of the syntheses for points at which they felt their flow of reading was interrupted because of an unusual burden of constructive processing. This subjective measure was conceptually related to Kintsch and van Dijk's (1978; van Dijk & Kintsch, 1983) and Kintsch and Vipond's (1979) notion of resource-consuming operations. The following are examples of problematic situations requiring connective operations:

The reader must work through illogical comparisons or modifications.

Resembling their parents at birth, the babies' shells do not harden until they are full grown.

The reader must infer why the writer has used a particular connective word. The connection is not clear, or it is not logical.

The armadillo is nocturnal, so it lives on insects, carrion, and vegetable matter.

The reader must resolve contradictory information.

Edentata means "lacking teeth." Armadillos have rootless, peglike teeth with no roots.

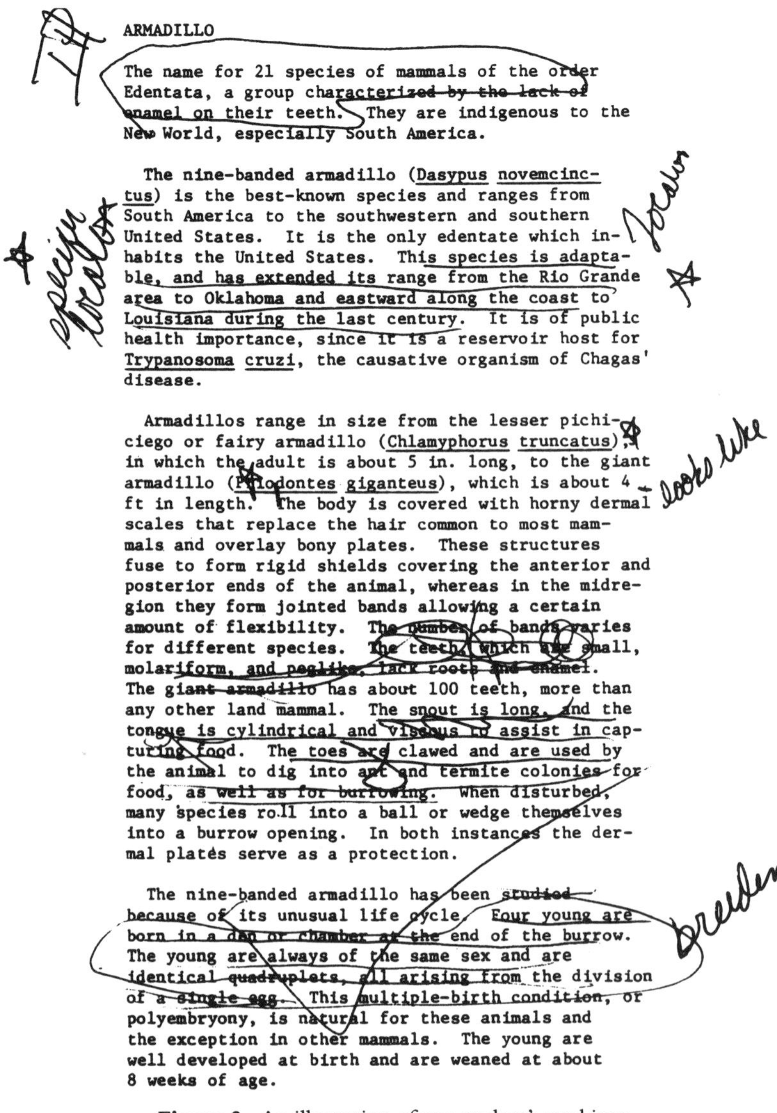

Figure 2. An illustration of one student's markings.

The reader must choose between two candidate antecedents.

> Armadillo, meaning "little armored thing," is in a class labeled Edentata, which means having an armor-type shell casing on its back. The name was given to the armadillo by the Spanish.

The reader must add a referent when one is not given.

> Armadillos tend to be frightened of man and other large predators. For this, the animals are equipped with a long third toe.

Like the organization measure, the connectivity measure was based on a ratio. It was calculated for each text by dividing the number of perceived connective operations (the mean for the three raters) by the number of content units scored. The average number of problems of this type was 6 for every 100 content units.

The reports also varied in how well they suggested connections for the reader. Excerpts from two of the students' reports, both of them about the armadillo's teeth, provide contrasts with respect to connectivity. The articles have provided these "facts" about armadillos: that the armadillo belongs to a group with few or no teeth; armadillos are edentates; edentates are toothless; edentates have teeth lacking tooth enamel; the armadillo's teeth are numerous, small, nearly useless, molariform, peglike, and simple; the teeth are missing roots and enamel; and the teeth are placed well back in the mouth. In the following sentences, one writer combines much of the (sometimes contradictory) information about teeth but leaves the reader the burden of making sense of what is said:

> The animal is known for its lack of teeth. Actually, the armadillo has numerous small, molariform, and peglike teeth. However, because of their uselessness and lack of roots, it is often misconstrued.

That illustration contrasts with an excerpt from another student's text that presents a more reader-based version of similar information for which no problems in connectivity were noted by the raters. The contradiction in the information is not actually resolved, but it is acknowledged by the writer:

> Armadillos have been given the order name Edentata (meaning toothless); however, they are not a toothless mammal. Their teeth are rootless and have no enamel on them.

A reader may still wonder why armadillos have teeth if they are classified as edentates, but he or she does not have to expend great mental effort before moving on.

Writers had to group together topically related material they selected as they read interrelated texts, material that was sometimes repetitive but was sometimes inconsistent. But synthesis is more than this centonistic selecting and grouping. It is also working out inconsistencies, making the parts really fit together and performing what Bartlett (1932) called *rationalization*. Because writers were composing as well as comprehending, these matters had to be worked out not only for oneself but also for one's own readers.

Quality of the Reports

To study the overall quality of synthesis, I elicited ratings again. These were holistic ratings from three people who were experts in this sort of informational writing, two professors of science education and the state science education coordinator. The procedure they followed, known as *general impression scoring*, had begun with a kind of socialization process, in which they rated practice papers, compared scores, and discussed differences. After they achieved a fairly high level of agreement with the practice papers, they independently rated the "real" papers—the ones for which the scores would be used (Cooper, 1977). Each rater gave each paper a single score, on a scale of 1 to 6, based on his or her holistic judgment of its overall quality relative to the range of quality of papers in the set. The holistic quality score I used in my analyses was the sum of the three raters' scores.

What makes a "good" synthesis? This study employed several measures that seemed to be associated with quality of the syntheses: the ratios for organization and connectivity and also a measure for quantity of content, which was simply a count of content units. There was also a measure for items judged to be "misinformation," although students averaged only one "inaccurate" item in their reports and, thus, there was little variance in this measure. When these four measures were tested in a multiple regression for their ability to predict the summed quality ratings, the results showed they did quite well in combination, accounting for 39 percent of the variance in the ratings. The standardized regression coefficients suggested that quantity of content made the most significant contribution to the equation—a finding that was not really surprising because one would expect educators to prefer a thorough presentation of the content. Nold and Freedman (1977), for example, found quantity to be a strong predictor for essay ratings. However, the measure for quantity of content was highly intercorrelated with the measures for organization and connectivity, and when I conducted a second regression in two steps (the other variables entered on a first step before quantity of content was entered on a second), results showed that the other measures in combination had almost as much predictive power without the measure for quantity as they did with it. In the absence of a measure for quantity, the measures for organization and connectivity could do quite well in predicting the holistic quality scores. This was because the writers who produced the more comprehensive treatments of the topic were the ones who tended to generate the more integrative organizational patterns and the writing that had fewer noticeable breaks in connectivity.

Summary of This Initial Study of Discourse Synthesis

This first study, conducted with college students, demonstrated the important role of organizing, selecting, and connecting in synthesizing discourse from multiple texts. Writers made organizational, selective, and connective transformations as they integrated content to produce informational reports. With respect to organization, all employed the same general organizational pattern, collection of topically arranged material, but differences lay in how much material they put together and how many chunks they created. And these quantitative differences were related to quality, as raters preferred a more integrative presentation achieved through topical chunking. With respect to selecting, writers selected a subset of the material offered by the set of texts, and those selections seemed to be made on the basis of an intertextual criterion, not only on staging within one text but also by repetition across texts. Those writers who produced more comprehensive treatments tended to receive higher scores. Finally, with respect to connecting, writers made inferences from their reading and cued the linkages for their own readers. And raters preferred those texts requiring readers to make fewer difficult inferences on their own. Thus, the study showed writers transforming text and achieving better results if their reports were characterized by tightness of organization and an absence of breaks in connectvity as well as by comprehensiveness of the treatment.

A Developmental Study of Discourse Synthesis

The next study, reported in more detail in Spivey and King (1989, 1994), was a replication with younger students and different texts. Participants were students in the sixth, eighth, and tenth grades—20 from each grade level—in a public school district in north-central Texas. At the time of the study, Texas was celebrating its Sesquicentennial (the anniversary of its independence from Mexico), and numerous activities in the schools were focused on "Texana." The writing task that James King and I devised required students to write a report about the rodeo to inform adults and teenagers in their community who were new to Texas and who did not know much about rodeos. This writing assignment was contextualized by school-district teachers into activities celebrating Texas events and traditions. In preparing the reports, the students had three encyclopedia articles to use, but they were to put the content in their own words. Report writing took place over three consecutive days in their English/language arts classes; students were asked to complete a final version sometime before the end of class the third day. We kept track of the time they spent.

The Texts Used in Composing

As in the previous study, the writers had three descriptive texts on the same topic. This time the topic was "Rodeo," and the texts were articles from reference sources intended for use in the middle school years: *World Book Encyclopedia* (World Book, 1986), *Britannica Junior Encyclopaedia* (Encyclopaedia Britannica, 1981), and *The New Book of Knowledge* (Rodeo News Bureau, 1985). Word counts for these texts were 931, 453, and 1226, respectively. All three texts were loosely organized with collection patterns, although each had a historical chronologically ordered section, which came at the end of the *World Book* article and at the beginning of the other two.

The *Britannica* article considers the history of the rodeo, five standard events (saddle bronc riding, bareback bronc riding, bull riding, calf roping, and steer wrestling), other activities at a rodeo (e.g., clowns, trick roping acts), rodeo sponsors, livestock, rodeo association, various kinds of rodeos, and popularity of the rodeo:

RODEO (rō' dē ō or rō dā' ō) is an event in which cowboys demonstrate their riding and roping skills in competition. The modern rodeo had its origin in the early days of the United States cattle industry. After the long months that cowboys spent on the range, they gathered to entertain themselves by competing with one another at roping and riding. Eventually these contests developed into public entertainment.

The actual time and place of the first rodeo is unknown, but several cities of western United States claim to be among the first to have held rodeos. One of the earliest known contests was at Deer Trail, Colorado, in 1869. It was a bronc riding contest among cowboys of the Hashknife, Mill Iron, and Camp Stool ranches. Other early contests were held at Cheyenne, Wyoming, in 1872 and Winfield, Kansas, in 1882. Denver, Colorado, is usually credited with holding the first paid spectator rodeo in 1887. Pecos, Texas; Prescott, Arizona; Dodge City, Kansas; and Miles City, Montana, also held early rodeo events.

Bronc riding and steer roping, the original rodeo events, were part of the cowboy's work. Other contests have evolved in the rodeo arenas. There are now five standard events for rodeos: saddle bronc riding; bareback bronc riding; bull riding; calf roping; and steer wrestling. Other events sometimes included are steer roping and team roping. These seven are the official rodeo events. There are a few variations, as in Canada where steer decorating replaces steer wrestling. Some rodeos have other events, such as wild cow milking or wild horse races.

In addition to contests, the modern rodeo usually includes other entertainment, such as trick riding, fancy roping, clowns, and dog and horse acts. These are called contract acts. A queen is usually chosen for each rodeo.

Rodeos are often staged by the local chamber of commerce or other civic groups. Sometimes a private promoter will sponsor a rodeo as a business venture. Good rodeo stock is valuable. Bucking horses, roping calves, and steers are contracted to the rodeo by men in that business.

Rules for the rodeo events are written by the Rodeo Cowboys Association, founded in 1936. It was originally organized as an association of competing cowboys, but it now includes all the professionals of the sport—cowboys, stock contractors, clowns, announcers, and contract acts.

Rodeo has become a popular amateur sport. There are now junior, high school, and intercollegiate rodeo associations. The sport has spread to other parts of the world and has become especially popular in Canada and Australia. Each year about 580 professional rodeos are held in the United States and Canada. About 80 are held each year in Australia and New Zealand. In many U. S. and Canadian cities, rodeos are annual events.[4]

---

[4]"Rodeo," *Britannica Junior Encyclopaedia*, 1981 (Vol. 13, pp. 127–128). Copyright © 1981 by Encyclopaedia Britannica, Inc. Reprinted with permission.

The *World Book* article begins with a discussion of the popularity of the rodeo, and then it discusses rodeo livestock, events (*rough stock* events, which include bareback bronc riding, saddle bronc riding, and bull riding, and *timed* events, which include calf roping, steer wrestling, team roping, steer roping, and barrel racing), all-girl rodeos and the events they feature, and the history of the rodeo. The *New Book of Knowledge* article moves through the history of rodeo, the rodeo association, popularity of rodeo, events (*bucking* events, which include bareback bronco riding, saddle bronco riding, and bull riding, and *timed* events, which include calf roping, steer wrestling, and team roping), rodeo skills, women in rodeo (events for women, all-cowgirl rodeos), and rodeos with young people as contestants. As in the previous study, we parsed the texts into content units and checked repetition across texts. As shown in Table 2, the three texts offered a composite of content, some of which was signaled by one text, some by two, and some by all three. Table 2 shows units and their intertextual repetition.

Transformations

As in the previous study, analyses focused on transformations involving organization, selection, and connectivity.

Organizing

Fifty-eight of the 60 participants in the study wrote texts with the same sort of organizational pattern, collection, as that of the source texts. Again, the variability within this pattern was measured with a breadth/depth ratio of number of topical chunks to number of content units. Content units were tagged for themes, such as location, popularity, history, rodeo associations, sponsors, events, and rodeo stock, and the themes were arranged in chains and divided into chunks. If a writer seemed to supply a link between two chains, the two so connected were considered to be a

Table 2
Content Units Associated with the Texts

	Text		
Content units	*World Book*	*Britannica*	*New Book of Knowledge*
This text only	105	71	124
This text and one of the other texts	59	26	52
This text and both of the other texts	16	16	16
Total	180	113	192

chunk. For example, one writer created a link between content about women's events and a discussion of association-sponsored rodeos: "Sometimes there are special rodeos instead of just special events for certain groups of people."

This variability in these breadth/depth ratios was associated with reading ability (as measured by a test of reading achievement), as in the previous study, with more accomplished readers producing tighter structures, but it was not associated with age or grade level. Younger students wrote briefer texts with fewer chunks, and older students wrote longer texts with more chunks, but the ratio was about the same across the years. It was 5.5 chunks to 50 content units (the papers averaged about 50 units), but it would translate to 11 chunks to 100 content units, quite similar to the 10 chunks per 100 content units of the college students in the previous study.

Almost all the students created collection patterns, which is a conventional way to pattern the descriptive content with which they were dealing and which was the approach used by the authors of the texts they read. However, 2 of the 60 students in the study did something quite different from the others in organizing their reports. In their efforts to meet the assignment, to inform adults and teenagers about the rodeo, one tenth grader wrote a comparison detailing similarities between a football game and a rodeo, and one eighth grader wrote a piece of advice, posing a problem (fitting into the crowd) and a solution (how to look and act "cool" at the rodeo). The following is the beginning of the latter piece:

> For people who don't know anything about rodeos: Some people think they are fun. If you really want to fit into the crowd and not look like a city boy, you will need the followin' items: a good pair of country style cowboy boots, a nice lookin' cowboy hat, some Wrangler jeans, a button-down shirt (cowboy patterns), and last of all, a can of Copenhagen (the choice is optional—depends on how much cowboy or cowgirl you want to be).

This student's interpretation of the task must have been quite different from the predominant interpretation that resulted in a conventional kind of report. The following is a more typical opening:

> Rodeo means "roundup" in Spanish. A rodeo is when cowboys or cowgirls compete in riding and/or roping events. Each rodeo has these five standard events: saddle bronc riding, bareback bronco riding, calf roping, bull riding, and steer wrestling.
>
> Rodeo origins go back to the mid to late nineteenth century. It is said that one of the earliest known rodeos was Deer Trail, Colorado, in 1869. In 1936 contestants started to organize. The Rodeo Cowboys Association, later renamed the Professional Rodeo Cowboys Association, was formed in 1945.
>
> Today the rodeo is big business. In Canada and the United States each year alone there are more than five hundred rodeos held. Millions of spectators attend rodeos. Several millions of dollars of prize money are awarded yearly.
>
> Now we are going to take a look at a rodeo. First is bareback riding.

Selecting

Like the college students in the previous study, these elementary and secondary students appeared to make selections on the basis of intertextual importance, defined in this study simply by repetition across texts. For all grade levels there was a significant linear trend in selections relative to number of repetitions across texts. Writers included larger proportions of content associated with two texts than proportions of content offered by only one, and they included still larger proportions of content associated with all three texts. However, there was an interaction between intertextual importance and grade level. As the content increased in intertextual importance, the older students included increasingly larger proportions. This finding seems related to research in summarizing by A. L. Brown and Day (1983), which indicated that after the seventh grade young people develop a heightened sensitivity to the textual importance of content. They also begin to use sophisticated summarizing strategies rather than the copy–delete strategy employed by younger students.

Connecting

For this study, too, three raters read the texts for connectivity and marked places where there seemed to be disruptions in the connective flow. Here, too, there was variability in connectivity. Comparisons showed a significant difference between the papers produced by writers from different grades, with the sixth grade students' texts requiring more inferencing on the part of readers. The following excerpt from one of the sixth graders' papers illustrates the inferencing that was sometimes required of readers if they were to achieve some kind of connectedness:

> A rodeo is an event in which cowboys compete against other cowboys. They go to several countries till in 1822 they went to Cheyenne, Wyoming. They used some wild bulls and cattle. The cowboy that is riding the bull or horse must hold the rope with one hand. If they hold it with two, they will have some seconds taken off. Some cowgirls have the color and spirit of the Old West. Cowboys and cowgirls ride on their horses, and they sometimes rope up cows. But we all know that most of the people come for the cheering up. That is why they use clowns. The clowns help the cowboys and cowgirls if they fall off the bull or horse. Clowns sometimes get in the barrel to protect himself from the bull or horse.

This writer has made use of the various sources. The information on the Cheyenne rodeo can be traced, for instance, to the *Britannica* article, the information about scoring of bull riding to the *New Book of Knowledge* article, and the note about "color and spirit of the Old West" to the *World Book* article. She brought the material together but did not present it in a reader-based form. Not only would a reader experience rapid shifts in topic, but would also have difficulty connecting material that is topically related because of violations in topic–comment patterning. Moreover, a reader would likely have problems with the unclear referents of pronouns, particularly "they" (cf. Piaget, 1923/1932). The writer, who may not have made the necessary connections for herself, did not provide cues to the connections that a reader would need to make. The developmental literature, discussed in other chapters, describes cognitive changes associated with increasing maturity that enable writers to provide connections in their discourse. They gain in the ability to make inferences that link content (A. L. Brown, Day, & Jones, 1983) and in the ability to make more explicit the relations they see by using various kinds of linguistic cues (McCutchen, 1986). They also develop an increasing awareness of an audience's particular needs for clarity or explicitness (e.g., Crowhurst & Piché, 1979; Kroll, 1985).

Quality of the Reports

The reports were judged for overall quality by three education professors whose specialties included content-area reading and writing. As before, the system used by raters was a form of general impression marking, in which each rater gave one score for quality relative to the whole sample. Differences in quality were associated with age (grade level), the older students receiving higher scores, as one would expect. And differences in the more specific features of connectivity and quantity of content were also associated with age (grade level).

Text quality was highly correlated not only with the various text measures for organization, connectivity, and amount of content but also with some process variables. These included the amount of time that a student spent on the task and the extensiveness of the written plan he or she developed. The latter finding is similar to that of A. L. Brown, et al. (1983), who found, in regard to summary writing, that people writing the better summaries tended to do more planning.

Summary of the Developmental Study

This developmental study extended the previous work by considering elementary and secondary students' performance in discourse synthesis to produce informational reports. The focus in this study, like the previous one, was on organizing, selecting, and connecting, and it was also on developmental patterns. In comparison to the younger students, older students selected more content, but students of all ages organized the material in much the same way. Younger students offered their readers less content in fewer topical chunks. Developmental differences were seen in selecting, as older students included more material and seemed to make more use of an *intertextual criterion,* although that criterion appeared to be employed by the younger students, too. And developmental differences were also seen in connecting, as younger students did less well than older students in providing the connective cues that readers need when reading a linear text. In addition, relations were found between text quality and the amount of time spent on the task and the extensiveness of the planning.

Discourse Synthesis and the Writing of Comparisons

Writers often approach texts with purposes that lead them to different ways of configuring semantic material, different ways of shaping meaning. Not only do they recombine and reorder, but they also generate different patterns to organize the content. This kind of structural transformation was the focus of another study of discourse synthesis, which I summarize here but report in more detail in Spivey (1991). This study was contextualized in a science education class for upper-level undergraduates preparing to be teachers at a public university in north-central Texas. The 30 students who participated were asked to write informational texts that provided comparisons of octopuses and squids, two marine animals that are often confused. They had as sources two descriptive texts, one on octopuses and one on squids, both of which, like the armadillo texts in the first study, were organized into collections of attributes.

The Texts Used in Composing

Both of these texts were based on articles from the *Encyclopedia Americana* (1986), but I had modified the articles slightly, deleting some material so that texts would be more equivalent in length and eliminating section headings as well as statements comparing the two animals, such as the phrase "like other cephalopods" from the Octopus article, which would have meant "like the squid." The Squid Text, adapted from Meglitsch (1986), was as follows:

> SQUID, any of a large group of marine mollusks that have a greatly reduced shell, a cylindrical body, and a well-developed head to which ten arms are attached. Two of these arms have long tentacles bearing suction cups near their tips. Below the head, the squid body is covered by a muscular mantle, or protective covering, that is equipped with lateral fins. The characteristic mollusk shell typically consists only of a horny "pen" entirely embedded in the mantle. Squids vary in size from about 2 inches (5 cm) to the giant squid *Architeuthis,* which reaches a length of up to 20 feet (6 meters) and is the largest of all invertebrates. They are widely distributed throughout the world, near the surface and at great depths.
>
> Squids are classified in the order Teuthoidea, class Cephalopoda, phylum Mollusca.

Usually gray with small red dots, the squid has the ability to 'change color. The squid's color change often involves becoming pale or losing color.

Squids have a complex circulatory system with an extensive set of arteries and veins. Flowing to the heart, the blood passes through capillaries in a pair of large gills located in the mantle cavity. Here oxygen is absorbed. Two kidneys, closely associated with the circulatory system, open through excretory pores into the mantle cavity. Ammonia is the chief excretory product.

Squids have a large brain protected by cartilagelike shields in the head. The brain is formed by the concentration of ganglia, which are separate in most other mollusks. The brain is complex, containing a number of definite centers for the control of specific body parts or activities. An interesting feature of the nervous system is a set of giant neurons that provide full coordination of the mantle musculature and arms. The huge nerve cells of the squid have been popular subjects for research. The excellent sense organs and complex brain of the squid are reflected in rather complex behavior patterns.

Water enters the squid's mantle cavity through spaces between the mantle and head. When the mantle is contracted, these spaces are closed. Water then is ejected forcibly through a siphon, propelling the squid through the water. Many squids are powerful swimmers, capable of capturing fish and other aquatic animals with ease. Squids travel and hunt in schools and are aggressive animals. The strongest swimmers are the so-called flying squids (family Onycoteuthidae), which have a slender body, relatively short arms, and large terminal fins. They achieve high speeds and are able to leap 10 feet (3 meters) or more above the surface of the sea.

Squids grasp their prey with the suction cups on the arms, bring it to the mouth, and attack it with their strong, horny jaws. The food is further fragmented by the radula, a toothed, tonguelike organ in the mouth cavity. The stomach opens into the intestine and a cecum. Skeletal remains and larger hard fragments pass directly into the intestine, while smaller fragments enter the cecum. Flat, leaflike plates in the cecum serve as sorting surfaces. Rejected particles are carried into the intestine. Food is digested and absorbed in the cecum and perhaps in the digestive gland.

Ink glands, forming a black or (in some deep-sea squids) a luminescent fluid, are located near the anus. When attacked, the squid ejects this ink to confuse the predator.

In squids the sexes are separate. Males store sperm in intricate spermatophores. One of the male's arms—the fourth on the left side—is modified into a hectocotylus, which the male uses to pluck out stored spermatophores and insert them into the female mantle cavity. The eggs, which are fertilized internally, are surrounded by an albuminous mass that hardens when it is later extruded and touches seawater. Many squids deposit their eggs singly, but *Loligo* produces egg strings. After breeding and laying eggs, the adults of many species die. The young squids hatch at a relatively advanced stage looking much like diminutive adults.

Squids are prized as seafood in the Mediterranean area and on the coasts of Asia, where they are of considerable economic importance. Squids are also an important part of the marine food chain. Giant squids, for example, are important food organisms for sperm whales.[5]

The Octopus Text presented its topics in the following order: classification, habitat, uses by humans, size and species, shell (pen), head, skirt, arms (including the male hectocotylus), mantle, circulatory system, ability to change colors, ability to eject ink, solitary lifestyle, method of movement, and method of reproduction.

I analyzed the texts into content units, as in the two previous studies. Then I checked the content for symmetry, seeing which units seemed to have matches in the other text, which could be either a similarity or a difference. Consider the following excerpts from the two texts:

Ink glands, forming a black or (in some deep-sea squids) a luminescent fluid are located near the anus. When attacked, the squid ejects this ink to confuse the predator.	An ink gland located in the intestines provides another defensive tool for the octopus. The gland opens through a duct to an ampulla near the anus. When alarmed, the octopus ejects brown or black inky fluid from the ampulla. The ink confuses enemies, anesthetizes their olfactory senses, and allows the octopus to escape.

Symmetrical content would include such matches (or close matches) as the black fluid, ability to eject ink, and the capacity of the ink to confuse an enemy or predator. But it would also include units that could be interpreted as either similarities or differences: The animal's having an ink gland or ink glands could be interpreted as either similarity or difference because of the ambiguity of the Squid Text. The ink gland's being near the ampulla (Octopus) and near the anus (Squid) could be interpreted as similarity or difference depending on what kind of inference a reader made. The contingency for ejecting ink "when attacked" (Squid) and "when alarmed" (Octopus) could be interpreted as either similarity or difference, again depending on the reader's inferencing. Examples of nonsymmetrical content, besides all the details about the octopus's gland, are colors of ink, the squid's fluid being luminescent in some species, and the octopus's fluid being brown in some instances.

Transformations

In this study, my focus was still on the same kinds of transformations, but this time writers performed the transformations in order to produce a different sort of text than the ones they read.

[5]Adapted from "Squid," by P. A. Meglitsch, *Encyclopedia Americana,* 1986 (Vol. 25, pp. 546–547). Copyright © 1986 by Grolier Incorporated. Reprinted with permission.

Organizing

To perform the task and shape content into comparison patterns, writers had to generate the organizing relation of comparison and reorder and recombine content so that points of similarity and difference would be apparent to, or could be inferred by, readers. In the comparison, *objects* are interrelated in terms of various *aspects,* which include similarities (shared features) and differences (differentiating features) (cf. J. B. Black, 1985; Kintsch & Yarbrough, 1982; Meyer, 1985; Mosenthal, 1985). As discussed previously, writers seem to have options within this conventional pattern in how to order content: They may use the object format or the aspect format (Schnotz, 1982, 1984) as illustrated in Figure 3. If organizing by object, the writer begins with one object and presents information about it before moving to the other, signaling similarities and differences, particularly when discussing the second object. But if organizing by aspect, the writer takes one aspect and discusses it with respect to each object, pointing out similarities and differences, then moves on to another aspect and discusses it with respect to each object, and so on. Of the 30 comparisons produced, only 2 were classified as the object format. The other 28 were classified as aspect format.

Yet, among the 28 writers who produced aspect-organized texts, there was an important difference in how they organized their comparisons. Fifteen used the aspects discussed in the articles to organize their comparisons, thus producing the form labeled as aspect format in Figure 3. However, the other 13 writers provided additional means of organizing these aspects. Among these writers, 6 grouped to-

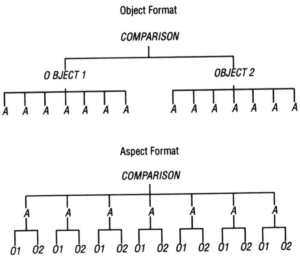

Figure 3. Patterns of comparing.

gether the aspects according to similarities and differences (which they inferred), considering similarities separately from differences, as illustrated in Figure 4. In addition, 7 writers generated macro-aspects, such as "lifestyle" and "internal organs," which subsumed several aspects. These macro-aspects, which some consider hyperthemes (cf. Firbas, 1974), would seem to have much the same effect as inter-chunk links in the previous studies. This pattern is also illustrated in Figure 4. A major distinction, then, among the various papers classified as aspect format was in regard to whether or not the writer provided additional means for chunking. Some aspect-organized comparisons signaled one of these two means for chunking, and some did not. Also illustrated in the figure is the object format with a macro-aspect grouping, to show how that would look, although neither of the writers using the object format produced it.

For writers producing their comparisons, organization was a major concern. They revealed this concern when responding to questionnaires administered after they completed their papers. In response to a question about their process of writing these papers, most responded with comments about their method of organizing the material. They mentioned wanting to accomplish such things as getting their points down in a logical order, providing a meaningful sequence, and sorting and classifying the information effectively. Twelve of the students produced written plans, and they were the writers who tended to provide more chunking in their texts (i.e., to use either macro-aspects or similarity–difference grouping).

Selecting and Balancing

As in the two previous studies, writers were quite selective in their use of source content. Not surprisingly, given the symmetrical nature of the comparison pattern, their selectivity was strongly related to symmetry. They averaged about 48 symmetrical units (approximately 38% of what was offered), and they averaged about 28 nonsymmetrical units (approximately 13% of what was offered) according to my analyses.

This *symmetry criterion* for writers is tied to the configuration of meaning for the new text, not to the structural characteristics of the texts that are read. Relevance of content is determined by its relation to an emergent pattern as the writer transforms the source material into a different shape. What might seem to be figure when a text is read for understanding can become ground when read in terms of other criteria. Writers did a balancing act in selecting source content, searching for content that was parallel for the two topics of the comparison. They apparently determined relevance in terms of similarities and differences. As they read and wrote, they noted relevant content by marking it or by writing notations in the margins about similar or contrasting attributes. For instance, one student wrote "Both are mollusks" in the margin of the Squid Text beside the phrase "large group of marine mollusks" and wrote "same" by the sentence stating that squids live "near the surface and at great depths." Some students who constructed written plans even put them in the form of matrices lining up the matching content, as shown in Figure 5.

Aspect Format with Similarity-Difference Grouping

Aspect Format with Macro-aspects

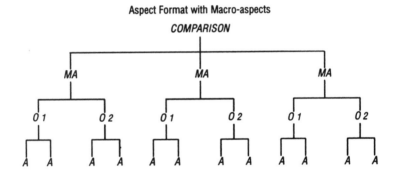

Object Format with Macro-aspects

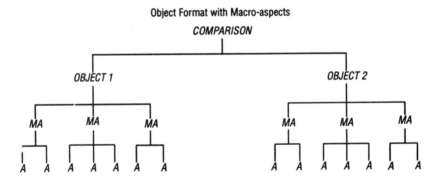

Figure 4. Similarity–difference grouping and macro–aspects within the comparison pattern.

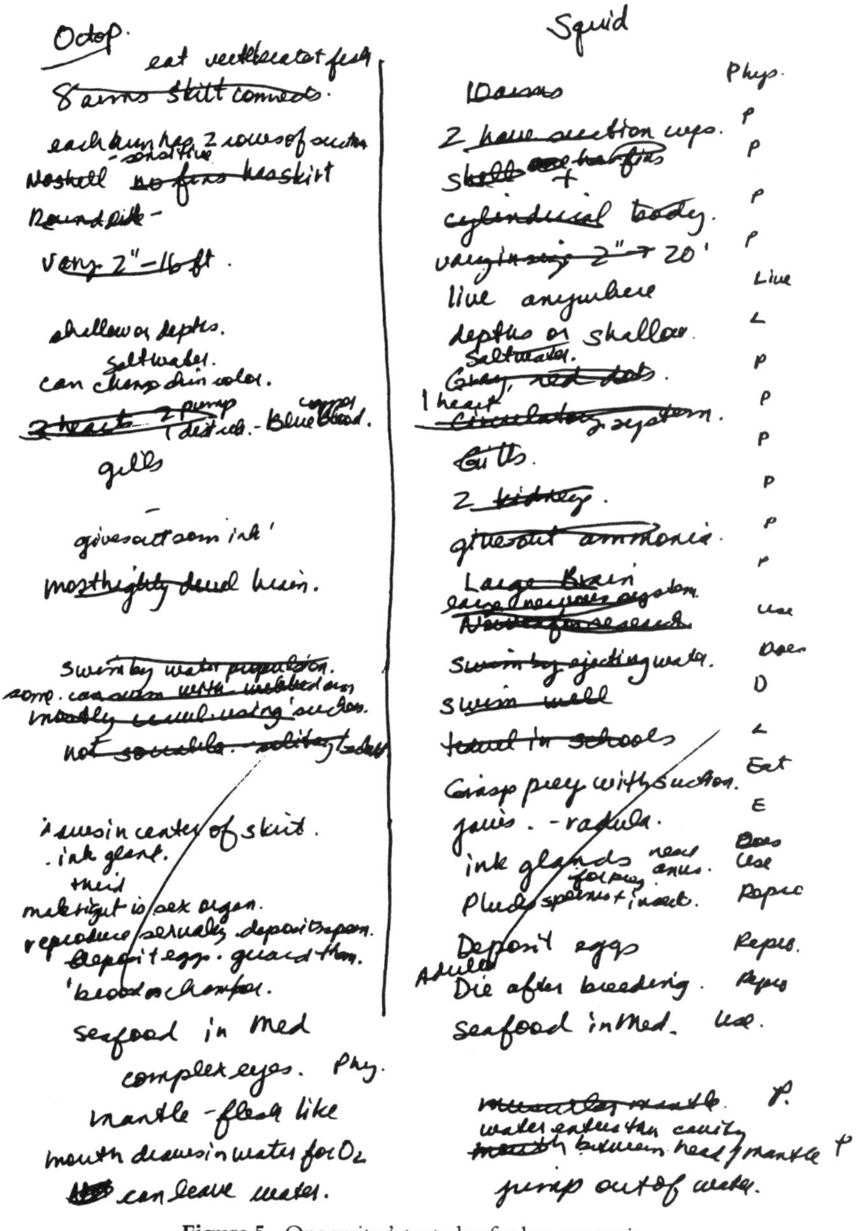

Figure 5. One writer's text plan for her comparison.

Writers also tried to achieve balance in their generation of content. Their reports typically included not only material suggested by the texts but also some content that the writers generated through inferential procedures. This occurred when one text provided a piece of information about one of the subjects of the comparison and the other text did not have parallel information about the other subject. Two examples will illustrate: one about aggressiveness and the other about color change. First, whereas the Squid Text discusses the squid's aggressiveness, the Octopus Text does not explicitly say whether or not the octopus is aggressive. It does, however, mention that the octopus tends to live a solitary life. Some writers inferred that the octopus was not aggressive and included that information to contrast with information about the squid. Second, both texts indicate that the animals change colors, but only the Octopus Text attributes the change to contractions in the wall of pigment cells. Some writers pointed out that wall-cell contractions cause color changes for both.

Quality of the Comparisons

Again, I had holistic quality ratings provided by three raters. As in the previous study, they were all university faculty members in a teacher educator program. Each gave a paper a score on a scale of 1 (low) to 4 (high) following the procedures of general impression marking discussed earlier, and the score I used was the sum of the three ratings. A multiple regression on these scores had the following as predictors: total content units, a measure for reliance on the texts, and two measures for organization. The measure for reliance on texts was the proportion of source content relative to the total, and the two organization measures were a dichotomous variable for whether or not the writer used the similarity–difference grouping and a dichotomous variable for whether or not the writer generated macro-aspects. All predictors were positively associated with quality, except for the measure for reliance on texts, which was negatively associated.

The regression suggested that the four measures in combination accounted for 60% of the variance in the ratings. What raters apparently preferred was the writer's grouping related aspects together to form fewer chunks as well as including more content overall and more added content relative to the total. I was particularly interested in the role of the organization variables, similarity–difference and macro-aspects, which were both methods of producing more integrative comparisons. Analyses showed that macro-aspects played a more important role than similarity–difference. By systematically removing one organizational variable and then the other, I found that the combination of macro-aspects and the content variables was a good model for predicting the raters' judgments.

The following comparison, written by the writer whose text plan is illustrated in Figure 5, demonstrates macro-aspects. This highly rated text was one of the longest (129 units) written by the students, and it also had a large number of added units (22).

People often confuse squids and octopuses. Though at first they may appear the same, they do have various differences.

First of all, as for physical attributes, the squid has a cylindrical body with a reduced shell. The octopus has no shell and a round body. The squid has ten arms, two of which have suction cups on the end, while the octopus has eight arms, each with two rows of sensitive touch receptors and suction cups. Though both have a mantle below the head, the squid has a "horny" pen embedded in it, and it is quite muscular. The octopus, on the other hand, has a fleshy mantle with a skirt and sometimes webbing between the arms. The squid also has lateral fins, which some use to swim. The octopus has no fins at all.

Both squid and octopus vary in size, though squids may be slightly larger—twenty feet compared to sixteen feet of the largest octopus. Both can change color to become paler by contracting the muscular walls of their pigment cells. The octopus ranges in color from gray to skin tone.

Secondly, these creatures are much the same inwardly with a few differences. The squid is known for its large nervous system, the large neurons that coordinate all muscular movement being popular in research. Both squid and octopus have highly complex brains, with the octopus having an advantage in being the most "highly developed brain of all the vertebrates." Both creatures use gills to breathe, the difference being in how water is brought in to be absorbed. The squid receives water in spaces between the mantle and the head, and the octopus draws in water through holes in the mantle.

Surprisingly, both have highly developed circulatory systems. The octopus stands out as having three hearts—two to pump and one to distribute blood. His blood is also blue due to a copper chemical present. The squid, on the other hand, has two kidneys, which excrete ammonia.

Thirdly, the squid and octopus live different lifestyles. The squid tends to travel and live in schools, while the octopus is a solitary unsociable creature. They both live in either shallow water or at great depths, but the octopus appears to stay more permanent, especially after laying eggs in a "brood chamber."

Both the squid and octopus swim by water ejection, but the octopus spends most of his time crawling on the ocean floor using the suction cups on his arms. They can also leave water and crawl about on land for short periods of time, whereas the squid (some species) can only jump (for a moment) out of water.

Both eat fish and smaller vertebrates. Both grasp their prey with suction cups. The octopus has very strong jaws at the base (center) of his skirt like the squid, but the squid also has a "toothed tongue" in his mouth cavity to "chew food." To fight off intruders or frighten prey, both let off an inky substance through their suction cups.

Lastly, another difference lies in their reproduction. Octopuses reproduce sexually, while male squids implant sperm via the fourth leg (on the right) into the female. For both, this arm is called a "hectocotylus." After squids breed and deposit eggs, they often die, while the female octopus sticks around to guard her eggs.

So the next time you savor squid or octopus (both a Mediterranean seafood treat), recognize which one you are eating and be thankful you didn't meet him alive.

This comparison illustrates the extensive inferencing that writers did as they interrelated the material and concluded in what ways the squid and octopus are similar and in what ways they are different. In this case, some of the inferred differences, such as numbers of hearts, numbers of kidneys, and type of reproduction, came when parallel information was not provided for both animals.

With respect to organization, we see that, after a brief introduction, the writer began her comparison with what she called "physical attributes," within which she included discussion of the animals' body shape, arms, mantle, fins, size, and color. After this she moved to internal systems, a theme that she did not actually state but instead implied by saying that "these creatures are much the same inwardly with a few differences." The internal system theme carried through her description of both animals' nervous, circulatory, and respiratory systems, and her description of the squid's excretory system. The third section dealing with "lifestyle" included discussions of locomotion, habitat, feeding, and protective devices. The final section focused on one of the aspects cued by the sources, "reproduction." The reader thus would have a text with a good amount of information organized in only four chunks. When the macro-aspects from the text are compared with those on the plan shown in Figure 5, some differences are apparent. In writing the text, the writer limited "physical" to external features and created another chunk for internal systems. She combined "use," "does," and "eat" into "lifestyle" but kept "reproduction" as it was. She was apparently not locked into her original plan, because she did some reorganizing as she wrote her text.

Summary of the Comparison Study

This study examined the synthesis of new texts, comparisons, from two texts on interrelated topics. In organizing comparisons, the writers had various options, which included focusing on aspects or focusing on objects. If using an aspect format, they could produce a more integrative presentation by generating macro-aspects or using a similarity–difference grouping. The symmetrical form of the comparison appeared to influence selecting and generating, as writers tended to use a symmetry principle, preferentially choosing content about one object that had a parallel for the other object. And they also made inferences to fill in when parallel information was not offered. Ratings suggested that the quality of a comparison, like the topical reports, was related to the tightness of its organization, as readers preferred the integrative presentation that results from use of large, inclusive themes, the generation of integrative material, and the comprehensiveness of treatment.

Discourse Synthesis and Disciplinary Tasks

Discourse synthesis is an important aspect of authorship in the disciplines of academe, as scholars make their own contributions by building upon, and moving beyond, what has been presented. They invent and discover intertextual links among texts in their topic or research area (e.g., Geisler, 1991), and position their own texts within an intertextual network of related texts (Latour, 1987), as discussed later in the chapter on authoring identity. For students, too, really learning an academic discipline means learning its content and also learning to use disciplinary texts, not only for purposes of reading but also for purposes of writing. They must learn to work within a disciplinary intertext to produce their own pieces that have some family resemblance to the texts produced by the scholars and researchers (Cochran, 1993; Mathison, 1993). What form do these pieces take? There is much variety in disciplinary texts that writers (students as well as their professors) produce through discourse synthesis: arguments, reports, proposals, critical essays, theoretical pieces, to name only a few (cf. Bridgeman & Carlson, 1984). And there is much choice for instructors regarding the kinds of writing-to-learn *tasks* they will assign their students. What transformations would students make if, for example, they wrote proposals instead of reports? What if they wrote reports instead of proposals? The following task study examined transformations when writers use the same texts to perform different tasks.

This was a comparison of two complex reading–writing tasks: writing a report and writing a research proposal. Writers would thus have different contexts to "read," and that "reading" of context would probably affect the meaning built for the texts and intertext they would read. The report task would seem to invite them to organize with a collection pattern in order to present major aspects of the topic. In contrast, the proposal task would seem to invite them to organize with a response pattern, posing a problem and offering a solution to it. Research in reading comprehension (e.g., Frederiksen, 1972, 1975a; Gauld & Stephenson, 1967; Rothkopf & Billington, 1979; Zwaan, 1993), discussed previously, has shown the impact that the nature of a task can have on the meaning that is built.

Participants in the study were 34 undergraduates taking a course in developmental psychology. When groups were formed, there were 18 in the proposal group and 17 in the report group. However, one student in the report group did not complete the paper and was subsequently dropped from the study, leaving 16 in the report group. All students received a written prompt for assigned writing based on the five sources. They were asked to write a paper of approximately three typed pages by using the five articles and were asked to credit the sources where appropriate and to include a reference list. Students in the proposal group received this assignment:

The nature of egocentrism is one focus of research in developmental psychology. Children, as they mature, are thought to "decenter" and to gain in the ability to take the perspectives of others. This perspective-taking ability is reflected not only in perception but also in verbal communication, both written and spoken. One unresolved problem, though, is that perspective-taking seems to be more delayed in writing than in speaking. Write a paper that considers this discrepancy and possible reasons for it and that proposes a good way to see if the difference in the two modalities is really there.

And students in the report group received this assignment:

The nature of egocentrism is one focus of research in developmental psychology. Children, as they mature, are thought to "decenter" and to gain in the ability to take the perspectives of others. This perspective-taking ability is reflected not only in perception but also in verbal communication, both written and spoken. Write a report that synthesizes information on this topic.

This paper, one of five for the course, was to be written outside of class and was due in ten days.

The Texts Used in Composing

Students had the following five articles on the topic of egocentrism in communication (ordered here according to year of publication):

Flavell, J. H. (1966). Role-taking and communication skills in children. *Young Children, 21,* 164–177.
Glucksberg, S., & Krauss, R. M. (1967). What do people say after they have learned to talk? Studies of the development of referential communication. *Merrill-Palmer Quarterly, 13,* 309–316.
Hoy, E. A. (1975). Measurement of egocentrism in children's communication. *Developmental Psychology, 11,* 392.
Donaldson, M. (1978). The ability to "decenter." In M. Donaldson, *Children's Minds* (pp. 9–25). New York: Norton.
Kroll, B. M. (1985). Rewriting a complex story for a young reader: The development of audience-adapted writing skills. *Research in the Teaching of English, 19,* 120–138.

The following are brief summaries:

Flavell (1966)

Flavell begins by citing Piaget's developmental work in children's nonsocial cognitive operations and then by stating a need for more research in social cognitive operations. One social-cognitive operation, according to Flavell, is role taking in communication: one's trying to deduce the attributes of listeners and to monitor what is said according to the perception of those attributes. This article, with ten references, presents summaries of relevant research conducted by others (including Piaget) in the areas of role-taking development and communication development and then that conducted by Flavell (and his colleagues). The article concludes with a theoretical conceptualization of five constituents of role-taking ability.

Glucksberg and Krauss (1967)

The Glucksberg and Krauss article is a report of a study focused on referential communication, a speaker's being able to communicate so that a listener can identify the referent. A distinction is made between nonsocial encoding, which is not responsive to effects upon the listener, and social encoding, which is. In the latter a speaker is thought to take "the role of the other," as George Herbert Mead said. These researchers examined the ability of children and adults in referential communication and found a developmental pattern in that young children, unlike older children and adults, failed to edit their messages to accommodate their listeners. The authors have five citations, four to their own work and one to a study by someone else. Mead is not listed as a formal reference.

Hoy (1975)

Hoy (1975) reports a study designed to examine whether children's listener-appropriate behavior, which seemed slight in studies such as Glucksberg and Krauss's (1967), might be increased by changing the context. In the study with children of three ages, Hoy manipulated the familiarity of the objects to which references were made and the restrictiveness of the speaker–listener interaction. Results indicated that percentage of listener-appropriate behavior varied with both object familiarity and condition restrictiveness, as well as with age. Hoy had only two citations, Glucksberg and Krauss (1967) and one other.

Donaldson (1978)

The Donaldson piece is a chapter from her book, *Children's Minds.* For this particular chapter she takes issue with Piaget's claim that children do not do well in communicating because they are highly egocentric. To show how Piaget might be wrong in his claims about children's extreme egocentrism, she contrasts Piaget's (1923/1932) studies with research conducted by others using tasks involving more intentionality. Some of these studies were in-progress pieces by her colleagues, such as Maratsos (1973) and Lloyd (1975), but she also cites the work of T. G. R. Bower (1977; T. G. R. Bower & Wishart, 1972) and refers to Bruner (1975). She concludes that preschool children are more capable of taking the point of view of other people than Piaget has maintained. There are nine references.

Kroll (1985)

Kroll's article begins with a comprehensive review of the literature on ego-centrism in communication, beginning with the work of Piaget and the studies conducted by Flavell and by Glucksberg and Krauss. He points out a paucity of research in audience-adapted writing and, thus, a need for his study. This study examined developmental trends between the end of elementary school and the beginning of college as groups of writers attempted to adapt a particular story for an audience of third graders. Developmental patterns were apparent in the writers' increasing ability to make lexical, syntactic, and syntactic changes that reduced complexity. This text has 24 references, including one citation of another study by the author himself.

Figure 6 portrays explicit interrelations among the texts with which the students were to work. The Flavell, Donaldson, and Kroll texts are interrelated in that all refer to Piaget, for whom the text is left uncolored because the students did not actually read it for this task. Kroll refers to Flavell and to Glucksberg and Krauss, also. The Glucksberg and Krauss article does not mention Piaget, but refers instead to Mead, whose text is colored like Piaget's because it was not read by the students. The brief report by Hoy cites only Glucksberg and Krauss out of the various texts in this intertext. A more complete representation of the intertext would include numerous other texts, cited and summarized by the various authors of the texts that were read.

Overall Patterns of Organization

Students' texts, produced in response to the two assignments, were analyzed for overall organizational pattern in general accordance with the rhetorical relations offered by Grimes (1975) and Meyer (1975, 1985) and discussed previously. Table 3 shows the results: some commonalities among students performing a particular task as well as variability within both groups, as was reported previously in Spivey and Greene (1989). Many students receiving the proposal assignment produced the expected kind of text, papers that could be classified as proposals. And many students receiving the report assignment also produced the expected, papers that could be classified as topical collections. However, there were several other sorts of texts written in response to the assignments—causal arguments, comparisons, critiques, and a collection organized according to researcher. Two types—collection and critique—were used for both tasks.

Papers Written for the Proposal Task

Figure 7 illustrates the patterns signaled by writers receiving the proposal assignment. Our analyses indicated that more than half of this group produced the

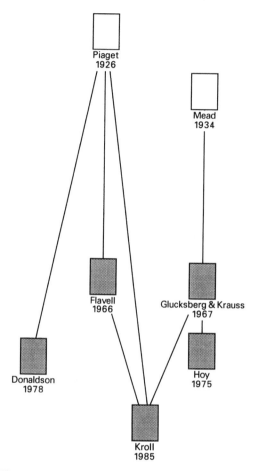

Figure 6. Citational links among the disciplinary texts.

Table 3
Numbers of Writers Generating Particular Patterns for the Two Tasks

	Proposal	Causal argument	Critique	Collection (topical)	Collection (author)	Comparison
Proposal task	8	7	1	2	0	0
Report task	0	0	1	7	1	7

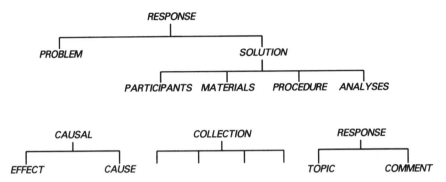

Figure 7. Patterns generated for the proposal task.

invited form, a response pattern, in which the problem (the apparent discrepancy in egocentrism between oral and written communication) was posed and a possible solution offered in the form of a study. Some writers produced fairly detailed studies. For example, one student, after discussing findings of prior research and considering differences between the processes of speech and writing, proposed an experiment taking into account the differing demands of speech and writing. This was to "isolate effects." The student proposed a series of tasks that involved the understanding and retelling of a story, "much as in the Kroll and Flavell articles—details would need to be developed." Three modes—speech with feedback, speech without feedback (no nodding or frowns), and written—would be compared for levels of egocentrism measured on a scale from low to high, and differences between modes could be ascribed to feedback or no feedback in the case of two speech modes and to famil-iarity or complexity in case of speech with feedback and written modes. This student even considered an expected result:

> As the mode of communication changes from speech with feedback to speech without feedback to written, the degree of apparent egocentrism exhibited would increase. In many cases, however, the increase would not be as great. In the case of written and speech with no feedback, the lesser differences should correspond to the children who have better writing skills. If this is the case, it suggests that writing skills are what makes the difference, particularly if the children display the same amount of egocentrism in the spoken portion but differ in the written.

The proposal concluded with issues to consider: the length and complexity of the stories ("should not exceed the child's ability to remember the entire story"), the sort of measures to use ("must be as objective and as consistent as possible"), and possible confounding variables such as writing ability ("must be considered and controlled").

Another writer, after a lengthy consideration of the problem, focused on differences in feedback for the two modalities as a possible explanation for apparent differences in egocentricity. This became the motivating issue for the proposed study. Participants in this study, aged 5 to 16, would have "written conversations" with a child and an adult. If participants "decenter" at ages younger than 14, which has been the age marked for decentering in writing, feedback would be demonstrated as an important variable.

These proposal writers included a number of the constituent elements of a study, as shown in Figure 7. Others, however, did not give as much attention to design specifics and to interpretation of results. Some proposal writers simply offered an idea for a study with few details. For instance, one suggested a study with children of several age groups. Two children of the same age would look at a picture and imagine how it would look from another angle. One would give the description orally and the other would give it in writing, and comparisons would be made.

The other major type of paper produced for this assignment was a causal argument. An effect (the apparent discrepancy in egocentrism between oral and written communication) was described, and then an argument was presented regarding the cause or causes. For the latter section, most writers taking this approach presented fairly well developed arguments in which they made claims based not only on what they read but also on their own experience and conclusions. Instead of proposing a possible solution to an unresolved problem, like the proposal writers, these students argued that there already was a "known" cause ("known" in that they knew it). They used reasoning to resolve the issue, instead of leaving open some part of the issue to motivate a study. Some texts were one-cause arguments. For instance, one student based his piece on the argument that a person has more experience communicating orally than communicating in written form. Others were multiple-cause arguments. For instance, another student argued that the apparent egocentricity results from the following causes: the child's inexperience in written communication relative to spoken, the child's inability to see another person's expression in written communication, and the child's difficulties in participating in research studies.

In addition, two writers produced papers classified as topical collections, which was, as Table 3 shows, the major pattern produced for the other assignment. One collection was organized around three kinds of differences between speech and writing, and the other centered on the topics of adolescence egocentrism, role taking on the part of children and adolescents, and egocentrism in written communication.

Finally, one student wrote a critique, which, like the proposals, was set up as a response in which the second part responded to the first. In contrast to the proposals, the critique had topic–comment patterning, with egocentrism as the topic about which evaluative commentary was offered. The writer began the commentary with the statement, "Overall, egocentrism is a concept that needs a closer scrutiny. It is a theory full of holes," and then went on to discuss flaws: problems in research design, variables not acknowledged in the theory, and the "major flaw," that all of us are egocentric to some extent.

Papers Written for the Report Task

For the report task, variability was also found in organizational pattern. As shown in Table 3, 7 in the report group produced reports with content organized in topical collections, which would be the form many of us would expect for the presentation of information. This pattern as well as others generated by the report group is shown in Figure 8. For these topical collections, the most common way to organize the material was to create topical chunks centered around large, subsuming topics (or hyperthemes): egocentrism in perception, egocentrism in oral communication, and egocentrism in written communication. (Actually, these particular topics were suggested by the assignment.) Within the discussion of a particular topic, various researchers' work would typically be included. However, instead of organizing thematically, one writer organized a collection according to researcher. The constituent parts were summaries of particular researchers' studies. This was a loose collection, as the researchers were not ordered chronologically or grouped together in any consistent way. The writer provided little to connect one to another

Besides collection, the other major pattern identified for the report assignment was the comparison. Like the collection just mentioned, it was organized on the basis of researchers, but, unlike the collection, writers taking this approach inferred similarities and differences among researchers as they aligned them. The researchers were grouped together according to a similarity in position, and one group was set in contrast to the other. These writers set up comparisons of positions, for and against Piaget and his notion of egocentrism, and put the various reseachers into Piaget-supporting and Piaget-opposing groups.

To see how these comparisons were set up, let us consider one of them, which is illustrated graphically in Figure 9. The writer begins with a presentation of the Piagetian position: Piaget's ideas, then "early work . . . carried out by Flavell (1966)," "a later study by Glucksberg and Krauss (1967)," and "children's written communication [which] was examined by Barry M. Kroll (1985)." These research-

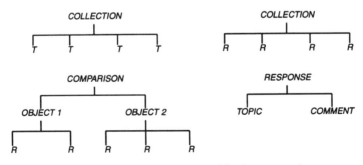

Figure 8. Patterns generated for the report task.

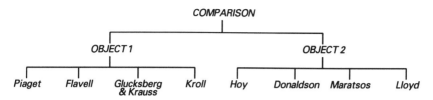

Figure 9. Illustration of intertextual links made in comparing.

ers are grouped together by their Piagetian position and ordered temporally. Kroll comes last, not only because of temporal order but also because of his contrasting focus on written instead of oral communication. Near the midpoint of the paper, the author sets up the major contrast: "These studies seem to confirm Piaget's claim that egocentrism is directly related to children's communication skills, but some researchers disagree." The writer then presents the other camp: Hoy and Donaldson, who is "another opponent," and brings two other researchers into the debate, Maratsos and Lloyd, whose work was cited by Donaldson.

As in the other group, one writer produced a critique. This student produced a paper strikingly similar in form to the critique, mentioned above, written by the student in the other group. The commentary for this one centered around the claim that egocentrism is an "obscure and ambiguous topic," which the writer supported with material from the reading as well as her own conclusions from them. A critique, like this, which argues for one perspective, contrasts with a comparison, which can incorporate more than one. Like the critique, a comparison can deal with critical comments, but, unlike the critique, both sides can receive a more symmetrical treatment.

Quality of the Syntheses

Rating Procedure

In the time period since this study was conducted, I have had the students' texts rated for quality by three psychologists who teach or have taught developmental psychology classes for undergraduates. After reading the texts and the assignments, each rater performed the ratings independently from the others and separately for the two sets. The raters made decisions about the quality of individual papers relative to the whole set by choosing the four they thought highest in quality and the four they thought lowest and putting the others in a medium-quality group. Attention in the study was mainly on the high-rated texts, and the low category was included as a check on consistency: to see if any of those considered high quality by one rater would be considered low by another. In addition to sorting the papers, the psychologists also made notes on those eight papers considered high and low for each set.

Interrater agreement was quite good. For the 18 texts produced in response to the proposal assignment, two of the three raters agreed on categories for 9 papers, and all three raters agreed on the ratings of the remaining 9 papers. In no case did one rater classify a paper as high in quality that another rater had classified as low. For the 16 texts produced in response to the report assignment, at least two of the three raters agreed on ratings, and all three raters agreed on the categories for 2 of them. As for the other set, no rater classified as high a paper that another had classified as low.

Quality and the Proposal Task

As mentioned above, the typical paper for the proposal task was set up with a response pattern, posing a problem and offering a possible solution in the form of a study. As it turned out, all six of the papers that received at least one high rating were set up in this way. The inclusion of a proposed study as a "solution" was a major criterion for the raters. Some of their comments on the high-rated proposals, all of which had studies proposed, were "reasonable experiment," "interesting suggestion," "pretty sophisticated," and "experiment sketchy but there is one." Texts receiving highest ratings, not surprisingly, were those that had a fairly well developed study, including a number of the conventional components (subjects, materials, design, measures, analyses, etc.). The two proposals unanimously named high quality included the proposal for a study of the three modes (oral communication, oral communication without feedback, and written communication) and the proposal for a study of "written conversation," both mentioned above.

What about the others? The causal arguments and the topical collections received nothing better than a medium rating. The critique about the "theory full of holes" did not fare well in the ratings, as it was given a unanimous low. Although one rater commented that it was an interesting paper, he, like the other raters, noted such things as "got off track," "no relevance to the task," and "did not stick to the assignment."

In a chi-square analysis the proposal/no-proposal dichotomy served as one categorical variable, and the individual ratings were combined to create another dichotomous variable for quality. The high category ($n = 6$) were those that received at least one high rating from the psychologists, and the not-high category were all others ($n = 12$). For the papers in this set, as expected, there was a difference in the quality ratings between those papers set up as proposals and those set up in some other fashion, $\chi^2(1) = 11.25$, $p < .001$.

Quality and the Report Task

The situation was not as clear-cut for the report task as it was for the proposal task. The six papers receiving at least one high rating included two topical collections, three comparisons, and the critique. It is not surprising that topical collections were acceptable to the raters because this approach to the task was implicit in the assignment. What is surprising is the variability among those papers considered highest in quality. Half of the highest rated papers were comparisons, for which raters noted as strengths such things as the presentation of opposing views and critical points. The lining up of researchers, achieved through such comparisons, seemed an appropriate way to deal with, and to report on, the opposing viewpoints. In fact, the one text receiving unanimous high ratings for this set was a comparison, the one illustrated in Figure 9 and used previously as an example.

For the report assignment, the raters did not require that the text be set up in a particular way with particular component parts. A topical report could meet the assignment, but so could a comparison. So, also, it seems, could a critique. The critique produced for the report assignment was well received by the raters (rated high by two and middle by the other), who, when rating papers for this other assignment, considered the writer's critical approach to be a strength. The raters' willingness to accept the critique as a report does support the idea that "report" can encompass a variety of text types.

The papers in this set were put into two large groups: (a) topical collections; (b) those taking some other form, which included the comparisons, the critique, and the collection set up according to researcher. Papers were also categorized according to quality, high or not high, as with the other set. For this set, when frequencies of high ($n = 6$) and not high ($n = 10$) ratings were compared for the two form categories, there was no statistically significant difference. One would expect this result because of the variable forms in both quality categories.

Intertextual Connections

In these acts of discourse synthesis students inferred intertextual connections among the researchers whose texts they read, and these inferences were important in the patterning of their texts. Let us first consider the connections made by a comparison writer, since the connections are most apparent for the comparison texts. Consider, for instance, the text already discussed and illustrated in Figure 9. From reading Flavell's text, the writer of this paper could see that Flavell had aligned himself with Piaget. Thus, the writer puts them together. From reading Kroll's text, he would see that Kroll had cited Piaget and Flavell and did not oppose their ideas. The writer lines Kroll up with them, too. (Even though Kroll did not present the Piagetian view as his position, he did cite the Piagetian work in a favorable way, and these connections can be considered as somewhat explicit in the intertext.) The connection the writer makes between Glucksberg and Krauss and others in the group may seem to be an inference, as Glucksberg and Krauss did not mention Piaget or Flavell. However, the person doing the inferencing would have some help from Kroll, who suggested the connection between Glucksberg and Krauss and the other two. The writer infers a relation between Hoy and Donaldson, two key figures in his opponent group, and also infers the relation between Hoy and Maratsos and Lloyd, whose work was cited by Donaldson. Although the connection between Maratsos and Lloyd was made rather explicitly by Donaldson, there was no referencing of Hoy by Donaldson. Even presenting Hoy as an anti-Piagetian figure is based on an inference, as Hoy did not mention Piaget. Simply setting up one group in opposition to the other involves inferencing, as many of the researchers in the two groups did not have anything to say about the work of those in the other group.

These various relations are quite obvious when one reads a comparison like this one. For the other patterns, the relations among various researchers are not as apparent; they are more embedded. Figure 10 illlustrates intertextual connections made by one of the proposal writers. The writer begins by setting up a contrast between oral and written communication with respect to egocentricity. A relation is established between Piaget and Donaldson and her colleagues in that they all have studied oral communication. However, the writer points to the theoretical disagreement, the contrast, between the Donaldson group and Piaget, which was stated explicitly by Donaldson. The writer then moves to written communication, for which he groups together Kroll and a pair of researchers Kroll cited, Crowhurst and Piché. This Kroll–Crowhurst–Piché group is set up in comparison to the other group, composed of Piaget, Donaldson, Maratos, and Hughes, who concentrated on oral instead of written communication. A possible cause is offered for the effect that has been considered by all these others, whom the student has now put together in one big group. The cause was suggested by Kroll (another colleague of Donaldson's), who discussed Piaget's work but never mentioned Donaldson, Hughes, or

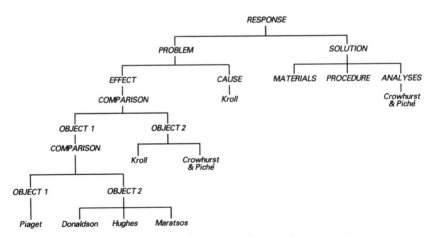

Figure 10. Illustration of intertextual links made in proposing.

Maratsos. The student concludes by suggesting a study, using a methodology similar to Crowhurst and Piché's. Their study was discussed in Kroll's article, but they did not address the particular issue this writer has set up. That connection, too, is an inference.

Summary of the Task Study

This task study examined synthesis as performed in disciplinary writing tasks. Students in a psychology class used the same disciplinary texts to perform different tasks, a proposal task and a report task. In general, different organizational patterns were generated in response to different assignments, although there were some text types, collection and critique, that were produced for both. Psychologists assessing the texts for quality required proposals to signal the form that is conventional in that discourse community if they were to receive high ratings, but reports could be set up in a number of different ways. Generating patterns for such texts involves making such global kinds of intertextual inferences as how the work or position of one author relates to the work or position of another.

Conclusion

These studies provide some glimpses into meaning making when texts are created from other texts. In discourse synthesis, writers shape their meanings with organizational patterns, make selections on the basis of some criterion or criteria of relevance, and generate inferences that integrate material that might seem inconsistent or even contradictory. In such acts writers read not only single texts but also an intertext, as they perceive intertextual cues and make connective inferences from one text to another. And they also read the context in which their act is situated, and that reading influences the other reading and writing that they do. Different tasks can lead to different kinds of new texts and different meanings.

These organizational, selective, and connective transformations can be "seen" in discourse synthesis when comparisons are made of the texts read and the texts produced. They are not so visible in some other literate acts. However, in many ways, as I attempt to show in subsequent chapters, they are the very basis of reading, writing, and learning in almost any domain of knowledge.

Chapter VII

. . . .

Textual Transformations
in Written Discourse

> The reader may well become the author's adversary, seeking to make the text over
> in a direction that the author did not anticipate.
>
> —Jay David Bolter, *Writing Space*

Suppose a social historian, a specialist in working-class history, is writing an essay to submit to a disciplinary journal on why the American working class did not generate a strong socialist movement. As one of numerous sources, she is using one of the manifestos issued in conjunction with the railroad strikes of 1877. Then suppose a sportswriter free-lancing for a sports magazine is writing an article comparing the run-and-shoot offense in football with the wishbone offense and is using, along with interview protocols, some printed material from Ellison's (1984) *Run and Shoot Football*. And finally, suppose a sophomore taking a course in developmental psychology is writing a research paper on the topic of autism as his final written project for the course. As one of several references, which include a couple of books as well as four or five articles, he is now using an article from the journal *Child Development*. All three writers would read others' texts as a part of the composing of their own texts, which would be conventional types of discourse for their own particular audiences and conventional practices in their discourse communities. This chapter is about transformations that writers such as these make as they perform constructive acts that involve reading other texts in order to produce new texts.

As we have seen, constructivists since Bartlett (1923, 1932) have focused their attention on transformations. Bartlett's work was particularly interesting because he considered such changes at the level of the individual and the level of society. He is well known for his study of individuals' transformations to make a text conform to their own frames, but he also considered larger transformations made by whole societies, as we have noted. An example he used was not a text but was another kind of cultural product, the peyote culture, which was transformed as it was appropriated by the Winnebagos. There has been much research, which I reviewed in Chapter III, examining transformations on the parts of readers, showing how particular transformations are associated with various factors, such as belonging to a particular group or having a particular kind of knowledge.

Of particular relevance to this chapter are those reading studies discussed earlier that focused on transformations associated with task: how people organize or reorganize, select particular material, and provide connectivity when they perform particular kinds of tasks as they make meaning from texts written by others. These studies have shown that particular kinds of transformations are made when people solve a problem instead of recounting the problem (Frederiksen, 1975a), when they are told to take one perspective instead of another (Pichert & Anderson, 1977), and when they expect one sort of assessment rather than another (Rothkopf & Billington, 1979). The tasks that people perform as they read influence their method of organizing, their criteria for selecting, and the extent of their inferencing. In this chapter I consider tasks that would fit into a category that might be labeled "writing from reading" or "composing from sources."

Textual Transformations and Conventional Practices

The hypothetical writers mentioned at the beginning of the chapter would, no doubt, approach other writers' texts with some ideas about their own to-be-written texts that would affect their reading. These ideas would likely include possible ways of organizing meaning. The historian might infer causal relations as she reads her source, the sportswriter might begin building contrastive patterns when reading about the run-and-shoot offense and relating it to the other offense, and the student might be satisfied merely to find, when reading this text as well as the others, a collection of major subtopics, such as etiology and treatment, around which to organize the report he is writing. Each writer, when reading, would give preferential attention to what has potential relevance to the text being written even though it might not be given most textual emphasis. In addition to organizing and selecting, the writer would make connections to topically related material associated with other texts or other experiences, making other inferences and elaborations. This generative process can be considered inferential and elaborative processing for reading. But it can also be considered an invention process for writing, as the content generated might become part of the potential meaning for the new piece that will be written. What writers do in such acts is both reading and writing. The transformations—organizational, selective, and connective—cannot be attributed simply to reading or simply to writing.

These writers, engaging in conventional practices, produce texts for their discourse communities. If analyzed and categorized, these texts might conform to particular *types* of discourse. The historian's article would likely be a causal argument, considering an effect and making the case for a particular cause or for particular causes; the sportswriter's article would be a report set up as a comparison, pointing out similarities and differences; and the student's paper would probably be a topical report, presenting various aspects of the topic. These writers would have generated form for their own texts as they transformed other writers' texts, and through their own texts they would suggest form for their own readers (who might very well make their own transformations). In such tasks we have some good illustrations of the social nature of composing as writers change texts written by some people to make them work for other people in different contexts.

Organizational Transformations

This section focuses on five kinds of academic practices involving such transformations: summarizing, reporting on a topic, solving a problem (or proposing a solution), critiquing, and making a causal argument. In such acts, people read the context and the intertext as well as the text, and, as they compose, they discover and invent relations as well as content. Some transformations are organizational, as writers frame content to meet their discourse goals, and others are selective and generative. Although these practices seem fairly common throughout academe, there are some differences among various groups.

Summarizing: Reducing *and* Adding

A reading–writing practice that has received much concentrated attention from researchers is summarizing, which is common to many communicative contexts. A person might give a capsule version of a film seen or a book read, might tell someone else what another person said, might present a compressed version of a longer paper for some audience. In academic discourse, it is conventional for abstracts to introduce long texts, such as journal articles, technical reports, and dissertations, and for these summaries to be used in indexes as well as attached to the full text. And the production of summaries is a conventional component of schooling, as summaries are frequently required of students to demonstrate their understanding of the informational texts that they have read (Applebee, 1984; Bridgeman & Carlson, 1984).

Even though there are various types of summaries, all have two characteristics in common: their *brevity* and their *selectivity* relative to what is summarized. A summary is a brief version of the gist of the text, those propositions that are deemed most central and essential according to some criterion. Much of the research on summarizing has examined summary writing when writers attempt to follow the original writer's guidance as they compress the text to its gist (cf. A. L. Brown & Day, 1983; Hidi & Anderson, 1986; Johns, 1985; van Dijk, 1977, 1980; P. N. Winograd, 1984). The texts so produced can be called *isomorphic summaries* because of the similarity in form to what is read.

When producing these isomorphic summaries, writers follow textual cues for organization, taking advantage of what seems to be offered structurally, and they attempt to reproduce those global organizational patterns. For example, an abstract of a psychological research report follows the organizational pattern of the full text, and an isomorphic summary of an essay with a causal pattern signals that pattern. Summary writers engaging in this kind of text-driven process choose to preserve the global patterns of the text, putting the content in a more compact but nevertheless similarly shaped package. They use authors' hierarchical placement to determine the relative importance of content, selecting the textually important material and deleting the more trivial and redundant information They adhere to the criterion that van Dijk (1979) called textual relevance, the same criterion that readers have often demonstrated in reading comprehension studies. In summarizing, we see the connection between organization and the selecting of content, as writers select what is most important structurally, most fitting to the text plan already established. Working through a text and deleting some content while preserving other content is an early-blooming strategy in summarizing, as demonstrated in research with writers as young as fifth graders. They use a copy–delete strategy when writing their summaries (A. L. Brown et al., 1983).

There are two important points to be made here about summaries. The first is that, even though the major task in producing summaries is to reduce the text, summarizing does involve generating. Summary writers *add* in the sense that they make inferences that become part of the summary. These inferences can be classified as two types, but both involve seeing commonalities and generating a larger, more inclusive item. One is inferring a superordinate concept to subsume items in a list, and the other is inferring a macroproposition to replace several propositions (A. L. Brown & Day, 1983; van Dijk, 1977, 1980). These generative operations are apparently more difficult to learn and perform than the selection and deletion operations, and they are rather late blooming, typically appearing in the summarizing of students in middle school or junior high (A. L. Brown et al., 1983). According to A. L. Brown and Day (1983), these connective kinds of operations are difficult for novice writers because they require writers to deviate most from copy–delete procedures. Inventing, which is much easier for experts than it is for novices, the researchers explained, requires writers to add instead of deleting or selecting what is already provided. And it is this use of invention that is the mark of effective summarization.

The second point is that, although many summaries fit this description of structural isomorphism, not all do. B. H. Smith (1980) discussed the diversity of gists that might be produced for a novel if it were summarized for different purposes and audiences, such as advertising it for potential buyers, deploring its sexism to a friend, or writing a critical biography of its author. Although all would simplify it and would delete some portions and emphasize others, these summaries would present different versions of the novel. In academic writing, there are different types of summaries shaped for particular purposes, contexts, and audiences, such as those summaries in indexes intended for people looking for particular kinds of information (Ratteray, 1985). And in scientific writing there is not only the "report in miniature" type of summary but also another type of summary indicating major topics included in the full text and serving as a kind of table of contents (Rathbone, 1972).

Particularly relevant to this discussion are summaries that are used rhetorically as components of a longer piece. Latour's (1987) studies of scholarly scientific writing suggest that writers sometimes make it appear that they are providing an isomorphic summary when, in fact, they restructure those texts and select content to accomplish their own purposes. In disciplinary writing texts are often "summarized" by means of a citation, and the kind of summary implied is a function of the context in which the citation appears. When citing that text, and thus summarizing it, a writer might also be, according to Weinstock (1971), paying homage, giving credit for related work, identifying methodology, providing background reading, correcting published work, criticizing published work, announcing forthcoming work, reporting poorly disseminated work, substantiating claims, authenticating data, and disputing priority claims (cf. Gilbert, 1977).

Reporting on a Topic

My own work has focused mainly on reporting, the presentation of different aspects of a topic for an audience. The discourse of reporting is quite common, particularly in educational settings (Armbruster, 1984), and reports are often produced, at least in part, by integrating material from several sources, using what other people have had to say on the topic. In my first two discourse-synthesis studies discussed in Chapter VI (cf. Spivey, 1984, 1992; Spivey & King, 1989, 1994), writers wrote topical reports organized as collections, as were the materials they read. The basis for organizing was topical, as writers noted repeated themes across texts and brought together the related material to create their own linear texts. The importance of making such topical connections as one reads a single text has been pointed out by a number of reading researchers (e.g., Kieras, 1985; R. F. Lorch, Jr., 1993), but identifying and linking topics is also a means of interrelating material associated with multiple texts. Writers identified recurring topics across texts, and they organized their own texts by combining the content on similar attributes. They were, it seems, creating chunks of topically related material and generating collection patterns. Their contributions came from providing an integrated presentation of the factual material, one text that cued the content selected from the composite offered by the sources.

The variability among texts was mainly in the manner in which a writer chose to order and combine content. In this way, each synthesis had the writer's structural stamp. For the armadillo topic, one writer might begin with classification, move to species, to habitat, to reproduction, and so on, whereas another might begin with habitat, move to diet, to reproduction, and so on. There was a quantitative difference associated with organization: the number of chunks of topically related content relative to the number of propositions cued. This variable, a ratio, seems to be a good predictor of quality ratings. In my studies, reports considered of higher quality were characterized by a more integrative presentation, with fewer chunks, or topical breaks, relative to quantity of content. Students, even as young as the sixth grade, seemed quite able to set up this kind of text using the same sort of collection pattern used by the older writers. The younger students tended to treat fewer topics and to say less about each topic, but their ratios of chunks to quantity were similar to those of older students and also similar to college students' performance in the previous study.

It is important to note that organizing is generative. What is generated is not only the overall pattern but also more specific inferences related to organization. Writers created larger topical chunks, for example, by inferring relations between topics. For instance, one writer inferred a connection between habitat and diet so that the two would become one more inclusive chunk. In the task study situated in a psychology class, students writing topical reports grouped together particular studies and particular researchers according to commonalities in topics as well as position on issues. Here, too, they inferred the relations.

These synthesis studies have focused, for the most part, on topical reports, but *reporting* seems to be a rather inclusive practice encompassing variable forms. In the task study, psychology students receiving the report task varied in the kinds of texts they produced. They seemed to have a variety of organizational options that were appropriate for the kind of paper called "report." For the reports there was no particular configuration the students produced that seemed to be preferred by the psychologist who rated the papers. Even the one paper critiquing instead of simply presenting the topic was received favorably. Most of the writers set up their reports according to topics, as students did in the report studies described above, and one set up his according to author, providing summaries of the authors' texts within his own text. For a number of writers, comparison became the dominant relation, and they set up their reports as comparisons, lining up researchers in two groups: those who supported Piaget and those who did not.

For reports set up as comparisons, the focus is on similarities and differences between two or more objects. In the comparison study (Spivey, 1991), writers generated the comparison patterns as they integrated content from informational texts organized as topical collections. To produce these reports, the writers had to reorder and recombine content and had to move the descriptive content to a lower level, to embed it in their comparison pattern. Again, writers used topics to create patterns, noting common themes across the two texts. And these became the aspects around which writers centered their descriptions in forming their comparisons. Most tended to discuss one aspect with respect to one object and then the other, to move to another aspect, which would be discussed with respect to both objects, and to move to another aspect, and so on.

Here, too, some writers generated inferences that affected organization. They inferred macro-aspects, larger topics that subsumed other topics, the sort of element that functions as a hypertheme. By generating these macro-aspects to portions of the text, writers achieved a more integrative presentation. The raters of these texts, like the raters of the topical reports, preferred texts that had fewer but more inclusive "chunks."

Proposing a Solution

Another practice involves offering solutions to problems (cf. Hoey, 1986). This might be the *presentation* of a particular solution in response to a problem, or it might instead be the *proposal* of a solution, which we shall consider here. In academic settings, the proposing of solutions as preliminary to solving problems is quite common for faculty performing their grantsmanship activities and students planning projects for courses or for theses and dissertations. In the "task study" situated in psychology, also discussed in Chapter VI, students receiving the proposal assignment were expected to produce a particular kind of text. The pattern was explicit in their assignment: "One unresolved problem . . . is that perspective-taking seems to be more delayed in writing than in speaking. Write a paper that considers this discrepancy and possible reasons for it and that proposes a good way to see if the difference in the two modalities is really there." Thus, writers were to develop a problem portion, presenting the discrepancy, and a solution part, proposing their solution. For the problem section, they summarized various researchers' findings relative to those of other researchers whose findings agreed or contrasted. For instance, Hoy's (1975) study might be "summarized" as a disagreement with Piaget's (1923/1932) egocentricity notion, or it might be "summarized" as an agreement with Glucksberg and Krauss (1967), or both. Particularly useful for the students with this assignment was the article by Kroll (1985), which was the only one that dealt specifically with writing, and, through that article, they were also able to bring in other studies that Kroll discussed.

The response to the problem was to be a means of determining whether or not there was a discrepancy, which in the context of psychology meant proposing a study. The inclusion of a proposed solution was the major factor influencing raters' judgment of quality. If a study was not proposed, the writer was considered to have left the task unfinished. Here, too, the articles were helpful. Some students suggested modifications of the methods used by these other researchers in their materials, procedure, or analyses.

A related study, conducted by Greene (1994, cf. 1993), compared undergraduates' writing of reports and proposals in another discipline, history. Here there was more consistency in the reports, as all seven writers given the report task produced topical collections focused on issues. Most students with the proposal assignment (six of eight) produced texts with a problem section followed by a solution section. For these proposals in history there were no set constituents for the solution, as there had been for the psychology proposals.

Critiquing: Commenting on a Topic

Another conventional practice in educational settings is critiquing, which involves presenting some representation of the object of critique and providing evaluative commentary about it. Critiquing is particularly important in the discipline of English, where it defines the large body of work known as literary criticism and the large number of people known as literary critics. In that discipline and others, critiques fill regulatory functions over other discourse and appear as reviews of new scholarly books, responses to published articles, and confidential reviews of submitted articles and proposals (cf. Myers, 1985a, 1985b). For students, too, critiquing seems to be a common practice in higher education (Bridgeman & Carlson, 1984). In the psychology task study the critique produced in response to the report assignment seemed quite acceptable. Critiquing is also, but probably to a lesser extent, a part of the practices in secondary and elementary education. Even young children write critiques, or protocritiques, when they prepare book reports, in which they typically summarize the text and tack on a commentary (cf. Durst, 1984). Critiques seem to have genre status not only in many different disciplinary communities but also in the wider mainstream culture, where we are quite accustomed to critiques of books, films, restaurants, and so on.

Through critiques, writers present two kinds of material: some kind of compressed version, or summary, of the text being critiqued and also some evaluative commentary about it. These can be thought of, respectively, as *topic,* what is being talked about, and *comment,* what is said about it. As such, they comprise the parts of the organizational pattern known as response. Critiques vary, as Mathison (1993) has pointed out, in the extensiveness of topical material relative to the extensiveness of commentary. Some critiques give emphasis to the topic and provide little commentary, and other critiques offer rather extensive commentary. (And then there are those that fall somewhere in between.) The writing of critiques was the focus of a recent study that Mathison conducted in a college course in the sociology of religion. The undergraduate students participating in the study critiqued an article on the topic of quasi religions, which their instructor had selected for them from an edited volume. Mathison analyzed the students' critiques in terms of response patterns, focusing on the ways in which they set up the critiqued text as the topic and provided their evaluative comments about it. These comments were either positive or negative and were backed up with either disciplinary or personal means of support.

Mathison was interested in what features would be valued by subject-matter experts, professors of sociology. She and her co-analysts had categorized the critiques according to which of the patterns in Figure 1 they resembled more closely. Some were more like the pattern on the left with an integrated configuration, and others were more like the pattern on the right with a separate configuration for topic and comment. Besides this dichotomous measure for organization, the other measures were for quantity of content, extensiveness of negative commentary, and extensiveness of disciplinary supports for commentary. When she used various text features as predictors of quality ratings by subject-matter experts, Mathison found that organizational configuration was a good predictor of those ratings provided by the sociologists. As might be expected, the sociology professors reading the critiques for quality gave higher ratings to those fitting the type illustrated on the left in Figure 1 (which had a brief orienting topical summary but an extensive evaluative commentary about selected subtopics) than to those fitting the type of critique illustrated on the right (which had an extensive treatment of the topic and little evaluative commentary). The configuration was important but so was extensiveness of negative commentary and disciplinary supports, which seemed often to co-occur with it. After the ratings, when interviewed individually, the raters reported that they were looking for an evaluative disposition as well as an understanding of the text.

What evaluative disposition translated to, when one examines the relationship of various text variables to the quality ratings, was not only presenting the more integrated sort of pattern but also providing negative commentary backed up with disciplinary means of support. The sociologists were looking for the generation of material that was evaluative in nature. These three features in concert were good predictors of the quality ratings. In contrast, the type of critique that these raters disliked for this writing assignment in sociology was what might be called a "response statement." This type of text is organized, like the critique, with a topic–comment sort of patterning, but a different sort of commentary is offered about the topic. Typically there is some sort of summary of the text followed by commentary in which the writer relates some aspect of the material to his or her own experience.

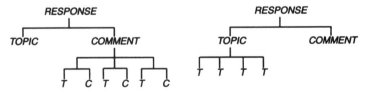

Figure 1. Patterns of critiquing.

The response statement, which is often a predominant form of discourse in literature classes, did not work well for this sociology class.

Making a Causal Argument

The final kind of practice to be considered here is the making of a causal argument, which has also received some research attention. Following G. E. Newell's (1984) initial study of writing and learning, Durst (1987) and Langer and Applebee (1987) investigated the transformations that writers make when they use narratives in writing causal arguments. Durst (1987) gave writers a task that involved either summarizing the text or writing an essay focusing on a particular aspect of the topic of the text. In either case writers used a text from a history textbook that was organized in chronological fashion; the topic was either the Great Depression or the McCarthy Era. The summary task was rather straightforward, simply asking them to summarize, and the essay task asked a writer to explain what he or she thought was the main lesson (which was an economic lesson for one text and a political lesson for the other text) to be learned from the events discussed in what they had read. The latter task also included defending points with evidence and excerpts from the reading.

Texts produced in response to the summary task were organized in chronological fashion, replicating the pattern of the text read, but those written in response to the essay task were set up differently, often, it seems, as causal arguments. The following excerpt is an example of the sort of stance taken: "One important cause of the crash was overproduction. This was because there was an excessive production of goods. So the prices fell, the profits decreased, unemployment grew." Many writers merely stated what they believed was the most important lesson to be learned without providing much support and then moved into a summary of the relevant portion of the text. The major transformation performed by essay writers occurred in their generation of a new organizing pattern into which they could fit relevant textual material. Langer and Applebee (1987), who produced similar findings, noted that summary writing tends to involve a superficial treatment of the entire text, whereas the writing of arguments involves more in-depth treatment of a particular portion.

Causal arguments were also produced by a number of the students given the proposal assignment in the psychology task study discussed in Chapter VI. Instead of proposing a study to provide answers about a possible cause, these students argued that a particular cause or set of causes was responsible. These arguments, which did not meet the expectations of the professors who rated them, provided an interesting contrast to the proposals, which did meet the professors' expectations. Through their causal arguments these students were arguing that a particular "known" cause was responsible, or particular "known" causes were responsible, for an effect. That was a different rhetorical stance than the stance taken by the proposal writers who presented themselves as not having that kind of knowledge and as proposing a study to gain it.

Selective Transformations

When performing these kinds of reading–writing acts, writers perform some transformations that are selective. They give preferential attention to some material, which they consider relevant for inclusion in their own texts. Sometimes they leave traces of the selective process in their markings, such as brackets, asterisks, stars, and underlinings, and in their notes (Kennedy, 1985; Spivey, 1984, 1991; Spivey & King, 1989). They use some principle or principles of relevance as they make selections. What are these relevance principles that writers use? What makes some content emerge as figure and other content fade into the ground?

Criteria: Textual and Otherwise

Studies of reading comprehension have provided many evidences of one criterion that people use when they read, the criterion of *textual relevance* (van Dijk, 1979), employed when readers attempt to follow a writer's cues to hierarchy and to staging. This is also the criterion that writers use when they produce what I call isomorphic summaries. In addition to this textual criterion, there also appears to be a kind of *intertextual relevance* for particular material when writers use multiple texts to present general information on a topic. The writers in my first discourse synthesis studies (Spivey, 1984, 1992) were selective regarding content, including on the average only about a third of the units offered. Writers apparently did much selecting on the basis of repetition across texts as well as placement in the textual hierarchies, especially the writers who were the better readers. The writers were more likely, for instance, to include a unit that was signaled by all three texts but played a moderately important role structurally in each, than to include a unit that was staged prominently in the hierarchy of a single text. In the developmental study (Spivey & King, 1989, 1994) younger students in secondary school also seemed to use an intertextual criterion.

A related criterion, also intertextual, is relevance to the particular configuration of meaning being constructed for the new text. We saw this criterion most clearly in the comparison study, where writers seemed to employ a *symmetry principle,* choosing parallel content for the two objects being compared.

And there are also social bases, as when particular texts or particular sorts of content are used to align oneself with certain people (e.g., Myers, 1985a) or when

they are used to have a particular effect on some audience. Cochran (1993) suggested the term *rhetorical relevance* for the use of particular texts or portions of texts
for particular audiences. And Many, Fyfe, Lewis, and Mitchell (1996), in a recent
study in Scotland, identified some children who were particularly sensitive to rhetorical relevance as they wrote from multiple texts over an extended period of time
to prepare reports. They selected material they thought would be appropriate for
their audience and attempted to make it accessible to them.

Selection and Generation

Texts produced by transforming other texts seem to be composed of two kinds of
material: some that is replicated (and usually paraphrased) from the texts that are
read and some that is added. Such mixing can be "seen" when the written material
is analyzed against a template for propositions and relations cued by texts. Generated
material not tied to the prior texts might be called *invented* (a term used by writing
people that goes back to classical rhetoric) or might be called *inferred* or *elaborated*
(terms used by reading people). It is difficult to make distinctions among the three
labels because one must make judgments as to how distant the content is from what
is considered explicitly cued. *Invented* might seem to be more distant than *elaborated,*
and *elaborated* more distant than *inferred,* but, to avoid such complications, one might
simply say *added*.

   It is important to remember, however, that all the content is really added, as
readers generate it on the basis of cues and it is not *in* the texts that were read. It is
also important to remember that, in a sense, the "added" material, too, can be
intertextual, because it, too, has links to prior experiences with other texts. Some
people might consider material that does not match up with textual content to be
"new," but in a sense it is older, at least to the person doing the generating, than
what has been generated in response to the text being read. It is inferred on the
basis of prior knowledge.

   If the texts being read cue ample content to meet the demands of the task, the
writer may not add much except what is needed for connectivity and organization.
In the two studies by Durst (1987) and Langer and Applebee (1987), high school
students added little to what a social studies text offered whether they were writing
summaries or causal essays. However, a difference between texts for the summary
task and essay task lay in the particular portion of the text used. For the summaries,
the writers made use of the entire text but did not go into depth about any portion,
and for the essays, the writers made use of a particular portion and did go into depth
about it. In my first two studies of report writing, writers relied mainly on the
published texts as they wrote informational reports for mature readers. Even
when they had fairly extensive topic knowledge, writers added content mainly to
provide the connective links, mentioned earlier, between clusters of content. Their

inventions (inferences), which led to a more integrated treatment, had some similarity to the inventions people make to produce integrated summaries (A. L. Brown & Day, 1983; van Dijk, 1977). And even when they restructured discourse in the comparison study, writers did not elaborate much. They often appeared to generate content to balance with the source material, as when one text provided a piece of information about one of the subjects of the comparison and the other text did not have parallel information about the other subject. For example, whereas the Squid Text discussed the squid's aggressiveness, the Octopus Text did not explicitly discuss whether or not the octopus was aggressive, although it did mention that the octopus tended to live a solitary life. As mentioned earlier, some writers inferred that the octopus was not aggressive and included that information to contrast with what they were saying about the squid.

Task Interpretations

In performing these acts some writers seem to defer to the authority of the texts and other writers seem to assume more authority themselves. This difference was noted, for example, by Hartman (1991) in his study of the reading of multiple literary texts, and more recently by Many et al. (1996) in students' report writing. It was also noted by McGinley (1992), who videotaped and audiotaped college students thinking aloud as they read some texts about a controversial issue and wrote arguments for a way to resolve the issue. The texts they read were two articles about mandatory drug testing, both organized as comparisons presenting pro and con regarding the issue. Striking contrasts in approach were noted among the students, and those approaches were reflected in their writing. For instance, one student seemed to deal almost exclusively with others' ideas as presented by the texts. Even though she started out with a position (con) on the issue, most of her sentences began with such acknowledgments as "many people see it," "some people believe . . . others feel," "others may see it as," "some feel," "those in favor believe." Not until the last two sentences did she state her own (pro) position, which was a change from the position she took initially. Her think-aloud protocols showed her changing her mind several times over the course of reading and finally taking a rather weak pro position. As she wrote her paper, she relied extensively on the sources, using them to get material for her paper. The other student ended up with a rather forceful solution to the mandatory drug problem: basing it on a notion of fairness. After presenting the problem and acknowledging the major positions, she devoted almost half of her paper to her solution, pulling the "authorities" in to support points she made. Her think-aloud protocols showed a different approach than that taken by the other student. As she read the texts, she noted the conflict among the positions but, instead of being convinced by one or the other, she spent some time mentally working out her position and generating her argument. Whereas the first student did more deferring to authority, the second did more assuming of authority herself. In an earlier study, Flower et al. (1990) also found differences among writers in the extent to which they deferred to others or assumed authority themselves.

Students' interpretations of their tasks not only differ among themselves, but also can differ from their instructors'. Greene's (1994) study, mentioned earlier, compared the interpretations that the students and the historians made of the task to write a proposal or a report. Before they began work on their papers, Greene had students verbalize their impressions of the task they had been given, and he also elicited impressions from three historians, including the instructor of the course. When he compared the impressions, Greene found the two groups agreed that the proposal task required a writer to assume the role of decision maker in developing an argument, while being accountable to the sources. However, he found that the groups did not agree on the report task. The professors expected a writer to assume authority by creating a causal section at the beginning explaining why he or she had chosen a particular set of issues as most relevant. In contrast, the students did not see their task in this way, but instead saw it as deferring to the authority of the sources. It was no surprise then that they did not generate that causal section.

Much the same thing had been noted earlier by J. Nelson (1990) in her inquiry into task interpretations, reported in an article she titled "This Was an Easy Assignment" (a quotation from one of the participants). One of the classroom cases she studied was a freshman-level orientation course in engineering for which students read articles and heard presentations on topics in that field. Of particular interest to Nelson was one assignment that the professor gave the students: to prepare a concise argument (no more than 200 words) from the texts, written and oral, they had experienced. This professor thought that he had developed a difficult assignment: Students would have to boil down the information to develop a concise argument and weigh the value of each word they included. He expected the students to do that kind of integrative inventing that A. L. Brown and Day (1983) said can be so challenging in the writing of summaries. However, in this case these students would do it across multiple texts, as writers had to do in my studies.

However, the students performing the task revealed, through oral interviews with Nelson and through reading–writing logs they kept, that their perceptions of the assignment were different from that of their instructor. They perceived it as a centonistic task of reiterating and putting together major points made by others. As one student put it:

> This was an easy assignment. All you had to do was reiterate what you'd read. I picked lots of names and cited important sounding incidents. . . . Essentially I paraphrased the reports I read. I think this assignment was another case of the instructor trying to have us learn through reiteration of read[ing] material. (p. 362)

Another student explained that she simply skimmed the articles looking for "blurbs about the topic" (p. 380).

Of course, generation of content also depends on one's knowledge that is relevant to the topic. Ackerman (1991) asked graduate students, some majoring in psychology and some in business, to write their own texts on a topic that was either in or out of their discipline. The psychology topic, dealt with by some students in each major, was rehearsal in memory; and the business topic, also dealt with by some in each major, was supply-side economics. For use in their writing, participants had excerpts from book chapters. They were asked to write an essay presenting and explaining their understanding of the topic and to base the essay on the passages *and* their "own ideas" on the topic. As might be expected, the extensiveness of their "own ideas" was a function of whether students were dealing with a topic in or out of their discipline. Those students reading and writing in their discipline made more elaborations when reading, as shown in think-aloud protocols. In addition, their written essays also revealed the effects of prior knowledge: more added material (not traceable to the texts that were read) at more prominent points in their essays. The staging of this generated material suggested that students assumed more authority to make major claims when writing on a topic in their field.

Form as Heuristic

Some of the studies reviewed thus far in this chapter illustrate the heuristic function of form (cf. Coe, 1987; D'Angelo, 1975). This was demonstrated years ago in Frederiksen's (1972, 1975a) study discussed earlier. A particular kind of task, such as the problem-solving task that Frederiksen gave his subjects, can invite a particular form, a configuration that creates a space to be filled in a particular way, and, for a text to "fit" the communicative context, it must fill the space. His subjects, who were writers as well as comprehenders, were producing discourse with a problem-solution pattern: They had to generate solutions to the problem posed by the text that they read.

For a meaning to "fit" the communicative context, it must fill the space perceived by people engaging in communication. Spaces are opened when such tasks as comparing, proposing, and critiquing are interpreted, and they are filled in as the tasks are performed, not in a mechanicial way but through active transformation and generation. If relevant material may be gained from reading, writers may select and transform content from their understanding of those texts to fill the spaces. If that is not the case, writers may generate content to fill the form if they have a knowledge base that allows them to do so and if they see their task as requiring that kind of pattern. (But they may also choose to search for other texts.) In this global sense, then, form can be heuristic. The studies seemed to show, in writing comparisons, writers generated content to fill in the empty portions of the symmetrical pattern, and, in producing critiques, they generated comments to fill the slots they created. In writing research proposals, some writers filled in the gaps in the solution portion, but other students either were not knowledgeable enough about research design to produce a detailed study or did not interpret their task as requiring the proposed study. They tended to create causal arguments instead.

These notions about form as heuristic relate to Bartlett's (1923, 1958) gap-filling metaphor. Bartlett, as mentioned earlier, saw his own writing as a matter of perceiving gaps and then coming up with material to fill them, sometimes by going to others and sometimes by developing ideas that might be called "his own."

This notion seems to have relevance for reading as well, particularly in respect to the critical reading of a text. When reading texts suggesting conventional patterns, readers sense the opening of rhetorical spaces. If the spaces are not filled, the text seems incomplete or inadequate. For example, in the task study, the psychologists reading the proposals had expectations set up by the first portion, which problematized the issue and established a need for a proposed study in the second portion. If the solution was inadequately developed and did not balance with the problem portion, their expectations were not met. The situation was much as it is in a conversation when a problem is posed and a space is created for a solution. There is an awkwardness that results when the space is left unfilled.

Connective Transformations

To form meaning that is internally coherent, writers make various kinds of connections when integrating material from texts they read. It happens in summarizing a single text as items are integrated to create more generalized statements, called macropropositions. It happens in synthesizing across texts as material, such as topical items or positions, as relations are generated and items are brought together.

Topical Connections

These connections include topical connections, which, in the case of multiple texts, are made across texts as well as within texts (cf. Walker & Meyer, 1980). In my report studies, writers inferred topical relations across texts, brought that material together, and made it fit for their readers. For example, when comparing the octopus and the squid, one writer created the following topical chunk about protective devices: "Both have the ability to protect themselves from predators. Each can change colors for camouflage, and each expels an inky substance when alarmed. The substance anesthetizes the predator and confuses it to help the octopus and squid escape." The writer brought together the information about color change and ink, which had been mentioned in both of the articles, but extended the notions of camouflage, anesthetizing, and escape, which had been mentioned only for the octopus, to the squid. These were inferences made in respect to the squid. In writing about the armadillo, one writer created a chunk on the topic of "interesting things about armadillos" that began "So the armadillo is a very interesting animal." Included were the Mayan Indians' believing that vultures turned into armadillos (mentioned in the *Americana* article) and the South Americans' considering armadillos a delicacy (mentioned in the *McGraw-Hill* article), as well as Texans' selecting the armadillo as their state animal (added). And yet another writer created a chunk on "service and disservice" to man, including as service their eating termites (all the articles) and their being eaten by South Americans (mentioned in the *Americana* article) and as disservice their being a host for Chagas disease (mentioned in the *McGraw-Hill* article).

Sometimes writers brought material together but did not provide (and perhaps did not generate) all the linking material that was needed. The writing that resulted was not well connected for a reader. Consider this rather confusing pair of sentences: "Armadillos tend to be frightened of man and other large predators. For this, the animals are equipped with a long third toe." The writer must have inferred the first portion from the *Encyclopedia Americana* article, which stated that armadillos are timid, and must have inferred the second portion from the *Collier's* article, which stated in the description of *Priodontes,* that "the third toe on its forefoot is armed with a great sicklelike claw used to tear rotten logs or to rip apart termite nests" (p. 661). From the latter, the writer apparently made two inferences: first, that the clawed toe was used for protecting oneself as well as for getting food and, second, that other armadillos besides *Priodontes* had this toe. With this sort of inferencing, there would be a connection between having the toe and protecting itself. But the connections would probably not be clear for readers. At least they were not for those who rated the text for connectivity. Is the toe for protection? How does the armadillo use this toe for protection?

Connectivity seemed to be the aspect of writing that presented the most difficulty for the younger students in the developmental study. They brought together related material, but quite often did not transform the material adequately to provide connective flow. They did not cue relations between the propositions they chose from the different sources, perhaps because they did not do all the necessary inferencing themselves or perhaps because they did not know how to transform others' ideas and provide connections. Bakhtin (1981) described texts, in general, as heteroglossic, or multivoiced, in that the words, phrases, and ideas have come from numerous other people (cf. Wolf & Hicks, 1989). However, what these younger students wrote, in a number of cases, remained *too much* in the voices of the various authors whose texts they used, a phrase from this one, two or three sentences from that one, and lacked an authorial voice providing the needed connections for the readers. To use Bakhtin's words, they had not "appropriated" the material, had not put it in their own "dialects." Here, again, we have that notion of assuming authority versus deferring to authority.

Whole-Text Connections

In the task study, the psychology students made rather large-scale intertextual inferences that involved whole texts. These were inferences about the alignment of the authors according to their positions on particular issues. The writers responding to the report and proposal assignments brought together researchers through either an inferred agreement or an inferred disagreement, and used them as a means of arranging content. For the most part these researchers were the six authors of texts they read for the assignment, but a few, including Piaget, were authors whose work was summarized by those authors. A number of report writers lined up these authors as to whether they agreed or disagreed with another author, Piaget. The dashed lines in Figure 2 illustrate the intertextual connections—the intertextual inferences—made by one of these writers, and the dark lines illustrate the crosscitations that were explicit in the set of texts. The texts by Piaget and Mead, cited by some of the authors, are left uncolored to distinguish them from texts students read for the task. The texts by Maratsos and Lloyd, also left uncolored, had been discussed by Donaldson, and it was Donaldson's summaries within her own text that the student read.

Text, Intertext, and Hypertext

These kinds of across-text connections are much the same as those made when people operate in hypertext computer environments. The hypertext concept is often attributed to Bush (1945), who devised a flexible means of keeping up with research through nonlinear connections, although the term was later coined by T. H. Nelson (1965). In talk about hypertext today (e.g., Landow, 1994) there is much figurative language that emphasizes the reader's movement, terms such as *navigation, traversal,* and *jump,* often reminiscent of Wittgenstein's (1945–1949/1973) comparison of writing to a crisscross kind of journey across a field that can be explored in various ways, not simply along a single path. McGinley and Tierney (1989) applied the landscape metaphor to reading–writing tasks in which students pursue their own topics, which they traverse in crisscross fashion.

    In performing these literacy acts I have described, people make across-text linkages and topical jumps, and they generate relations from one text to another as they make their transformations. The kinds of intertextual connections that are so visible when people work in hypertext environments are the kinds of transformations that we have been considering in this chapter. A difference, of course, is that

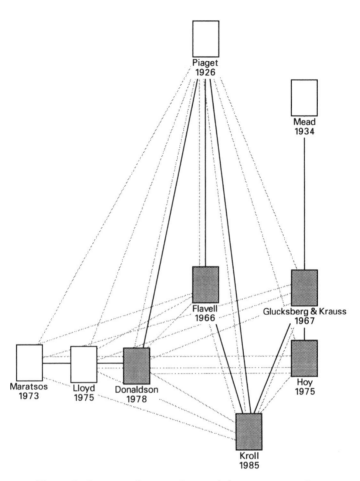

Figure 2. Intertextual connections made by one report writer.

there has not been a programmer who built the interconnecting links into the database, and writers (readers) have to generate such links themselves, making such inferences as "This supports . . . ," "This adds to . . . ," and "This contradicts . . . ." It is not just in a hypertext computer environment that people do this relating and embedding, as Spiro, Feltovich, Jacobson, and Coulson (1995) have also noted. It happens with conventional texts and in conventional tasks as well. In making their case for "cognitive flexibility theory," Spiro et al. have demonstrated the cognitive benefits that can come from such crisscrossing and from experiencing related material in different texts or other semiotic materials.

Conclusion: Readers as Writers

As we have seen, when readers are writers using others' texts to create their own, they make transformations that are not so apparent in other kinds of reading, because in these hybrid acts writers read to construct different meanings in their particular situational context. Sometimes these transformations consist only of reordering and recombining within global patterns similar to those cued by the text, and other times the transformations entail generating a different kind of organizational pattern. When readers are writers, they make selections and generate other material on such bases as intertextual relevance and symmetry that are relevant to the new text that is being created. And when readers are writers, they make various kinds of global inferences as they bring "subject matter to subject matter," to use Bartlett's (1958) phrase. This bringing together does result in constructiveness, the generation of inferences as well as new patterns.

Chapter VIII

· ·

Authoring Identity

There is not author without first a concept of personal property and hence of person.

— Francoise Meltzer, *Hot Property*

Are we for ever to be twisting and untwisting the same rope?

— Laurence Sterne, *Tristram Shandy*

My topic here is *authoring identity,* the identification of a person (or pair or team) as the author of particular work and the identification of work with a particular author. Authoring identities are established for producers of various kinds of texts, most notably literary texts and disciplinary texts, but also other creations such as musical, cinematic, artistic, or architectural. Gabriel García Márquez, Jane Austin, James Taylor, Georgia O'Keefe, David Pearson, Oliver Stone, Janet Emig, Joan Miró, Mies van der Rohe, Donna Karan, and Antonio Gaudí are all known for particular bodies of work. A corpus identified with a particular author has a perceived sameness among its constituents; they are identifiable in some way. It also has a perceived sameness with the work of some other people, but, despite the similarity, it is also unique, differentiated from that work. That is where the tension has been in respect to authoring identity: the author's similarity to others and the author's distinctiveness from others. This chapter develops this constructivist conception of authorship, with respect to written texts, which was introduced in the first chapters and which incorporates many of the other notions that have also been presented: textual transformations, topical links across texts, and social connections from one author to another. After a historical review of some other conceptions of authorship, more detail is provided for the constructivist conception guiding this book. Finally, that conception is illustrated with a longitudinal inquiry into identity construction that Maureen Mathison and I conducted and are reporting in more detail elsewhere. It is from the Writing from Academic Sources Project for the Center for the Study of Writing and Literacy at the University of California, Berkeley, and Carnegie Mellon University.

Changing Conceptions of Authorship over the Years

An author is known for his or her work, and texts can be attributed to a particular author. That would be all we might need to say about authoring identity if there were not certain interesting complications: that authors are also readers who transform others' texts and that authors are social beings who produce their work in a social fashion. At this point we will consider how authoring identity has been conceptualized through the years, and how such complications have been treated.

The Medieval Author

Before the printing press, much literature was communal and oral and was not tied to a particular author, as tales were told and retold, and transformed in the telling. However, some important texts were preserved in written manuscripts, often from generation to generation, as they were reproduced by scribes. And some, by no means all, of these manuscripts had named authors. During the middle ages, the manuscript texts with named authors were considered "authentic" and were privileged in the culture. According to Minnis (1984), *author* was "an accolade" given to a popular writer by scholars who came later and who used the author's texts as models, lectured on them, or quoted from them. But even those named as authors did much borrowing and sharing, and the named authors were not always the ones who generated material for the texts attributed to them. After it had been around for some time, a popular text, even one that was a communal product of unknown origin, could be attributed to a favorite author, even if there was little to support that attribution. To people of that time, if it was a valuable text, it had an author. Thus, even before the printing press, there was an identity of a text with an author, at least for some texts, and a named author had a kind of authority.

There was much sharing, borrowing, and imitation, and the author did not own the text. Not only did authors borrow from one another, but scribes and readers got in the act, too. Scribes often made changes in the wording from one manuscript to another as they made new copies, and this was something that authors knew was likely to happen. In addition, scribes sometimes also provided glosses in the margins, giving guidance as to how a text should be read. And then readers from one generation to another added their own glosses, which might be about the text or about another person's gloss, perhaps a correction of what someone else had said. Dagenais (1994), in his historical treatment of glosses, described glossing as a "dialogue across generations, miles, and cultures" (p. 36). A particular reader would read not only the writer's text but also what other readers through the years had to say about it, what they thought was important. And that reader might, in turn, write his or her own opinions or provide commentary from a teacher or from another book. Sometimes these glosses would be interlinear, and the text and the gloss would eventually merge as subsequent copies were made.

Authorship after the Printing Press

The dialogue in the margins, the transformations of authors' works, and the blending of authors' words and readers' interpretations *seemed* to stop with the printing press. With the printing press, authorship came to be conceived more in terms of individual ownership and originality. An author was now seen as someone who originates the material (it is original with that person) and who "owns" it, or in the case of co-authors, co-owns it with that other person or those other people. A particular text became an author's individual property. As Mallon (1990) put it, "The Writer, a new professional was invented by a machine. Suddenly his capital and identity were at stake" (p. 4). During the Renaissance there was growing concern about theft of one's property, and authors began using their prefaces for self-authorization (Dunn, 1994). The seventeenth and eighteenth centuries were marked by assertions of authorship and ownership, and there were accusations and scandals concerning people's stealing ideas and words from others. Attempts were made to define what was and was not theft, which was rather difficult to do because imitation was then, as it had been before and still is now, such a large part of writing, and because writers read the works of other writers. The term *plagiarism,* which had been used for kidnapping, came to be used for literary theft, and it entered the dictionaries in the mid-eighteenth century.

One scandal recounted by Mallon (1990) was that of Sterne (1779/1925) and his *Tristram Shandy,* the book that would later be so admired by the Russian formalist Shklovsky (1921/1965b) and that seems so postmodern today. This massive work incorporated numerous passages that were changed only slightly from other writers' texts, especially Burton's (1651/1852) *The Anatomy of Melancholy.* One replicated passage was even about plagiarism. Burton had said:

> As apothecaries, we make new mixtures every day, pour out of one vessel into another; and as those old Romans robbed all the cities of the world, to set out their bad-sited Rome, we skim off the cream of other men's wits, pick the choice flowers off their tilled gardens to set out our own sterile plots. . . . We weave the same web still, twist the same rope again and again. (p. 19)

Sterne's (1779/1925) version in *Tristram Shandy* was as follows:

> Shall we for ever make new books, as apothecaries make new mixtures, by pouring only out of one vessel into another?

> Are we for ever to be twisting, and untwisting the same rope? for ever in the
> same track—for ever at the same pace? (p. 175)

Although there were accusations during Sterne's lifetime, a scandal erupted after his
death despite his defenders' arguments that the borrowings were playful and intentional. Ferrier (1798/1974), in a piece of literary detective work, conducted micro-
analyses and located numerous instances of replication with little transformation.

The Romantic Conception

The Romantic Period was marked by glorification of the author, as Abrams (1953)
has shown in his detailed treatment. Authors were seen as gifted individuals, natural
geniuses, who had special, sometimes divine inspiration, and this was a conception
to which the authors themselves contributed, as they glorified the work of authors
in general or of one author in particular or described their own creative process.
For example, Coleridge (1817/1907) described poets' emotional depth and the
energy of their thought, and Wordsworth (1805/1974) described their "more than
usual organic sensibility" (p. 72). The Romantics offered an idealized conception of
who an individual author was and how a text was created solely by that individual
in a process that was likened to growth of a plant. But, when it came to practice,
they, too, did much reading of other authors' works. There was much imitation and
"borrowing," and some seemed to cross the plagiarism line. For instance, persistent
questions were asked about the similarities between Coleridge's philosophical writing and the writing of Schelling and other German philosophers. It seems that
Coleridge was a very active reader. Not only did he make copious notes in the
margins of books, but he also kept a notebook in which he took notes from his
reading and made notes for his writing. It is possible that he did not keep straight
what was "his" and what was "others'."

The idea of author as unique, special, and original person, as single originator
of a literary work, was reified in the literary studies that followed the Romantic
Period. The late eighteenth century began the biographical approach to literature
that dominated literary studies until the early part of the twentieth century and
continues in many settings today as the traditional approach. Some scholars through
the years, however, have conducted "source-based" studies, tracing links from one
text to another and influences of one author on another author.

Deemphasis of the Author

Although author-based interpretation was (and still is) influential in many contexts,
some major movements in literary studies—New Criticism, reader response, and
poststructuralism—were attempts to break the strong identity of a text with an

author and to undermine the authority of the author. The New Criticism (which began its influence in the 1930s and peaked during the 1950s), can be seen as an attempt to wrest attention away from the author to the literary text. What was important to the New Critics was not the author's intention or the reader's response but the text itself, and the text of choice was often a poem to be studied—*closely* studied (Brooks, 1947). Attending too much to the author was called "the intentional fallacy" (Wimsatt & Beardsley, 1946), and attending too much to the reader was called "the affective fallacy" (Beardsley & Wimsatt, 1949).

Reader response theory, which came in the 1970s, elevated the reader—the individual reader—to the source of meaning and kept the author in the background (Bleich, 1975, 1978; Fish, 1970; Holland, 1968, 1975a, 1975b; Rosenblatt, 1978). For instance, in Holland's (1975b) theory, the reader was the originator of meaning, and it was the reader's identity, not the author's, that influenced the nature of the meaning. Numerous studies of readers' responses have dealt with the reading of literary texts, particularly fiction and poetry, and have addressed such questions as how the readers relate what they read to their own experience and how they feel about what they read (reviewed by Beach & Hynds, 1991). Several different categorical schemes have been developed to classify the various responses (e.g., Purves & Rippere, 1968).

At about the same time that reader response theorists challenged the literary conception of author, the poststructuralists, whose work was discussed previously, also challenged the authority of the author. Barthes (1968/1977) and Kristeva (1967/1986, 1968), for example, eliminated the author as the source of meaning, as mentioned in a previous chapter. Echoing Nietzsche's pronouncement of the death of God, Barthes declared the death of the "author–god" and announced the end to a single, predetermined meaning for a text. By undermining the notion of author, these poststructuralists were undermining ideology, since the traditional conception of author was considered a function of ideology. As to a source for writing, the poststructuralists pointed not to author but to intertextuality, relations among texts and the traces of other texts that are a part of any writing. Writing was seen as autonomous, disconnected from a particular author and from determinate meaning. Most poststructuralists would see as senseless any scholarly attempts to identify particular authors as sources of those traces, since one source would be influenced by another, which would be influenced by another, and so on.

The Rebirth of the Author

Authoring identity, the target of attack by some literary theorists, has received more positive attention in other quarters: sociology of knowledge, sociology of science, philosophy of science, and social psychology, as well as the study of rhetoric, which has since classical times considered author–audience relations. The focus in this work is a disciplinary author, often a scientist or social scientist, who engages in a social process, reads the writings of others, builds on their ideas, and "belongs" to a group or to groups of people who do similar work.

As discussed previously, these disciplinary groups and subgroups are often called communities or even discourse communities because, to a great extent, it is their discourses, the topics that are talked or written about and the conventions for speaking or writing about those topics, that define and differentiate them (Bizzell, 1982; Porter, 1986). The members of a particular community are seen as similar, as having a common identity. They share *ways,* which include common interests, common philosophical orientations, a common literature, and a common "language." And they share assumptions about what is valuable and what is "true." They are involved in a collective endeavor, and, if a global kind of perspective is taken on their work, a particular community can be seen as a single collective author, creating and constraining its literature. But if the focus is on activity of individuals within the group, members can be seen writing their texts in a highly social fashion, reading each others' work, commenting on drafts, and so on, as illustrated in Reither and Vipond's (1989) study, described earlier.

All this seems quite different from the solitary process attributed to literary authors. However, some recent accounts of literary authorship, such as that by Stillinger (1991) on "the myth of solitary genius," suggest that, like disciplinary writing, that practice often involves much reading of other authors' work and much sharing (cf. D. Brown, 1991). Joyce Carol Oates (1973), who has a certain kind of authority on the topic of literary authors, as she is one herself, has made the argument that literary authors have much in common with scientists. This is the way she put it:

> Scientists have always known and acknowledged their dependence upon one another. . . . The complex of theories and facts that goes by the term science is a vast, collective venture, running parallel with civilization itself, and not even a maddened scientist would imagine that he, alone, had achieved anything significant. Immense bibliographies are appended to all books of a nonfiction type, in which the author acknowledges his dependence upon everyone. Works of fiction never contain bibliographies: they would be too lengthy, perhaps, but most of all they are just not traditional. The creative artist is told that he is original, highly individual, solitary, and that his successes and failures are totally his. . . . If I were to suggest, in utter seriousness, that my fiction is the creation of thousands upon thousands of processes of consciousness, synthesized somehow in me, I would be greeted with astonishment or disbelief, or dismissed as being "too modest." (pp. 74–75)

She may be overstating her case in several respects, saying, for instance, that scientific authors credit "everyone," when there is evidence that they can be selective about their crediting (e.g. Myers, 1985a). And she does not mention the mechanism, which seems well established, by which literary authors can and do give some credit—the acknowledgments. In her brief essay Oates did not get into the details of either kind of writing, but she did make a point about the social nature of literary authorship and its parallels with disciplinary writing.

A recent event in the literary world gives evidence of the social nature of much literary authorship. According to a front-page story in *The New York Times* (Honan, 1996), an elegy printed in 1612 has just recently been attributed to Shakespeare, and that attribution has been accepted, it seems, by many Shakespearean scholars. Foster, the scholar who identified the poem as Shakespeare's was not particularly successful in his first attempt in 1989, which was based on stylistic idiosyncracies associated with Shakespeare, for instance using "who" instead of "which" or "that." However, Foster was able to persuade many this time through a computer analysis of words. First, he created a database indexing all the rather rare words, such as "widow" as a verb and adjectives such as "abandoned" and "unprevailing," that appear 12 or fewer times in Shakespeare's plays. He then compared a computer analysis of the elegy with Shakespeare's recognized work published in the same period, and also compared analyses of the elegy with the works of other authors who published at about that same time. Such analyses revealed that the author of the elegy and Shakespeare had used the same rare words too often to be coincidence, and were thus the same person. And, of particular relevance to the point I am making here, the rare words could be traced to particular readings that both the unknown author and Shakespeare were engaging in at the time. Uses of such expressions as "seeled dove," "concourse," and "partage" suggested that both had been reading Sidney's (c. 1590/1599) "Arcadia" and Cary's (c. 1610/1613) "The Tragedy of Mariam" as well as a certain French–English dictionary.

In disciplinary writing, transforming other writers' texts is valued and sanctioned (that is, if they are transformed enough, but not *too* transformed and are credited properly). Authors select relevant material from their reading of other authors' texts, which may mean summarizing major points or selecting something that was not given much prominence by the other author, or may mean synthesizing across various texts. They cite related work conducted by others, often using those citations rhetorically (Cronin, 1984), as they write their own texts and attempt to get them included in the communal literature so that they, too, can be cited, summarized, and transformed.

What, then, about *originality* if writing involves so much use of prior texts? It seems that, to get in print, disciplinary authors must have something "new" to say, but they can have difficulty getting their work published and accepted if it is *too* new. Originality is valued, but, as Mulkay (1972) pointed out, this value is conditional in that a piece must contribute to the "predictable extension of knowledge" (p. 18). It must be presented and interpreted relative to others' work. Mulkay concluded from his studies that there tends to be a bias against radical shifts of perspective and a bias for gradual accumulation of knowledge within accepted ways of knowing. Is the situation at all similar for literary writing? At first glance, it seems quite different, as, generally speaking, literary authors do not do much explicit summarizing of prior work and do not make such obvious connections to others' work. However, authors considered to be part of a particular group or school do repeat themes and discourse features, and some literary authors make noticeable transformations of others' texts. The most dramatic are postmodern authors who blatantly lift others' writing as they create their pastiches. In doing so, they parody the transformational process that is a large part of writing even as they parody notions of originality.

Authoring Identity as Construct

This social constructivist work undergirds my conception of authoring identity, which gives emphasis to author as reader as well as writer, to transformations made in texts that are read, and to connections from one text to another. Authors are considered to be in a social process, much as that described in the work on disciplinary discourse communities, and they can be seen as original, as originators, even though they use others' texts in producing their own.

An author's identity is most often based on a set of texts. A person becomes a specialist in a certain kind of knowledge or in certain types of texts, or both, which might, for instance, be interactive fiction, film critiques, or experimental research reports. An author becomes identifiable by producing texts with some kind of commonality, texts that are the "same" or similar in some way or ways. The texts are identifiable with that author and identified by that author's name. The texts in the set may be similar in content (e.g., repeated topics) or may have certain identifiable genre features, or both. Analogies might be made with a songwriter's corpus, with a hairdresser's stylings, with an architect's products, and with a clothing designer's collection.

For discourse, let us imagine a vast network of interrelated texts produced by *all* authors. Within a portion of that network are some texts that were written by some particular author (and have that author's name affixed), and the texts within this author's set are interconnected because they have similarities, which might be repeated themes and similar discourse features. Figure 1 represents this portion of an intertext with a particular author's corpus darkened. An author's identity is constructed, in part, by perceived similarities among texts that comprise a set. The figure also illustrates connections with the texts of other authors, which is another aspect of authoring identity. The texts identified with this author are related to the texts of others in the community who have done related work, which are dotted in the figure. An author makes connections to people who discuss the same topics, say

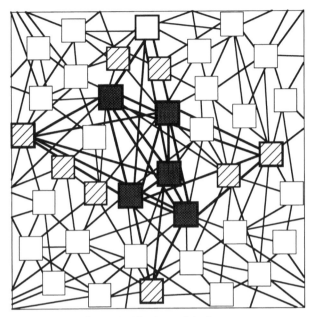

Figure 1. Identity and the intertext.

similar things, take similar positions, or study the topics in similar ways. These may be made consciously and rather explicitly through referencing, citing, or acknowledging, or less explicitly through alluding, or may be made consciously but less explicitly than what might be called an allusion. Moreover, they may be made unconsciously and not explicitly. Some connections to others are effected by using the same specialized discourse forms that they use. These can be ties to a whole community of authors if the author uses that community's forms and produces discourse identifiable with that of the large group. Or they can be ties to particular authors. Saying similar things and saying them in similar ways are components of the "identity kits" that Gee (1989) described for community members, their "saying-(writing)-doing-being-valuing-believing" combinations (p. 178).

Thus, to some extent, a person's authoring identity may be "seen" in his or her body of authored texts, which are interlinked within the set and linked outside the set with other authors' texts through repeated topics and approaches. An author identifies himself or herself, and becomes identified, with a particular part of the textual territory and with particular other authors. The similarity aspect of identity is important, but the distinctiveness aspect is important, too. Community members create, or are given, rather specialized identities associated, at least in part, with the niches claimed for their work relative to others' niches, and, of course, some members have bodies of work that are larger and more influential—more identifiable and visible—than those of others. There are other facets of a person's identity, which can be described in terms of membership in particular groups, as social identity theorists (Hogg & McGarty, 1990; J. C. Turner, Hogg, Oakes, Reicher, & Wetherell, 1987) would tell us. In the case of authoring identity, other aspects of the identity might include institutional identities, gender identity, identity with a particular publishing house, and so on (e.g., D. L. Rubin, 1995).

Writers do much to create their identities through what they write, how they write it, and with whom they associate, but their readers participate in the identity construction process. An author's identity is very much a construction on the part of readers. When reading one author's work, an individual reader might focus on one part of it, rather than the totality, and identify the author in that way. Or that reader might see that author as similar to other authors of whom that author was unaware. (Perhaps those authors came later.) The constructions have strong social component, since citations and critiques in the community's literature play an important role in shaping the identity that is constructed. Other people's representations affect how a particular author is perceived, and perception of an author would be part of the interpretive process conducted by members of a particular "interpretive community" (Fish, 1976). We have considered already how Bartlett's identity in cognitive psychology and in education has been shaped through the years by means of others' representations. Today for many people his identity is, no doubt, tied to the topic of knowledge structures in reading and memory, and he is interlinked with Neisser (1967), who reintroduced him in a particular way, with Zangwill (1972), who critiqued him, and with those researchers and theorists in the 1970s who built upon a particular part of his work. The only people he cited who are probably still identified with him are Head (1920), from whom he got the term *schema,* and Philippe (1897), from whom he borrowed his method, and Ebbinghaus (1895/1913), with whom he disagreed. His Cambridge (and sociologist/anthropologist) identification with Rivers, Haddon, and others doing socially oriented studies has faded over time.

This conception of authoring identity, which applies to disciplinary writing and can be extended to literary writing as well, contrasts with the other conceptions mentioned earlier. If we return to Figure 1, we can see how certain other orientations foregrounded some parts of the figure and put other parts in the background. The Romantic conception foregrounded an individual author's interrelated set of texts and presented that set as separate from others', because an author was viewed as a unique talent. The author was perceived as unique, even though considered to be in the rather large abstract group of all those other special individuals who were authors. All else is in the background, except for a certain kind of abstract relation between one author and another: the genius that they were thought to share.

The other conceptions—New Criticism, reader response, and poststructuralism—highlighted other parts. New Criticism foregrounded an individual text and attempted to separate it from an author's corpus and from other texts. This separation of the text of interest from other texts was central to the "theory" of the New Critics, but their practice contradicted their theory by requiring them to make connections to other texts. Only by making such connections could they interpret particular literary devices, such as metaphors and other kinds of figurative language, and only by making such connections could they favor certain *kinds* of texts, modernist literature, particularly metaphysical poems, over others. Reader response theory, while putting its emphasis on an individual reader, also foregrounded a single text, which was not necessarily considered to be part of a corpus or as related to other texts. Although it was the individual text with which the reader interacted (or transacted), the responding reader was thought to relate his or her reading to prior experiences, including reading of other texts. And then, unlike any of the others, the poststructuralist conception foregrounded the connections themselves, not a text and not a corpus of texts. A single text in this conception lost its identity as it regressed infinitely into the intertext. And authoring identity was also undone.

The conception I offer has some similarity, as pointed out previously, to the notion of author-function presented by Foucault (1969/1979). In his paper Foucault was speaking of literary discourse, but the idea can be extended to disciplinary discourse as well. Foucault spoke of the sameness and relation—"homogeneity" and "filiation"—among texts to whom the same author's name is affixed: "A name permits one to group together a certain number of texts, define them, differentiate them from and contrast them to others. In addition, it establishes a relationship among the texts" (p. 147). Foucault, who had his attention on systems, did not speak much about readers' cognition, but nevertheless he seemed to be describing authors as abstract constructs by means of which readers familiar with the literature can "chunk" sets of texts.

There has been much scholarly attention to authors and to authorship, focusing on authors whose identities are already established. This scholarship tends to move in a backwards fashion: A person acquires a certain status, and then the development of that person's body of work is traced historically from the artifacts that remain. For example, in an earlier chapter, for my treatment of Bartlett, I used his writings as well as articles that had been written about him. I noted certain themes that he developed over time in much of his work and also noted relations to the writings of others, some of which I also read. It seemed that the themes he emphasized in *Remembering,* the book for which he is best known, had been developing for years and had run through much of his prior work. They can be seen, for instance, in the studies he conducted for his fellowship dissertation. That is one way to study development, but another would be to start collecting writings and to conduct interviews as a person begins to produce an identifiable set of work.

What is the nature of authorship when one first begins to develop a corpus of interrelated work? What does it look like when one begins to identify and claim particular topics and create a specialization within a community's textual network? How does one begin to assume the authority to transform the texts published by others and use them for one's own purposes? Do people create social alliances that persist? Maureen Mathison and I tried to get some glimpses into this developmental process by following students from the point when they first declared a disciplinary major, through their graduation, and the next year, when some were pursuing graduate work in subfields.

Development of Authoring Identity

by Nancy Nelson Spivey and Maureen A. Mathison

To study possible beginnings of authoring identity, we followed six undergraduate students, all psychology majors, through the course of their undergraduate careers. Our inquiry started during the students' freshman year, continued for the next three years through their graduation, and followed up one year later, after they had begun graduate programs or careers. It was a longitudinal inquiry with multiple cases, as we wanted to capture glimpses of diversity as well as commonalities across individuals within the same setting (Spivey & Mathison, 1997).

Our interest was in long-term developmental patterns, seeing how the students' writing fit into their overall identity construction process in their chosen discipline. We were quite confident that one way in which students would demonstrate their identification with the larger discipline would be by beginning to use the discipline's genres and to adopt some of its formal conventions as they met assignments for their courses. Some previous research has shown that students, even as undergraduates, can adopt many of the surface features of specialized disciplinary genres over the course of a semester (e.g., Faigley & Hansen, 1985). But we were most interested in the extent to which they might begin to create the specialized kinds of authoring identities, described above, by building an interrelated body of work and making repeated connections to particular disciplinary authors. In order to learn about their production of disciplinary discourse—their own authorship— we collected all the papers they wrote for their psychology classes, and we analyzed them for genres and surface conventions that tied them to the community of psychology, for creation of thematic categories through recurrent topics, and for repeated citations or repeated transformations of others' texts.

The Students and Their Course of Study

As undergraduates, these students majored in psychology at Carnegie Mellon, a private research-oriented university. The psychology department there seemed, to us, to be a context conducive to students' developing disciplinary identities and authoring identities. Authorship is highly valued in that department, which has been acknowledged for its high *impact index* (number of citations relative to number of papers published). In addition to its major in psychology, the psychology department also offers an interdisciplinary major in cognitive science, which requires fewer courses in psychology but has requirements in such areas as computer science, philosophy, linguistics, and decision sciences. Five of the students in our study were in the regular psychology major, and one of them was in cognitive science.

They were all born in the same year and were 17 or 18 when they entered the university. All were ranked very high in their class in high school—one was first in his class, but all were in the top fifth—and all had high scores on the SAT, which averaged 1247 and ranged from 1080 to 1460 for the total score. When they were freshmen, the psychology department asked students who were thinking of majoring in psychology to sign a list in the departmental office. Our participants' names came to us from this source, not from an official university list, because students would not be formally declaring their major until the spring semester of their second year. These participants were high-achieving students who were making early decisions about their courses of study and future careers. Initially there were two other students on the list and in the study. One of them transferred, and the other changed his major to Creative Writing.

Adoption of Disciplinary Genres and Conventions

Through their undergraduate years, these six students wrote a number of texts for their psychology classes, of the types discussed in previous chapters, including topical reports (literature reviews or syntheses of research), research reports, research proposals, and one student wrote a proposal for a program. These types can be categorized as psychology genres. The students also wrote summaries and summaries with critical comments attached, common forms of school discourse in which students demonstrate their understandings of particular texts (cf. Bridgeman & Carlson, 1984). Students wrote on the average 15 papers for their psychology classes, of which more than half were papers on topics of their own choice. Four of them also wrote honors theses. The most common form overall was the research report (a report of a study), and students averaged 7 of these.

In meeting the assignments of their instructors, these undergraduates were beginning to produce genres used by psychologists and to incorporate the stylistic features that accompany those forms in psychology. This conventionalization started rather immediately when they began taking courses for their major, as they were required to use the APA format, as outlined in the 1983 manual of the American Psychological Association, which was the edition still in use when they were undergraduates. Their attempts to use the format were obvious in the textual components (cover page, abstract, reference list instead of bibliography, etc.), use of subheadings and running heads, and use of internal citations. The addition of these textual components was not at all surprising because the students were given much formal and informal instruction in writing according to APA style in research methods classes and other classes as well. Their research methods courses included explicit instruction in writing the research report with its four parts: introduction, method, results, and discussion. They also received (co-constructive) response to their papers. This commentary, which was often quite extensive, included marginal commentary on specific points as well as more general commentary at the end of a paper.

Creation of an Interrelated Body of Work

By adopting some forms and conventions of psychology, the students were beginning to produce language identifiable as that of their discipline and were beginning a process of identification with psychologists through their writing. But would they also begin to create more specialized identities by creating thematic categories for their work? Would they build one text on another, pursuing in one paper an issue that was raised in a previous one? They had much choice of topics within the courses they took, although some took more courses and had more opportunity for topic choice than others. The fifth year three of the six were still pursuing in some way topics that they had identified as undergraduates, and the following are summaries of their work (names have been changed). One of the other students also entered graduate school that year, but he had not settled on particular topics to pursue in his writing. The other two did not continue their work in psychology the year after they graduated.

Barbara: Clinical Psychologist

As a freshman Barbara decided on psychology as her major but not necessarily as her career. During the next year she decided on psychology for her career and clinical psychology as her area of the discipline. She wanted a career as both a practitioner and a researcher, wanted not only to have a clinical practice but also to do research and publish results of her studies. Barbara's corpus of papers, illustrated in Figure 2, is unique among the collections in that she had two major interrelated and fairly well developed sets of papers in psychology. One of them was relevant to her identity as a woman, and the other was related more to her emerging identity as a clinical therapist. The first set of three papers was on gender-related issues, topics that she explained were of specific interest to her as a woman as well as of general interest to her as a prospective psychologist. These topics were cross-cultural sex roles, depression in women, and premenstrual syndrome (written for classes in Cognitive Processes, Abnormal Psychology, and Personality and Health, respectively). What tied the three together so tightly was the attention she gave to cultural influences on phenomena often thought to be biological and gender. Her conclusion in all three was that gender phenomena that seem to be biological are, in fact, strongly influenced by social factors.

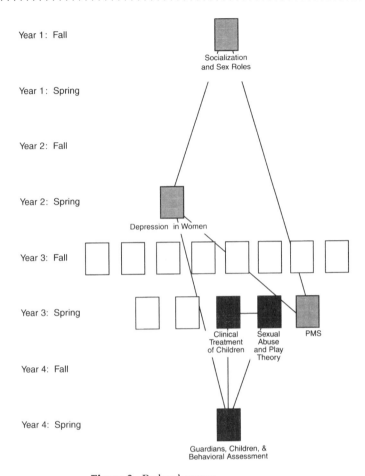

Figure 2. Barbara's corpus.

The other interrelated set, which was tied to her emerging specialized identity as a clinical psychologist, dealt with children's problems. What linked the texts in this set together so closely was her emphasis on reports of children's behavior. For a class in Clinical Psychology she reviewed studies of behavioral reports in clinical treatment of children, and she wrote a paper on the topic of sexual abuse in children, noting that abusive parents tend to overreport behavior problems of children. Her honors thesis, completed her last semester, "Guardians and Children as Sources and Targets of Behavioral Assessments," pursued the issue of behavior reporting from the two previous texts, and it also had intertextual ties with a paper in the other set, the paper on depression in women written two years earlier. Barbara pointed out in the thesis that maternal depression was a variable that might bias mothers' reports.

Barbara had two major authorities, one for each of her two sets: The authority for her woman-identity set was Milner (1949), and the one for her clinical psychology-identity set was Kazdin (1977; Kazdin, Bass, Siegel, & Thomas, 1989; Kazdin, French, Unis, Esveldt-Dawson, & Sherick, 1983). In her freshman paper on sex roles, a major point that she made was how the female role differs across cultures. She used the work of Milner when she pointed out that the Samoan girl does not experience the same tensions as the American girl. She provided a table comparing American and Samoan adolescents and a quotation presenting the Samoan perspective:

> Life was never very difficult for me. . . . If I am momentarily angry or disappointed there is always some relative nearby to whom I can go and get understanding and a jolly word. My world is simple and orderly and accepting. It allows me to express my emotions freely. . . . All I want from life is to remain as I am now, a girl with little work and many lovers, as long as possible. (Milner, 1949, p. 309)

A year and a half later, when she wrote her paper on depression, she made an interesting transformation in her claims about conclusions to be drawn from Milner's study. She used the same table and an excerpt from that same quotation, "My world is simple and orderly and accepting. It allows me to express my emotions freely." She was "summarizing" Milner's work, but this was a different sort of summary. She slanted her summary of Milner in this paper to support a different argument: that female depression is linked to cultural factors. Barbara was using Milner as an authority, but she was also assuming authority herself, as she transformed his text and used it to support a different point.

Kazdin became Barbara's major authority about behavioral reporting in the clinical psychology papers she wrote, and she seemed to find his work particularly relevant when she pointed out the limitations of behavior reports for the study of behavior changes. When she needed an explanation for her finding of no significant differences for the treatment in her study, Kazdin (1977) became important because of this "authoritative" statement that he had made: "Changing the behavior of clients will not necessarily alter the evaluations of individuals with whom the target clients have interacted" (p. 447). His statement provided support for the possibility that change may have occurred but that it was not reflected in the reports she collected.

The fall after graduation, Barbara entered a graduate program in clinical psychology at a public university in the Midwest, where she planned to prepare herself for both roles, therapist and researcher. During her first year of graduate school Barbara produced only a few papers for her courses. Most of them were psychological assessments; she wrote four of these. She also wrote a literature review essay on coping with stress, the topic that she would be investigating for her thesis. It was a topic that fit with her advisor's work. This review was thus an important paper for her, because she was getting to know that work and that community. Through this literature review she was making an intertextual link to a future text, her own thesis. This future text, we discovered, would also be linked, to some extent, with prior texts from her undergraduate work: her clinical psychologist set. As in her undergraduate honors thesis, she would be using behavioral reports from both children and adults.

Hiro: Counseling Psychologist

Hiro saw psychology as a discipline that helped people, and he wanted a career in which he could provide help. During his sophomore year, when he thought he would be going into clinical psychology, he began to pursue an issue where he could provide help as a psychologist: trauma from rape. He had become interested in the issue of rape when he took an elective course that year in Abnormal Psychology taught by an adjunct professor, and rape was discussed in that class. Over the next two years, as shown in Figure 3, he produced a set of texts related to this topic. In his junior year he really got into his coursework for his major and decided that he would probably go into counseling psychology for his career. That year he also began studying the topic that interested him. For a class in Individual Differences he conducted a study that involved surveys, eliciting self-reports of perceptions of rape. At the end of his report of that study he pointed to future work that he would do:

> On the "Comments and Ideas" section of the surveys, I received many positive responses concerning the study, and many participants pointed out that it made them feel and think more deeply about the subject of rape. One of my goals in the future is to conduct rape awareness programs on the CMU campus.

The figure shows interconnections within this subset of his writing: issues of gender and trauma. During the fall semester of his senior year he conducted a related study on the topic of gender and trauma for his course in Research Methods in Social Psychology. And then his honors paper the final semester, supervised by the same professor who had taught the Abnormal Psychology course, was "A Date Rape Prevention Program: Rationale and Design." This thesis was thematically related to both of the prior texts. In fact, the program he proposed was motivated by findings from his first survey and was foreshadowed at the end of his report of that survey.

Hiro's connections with other authors were interesting not in a citation that he made but in a citation that he did not make. He actually had no repeated citations across his texts but had some redundant source material that he attributed to different sources. That switch in attribution was some evidence, we thought, of his growing sophistication in psychology. The redundant source material was about how a potential rapist does not have a distinct psychological profile. This is what he said in the report of his first survey in his junior year:

> Furthermore, researchers indicate that most rapists do not fit into any specific psychopathological type, nor are they more disturbed, sexually abnormal, or physically different from any man on the street (Griffin, 1971). This, in turn, places

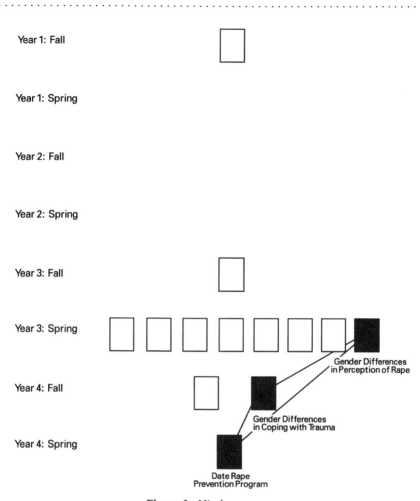

Figure 3. Hiro's corpus.

more impact on a statement made by Griffin that "all men are potential rapists, and every woman is a potential victim."

The Griffin (1971) citation was to an article in the periodical *Ramparts*.

In his honors thesis his senior year Hiro presented similar content but with more supporting detail and different references:

[Rape] should not be thought of as a violent sexual act committed by a few mentally ill men. Studies have indicated that convicted rapists are not significantly different from any other man in terms of their psychological or physical functioning

(Kanin, 1983). Studies utilizing the MMPI (Minnesota Multiphasic Personality Inventory) have also shown no evidence for the presence of personality disorder or neurotic/psychotic psychopathology (Koss, Leonard, Beezley, & Oros, 1985). This supports the idea that every man is a potential rapist, and the characteristics of rapists are similar in all rape categories.

One of the claims (rapists are not that different from nonrapists) attributed in the earlier paper to Griffin's article in *Ramparts* was no longer attributed to that author and that source. It was now supported by citations of two studies published in more scholarly journals that did report *some* differences between rapists and nonrapists. Hiro was changing to sources that were more appropriate for the disciplinary community of psychology. And the related claim (every man as potential rapist) was now put in the realm of shared knowledge as a claim that did not need citational support.

After graduation Hiro began studies at a state university in the West, where he entered a counseling psychology program that would lead to a Ph.D. During his first year there he produced a formidable set of papers, most of which were practitioner-oriented forms and responses to texts that he read for his courses. The most direct link between his identifiable body of work (on trauma and rape) and his current work was the volunteer work he was doing with support groups at a rape crisis center. He was maintaining that identity—that specialization from his under-graduate years—but not in his written texts.

Through much of his coursework that year Hiro, like Barbara, was learning another kind of discourse in psychology, the discourse of therapy/practice. Instead of research reports, the writing of both Barbara and Hiro involved practitioner-related forms (cf. J. F. Reynolds, Mair, & Fischer, 1996). They had been aware of such forms, such as psychological assessments, when they were in their undergrad-uate program. They had encountered them in their internships, but they did not produce them. In their graduate work they were learning the specialized discourse of another subcommunity within the discipline.

Arjun: Cognitive Scientist

For Arjun cognition was the "best part of psychology"—best not only in terms of what was interesting to him but also in terms of its importance. He was commit-ted to his major in cognitive science throughout his undergraduate career, but he was not sure that he would go into a career in psychology. Arjun, the "possible" cognitive scientist, wrote three major papers during his undergraduate career. All were attempts to contribute to theory building (or theory testing) by extending or proposing models of cognition. His psychology papers, illustrated in Figure 4, show his interest in theoretical issues at the intersections of cognition, mathematics, and computers and also illustrate his developing identity as a cognitive scientist. A par-ticular focus was on the relations among competing models. His first long paper, written the spring semester of his freshman year, reported a simulation of the spread-

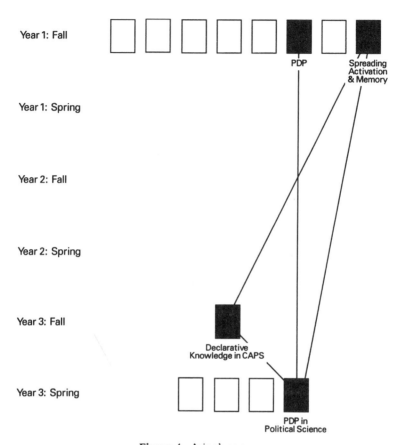

Figure 4. Arjun's corpus.

ing activation model of memory, giving special attention to J. R. Anderson's (1976) theory of adaptive control of thought (ACT). For it he wrote a program to test specific aspects of that model of memory on the computer, which involved building a memory structure and creating an algorithm to spread activation. Related work included one report of a study modeling the learning of declarative knowledge in a collaboration activation-based production system (CAPS) and another paper proposing the use of parallel distributed processing (PDP) networks (used most often as models of knowledge and memory) to account for phenomena in political science, again with computer modeling as means of testing. The latter was his final undergraduate paper, as he graduated with university honors after only three years.

Arjun made connections to authors in the community, but, instead of people he knew only through their texts, many of the authors he cited were people with whom he studied and, in some cases, worked. Although Arjun worked with different theories—ACT, CAPS, and PDP—the same names kept coming up: Anderson, Just and Carpenter, Newell, Simon, and McClelland, all on the faculty of the psychology department where he was doing his work. Arjun was creating an institutional identity. Even in his first paper during the second semester of his freshman year, as he made his attempt to simulate J. R. Anderson's (1976) spreading activation, Arjun (boldly) referred to the work of A. Newell and Simon (e.g., A. Newell & Simon, 1972) as well as Anderson as he attempted to make his contribution:

> There is one major addition that I feel is definitely worth making: better control of initial activation. On each pass, the user could determine where attention is being focused. . . . Hopefully, this could lead to the program itself going with and directing the activation down the best (strongest connection strength) routes or the routes which seem closest to a pre-stated goal node. This would be analogous to searching in a problem space, and might unite the spreading activation model with Newell and Simon's theories.

The sources used as points of departure for all three of Arjun's papers were major pieces authored or co-authored by cognitive scientists at the university he was attending. They were people whom he knew. He worked as a research assistant for Just and Carpenter, who developed the CAPS model, and took a course from Carpenter, and he also took courses from Simon and from McClelland, who with Rumelhart developed the PDP model. In writing his CAPS paper for the course with Simon, he pulled in Simon's own work (e.g., Anzai & Simon, 1979; Simon, 1989) and J. R. Anderson's (1985) but drew mainly from the work he was doing in his research assistantship with Just:

> Psychologists have traditionally approached the issue of learning in production systems by focusing on the acquisition of procedural knowledge. Their investigations have led quite naturally to the formation of adaptive production systems. [At this point Arjun cited four examples, including J. R. Anderson (1985) and Anzai and Simon (1979) before he set up his issue.] In contrast the issue of learning declarative knowledge in production systems has not been investigated as extensively. This fact is surprising considering the plethora of both theoretical and experimental research during the last thirty years exploring how humans acquire declarative knowledge. I claim that this research has not been instantiated in production systems because, until now, we have lacked the correct production system architecture. [Then he went into CAPS, citing Thibadeau, Just, and Carpenter (1982).]

For the PDP paper, major sources were, of course, McClelland and Rumelhart (1986) and Rumelhart and McClelland (1986), who proposed the PDP theory. For this paper, while trying to show the utility of PDP networks for models in policy studies, Arjun made intellectual connections across disciplines, and he also brought together the two disciplines he was thinking about for his own identity.

Through his research and writing he attempted to extend or test aspects of the work of these psychologists. The community he was constructing, and placing himself within, was composed of cognitive scientists, with certain psychologists at his university playing very important roles. He connected himself to cognitive psychology and to his institution and constructed an institutional authoring identity for his work, to some extent the way a graduate student would (cf. Bickman & Ellis, 1990), although he was probably freer to move around among theories than many graduate students would be.

Arjun's CMU cognitive-science identity was apparent in methods, themes, and citations/allusions of much of the writing that he produced the fifth year of our study, when he was employed as a programmer at a university research center in the South. Although ambivalent at that time about further studies and a career in the discipline of psychology, he was working actively on two psychology projects. The 20 informal papers that he wrote for the projects that provided his support were internal pieces, intended for the other members of the research teams to read and, in some instances, use in reports to funding agencies. These papers included responses to research ideas, descriptions of work being done, and proposals for taking a particular kind of direction on a project. And he produced four additional texts on his own that were linked to his prior work: a manual for data collection software, a theoretical proposal for a universal architecture based on CAPS, and two comparisons of Newell's and Anderson's architectures. He was trying out a different approach to theory testing and a different way to write a report: attempting, as he put it, "to differentiate between theories by finding the crucial test of experimental data to do that" instead of the way in which he had tried to argue psychologically during his undergraduate program, accounting "for a bunch of data with a clear theory or mechanism."

Identities and Niches

Here we have presented the connections that three of the six students made as they produced interrelated texts and began creating specialized identities through their writing—"possible selves" (Markus & Nurius, 1986)—that they might or might not continue to develop. But we should point out that all six students were involved in a complex identification process that involved much more than writing. Their major was like the general layout of a painting without the details. The details were the choices that they needed to make regarding subgroups they might join: groups of people belonging to particular subfields, people filling particular roles, and so on. All the students were becoming specialists even as they were becoming generalists, but the decisions they made were often quite tentative, as they were seeing what it would be like to be that kind of psychologist, to do that kind of research.

Writing can play a role in the overall social identification process, serving as a means of aligning oneself with groups or communities. Through their writing these students were trying out an identity, beginning to place themselves in the large disciplinary community of psychology, as they started to produce its forms and to use its conventions, as outlined in the APA manual. They were learning its discourse, and they were building on others' work as well as, in some cases, their own prior work. Some were even beginning to produce interrelated work to some extent the way that psychologists in the large community would do, were beginning to create more specialized identities by choosing particular topics in which they were intellectually invested. These students could give their topic a developmental twist, or a social twist, or a clinical twist to make it fit a project for a particular course. They were also, in some cases, beginning to connect with others in the larger community, authors in the discipline who did related work and whose texts they could use as they produced their own.

Conclusion

Here, with respect to authoring identity, not only for those published authors discussed earlier, but also these emerging authors in this longitudinal inquiry, is the interplay between the social and the individual that has often come up in this book. An author creates an interrelated body of work, following social conventions, and, in doing so, becomes socially aligned by repeating the themes and forms used by various other people. This alignment may be intentional on the part of the author, but may instead be inferred by others as they seek ways to classify particular works. An author achieves individuality through relations with others. The topics, methods, and sources do not belong only to that one author, but the particular configuration does.

Here is also the interplay between reading and writing that comprises literate behavior. The authoring identity of an individual is created, to a great extent, by his or her use of other people's texts that have been read and replication of some features and content. This chapter has been about authoring identity created through one's own writing, but it has also been about transformations that people make as readers of other writers' texts. And these transformations and the resulting synthesis can result in what we call *originality*. Bartlett (1932) was original when he extended others' ideas about social processes to cognitive processes. Barbara was original when she applied Milner's (1949) notions about cultural differences to women's depression. Hiro was original when he created a date rape prevention program, based on prior research, that was different from any other program developed previously. Arjun was original when he applied PDP to policy studies. Joyce Carol Oates's writing is original, even though she attributes her thoughts to the consciousnesses of others who preceded her. An author originates something "new" through inferencing, through seeing relations.

Chapter IX

· ·

Constructive Criticism

Metaphor participates fully in the progress of knowledge: in replacing some stale "natural" kinds with novel and illuminating categories, in contriving facts, in revising theory, and in bringing us new worlds.

—Nelson Goodman, "Metaphor as Moonlighting"

This book has dealt with a number of interrelated topics, all addressing some aspect of constructivism in discourse theory. We began with a consideration of the *underlying metaphor*: its historical antecedents, its major forms, and different ways of focusing one's lens when viewing constructive processes. Then we revisited the *work of Frederic Bartlett,* giving special attention to how his theory of construction on the part of individuals originated in his conception of the constructiveness of societal knowledge, how his own writing process was affected by social contact, and how his work has been (constructively) remembered. Next we reviewed the large body of research conducted on *the reading process*—the reading of texts, the reading of contexts, and the reading of intertexts. We looked at work taking different perspectives, not only the perspective focused on individual agents but also those focusing on micro and macro social agents. That treatment of reading was followed by a comparison with *other metaphorical conceptions* of discourse, structuralism and poststructuralism (including deconstruction), which are also based on a building metaphor.

At that point, we moved to the topic of *writing,* considering three dimensions—the author–audience dimension, the intertextual dimension, and the co-constructive dimension. The point here was that these dimensions are cognitive as well as social and they involve comprehending texts as well as composing texts. That was followed by a treatment of my special research interest, *discourse synthesis,* acts that are both comprehension and composition and involve writing based on the reading of multiple texts. The next focal topic was a theme that had run through other chapters and is central to constructivism, *textual transformations.* There we reviewed some conventional kinds of practices involving transformations of others' texts, such

235

as summarizing, reporting, proposing, and critiquing, which are performed in written as well as oral discourse. And finally we took up the issue of *authoring identity* and speculated about the construction of an identity through repetition of themes and creation of social links with other authors.

Various Ways of Reading This Book

Like any book, this book can be—and will be—understood in various ways. One way is to follow this overall layout of chapters, this set of topics. This would be a conventional sort of "reading," but other kinds of understandings are also possible, as we shall now consider.

The book might be seen instead as a kind of intellectual history. Readers might construct a history of the constructivist movement from various chapters and sections of chapters, even though the overall organization is topical. If it is a history, it is a history reflecting, as histories must, the historian's own perspective and focus (cf. Callinicos, 1995; Carr, 1990; Goldstein, 1976, 1977). As Goldstein (1977) argued, "The procedures whereby we come to know the human past remain always cognitive-constructive" (p. 35), in which the historian draws conclusions, on the basis of his or her rationality, about what is reasonable to assume took place. In part, as acknowledged in the first chapter, it is a history with an agenda: I wanted to show that there are some similarities and complementarities among three major forms of construction, even though they do have different foci and emphases. And as also acknowledged earlier, it is a revisionist history, particularly with respect to Bartlett, whose constructivist work could fit in all three categories, even though it has been mainly remembered only for one. My book might have been organized more explicitly as a history, and that approach was certainly one of the possibilities that I dealt with in writing it. Wittgenstein (1945–1949/1973) spoke rather passionately about the tension a writer experiences when choosing among various ways of organizing one's writing.

Another way to understand it is as an autobiography. A "subtext" can be read from my acknowledgments, dedication, illustrations, citations, and references, and even from the issues that were examined. In a certain sense, this is an account of my life for the past 15 years or so, beginning when I was a graduate student in Texas reading the *new* and exciting work in reading comprehension and also the *really new* work in the composing process. Even then, my quest was to find relations between comprehending and composing, and my dissertation in discourse synthesis was one way to study those relations. The follow-up studies conducted over the next few years continued with the same issue but examined other variables. A reader might see how my work became more "situated" in academic disciplines when I joined the Carnegie Mellon faculty and, while at CMU, directed a set of studies for the

Center for the Study of Writing into disciplinary practices and the development of disciplinary authorship. No doubt, some readers would also note the effects of that university's literary and cultural studies program on my interest in poststructural conceptions and my efforts to compare them with constructivist theory. There are also some evidences of two years in Virginia and my year and a half in Louisiana in my acknowledgments and examples. And perhaps running through it all is a Texan's willingness to take risks combined with a newly acquired Louisiana belief in the power of the gumbo.

Some readers could perform a reading that is even more rhetorical than that. They could read even more into the person behind the text, speculating about my purposes and strategies as well as about the contexts in which I have worked and the people to whom I relate in some way, and asking such questions as these: How does the author align herself? Why is one set of texts emphasized instead of another set? Whose work does she support? Whose work is this piece set in contrast with? What move is she trying to make here? Why were particular terms chosen over others? Why were particular citations made instead of others? What was she trying to accomplish with particular epigraphs? How were studies summarized this time in contrast to their previous summaries? What material is included because of reviewers' comments? What material is included to satisfy a particular sort of audience?

And it could be a different kind of rhetorical reading: a deconstruction, which would mean finding contradictions, gaps, and places where ideology is revealed, and tying them not to me as an individual author but to an ideology. Where, for instance, does the conduit metaphor (which any constructivist must try to stifle, but cannot completely) slip through? There are these possibilities, and there are many others, perhaps even a Shandean kind of postmodern reading, following the method of Sterne's (1779/1925) *Tristram* and going back through all the documents cited in this book and all those cited in those works (and all those that were cited there and so on), only to find that my claims were actually made earlier by someone else (cf. Merton, 1965).

I shall leave any or all of this to my readers. Here, however, as a way of concluding, I would like to do some rearranging of topics, do some pulling together, reconsidering, and developing of major constructivist themes mentioned at various points throughout the book. That will be done by seeing what constructivism has to say about some issues in discourse theory: the social versus the cognitive, product versus process, and originality versus conventionality.

Response to Issues

The metaphor of constructivism does us no good if it leads only to statements that seem so final, so "true," and so universally acceptable that there is no surprise in hearing them and no questioning of them. The constructivist metaphor would be a "dead" metaphor, a cliché in the "trop(e)ical jungle", in which we all work (W. Taylor, 1984). I am thinking here of the truisms that "reading (or writing) is a (socially) constructive process" and "knowledge is (socially) constructed." If that is all that can be said, then our constructivist metaphor has become "stale" and is no longer generative. I would argue, however, that constructivism is generative and that it leads not only to continued research and theory development, as illustrated in previous chapters, but also to positions on controversial social and educational issues. The following discussion provides a constructivist response to three such issues in discourse theory, all of which are based on socially constructed dichotomies: the social versus the cognitive, process versus product, and originality versus conventionality. Instead of deconstructing these pairs, I attempt to show how a constructivist might see the relation between the two.

The Social and Cognitive Issue

One continuing issue to which constructivists must respond is a dichotomy that has been established between the cognitive and the social: Some theories, research, and pedagogies are considered cognitive, and other theories, research, and pedagogies are considered social (cf. Bruffee, 1984). The issue has become so important that a number of people in literacy education have attempted to bring the social and the cognitive together, have tried to supply a hyphen between the two (e.g., Geisler, 1991, 1994; cf. Nystrand, 1986). Historically, constructivism in its various forms has been an epistemology that resists attempts to be neatly classified as either cognitive or social.

All forms emphasize cognition, or the process of knowing, and all give attention to social aspects of knowing. The form I called *cognitive* in Chapter I turned out, when traced back to Bartlett (1923, 1932), to have originated from a social theory based on anthropological and sociological work before it was taken to the psychological level. And throughout its two incarnations, much attention has been given to socially valued forms and conventions and to the ways of different groups. Piaget (1923/1932) gave attention to the author–audience relationship when studying perspective taking. Kelly's (1955) theory, which offers a conception of mental categories, focuses on individuals' intersubjective interpretations of other people, and N. Goodman's (1978) theory of "worlds" describes the transformations in theories, or ways of knowing, constructed cognitively by individuals as well as socially by societies and other groups. The forms often called *social construction* have focused on the the cognitive as well as the social. Theories dealing with dyads and small groups have knowledge that is socially constructed result eventually in cognitive change in individuals (e.g., Vygotsky, 1978, 1986), and the systems-oriented work portrays cognition as distributed across members (e.g., Salomon, 1993a). Even the macro social constructivism focusing on disciplinary constructions and literary constructions has a cognitive orientation, as the interest is in societies' processes of socially constructing knowledge (Leenhardt, 1992; Otter, 1991; Schmidt, 1992) and in the cognitive differences, or differing ways of knowing, among different societies.

I think almost any constructivist would wonder why some people had such difficulty bringing the two together when it seems impossible to separate them in any consideration of discourse. To constructivists, I think, the social-cognitive issue is a nonissue, and the real issue is which way to adjust the lens: to focus on the individual, the small group, or on a more abstract community as an agent.

Constructivist pedagogy has followed from this theoretical attention to cognitive and social factors. For instance, many of the methods developed in the 1980s (and generally endorsed in *Becoming a Nation of Readers*) emphasized the social conventions of discourse in our society, particularly those used in academic settings, and pointed to the recurring patterns that one will experience in reading texts (R. C. Anderson et al., 1985). Some pedagogy has given attention to metacognitive knowledge, helping students to become aware of strategies and options and to be able to decide when to use one over another (e.g., A. L. Brown, 1987; Palincsar & Brown, 1984; Paris, Lipson, & Wixson, 1983; Pressley, Harris, & Guthrie, 1992). Other approaches focus on social relations between reader and author to facilitate cognitive understandings. For example, a method called "questioning the author" helps students become more aware of a (fallible) textbook author who wrote the text and made various choices in how to present material (Beck, McKeown, Sandora, Kucan, & Worthy, 1996). This work is particularly timely, as educators are realizing that "authorless" and yet authoritative textbooks present problems to students and do not prepare them for reading "authored" books in a discipline. By suppressing the human aspects of communication, these books seem to make it difficult for readers to build coherent understandings, as pointed out by Beck et al. (1995) and Wineburg (1994). A great deal of emphasis is put today on activities that are "authentic" for a particular domain or discipline as students learn the ways of knowing in that community (cf. J. S. Brown et al., 1989). Saying that students "learn ways" comes down to saying that they "build particular kinds of knowledge."

The Process and Product Issue

Another dichotomy that has become a critical issue is that of process versus product. Some pedagogies and research methods are considered process approaches, and others are considered product approaches. To understand this one, we have to go back again to the 1960s and the 1970s when the organic plant metaphor of Romanticism began to blossom once more in discourse theory. Rohman and Wlecke (1964) gave that metaphor of Wordsworth and Coleridge new life in their influential model of the composing process, which likened the composing of a text to the growth of a plant. They went to Abrams's (1953) *Mirror and the Lamp* where they discovered the following "parallels" between the process of writing and the process of growth: Writing, like a plant, was seen as originating in a seed, growing, assimilating diverse elements, evolving "spontaneously from an internal source of energy," and achieving a structure that is an "organic unit" (pp. 171–175). Rohman and Wlecke's work was important because it was one of the first attempts to offer a model of the process, which they based on three components: prewriting, writing, and rewriting. Other early models of composing were undergirded with a growth conception, sometimes with a notion of "incubation" (e.g., J. Britton, Burgess, Martin, McLeod, & Rosen, 1975). And in respect to the reading of literature, the plant metaphor also began to play a major role. In her transactional theory, Rosenblatt (1978) described a continuum of reader response with aesthetic at one end and efferent at the other. Aesthetic reading, which was described in organic terms, gave emphasis to the process, whereas in efferent reading the emphasis was on the product, the mental product that remained after one read.

All this new attention to organic growth contrasted dramatically with old thinking about literacy that was based on a notion of correctness. The process orientation in writing contrasted with old red-ink methodologies of teaching writing that consisted of marking errors on a final product, and the process emphasis on aesthetic reading contrasted with the careful, close, determinate readings of the New Criticism in college or correct answers to comprehension questions. A person's own natural response could blossom as constraints were removed and the context was more conducive. The new slogan in writing became "Teach process, not product" (D. Murray, 1972) and much attention was given to students' prewriting and revising. And in literature classes, students began writing response statements to the works they read. These statements were considered to be "process" oriented in that they facilitated the students' responses rather than assessing their ability to produce a predetermined correct interpretation (Bleich, 1975). Even research methods were set in opposition, particularly in respect to writing research: "Product" methodologies were those that involve analysis of a written text, and "process" methodologies were those employing such methods as think-aloud procedures and observations. Many seemed not to notice that the process methodologies result in products, such as think-aloud protocols, which have to be subjected to meticulous parsings and codings, just as they seemed not to notice that pedagogical approaches labeled "process," such as peer conferences, and those labeled "product," such as teachers' written commentary, involved verbal products as well as social and cognitive processes.

The process–product issue has been particularly prominent with respect to writing. It has not been as contentious for reading, I think, because of the constructivists' traditional use of products to study the process of reading (e.g., R. C. Anderson, Reynolds et al., 1977; Kintsch, 1974). The comprehension studies of the

1970s and 1980s, which were clearly focused on process, involved analysis of products, even written products, and the nature of the process was inferred from those
products. That attention to products to infer process continues even as other kinds
of products, such as conversations, are examined. Constructivists are interested in
the products of cognition, which, for some, might be a mental product constructed
by an individual, and which, for others, calling themselves social constructivists,
might be a particular kind of theory being developed collaboratively by a community. The process of constructing those cognitive products is inferred by studying
other products, which might be written or oral texts or might be something else.

The constructivist epistemology includes a valuing of human products as well
as the processes people undergo to produce them. And it portrays the constructive
agent as engaged in an effortful process, as in Bartlett's "effort after meaning,"
although it may not be a conscious effort. Here, the constructivist portrayal of
process, giving attention to agency, would seem to differ from that of an organic,
plant-metaphor "process," in which the "natural process" could come from within
if only the constraints were removed. These different conceptions would lead, of
course, to different pedagogies.

As we have seen, constructivists have given a great deal of attention to textual
products of various types. Many do so with the goal of improving materials that
students read in their schooling. One issue that persists is the readability issue. Even
though constructivist research, reviewed in Spivey (1987), has demonstrated how
slippery the ground is on which readability formulas are based, the very notion of
readability levels remains so firmly entrenched in the culture of schooling that
sometimes people who argue vehemently against them continue to report them.

The Originality and Conventionality Issue

The final issue to be noted here is originality versus conventionality. This particular
dichotomy, unlike the other two, might seem on the surface to be intuitive and
unarguable: If something is conventional, it is not original, and, if it is original, it is
not conventional. In the previous chapter we considered the Romantic conception
of authorship based on this sort of dichotomy, in which an author was viewed as
the unique creator of an original literary work, as someone who was not conventional. The problem here was that this idealized conception did not match up with
the practice. Authors, creating their "original" works, followed conventions of their
time as they worked in particular traditions, and they engaged in social processes of
reading, responding to and borrowing from each other's writing. When literary
works are analyzed, the borrowings and the conventions can be seen in their "original" work. Even postmodern writers of our time, who seem quite original, are
actually, as we saw earlier, making transformations in accepted conventions (some
of which have been made before) and even joining other postmodern writers in

following the same sorts of discourse conventions. It is *human* to be social and to be conventional.

Pedagogy today is often based on an idealized conception of author, and students are encouraged to be original, come up with their "own ideas," and create their own forms. Does constructivism, with its value on social conventions and artifacts and its attention to socially established forms, stand in opposition to originality? No, it does not stand in opposition to originality, but instead presents a different conception of what it is to be original. Originality is achieved, not by coming up with something totally new, but by making transformations in what is known and in what is read and by making connections across domains (cf. Bereiter & Scardamalia, 1985). Originality can come through synthesis as new connections and possibilities are perceived by people as they engage in their social practices. At the theoretical level originality has often resulted from taking a metaphor from some domain of knowledge, applying it to one's own, and making it work within new constraints (e.g., Edge, 1974), for example, discourse theories based on such conceptions as hypothesis testing (K. S. Goodman, 1967), problem solving (Flower & Hayes, 1981), and computer processing (Rumelhart, 1977). Whether something is seen as original can depend on the context and the audience. For example, a feminist reading of Bly's (1990) *Iron John* might be original in some settings but rather conventional in others. Moreover, whether something is seen as original by a discourse community can depend to a great extent, it seems, on how it is presented rhetorically. Is it claimed as original? Does the "originator" assert authority? Or does he or she defer to the authority of others?

Here, in respect to originality within conventionality, is where the theory needs to guide development of pedagogical approaches. Much attention has gone to the summarizing of texts, but not to the synthesizing of material (see, however, Kaufer et al., 1989; Many et al., 1996; Raphael, Kirschner, & Englert, 1988). A pedagogy based on the constructivist theory presented in this book would help students learn *how* to make transformations and, in doing so, to employ knowledge of social conventions for crediting others. It would help them learn to build on their own prior intellectual work (as well as others' work) and lessen the pressure to come up with something that seems totally new for each assignment they receive. And it would also give attention to learning the conventional ways of assertion and deferral of authority. Moreover, it would encourage those "original" connections across domains.

Conclusion

My major purpose in writing this book was a synthetic one: to highlight parallels in constructivism as it has developed and to bring the various versions in closer contact. I believe that the shifting lens is healthy for theory development: The shifts in perspective can lead to new ideas as well as criticism, both of which keep constructivism from becoming some kind of doctrine. My other purpose has been to offer an integrative conception of discourse that encompasses both composing and comprehending and that challenges some conventional boundaries between reading and writing. To accomplish this integration, attention has been given to the following: the role of comprehending in the composing processes of individuals and of groups (both micro and macro), the numerous conventional practices that involve both reading and writing, and the part that reading plays in the creation of authoring identities. The theme here in this constructivist conception of discourse has been *transformation*: Texts are transformed to create new texts, and knowledge is transformed to create new knowledge.

References

Abrams, M. H. (1953). *The mirror and the lamp.* Oxford: Oxford University Press.

Ach, N. (1905). *Über die Willenstätigkeit und das Denken.* Göttingen: Vandenhoeck.

Ackerman, J. (1991). Reading, writing, and knowing: The role of disciplinary knowledge in comprehension and composing. *Research in the Teaching of English, 25,* 133–178.

Afflerbach, P. (1990). The influence of prior knowledge on expert readers' main idea construction strategies. *Reading Research Quarterly, 25,* 31–46.

Alexander, P. A., Jetton, T. L., Kulikowich, J. M., & Woehler, C. A. (1994). Contrasting instructional and structural importance: The seductive effect of teacher questions. *Journal of Reading Behavior, 26,* 19–45.

Alexander, P. A., Schallert, D. L., & Hare, V. C. (1991). Coming to terms: How researchers in learning and literacy talk about knowledge. *Review of Educational Research, 61,* 315–343.

Almasi, J. (1995). The nature of fourth-graders' sociocognitive conflicts in peer-led and teacher-led discussions of literature. *Reading Research Quarterly, 30,* 313–351.

American Psychological Association. (1983). *Publication manual* (3rd ed.). Washington, DC: Author.

Anderson, J. R. (1976). *Language, memory, and thought.* Hillsdale, NJ: Erlbaum.

Anderson, J. R. (1983). *The architecture of cognition.* Cambridge, MA: Harvard University Press.

Anderson, J. R. (1985). *Cognitive psychology and its implications* (2nd ed.). New York: Freeman.

Anderson, R. C. (1977). The notion of schemata and the educational enterprise: General discussion of the conference. In R. C. Anderson, R. J. Spiro, & W. E. Montague (Eds.), *Schooling and the acquisition of knowledge* (pp. 415–431). Hillsdale, NJ: Erlbaum.

Anderson, R. C., Hiebert, E. H., Scott, J. A., & Wilkinson, I. A. G. (1985). *Becoming a nation of readers.* Washington, DC: National Institute of Education.

Anderson, R. C., & Ortony, A. (1975). On putting apples into bottles—a problem of polysemy. *Cognitive Psychology, 7,* 17–180.

Anderson, R. C., & Pichert, J. W. (1978). Recall of previously unrecallable information following a shift in perspective. *Journal of Verbal Learning and Verbal Behavior, 17,* 1–12.

Anderson, R. C., Reynolds, R. E., Schallert, D. L., & Goetz, E. T. (1977). Frameworks for comprehending discourse. *American Educational Research Journal, 14,* 367–382.

Anderson, R. C., Spiro, R. J., & Montague, W. E. (Eds.). (1977). *Schooling and the acquisition of knowledge.* Hillsdale, NJ: Erlbaum.

Angenot, M. (1984). Structuralism as syncretism: Institutional distortions of Saussure. In J. Fekete (Ed.), *The structural allegory: Reconstructive encounters with the new French thought* (pp. 150–163). Minneapolis: University of Minnesota Press.

244

Anzai, Y., & Simon, H. A. (1979). The theory of learning by doing. *Psychological Review, 86,* 124–140.

Applebee, A. N. (1978). *The child's concept of story: Ages two to seventeen.* Chicago: University of Chicago Press.

Applebee, A. N. (1984). *Contexts for learning to write: Studies of secondary school instruction.* Norwood, NJ: Ablex.

Armbruster, B. B. (1984). The problem of "inconsiderate text." In G. G. Duffy, L. R. Roehler, & J. Mason (Eds.), *Comprehension instruction: Perspectives and suggestions* (pp. 202–217). New York: Longman.

Armbruster, B. B., Anderson, T. H., & Ostertag, J. (1987). Does text structure/summarization instruction facilitate learning from expository text? *Reading Research Quarterly, 22,* 331–346.

Armstrong, W. E. (1928). Social constructiveness: III. *British Journal of Psychology, 18,* 396–399.

Asch, S. (1952). *Social psychology.* Englewood Cliffs, NJ: Prentice-Hall.

Au, K. H. (1980). Participation structures in a reading lesson with Hawaiian children: Analysis of a culturally appropriate instructional event. *Anthropology and Education Quarterly, 11,* 91–115.

Bakhtin, M. M. (1981). *The dialogic imagination* (M. Holquist, Ed.; C. Emerson & M. Holquist, Trans.). Austin: University of Texas Press.

Bakhtin, M. M. (1984). *Problems of Dostoevsky's poetics* (C. Emerson, Ed. and Trans.). Minneapolis: University of Minnesota Press. (Original work published in Russian 1929)

Bakhtin, M. M. (1986). *Speech genres and other late essays* (C. Emerson & M. Holquist, Eds.; V. W. McGee, Trans.). Austin: University of Texas Press.

Bally, C., & Sechehaye, A. (1983). Preface to the first edition. In F. de Saussure, *Course in general linguistics* (R. Harris, Trans.) (pp. xvii–xx). London: Duckworth. (Original work published in French 1916)

Barth, J. (1967, August). The literature of exhaustion. *Atlantic Monthly, 220,* 29–54.

Barth, J. (1968). *Lost in the funhouse.* New York: Doubleday.

Barthes, R. (1964). *On Racine* (R. Howard, Trans.). New York: Hill & Wang. (Original work published in French 1963)

Barthes, R. (1967). *Elements of semiology* (A. Lavers & C. Smith, Trans.). London: Cape. (Original work published in French 1964)

Barthes, R. (1968). *Writing degree zero* (A. Lavers & C. Smith, Trans.). New York: Hill & Wang. (Original work published in French 1953)

Barthes, R. (1972). *Mythologies* (A. Lavers, Trans.). New York: Hill & Wang. (Original work published in French 1957)

Barthes, R. (1974). *S/Z* (R. Miller, Trans.). New York: Hill & Wang. (Original work published in French 1973)

Barthes, R. (1975). An introduction to the structural analysis of narrative. *New Literary History, 6,* 237–272.

Barthes, R. (1977). The death of the author. In S. B. Heath (Ed. and Trans.), *Image-music-text* (pp. 142–148). New York: Hill & Wang. (Original work published in French 1968)

Barthes, R. (1979). From work to text. In J. V. Harari (Ed.), *Textual strategies: Perspectives in post-structural criticism* (pp. 73–81). Ithaca, NY: Cornell University Press. (Original work published in French 1971)

Bartlett, F. C. (1916a). An experimental study of some problems of perceiving and imaging. *British Journal of Psychology, 8,* 222–266.

Bartlett, F. C. (1916b). *Transformations arising from repeated representations: A contribution towards an experimental study of the process of conventionalization.* Unpublished fellowship dissertation, St. John's College, Cambridge University, Cambridge, England.

Bartlett, F. C. (1920a). Some experiments on the reproduction of folk–stories. *Folk-Lore, 31,* 30–47.

Bartlett, F. C. (1920b). Psychology in relation to the popular story. *Folk-Lore, 31,* 264–293.

Bartlett, F. C. (1923). *Psychology and primitive culture.* Cambridge: Cambridge University Press.

Bartlett, F. C. (1927). *Psychology and the soldier.* Cambridge: Cambridge University Press.

Bartlett, F. C. (1928). Social constructiveness: I. *British Journal of Psychology, 18,* 388–391.

Bartlett, F. C. (1932). *Remembering: A study in experimental and social psychology.* Cambridge: Cambridge University Press. (Reissued 1995)

Bartlett, F. C. (1937a). Cambridge England, 1887–1937. *American Journal of Psychology, 50,* 97–110.

Bartlett, F. C. (1937b). Psychological methods and anthropological problems. *Africa, 10,* 401–420.

Bartlett, F. C. (1958). *Thinking: An experimental and social study.* New York: Basic Books.

Bazerman, C. (1985). Physicists reading physics: Schema-laden purposes and purpose-laden schema. *Written Communication, 2,* 3–23.

Bazerman, C. (1987). Codifying the social scientific style: The APA publication manual as a behaviorist rhetoric. In J. S. Nelson, A. Megill, & D. N. McCloskey (Eds.), *The rhetoric of the human sciences* (pp. 125–144). Madison: University of Wisconsin Press.

Beach, R., Appleman, D., & Dorsey, S. (1994). Adolescent uses of intertextual links to understand literature. In R. B. Ruddell, M. R. Ruddell, & H. Singer (Eds.), *Theoretical models and processes of reading* (4th ed., pp. 695–714). Newark, DE: International Reading Association.

Beach, R., & Hynds, S. (1991). Research on response to literature. In R. Barr, M. L. Kamil, P. B. Mosenthal, & P. D. Pearson (Eds.), *Handbook of reading research* (Vol. 2, pp. 453–489). New York: Longman.

Beardsley, M. C., & Wimsatt, W. K., Jr. (1949). The affective fallacy. *Sewanee Review, 57,* 31–55.

Beaugrande, R. de (1980). *Text, discourse, and process.* Norwood, NJ: Ablex.

Becher, T. (1989). *Academic tribes and territories.* Milton Keynes, Great Britain: Open University Press.

Beck, I. L., McKeown, M. G., Omanson, R. C., & Pople, M. T. (1984). Improving the comprehensibility of stories: The effects of revisions that improve coherence. *Reading Research Quarterly, 19,* 263–277.

Beck, I. L., McKeown, M. G., & Worthy, J. (1995). Giving a text voice can improve students' understanding. *Reading Research Quarterly, 30,* 220–238.

Beck, I. L., McKeown, M. G., Sandora, C., Kucan, L., & Worthy, J. (1996). Questioning the author: A year-long implementation to engage students with text. *Elementary School Journal, 96,* 385–414.

Beckett, S. (1972). *The lost ones.* New York: Grove Press.

Bereiter, C. (1994). Constructivism, socioculturalism, and Popper's World 3. *Educational Researcher, 23*(7), 21–23.

Bereiter, C., & Scardamalia, M. (1984). Learning about writing from reading. *Written Communication, 1,* 163–188.

Bereiter, C., & Scardamalia, M. (1985). Cognitive coping strategies and the problem of "inert knowledge." In S. F. Chipman, J. W. Segal, & R. Glaser (Eds.), *Thinking and learning skills: Current research and open questions* (Vol. 2, pp. 65–80). Hillsdale, NJ: Erlbaum.

Berger, J. (1972). *G.* New York: Viking.

Berger, P. L., & Luckmann, T. (1966). *The social construction of reality.* New York: Doubleday.

Berkenkotter, C., Huckin, T. N., & Ackerman, J. (1988). Conventions, conversations, and the writer: Case study of a student in a rhetoric Ph. D. program. *Research in the Teaching of English, 22,* 9–44.

Berkenkotter, C., & Huckin, T. N. (1993). Rethinking genre from a sociocognitive perspective. *Written Communication, 10,* 475–509.

Betz, A. (1910). Vorstellung und Einstellung: I. Weidererkennen. *Archiv für die gesamte Psychologie, 17,* 266–296.

Bickman, L., & Ellis, H. (Eds.). (1990). *Preparing psychologists for the 21st century: Proceedings of the National Conference on Graduate Education in Psychology.* Hillsdale, NJ: Erlbaum.

Bizzell, P. (1982). Cognition, convention, and certainty: What we need to know about writing. *PRE/TEXT, 3,* 213–243.

Black, J. B. (1985). An exposition on understanding expository text. In B. K. Britton & J. B. Black (Eds.), *Understanding expository text* (pp. 249–267). Hillsdale, NJ: Erlbaum.

Black, J. B., & Bern, H. (1981). Causal coherence and memory for events in narratives. *Journal of Verbal Learning and Verbal Behavior, 20,* 267–275.

Black, J. B., & Bower, G. H. (1980). Story understanding as problem solving. *Poetics, 9,* 223–250.

Black, M. (1979). More about metaphor. In A. Ortony (Ed.), *Metaphor and thought* (pp. 356–408). Cambridge: Cambridge University Press.

Bleich, D. (1975). *Readings and feelings: An introduction to subjective criticism.* Urbana, IL: National Council of Teachers of English.

Bleich, D. (1978). *Subjective criticism.* Baltimore: Johns Hopkins University Press.

Bloome, D., & Egan-Robertson, A. (1993). The social construction of intertextuality in classroom reading and writing lessons. *Reading Research Quarterly, 28,* 304–333.

Bloomfield, L. (1933). *Language.* New York: Allen & Unwin.

Bly, R. (1990). *Iron John: A book about men.* Reading, MA: Addison-Wesley.

Boas, F. (1901). *Kathlamet texts* (Bull. No. 26). Washington, DC: Bureau of American Ethnology.

Boas, F. (1909–1910). *Thirty-first annual report of the Bureau of American Ethnology.* Washington, DC: U.S. Government Printing Office.

Boas, F. (1910). Psychological problems in anthropology. *American Journal of Psychology, 21,* 371–384.

Bolter, J. D. (1991). *Writing space: The computer, hypertext, and the history of writing.* Hillsdale, NJ: Erlbaum.

Boring, E. G. (1950). *A history of experimental psychology.* New York: Appleton-Century-Crofts.

Bower, G. H. (1976). Experiments on story understanding and recall. *Quarterly Journal of Experimental Psychology, 28,* 511–534.

Bower, G. H., Black, J. B., & Turner, T. J. (1979). Scripts in memory for text. *Cognitive Psychology, 11,* 177–220.

Bower, T. G. R. (1977). *A primer of infant development.* San Francisco: Freeman.

Bower, T. G. R., & Wishart, J. G. (1972). The effects of motor skill on object permanence. *Cognition, 1,* 165–172.

Boyd, R. (1993). Metaphor and theory change: What is a "metaphor" a metaphor for? In A. Ortony (Ed.), *Metaphor and thought* (2nd ed., pp. 481–532). New York: Cambridge University Press.

Bracewell, R. J., Frederiksen, C. H., & Frederiksen, J. D. (1982). Cognitive processes in composing and comprehending discourse. *Educational Psychologist, 17,* 146–164.

Bransford, J. D., Barclay, J. R., & Franks, J. J. (1972). Sentence memory: A constructive versus interpretive approach. *Cognitive Psychology, 3,* 193–209.

Bransford, J. D., & Franks, J. J. (1971). The abstraction of linguistic ideas. *Cognitive Psychology, 2,* 331–350.

Bransford, J. D., & Johnson, M. K. (1972). Contextual prerequisites for understanding. *Journal of Verbal Learning and Verbal Behavior, 11,* 717–726.

Bransford, J. D., Nitsch, K. E., & Franks, J. J. (1977). Schooling and the facilitation of knowing. In R. C. Anderson, R. J. Spiro, & W. E. Montague (Eds.), *Schooling and the acquisition of knowledge* (pp. 31–60). Hillsdale, NJ: Erlbaum.

Bremond, C. (1964). Le message narratif. *Communications, 4,* 4–32.

Bremond, C. (1966). La logique des possibles narratifs. *Communications, 8,* 60–76.

Brewer, W. F. (1985). The story schema: Universal and culture-specific properties. In D. R. Olson, N. Torrance, & A. Hildyard (Eds.), *Literacy, language, and learning: The nature and consequences of reading and writing* (pp. 167–194). New York: Cambridge University Press.

Brewer, W. F., & Lichtenstein, E. H. (1982). Stories are to entertain: A structural-affect theory of stories. *Journal of Pragmatics, 6,* 473–486.

Bridgeman, B., & Carlson, S. B. (1984). Survey of academic writing tasks. *Written Communication, 1,* 247–280.

Britton, B. K., Glynn, S. M., Meyer, B. J. F., & Penland, M. J. (1982). Effects of text structure on use of cognitive capacity during reading. *Journal of Educational Psychology, 74,* 51–61.

Britton, B. K., van Dusen, L., Gulgoz, S., & Glynn, S. M. (1989). Instructional texts rewritten by five expert teams: Revisions and retention improvements. *Journal of Educational Psychology, 81,* 226–239.

Britton, J. (1978). The composing processes and the functions of writing. In C. R. Cooper & L. Odell (Eds.), *Research on composing: Points of departure* (pp. 13–28). Urbana, IL: National Council of Teachers of English.

Britton, J., Burgess, A., Martin, N., McLeod, A., & Rosen, H. (1975). *The development of writing abilities (11–18).* London: Macmillan Education.

Broadbent, D. E. (1970). Frederic Charles Bartlett, 1886–1969. *Biographical Memoirs of Fellows of the Royal Society, 16,* 1–13.

Brooks, C. (1947). *The well wrought urn: Studies in the structure of poetry.* New York: Reynal & Hitchcock.

Brown, A. L. (1987). Metacognition, executive control, self-regulation, and other more mysterious mechanisms. In F. E. Weinert & R. H. Kluwe (Eds.), *Metacognition, motivation, and understanding* (pp. 65–116). Hillsdale, NJ: Erlbaum.

Brown, A. L., & Day, J. D. (1983). Macrorules for summarizing texts: The development of expertise. *Journal of Verbal Learning and Verbal Behavior, 22,* 1–14.

Brown, A. L., Day, J. D., & Jones, R. S. (1983). The development of plans for summarizing texts. *Child Development, 54,* 968–979.

Brown, D. (1991). *Intertextual dynamics within the literary group—Joyce, Lewis, Pound, and Eliot: The men of 1914.* New York: St. Martin's Press.

Brown, J. S., Collins, A., & Duguid, P. (1989). Situated cognition and the culture of learning. *Educational Researcher, 18*(1), 32–42.

Bruce, B. C. (1993). *Network-based classrooms: Promises and realities.* New York: Cambridge University Press.

Bruce, B. C., Collins, A., Rubin, A. D., & Gentner, D. (1978). *A cognitive science approach to writing* (Tech. Rep. No. 89). Urbana: University of Illinois, Center for the Study of Reading.

Bruffee, K. A. (1984). Collaborative learning and the conversation of mankind. *College English, 46,* 635–662.

Bruner, J. (1973). *Beyond the information given.* New York: Norton.

Bruner, J. (1975). The ontogenesis of speech acts. *Journal of Child Language, 2,* 1–19.

Bruner, J. (1985). Narrative and paradigmatic modes of thought. In E. Eisner (Ed.), *Learning and teaching the ways of knowing* (84th Yearbook of National Society for the Study of Education, pp. 97–115). Chicago: National Society for the Study of Education.

Bruner, J. (1986). *Actual minds, possible worlds.* Cambridge, MA: Harvard University Press.

Bruner, J. (1990). *Acts of meaning.* Cambridge, MA.: Harvard University Press.

Bruner, J. (1992). The narrative construction of reality. In H. Beilin & P. Pufall (Eds.), *Piaget's theory: Prospects and possibilities* (pp. 229–248). Hillsdale, NJ: Erlbaum.

Bruner, J., & Feldman, C. F. (1990). Metaphors of consciousness and cognition in the history of psychology. In D. E. Leary (Ed.), *Metaphors in the history of psychology* (pp. 230–238). New York: Cambridge University Press.

Burke, P. (1986). Strengths and weaknesses of the history of mentalities. *History of European Ideas, 7,* 439–451.

Burton, R. (1852). *The anatomy of melancholy, what it is, with all the kinds, causes, symptoms, prognostics, and several causes of it* (5th ed.). Philadelphia: J. W. Moore. (Original work published 1651)

Bush, V. (1945). As we may think. *Atlantic Monthly, 176*(7), 101–108.

Cage, J. (1982). *A John Cage reader* (P. Gena & J. Brent, Eds.). New York: C. F. Peters.

Cairney, T. (1990). Intertextuality: Infectious echoes from the past. *The Reading Teacher, 43,* 478–484.

Calfee, R. C., & Chambliss, M. J. (1987). The structural design features of large texts. *Educational Psychologist, 22,* 357–378.

Callinicos, A. (1995). *Theories and narratives: Reflections on the philosophy of history.* Durham, NC: Duke University Press.

Calvino, I. (1981). *If on a winter's night a traveler* (W. Weaver, Trans.). New York: Harcourt Brace Jovanovich.

Carr, E. H. (1990). *What is history?* (2nd rev. ed.). Harmondsworth, Great Britain: Penguin.

Cary, E. (1613). *The tragedie of Mariam, the faire queene of jewry.* London: Thomas Creede for Richard Hawkins. (Original work published circa 1610)

Cazden, C. B. (1988). *Classroom discourse: The language of teaching and learning.* Portsmouth, NH: Heinemann.

Cazden, C. B. (1989). The myth of autonomous text. In D. M. Topping, D. C. Crowell, & V. N. Kobayashi (Eds.), *Thinking across cultures* (pp. 109–122). Hillsdale, NJ: Erlbaum.

Chafe, W. L. (1977). Giveness, contrastiveness, definiteness, subjects, topics, and points of view. In C. N. Li (Ed.), *Subject and topic* (pp. 25–56). New York: Academic Press.

Chapman, M. (1986). The structure of exchange: Piaget's sociological theory. *Human Development, 29,* 181–184.

Chapman, M. (1992). Equilibration and the dialectics of organization. In H. Beilin & P. Pufall (Eds.), *Piaget's theory: Prospects and possibilities* (pp. 39–59). Hillsdale, NJ: Erlbaum.

Charney, D. H., & Carlson, R. A. (1995). Learning to write in a genre: What student writers take from model texts. *Research in the Teaching of English, 29,* 88–125.

Chatman, S. (1978). *Story and discourse: Narrative structure in fiction and film.* Ithaca, NY: Cornell University Press.

Chomsky, N. (1957). *Syntactic structures.* The Hague: Mouton.

Chomsky, N. (1965). *Aspects of the theory of syntax.* Cambridge, MA: MIT Press.

Cicourel, A. V. (1981). Notes on the integration of micro- and macro-levels of analysis. In K. Knorr-Cetina & A. V. Cicourel (Eds.), *Advances in social theory and methodology: Toward an integration of micro- and macro-sociologies* (pp. 51–80). Boston: Routledge.

Clark, H. H. (1977). Inferences in comprehension. In D. LaBerge & S. J. Samuels (Eds.), *Basic processes in reading: Perception and comprehension* (pp. 243–263). Hillsdale, NJ: Erlbaum.

Clark, H. H., & Haviland, S. F. (1977). Comprehension and the given-new contract. In R. O. Freedle (Ed.), *Discourse production and comprehension* (pp. 1–40). Norwood, NJ: Ablex.

Cobb, P. (1994). Where is the mind? Constructivist and sociocultural perspectives on mathematical development. *Educational Researcher, 23,* 13–20.

Cochran, C. A. (1993). *Rhetorical relevance in reading and writing.* Unpublished doctoral dissertation, Carnegie Mellon University, Pittsburgh, PA.

Coe, R. (1987). An apology for form; or, who took the form out of the process? *College English, 49,* 13–28.

Colby, B. N. (1973). A partial grammar of Eskimo folktales. *American Anthropologist, 75,* 645–662.

Cole, M. (1985). Mind as a cultural achievement: Implications for IQ testing. In E. Eisner (Ed.), *Learning and teaching the ways of knowing* (84th Yearbook of the National Society for the Study of Education, pp. 218–249). Chicago: National Society for the Study of Education.

Cole, M., & Scribner, S. (1974). *Culture and thought.* New York: Wiley.

Coleridge, S. T. (1907). *Biographia literaria* (J. Shawcross, Ed.). Oxford: Clarendon. (Original work published 1817)

Collins, A., & Gentner, D. (1980). A framework for a cognitive theory of writing. In L. W. Gregg & E. R. Steinberg (Eds.), *Cognitive processes in writing* (pp. 51–72). Hillsdale, NJ: Erlbaum.

Cooper, C. R. (1977). Holistic evaluation of writing. In C. R. Cooper & L. Odell (Eds.), *Evaluating writing: Describing, measuring, judging* (pp. 3–31). Urbana, IL: National Council of Teachers of English.

Corbett, E. P. J. (1971). *Classical rhetoric for the modern student* (2nd ed.). New York: Oxford University Press.

Crismore, A. (1984). The rhetoric of textbooks: Metadiscourse. *Journal of Curriculum Studies, 16,* 279–296.

Crismore, A. (1990). Metadiscourse and discourse processes: Introduction and issues. *Discourse Processes, 13,* 191–205.

Cronin, B. (1984). *The citation process.* London: Taylor Graham.

Crowhurst, M., & Piché, G.I. (1979). Audience and mode of discourse effects on syntactic complexity in writing at two grade levels. *Research in the Teaching of English, 13,* 101–109.

Culler, J. (1975). *Structuralist poetics: Structuralism, linguistics and the study of literature.* London: Routledge.

Cunningham, J. W., & Fitzgerald, J. (1996). Epistemology and reading. *Reading Research Quarterly, 31,* 36–60.

Curtin, C. B. (1982). Armadillo. In *McGraw-Hill encyclopedia of science and technology* (Vol. 1, pp. 705–706). New York: McGraw-Hill.

Dagenais, J. (1994). *The ethics of reading in manuscript culture: Glossing the Libro de Buen Amor.* Princeton, NJ: Princeton University Press.

Daiute, C. (1986). Do 1 and 1 make 2? Patterns of influence by collaborative writers. *Written Communication, 3,* 382–408.

Daneš, F. (1974). Functional sentence perspective and the organization of the text. In F. Daneš (Ed.), *Papers on functional sentence perspective* (pp. 106–128). The Hague: Mouton.

Danesi, M. (1995). Cognitive science: Toward a Vichian perspective. In M. Danesi (Ed.), *Giambattista Vico and Anglo-American science: Philosophy and writing* (pp. 63–85). Berlin: Mouton de Gruyter.

D'Angelo, F. J. (1975). *A conceptual theory of rhetoric.* Cambridge, MA: Winthrop.

Danziger, K. (1990). Generative metaphor and the history of psychology. In D. E. Leary (Ed.), *Metaphors in the history of psychology* (pp. 331–346). New York: Cambridge University Press.

Dawes, R. M. (1966). Memory and distortion of meaningful written material. *British Journal of Psychology, 57,* 77–86.

de Man, P. (1979). Semiology and rhetoric. In J. V. Harari (Ed.), *Textual strategies: Perspectives in post-structural criticism* (pp. 121–140). Ithaca, NY: Cornell University Press.

Denis, M. (1984). Imagery and prose: A critical review of research on adults and children. *Text, 4,* 381–401.

Derrida, J. (1970). Structure, sign, and play in the discourse of the human sciences. In R. Macksey & E. Donato (Eds.), *The structuralist controversy: The language of criticism and the discourse of the human sciences* (pp. 247–272). Baltimore: Johns Hopkins University Press.

Derrida, J. (1976). *Of grammatology* (G. C. Spivak, Trans.). Baltimore: Johns Hopkins University Press. (Original work published in French 1967)

Derrida, J. (1978). *Writing and difference* (A. Bass, Trans.). Chicago: University of Chicago Press. (Original work published in French 1967)

Derrida, J. (1992a). The law of genre. In D. Attridge (Ed.) *Acts of literature* (pp. 221–252). New York: Routledge. (Original work published in French 1980)

Derrida, J. (1992b). The strange institution called literature: An interview with Jacques Derrida. In D. Attridge (Ed.); G. Bennington & R. Bowlby (Trans.), *Acts of literature* (pp. 33–75). New York: Routledge.

Derrida, J. (1995). The time is out of joint. In A. Haverkamp (Ed.), *Deconstruction is/in America* (pp. 14–38). New York: New York University Press.

DiSibio, M. (1982). Memory for connected discourse: A constructivist view. *Review of Educational Research, 52,* 149–174.

Dobson, M., Rada, R., Chen, C., Michailidis, A, & Ulloa, A. (1993). Towards a consolidated model for a collaborative courseware authoring system. *Journal of Computer Assisted Learning, 9,* 34–50.

Donaldson, M. (1978). *Children's minds.* New York: Norton.

Dooling, D. J., & Lachman, R. (1971). Effects of comprehension on retention of prose. *Journal of Experimental Psychology, 88,* 216–222.

Douglas, M. (1986). *How institutions think.* Syracuse, NY: Syracuse University Press.

Duffy, T. M., Higgins, L., Mehlenbacher, B., Cochran, C. A., Wallace, D., Hill, C., Haugen, D., McCaffrey, M., Burnett, R., Sloane, S., & Smith, S. (1989). Models for the design of instructional text. *Reading Research Quarterly, 24,* 434–457.

Dunn, K. (1994). *Pretexts of authority: The rhetoric of authorship in the Renaissance preface.* Stanford, CA: Stanford University Press.

Durkheim, E. (1953). Individual and collective representations. D. F. Pocock (Trans.) *Sociology and philosophy* (pp. 1–34). Glencoe, IL: Free Press. (Original work published in French 1898)

Durkheim, E. (1968). *The elementary forms of the religious life* (J. W. Swain, Trans.). New York: Free Press. (Original work published in French 1912)

Durkheim, E. (1984). *The division of labor in society* (W. D. Halls, Trans.). New York: Free Press. (Original work published in French 1893)

Durkheim, E., & Mauss, M. (1963). *Primitive classification* (R. Needham, Trans.). Chicago: University of Chicago Press. (Original work published in French 1901–1902)

Durst, R. K. (1984). The development of analytic writing. In A. N. Applebee, *Contexts for learning to write: Studies of secondary school instruction* (pp. 79–102). Norwood, NJ: Ablex.

Durst, R. K. (1987). Cognitive and linguistic demands of analytic writing. *Research in the Teaching of English, 21,* 347–376.

Dyson, A. H. (1986). Transitions and tensions: Interrelationships between the drawing, talking, and dictating of young children. *Research in the Teaching of English, 20,* 379–409.

Ebbinghaus, H. (1913). *Memory: A contribution to experimental psychology* (H. A. Ruger & C. E. Bussenius, Trans.). New York: Dover. (Original work published in German 1895)

Eco, U. (1976). *A theory of semiotics.* Bloomington: Indiana University Press.

Eco, U. (1979). *The role of the reader: Explorations in the semiotics of texts.* Bloomington: Indiana University Press.

Eco, U. (1984). *Semiotics and the philosophy of language.* London: Macmillan.

Ede, L., & Lunsford, A. (1984). Audience addressed/audience invoked: The role of audience in composition theory and pedagogy. *College Composition and Communication, 35,* 155–171.

Ede, L., & Lunsford, A. (1990). *Singular texts/plural authors.* Carbondale: Southern Illinois University Press.

Edge, D. O. (1974). Technological metaphor and social control. *New Literary History, 6,* 135–147.

Eichenbaum, B. (1965). The theory of the formal method. In L. T. Lemon & M. J. Reis (Eds.), *Russian formalist criticism: Four essays* (pp. 99–139). Lincoln: University of Nebraska Press. (Original work published in Ukranian 1926)

Ellison, R. (1984). *Run and shoot football: The offense of the future* (2nd ed.). West Nyack, NY: Parker.

Emerson, R. W. (1968). Plato; or, the philosophers. In *The complete works of Ralph Waldo Emerson: Vol. 4. Representative men: Seven lectures* (pp. 39–79). New York: AMS Press. (Original work published 1903)

Emig, J. (1971). *The composing processes of twelfth graders* (Research Rep. No. 13). Urbana, IL: National Council of Teachers of English.

Encyclopaedia Britannica. (1981). Rodeo. In *Britannica junior encyclopaedia* (Vol. 13, pp. 127–128). Chicago: Author.

Encyclopedia Americana. (1986). Octopus. In *Encyclopedia Americana* (Vol. 20, pp. 631–632). Danbury, CT: Grolier.

Englert, C. S., & Hiebert, E. H. (1984). Children's developing awareness of text structures in expository materials. *Journal of Educational Psychology, 76,* 65–74.

Faigley, L., & Hansen, K. (1985). Learning to write in the social sciences. *College Composition and Communication, 36,* 140–149.

Fekete, J. (1984). Introduction: The new maelstrom. In J. Fekete (Ed.), *The structural allegory: Reconstructive encounters with the new French thought* (pp. xi–xxii). Minneapolis: University of Minnesota Press.

Ferriar, J. (1974). *Illustrations of Sterne.* New York: Garland. (Original work published 1798)

Fillmore, C. J. (1968). The case for case. In E. Bach & R. T. Harms (Eds.), *Universals in linguistic theory* (pp. 1–88). New York: Holt, Rinehart & Winston.

Firbas, J. (1974). Some aspects of the Czechoslovak approach to problems in functional sentence perspective. In F. Daneš (Ed.), *Papers on functional sentence perspective* (pp. 11–37). The Hague: Mouton.

Fish, S. (1970). Literature in the reader: Affective sylistics. *New Literary History, 2*(1), 123–162.

Fish, S. (1976). Interpreting the *Variorum. Critical Inquiry, 2,* 465–485.

Fish, S. (1980). *Is there a text in this class? The authority of interpretive communities.* Cambridge, MA: Harvard University Press.

Fitzgerald, J., & Spiegel, D. L. (1983). Enhancing children's reading comprehension through instruction in narrative structure. *Journal of Reading Behavior, 15,* 1–17.

Flavell, J. H. (1966). Role-taking and communication skills in children. *Young Children, 21,* 164–177.

Flavell, J. H. (1992). Perspectives on perspective taking. In H. Beilin & P. Pufall (Eds.), *Piaget's theory: Prospects and possibilities* (pp. 107–139). Hillsdale, NJ: Erlbaum.

Flavell, J. H., Botkin, P. T., Fry, C. L., Wright, J. W., & Jarvis, P. E. (1968). *The development of role-taking and communication skills in children.* New York: Wiley.

Fleck, L. (1979). *Genesis and development of a scientific fact* (T. J. Trenn & R. K. Merton, Eds.; F. Bradley & T. J. Trenn, Trans.). Chicago: University of Chicago Press. (Original work published in German 1935).

Flower, L., Burnett, R., Hajduk, T., Wallace, D., Norris, L., Peck, W., & Spivey, N. N. (1989). *Classroom inquiry in collaborative planning.* Pittsburgh, PA: Center for the Study of Writing at Berkeley, CA, and at Carnegie Mellon.

Flower, L., & Hayes, J. R. (1981). A cognitive process theory of writing. *College Composition and Communication, 32,* 365–387.

Flower, L., & Hayes, J. R. (1984). Images, plans, and prose: The representation of meaning in writing. *Written Communication, 1,* 120–160.

Flower, L., Stein, V., Ackerman, J., Kantz, M., McCormick, K., & Peck, W. (1990). *Reading to write: Exploring a cognitive and social process.* New York: Oxford University Press.

Foster, D. (1989). *Elegy by W. S.—A study in attribution.* Newark: University of Delaware Press.

Foucault, M. (1970). *The order of things: An archeology of the human sciences.* New York: Pantheon. (Original work published in French 1966)

Foucault, M. (1972). *The archeology of knowledge* (A. M. S. Smith, Trans.). New York: Pantheon. (Original work published in French 1969)

Foucault, M. (1979). What is an author? In J. V. Harari (Ed.), *Textual strategies: Perspectives in post-structuralist criticism* (pp. 141–160). Ithaca, NY: Cornell University Press. (Original work published in French 1969)

Foucault, M. (1989). *Foucault live (Interviews 1966–84)* (S. Lotringer, Ed.; J. Johnston, Trans.). New York: Semiotexte.

Frawley, W. (1987). *Text and epistemology.* Norwood, NJ: Ablex.

Frederiksen, C. H. (1972). Effects of task-induced operations on comprehension and memory processes. In R. O. Freedle & J. B. Carroll (Eds.), *Language comprehension and the acquisition of knowledge* (pp. 211–245). Washington, DC: Winston.

Frederiksen, C. H. (1975a). Effects of context-induced processing operations on semantic information acquired from discourse. *Cognitive Psychology, 7,* 139–166.

Frederiksen, C. H. (1975b). Representing logical and semantic structure of knowledge acquired from discourse. *Cognitive Psychology, 7,* 317–458.

Frederiksen, C. H. (1977). Semantic processing units in understanding text. In R. O. Freedle (Ed.), *Discourse production and comprehension* (pp. 57–87). Norwood, NJ: Ablex.

Freedle, R. O., & Carroll, J. B. (Eds.). (1972). *Language comprehension and the acquisition of knowledge.* Washington, DC: Winston.

Freedle, R. O., Naus, M., & Schwartz, L. (1977). Prose pocessing from a psychosocial perspective. In R. O. Freedle (Ed.), *Discourse production and comprehension* (pp. 175–192). Norwood, NJ: Ablex.

Freedman, S. W., & Sperling, M. (1985). Written language acquisition: The role of response and the writing conference. In S. W. Freedman (Ed.), *The acquisition of written language* (pp. 106–130). Norwood, NJ: Ablex.

Frye, N. (1969). *Fearful symmetry: A study of William Blake.* Princeton, NJ: Princeton University Press.

Gadamer, H.-G. (1975). *Truth and method* (2nd ed.). New York: Seabury. (Original work published in German 1960)

Galda, L. (1984). The relations between reading and writing in young children. In R. Beach & L. Bridwell (Eds.), *New directions in composition research* (pp. 193–204). New York: Guilford.

Gardner, H. (1981). *The quest for mind: Piaget, Lévi-Strauss, and the structuralist movement* (2nd ed.). Chicago: University of Chicago Press.

Garner, R., Gillingham, M. G., & White, J. (1989). Effects of "seductive details" on macroprocessing and microprocessing in adults and children. *Cognition and Instruction, 6,* 41–57.

Gauld, A., & Stephenson, G. M. (1967). Some experiments relating to Bartlett's theory of remembering. *British Journal of Psychology, 58,* 39–49.

Gee, J. (1989). Self, society, mushfake, and Vygotsky: Meditations on papers redefining the social in composition theory. *The Writing Instructor, 8,* 177–183.

Geertz, C. (1983). *Local knowledge: Further essays in interpretive anthropology.* New York: Basic Books.

Geisler, C. (1991). Toward a sociocognitive model of literacy: Constructing mental models in a philosophical conversation. In C. Bazerman & J. Paradis (Eds.), *Textual dynamics and the professions: Historical and contemporary studies of writing in professional communities* (pp. 171–190). Madison: University of Wisconsin Press.

Geisler, C. (1994). *Academic literacy and the nature of expertise: Reading, writing, and knowing in academic philosophy.* Hillsdale, NJ: Erlbaum.

Gere, A. R., & Stevens, R. S. (1985). The language of writing groups: How oral response shapes revision. In S. W. Freedman (Ed.), *The acquisition of written language* (pp. 85–105). Norwood, NJ: Ablex.

Gergen, K. J. (1985). The social constructionist movement in modern psychology. *American Psychologist, 40,* 266–275.

Gergen, K. J. (1995). Social construction and the educational process. In L. P. Steffe & J. Gale (Eds.), *Constructivism in education* (pp. 17–39). Hillsdale, NJ: Erlbaum.

Gibson, J. J. (1979). *The ecological approach to visual perception.* Boston: Houghton Mifflin.

Gilbert, G. N. (1977). Referencing as persuasion. *Social Studies of Science, 7,* 113–122.

Gilbert, G. N., & Mulkay, M. J. (1984). *Opening Pandora's box: A sociological analysis of scientists' discourse.* Cambridge: Cambridge University Press.

Glucksberg, S., & Krauss, R. M. (1967). What do people say after they have learned to talk? Studies of the development of referential communication. *Merrill-Palmer Quarterly, 13,* 309–316.

Goetz, E. T., & Armbruster, B. B. (1980). Psychological correlates of text structure. In R. J. Spiro, B. C. Bruce, & W. F. Brewer (Eds.), *Theoretical issues in reading comprehension* (pp. 201–220). Hillsdale, NJ: Erlbaum.

Goldman, S. R., & Varnhagen, C. K. (1986). Memory for embedded and sequential story structures. *Journal of Memory and Language, 25,* 401–418.

Goldstein, L. J. (1976). *Historical knowing.* Austin: University of Texas Press.

Goldstein, L. J. (1977). History and the primacy of knowing. *History and Theory, 16*(4), 29–52.

Gomulicki, B. R. (1956). Recall as an abstractive process. *Acta Psychologica, 12,* 77–94.

Goodman, K. S. (1967). Reading: A psycholinguistic guessing game. *Journal of the Reading Specialist, 4,* 126–135.

Goodman, N. (1951). *The structure of appearance*. Indianapolis, IN: Bobbs-Merrill.

Goodman, N. (1978). *Ways of worldmaking*. Indianapolis, IN: Hackett.

Goodman, N. (1979). Metaphor as moonlighting. In S. Sachs (Ed.), *On metaphor* (pp. 175–180). Chicago: University of Chicago Press.

Goodman, N. (1980). Twisted tales; or, story, study, and symphony. *Critical Inquiry, 7,* 103–119.

Goodman, N. (1984). *Of mind and other matters*. Cambridge, MA: Harvard University Press.

Goodwin, G. G. (1983). Armadillo. In *Collier's encyclopedia* (Vol. 2, p. 66). New York: Collier's.

Graesser, A. C. (1981). *Prose comprehension beyond the word*. New York: Springer-Verlag.

Graesser, A. C., Bertus, E. L., & Magliano, J. P. (1995). Inference generation during the comprehension of narrative text. In R. F. Lorch, Jr., & E. J. O'Brien (Eds.), *Sources of coherence in reading* (pp. 295–320). Hillsdale, NJ: Erlbaum.

Graesser, A. C., & Kreuz, R. J. (1993). A theory of inference generation during text comprehension. *Discourse Processes, 16,* 145–160.

Green, G. M. (1989). *Pragmatics and natural language understanding*. Hillsdale, NJ: Erlbaum.

Green, J. L., & Wallat, C. (1981). Mapping instructional conversations—a sociolinguistic ethnography. In J. L. Green & C. Wallat (Eds.), *Ethnography and language in educational settings* (pp. 161–205). Norwood, NJ: Ablex.

Green, J. L., Weade, R., & Graham, K. (1988). Lesson construction and student participation: A sociolinguistic analysis. In J. L. Green & J. O. Harker (Eds.), *Multiple perspective analyses of classroom discourse* (pp. 11–47). Norwood, NJ: Ablex.

Greene, S. (1993). The role of task in the development of academic thinking through reading and writing in a college history course. *Research in the Teaching of English, 27,* 46–75.

Greene, S. (1994). Students as authors in the study of history. In G. Leinhardt, I. L. Beck, & C. Stainton (Eds.), *Teaching and learning in history* (pp. 137–170). Hillsdale, NJ: Erlbaum.

Greenleaf, C., & Freedman, S. W. (1993). Linking classroom discourse and classroom content: Following the trail of intellectual work in a writing lesson. *Discourse Processes, 16,* 465–505.

Greimas, A. J. (1966). *Sémantique structurale: Recherche de méthode*. Paris: Larousse.

Greimas, A. J. (1987). *On meaning: Selected writings in semiotic theory* (P. J. Perron & F. H. Collins, Trans.). Minneapolis: University of Minnesota Press.

Griffin, S. (1971). Rape: The all-American crime. *Ramparts, 10*(13), 26–35.

Grimes, J. E. (1975). *The thread of discourse*. The Hague: Mouton.

Gumperz, J. J., Kaltman, H., & O'Connor, M. C. (1984). Cohesion in spoken and written discourse: Ethnic style and the transition to literacy. In D. Tannen (Ed.), *Coherence in spoken and written discourse* (pp. 3–19). Norwood, NJ: Ablex.

Haas, C. (1989). How the writing medium shapes the writing process: Effects of word processing on planning. *Research in the Teaching of English, 23,* 181–207.

Haas, C. (1994). Learning to read biology: One student's rhetorical development in college. *Written Communication, 11,* 43–84.

Haas, C., & Flower, L. (1988). Rhetorical reading strategies and the construction of meaning. *College Composition and Communication, 39,* 167–183.

Haas, C., & Hayes, J. R. (1986). What did I just say? Reading problems in writing with the machine. *Research in the Teaching of English, 20,* 22–35.

Haddon, A. C. (1894). *The decorative art of British New Guinea* (Cunningham Memoirs No. 10). Dublin: Royal Irish Academy.

Haddon, A. C. (1901). *Reports of the Cambridge anthropological expedition to Torres Straits* (Vol. 1). Cambridge: Cambridge University Press.

Haddon, A. C. (1920). *Migrations of cultures in British New Guinea* (Huxley Memorial Lecture). London: Royal Anthropological Institute.

Haddon, A. C. (1928). Social constructiveness: IV. *British Journal of Psychology, 18,* 400–404.

Halász, L. (1988). Affective-structural effect and the characters' perception in reception of short stories: An American–Hungarian cross-cultural study. *Poetics, 17,* 417–438.

Halbwachs, M. (1975). *Les Cadres sociaux de la mémoire.* New York: Arno. (Original work published 1925)

Halbwachs, M. (1980). *The collective memory* (F. J. Ditter, Jr., & V. Y. Ditter, Trans.). New York: Harper & Row. (Original work published in French 1950)

Halliday, M. A. K. (1994). The place of dialogue in children's construction of meaning. In R. B. Ruddell, M. R. Ruddell, & H. Singer (Eds.), *Theoretical models and processes of reading* (4th ed., pp. 70–82). Newark, DE: International Reading Association.

Halliday, M. A. K., & Hasan, R. (1976). *Cohesion in English.* London: Longman.

Harris, R. (1983). Translator's introduction. In F. de Saussure, *Course in general linguistics* (pp. ix–xvi). London: Duckworth.

Harris, Z. S. (1951). *Methods in structural linguistics.* Chicago: University of Chicago Press.

Hartman, D. K. (1991). The intertextual links of readers using multiple passages: A postmodern/semiotic/cognitive view of meaning-making. In J. Zutell & S. McCormick (Eds.), *Learner factors/teacher factors: Issues in literacy research and instruction* (40th Yearbook of the National Reading Conference, pp. 49–66). Chicago: National Reading Conference.

Hawkes, T. (1977). *Structuralism and semiotics.* Berkeley: University of California Press.

Hayes, J. R., & Flower, L. S. (1980). Identifying the organization of writing processes. In L. W. Gregg & E. R. Steinberg (Eds.), *Cognitive processes in writing* (pp. 3–28). Hillsdale, NJ: Erlbaum.

Head, H. (1920). *Studies in neurology.* Oxford: Oxford University Press.

Head, H. (1926). *Aphasia and kindred disorders of speech.* Cambridge: Cambridge University Press.

Head, H., & Holmes, G. (1911–1912). Sensory disturbances from cerebral lesions. *Brain, 34,* 102–254.

Heath, S. B. (1982). *Ways with words: Language, life, and work in communities and classrooms.* New York: Cambridge University Press.

Hegel, G. W. F. (1874). *The logic of Hegel translated from the encyclopaedia of the philosophical sciences with prolegomena* (W. Wallace, Trans). Oxford: Clarendon. (Original work published in German 1843)

Hegel, G. W. F. (1894). *Hegel's philosophy of mind translated from the encyclopaedia of the philosophical sciences with five introductory essays* (W. Wallace, Trans.). Oxford: Clarendon. (Original work published in German 1827 and 1830)

Hegel, G. W. F. (1929). *Hegel's science of logic* (W. H. Johnston & L. G. Struthers, Trans.). New York: Macmillan. (Original work published in German 1812–1816)

Hegel, G. W. F. (1931). *The phenomenology of mind* (J. B. Baille, Trans.) (2nd ed.). New York: Macmillan. (Original work published in German 1807)

Hidi, S., & Anderson, V. (1986). Producing written summaries: Task demands, cognitive operations, and implications for instruction. *Review of Educational Research, 56,* 473–493.

Hidi, S., & Baird, W. (1988). Strategies for increasing text-based interest and students' recall of expository texts. *Reading Research Quarterly, 20,* 465–483.

Hidi, S., Baird, W., & Hildyard, A. (1982). That's important but is it interesting? Two factors in processing. In A. Flammer & W. Kintsch (Eds.), *Discourse processing* (pp. 63–75). Amsterdam: North Holland.

Hodge, R., & Kress, G. (1988). *Social semiotics.* Ithaca, NY: Cornell University Press.

Hoey, M. (1986). Overlapping patterns of discourse organization and their implications for clause relational analysis of problem-solution texts. In C. R. Cooper & S. Greenbaum (Eds.), *Studying writing: Linguistic approaches* (pp. 187–214). Beverly Hills, CA: Sage.

Hogg, M. A., & McGarty, C. (1990). Self-categorization and social identity. In D. Abrams & M. A. Hogg (Eds.), *Social identity theory: Constructive and critical advances* (pp. 10–27). New York: Springer-Verlag.

Holland, N. N. (1968). *The dynamics of literary response.* New York: Oxford University Press.

Holland, N. N. (1975a). *5 readers reading.* New Haven, CT: Yale University Press.

Holland, N. N. (1975b). Unity identity text self. *Publications of the Modern Language Association, 90,* 813–822.

Holland, N. N. (1992). *The critical I.* New York: Columbia University Press.

Honan, W. H. (1996, January 14). A sleuth gets his man: It's Shakespeare. *New York Times,* pp. 1A, 12A.

Horowitz, R., & Samuels, S. J. (Eds.). (1987). *Comprehending oral and written language.* New York: Academic Press.

Hoy, E. A. (1975). Measurement of egocentrism in children's communication. *Developmental Psychology, 11,* 392.

Hume, D. (1907). *A treatise on human nature.* Chicago: Open Court. (Original work published in 3 books, 1739–1740)

Hunt, K. (1965). *Grammatical structures written at three grade levels* (Research Rep. No. 3). Champaign, IL: National Council of Teachers of English.

Hunt, R. A., & Vipond, D. (1986). Evaluations in literary reading. *Text, 6,* 53–71.

Huxley, A. (1937). In B. R. Haydon (Ed.), *The olive tree* (pp. 243–265). New York: Harper.

Hymes, D. (1974a). *Foundations in sociolinguistics: An ethnographic approach.* Philadelphia: University of Pennsylvania Press.

Hymes, D. (1974b). Ways of speaking. In R. Bauman & J. Sherzer (Eds.), *Explorations in the ethnography of speaking* (pp. 433–451). London: Cambridge University Press.

Hynds, S. (1985). Interpersonal cognitive complexity and the literary response processes of adolescent readers. *Research in the Teaching of English, 19,* 386–404.

Iser, W. (1978). *The act of reading: A theory of aesthetic response.* Baltimore: Johns Hopkins University Press.

Jacoby, R. (1975). *Social amnesia: A critique of conformist psychology from Adler to Laing.* Boston: Beacon.

Jakobson, R. (1956). Two aspects of language and two types of aphasia disturbances. In R. Jakobson & M. Halle, *Fundamentals of language* (Part 2, pp. 55–82). The Hague: Mouton.

Jakobson, R. (1971a). The dominant. In L. Matejka & K. Pomorska (Eds.), *Readings in Russian poetics: Formalist and structuralist views* (pp. 82–87). Cambridge, MA: MIT Press. (Original paper presented in Czech 1935)

Jakobson, R. (1971b). Results of a joint conference of anthropologists. In *Selected writings: Vol. II. Words and language* (pp. 554–568). The Hague: Mouton. (Original work published 1953)

Jakobson, R. (1971c). Shifters, verbal categories, and the Russian verb. In *Selected writings: Vol. II. Words and language* (pp. 130–147). The Hague: Mouton. (Original work published 1956)

Johns, A. M. (1985). Summary protocols of "unprepared" and "adept" university students: Replications and distortions of the original. *Language Learning, 35,* 495–517.

Johnson, B. (1987). *A world of difference.* Baltimore: Johns Hopkins University Press.

Johnson, R. (1970). Recall of prose as a function of the structural importance of the linguistic units. *Journal of Verbal Learning and Verbal Behavior, 9,* 12–20.

Johnson-Laird, P. N. (1983). *Mental models: Towards a cognitive science of language, inference, and consciousness.* Cambridge: Cambridge University Press.

Jung, C. G. (1916). La structure de l'inconscient. *Archives de Psychologie, 16,* 152–179.

Kanin, E. J. (1983). Rape as a function of relative sexual frustration. *Psychological Reports, 52,* 133–134.

Kant, E. (1946). *Critique of pure reason.* (J. M. D. Meiklejohn, Trans.). New York: Dutton. (Original work published in German 1781)

Kaufer, D., & Geisler, C. (1989). Novelty in academic writing. *Written Communication, 6,* 286–311.

Kaufer, D., Geisler, C., & Neuwirth, C. (1989). *Arguing from sources: Exploring issues through reading and writing.* San Diego, CA: Harcourt Brace Jovanovich.

Kay, H. (1955). Learning and retaining verbal material. *British Journal of Psychology, 46,* 81–100.

Kazdin, A. E. (1977). Assessing the clinical or applied importance of behavior change through social validation. *Behavior Modification, 1,* 427–451.

Kazdin, A. E., Bass, D., Siegel, T., & Thomas, C. (1989). Cognitive-behavioral therapy and relationship therapy in the treatment of children referred for antisocial behavior. *Journal of Consulting and Clinical Psychology, 57,* 522–535.

Kazdin, A. E., French, N. H., Unis, A. S., Esveldt-Dawson, K., & Sherick, R. B. (1983). Hopelessness, depression, and suicidal intent among psychiatrically disturbed inpatient children. *Journal of Consulting and Clinical Psychology, 51,* 504–510.

Kearsley, G. (1988). Authoring considerations for hypertext. *Educational Technology, 28*(11), 21–24.

Kelly, G. A. (1955). *The psychology of personal constructs.* New York: Norton.

Kennedy, M. L. (1985). The composing process of college students writing from sources. *Written Communication, 2,* 434–456.

Kermode, F. (1980). Secrets and narrative sequence. *Critical Inquiry, 7,* 83–101.

Kieras, D. E. (1980). Initial mention as a signal to thematic content in technical passages. *Memory & Cognition, 8,* 345–353.

Kieras, D. E. (1981). A model of reader strategy for abstracting main ideas from simple technical prose. *Text, 2,* 47–82.

Kieras, D. E. (1985). Thematic processes in the comprehension of technical prose. In B. K. Britton & J. B. Black (Eds.), *Understanding expository text* (pp. 89–107). Hillsdale, NJ: Erlbaum.

Kinneavy, J. L. (1971). *A theory of discourse.* Englewood Cliffs, NJ: Prentice-Hall.

Kintsch, W. (1974). *The representation of meaning in memory.* Hillsdale, NJ: Erlbaum.

Kintsch, W. (1988). The role of knowledge in discourse comprehension: A construction-integration model. *Psychological Review, 95,* 163–182.

Kintsch, W., & Greene, E. (1978). The role of culture-specific schemata in the comprehension and recall of stories. *Discourse Processes, 1,* 1–13.

Kintsch, W., & van Dijk, T. A. (1975). Comment on se rappelle et on résume des histoires. *Langages, 40,* 98–128.

Kintsch, W., & van Dijk, T. A. (1978). Toward a model of text comprehension and production. *Psychological Review, 85,* 363–394.

Kintsch, W., & Vipond, D. (1979). Reading comprehension and readability in educational practice and psychological theory. In L. G. Nilsson (Ed.), *Perspectives in memory research* (pp. 329–365). Hillsdale, NJ: Erlbaum.

Kintsch, W., & Yarbrough, J. C. (1982). The role of rhetorical structure in text comprehension. *Journal of Educational Psychology, 74,* 828–834.

Knapp, P. A. (1990). *Chaucer and the social contest.* New York: Routledge.

Koffka, K. (1935). *Principles of gestalt psychology.* New York: Harcourt, Brace.

Köhler, W. (1929). *Gestalt psychology.* New York: Liveright.

Koss, M. P., Leonard, K. E., Beezley, D. A., & Oros, C. J. (1985). Nonstranger sexual aggression: A discriminant analysis of the psychological characteristics of undetected offenders. *Sex Roles, 12,* 981–992.

Kristeva, J. (1968). Problèmes de la structuration du texte. *Théorie d'ensemble* (pp. 297–316). Paris: Éditions du Seuil.

Kristeva, J. (1969). Narration et transformation. *Semiotica, 1,* 422–448.

Kristeva, J. (1980). *Desire in language: A semiotic approach to literature and art* (L. S. Roudiez, Ed.; A. Jardine, T. Gora, & L. S. Roudiez, Trans.). New York: Columbia University Press.

Kristeva, J. (1986). Word, dialogue and novel (A. Jardine, T. Gora, & L. S. Roudiez, Trans.). *The Kristeva reader* (T. Moi, Ed.) (pp. 34–61). New York: Columbia University Press. (Original work published in French 1967)

Kristof, A. (1986). *Le grand cahier* [The notebook]. Paris: Seuil.

Kroll, B. M. (1985). Rewriting a complex story for a young reader: The development of audience-adapted writing skills. *Research in the Teaching of English, 19,* 120–139.

Kucer, S. (1985). The making of meaning: Reading and writing as parallel processes. *Written Communication, 2,* 317–336.

Kuhn, T. (1962). *The structure of scientific revolutions.* Chicago: University of Chicago Press.

Labov, W. (1972). *Language in the inner city: Studies in the Black English vernacular.* Philadelphia: University of Pennsylvania Press.

Lacan, J. (1968). *The language of the self: The function of language in psychoanalysis* (A. Wilden, Trans.). Baltimore: Johns Hopkins University Press. (Original work published in French 1956)

Lacan, J. (1970). Of structure as an inmixing of an otherness prerequisite to any subject whatever. In R. Macksey & E. Donato (Eds.), *The structuralist controversy: The language of criticism and the discourse of the human sciences* (pp. 186–195). Baltimore: Johns Hopkins University Press.

Lacan, J. (1977). *Écrits: A selection* (A. Sheridan, Trans.). New York: Norton. (Original work published in French 1966)

Laclos, C. de (1929). *Les liaisons dangereuses* [Dangerous liaisons]. Paris: Black Sun.

Lakoff, G., & Turner, M. (1988). *More than cool reason: A field guide to poetic metaphor.* Chicago: University of Chicago Press.

Landow, G. P. (Ed.). (1994). *Hyper/text/theory.* Baltimore: Johns Hopkins University Press.

Langer, J. A. (1984). The effects of available knowledge on responses to school writing tasks. *Research in the Teaching of English, 18,* 27–44.

Langer, J. A., & Applebee, A. N. (1987). *How writing shapes thinking: A study of teaching and learning* (Research Rep. No. 22). Urbana, IL: National Council of Teachers of English.

Latour, B. (1987). *Science in action.* Cambridge, MA: Harvard University Press.

Leeds-Hurwitz, W. (1993). *Semiotics and communication: Signs, codes, cultures.* Hillsdale, NJ: Erlbaum.

Leenhardt, J. (1992). Does there exist a European reader? *Poetics, 21,* 117–128.

Leibniz, G. W. F. von (1981). *New essays on understanding* (R. Remnant & J. Bennett, Eds. and Trans.). Cambridge: Cambridge University Press. (Original work published in German 1704)

Lemke, J. (1988). Genres, semantics, and classroom education. *Linguistics and Education, 1,* 81–99.

Leont'ev, A. N. (1981). *Problems of the development of mind.* Moscow: Progress Publishers.

Levin, S. R. (1988). *Metaphoric worlds: Conceptions of a Romantic nature.* New Haven, CT: Yale University Press.

Lévi-Strauss, C. (1963). *Structural anthropology* (C. Jacobson & G. Schoepf, Trans.). New York: Basic Books. (Original work published in French 1958)

Lévi-Strauss, C. (1966). *The savage mind* (G. Weidenfeld, Trans.). Chicago: University of Chicago Press. (Original work published in French 1962)

Lévi-Strauss, C. (1969). *The elementary structures of kinship* (J. Bell, J. von Sturmer, & R. Needham, Trans.). Boston: Beacon. (Original work published in French 1960)

Lévi-Strauss, C. (1973). *From honey to ashes* (J. Weightman & D. Weightman, Trans.). New York: Harper & Row. (Original work published in French 1966)

Lévi-Strauss, C. (1983). *The raw and the cooked* (J. Weightman & D. Weightman, Trans.). Chicago: University of Chicago Press. (Original work published in French 1964)

Lévy-Bruhl, L. (1923). *Primitive mentality* (L. A. Clare, Trans.). New York: Macmillan. (Original work published in French 1922)

Lévy-Bruhl, L. (1926). *How natives think* (L. A. Clare, Trans.). London: Allen & Unwin. (Original work published in French 1910)

Lloyd, P. (1975). *Communication in pre-school children.* Unpublished doctoral dissertation, Edinburgh University, Scotland.

Loban, W. D. (1976). *Language development: Kindergarten through grade twelve* (Research Rep. No. 18). Urbana, IL: National Council of Teachers of English.

Lodge, D. (1977). *The modes of modern writing: Metaphor, metonymy, and the typology of modern literature*. London: Edward Arnold.

Longacre, R. E. (1979). The paragraph as a grammatical unit. In T. Givon (Ed.), *Syntax and semantics: XII. Discourse and syntax* (pp. 115–134). New York: Academic Press.

Lorch, E. P., Lorch, R. F., Jr., Gretter, M. L., & Horn, D. G. (1987). On-line processing of topic structure by children and adults. *Journal of Experimental Child Psychology, 43*, 81–95.

Lorch, R. F., Jr. (1993). Integration of topic and subordinate information during reading. *Journal of Experimental Psychology: Learning, Memory, and Cognition, 32*, 1071–1081.

Lorch, R. F., Jr., Klusewitz, M. A., & Lorch, E. P. (1995). Distinctions among reading situations. In R. F. Lorch, Jr., & E. J. O'Brien (Eds.), *Sources of coherence in reading* (pp. 375–398). Hillsdale, NJ: Erlbaum.

Lotze, H. (1852). *Medicinische Psychologie; oder, Physiologie der Seele*. Leipzig: Weidmann.

Lyotard, J. F. (1984). *The postmodern condition: A report on knowledge* (G. Bennington & B. Massumi, Trans.). Minneapolis: University of Minnesota Press. (Original work published in French 1979)

MacCurdy, J. T. (1928). Social constructiveness: II. *British Journal of Psychology, 18*, 392–395.

Mahoney, M. J. (1991). *Human change processes: The scientific foundations of psychotherapy*. New York: Basic Books.

Mallon, T. (1990). *Stolen words: Forays into the origins and ravages of plagiarism*. New York: Ticknor & Fields.

Mandler, J. M., & Goodman, M. S. (1982). On the psychological validity of story structure. *Journal of Verbal Learning and Verbal Behavior, 21*, 507–523.

Mandler, J. M., & Johnson, N. S. (1977). Remembrance of things parsed: Story structure and recall. *Cognitive Psychology, 9*, 111–151.

Mann, W. C., & Thompson, S. A. (1988). Rhetorical structure theory. *Text, 8*, 243–281.

Mannheim, K. (1936). *Ideology and utopia: An introduction to the sociology of knowledge* (L. Wirth & E. Shils, Trans.). London: Routledge. (Original work published in German 1929)

Mannheim, K. (1952). *Essays on the sociology of knowledge* (P. Kecskemeti, Ed.). New York: Oxford University Press.

Mannheim, K. (1956). *Essays on the sociology of culture*. New York: Oxford University Press.

Many, J. E., Fyfe, R., Lewis, G., & Mitchell, E. (1996). Traversing the topical landscape: Exploring students self-directed reading-writing-research processes. *Reading Research Quarterly, 31*, 12–35.

Maratsos, M. P. (1973). Nonegocentric communication abilities in preschool children. *Child Development, 44*, 697–700.

Markus, H., & Nurius, P. (1986). Possible selves. *American Psychologist, 41*, 954–969.

Marshall, N., & Glock, M. D. (1978–1979). Comprehension of connected discourse: A study into the relationships between the structure of text and information recalled. *Reading Research Quarterly, 14*, 10–56.

Mathesius, V. (1964). On linguistic characterology with illustrations from modern English. In J. Vachek (Ed.), *A Prague school reader in linguistics* (pp. 59–67). Bloomington: Indiana University Press. (Original work published 1928)

Mathison, M. A. (1993). *Writing the critique: Taking critical stances on disciplinary texts*. Unpublished doctoral dissertation, Carnegie Mellon University, Pittsburgh, PA.

McClelland, J. L., & Rumelhart, D. E. (1986). *Parallel distributed processing: Explorations in the microstructure of cognition: Vol. 1. Foundations.* Cambridge, MA: MIT Press.

McCormick, K. (1987). Task representation in writing about literature. *Poetics, 16,* 131–154.

McCutchen, D. (1986). Domain knowledge and linguistic knowledge in the development of writing ability. *Journal of Memory and Language, 25,* 431–444.

McGee, L. M. (1982). Awareness of text structure: Effects on children's recall of expository text. *Reading Research Quarterly, 17,* 581–590.

McGinley, W. (1992). The role of reading and writing while composing from sources. *Reading Research Quarterly, 27,* 226–249.

McGinley, W., & Tierney, R. J. (1989). Traversing the topical landscape: Reading and writing as ways of knowing. *Written Communication, 6,* 243–269.

McNamara, T. P., Miller, D. L., & Bransford, J. D. (1991). Mental models and reading comprehension. In R. B. Barr, M. L. Kamil, P. B. Mosenthal, & P. D. Pearson (Eds.), *Handbook of reading research* (Vol. 2, pp. 490–511). New York: Longman.

Medvedev, P. N. (1978). *The formal method in literary scholarship: A critical introduction to sociological poetics* (A. J. Wehrle, Trans.). Baltimore: Johns Hopkins University Press. (Original work published in Russian 1928)

Meglitsch, P. A. (1986). Squid. In *Encyclopedia Americana* (Vol. 25, pp. 546–547). Danbury, CT: Grolier.

Mehan, H. (1979). *Learning lessons: Social organization in the classroom.* Cambridge, MA: Harvard University Press.

Meltzer, F. (1994). *Hot property: The stakes and claims of literary originality.* Chicago: University of Chicago Press.

Mendelbaum, M. (1982). Subjective, objective, and conceptual relativisms. In J. W. Meiland & M. Krausz (Eds.), *Relativism: Cognitive and moral* (pp. 34–61). Notre Dame, IN: University of Notre Dame Press.

Merrell, F. (1992). *Sign, textuality, world.* Bloomington: Indiana University Press.

Merton, R. K. (1965). *On the shoulders of giants: A Shandean postscript.* New York: Free Press.

Merton, R. K. (1973). *The sociology of science: Theoretical and empirical investigations.* Chicago: University of Chicago Press.

Meutsch, D., & Schmidt, S. J. (1985). On the role of conventions in understanding literary texts. *Poetics, 14,* 551–574.

Meyer, B. J. F. (1971). *Idea units recalled from prose in relation to their position in the logical structure, importance, stability and order in the passage.* Unpublished master's thesis, Cornell University, Ithaca, NY.

Meyer, B. J. F. (1975). *The organization of prose and its effects on memory.* Amsterdam: North Holland.

Meyer, B. J. F. (1977). The structure of prose: Effects on learing and memory and implications for educational practice. In R. C. Anderson, R. J. Spiro, & W. E. Montague (Eds.), *Schooling and the acquisition of knowledge* (pp. 179–200). Hillsdale, NJ: Erlbaum.

Meyer, B. J. F. (1985). Prose analysis: Purposes, procedures, and problems. In B. K. Britton & J. B. Black (Eds.), *Understanding expository text* (pp. 11–64). Hillsdale, NJ: Erlbaum.

Meyer, B. J. F., Brandt, D. M., & Bluth, G. J. (1980). Use of top-level structure in text: Key for reading comprehension of ninth-grade students. *Reading Research Quarterly, 16,* 72–103.

Meyer, B. J. F., & Freedle, R. O. (1984). Effects of discourse type on recall. *American Educational Research Journal, 21,* 121–143.

Meyer, B. J. F., & McConkie, G. (1973). What is recalled after hearing a passage? *Journal of Educational Psychology, 65,* 109–117.

Meyer, B. J. F., & Rice, G. E. (1989). Prose processing in adulthood: The text, the reader, and the task. In L. W. Poon, D. C. Rubin, & B. A. Wilson (Eds.), *Everyday cognition in adulthood and late life* (pp. 157–194). Cambridge: Cambridge University Press.

Miall, D. S., & Kuiken, D. (1994). Beyond text theory: Understanding literary response. *Discourse Processes, 17,* 337–352.

Middleton, D., & Edwards, D. (1990). Conversational remembering: A social psychological approach. In D. Middleton & D. Edwards (Eds.), *Collective remembering* (pp. 23–45). London: Sage.

Miller, O. (1985). Intertextual identity. In M. J. Valdés & O. Miller (Eds.), *Identity of the literary text* (pp. 19–40). Toronto, Canada: University of Toronto Press.

Millis, K. K., Graesser, A. C., & Haberlandt, K. (1993). The impact of connectives on the memory for expository texts. *Applied Cognitive Psychology, 7,* 317–339.

Milner, E. (1949). Effects of sex role and social status on the early adolescent. *Genetic Psychology Monographs, 40,* 231–325.

Minnis, A. J. (1984). *Medieval theory of authorship: Scholastic literary attitudes in the later Middle Ages.* London: Scolar Press.

Minsky, M. (1975). A framework for representing knowledge. In P. H. Winston (Ed.), *The psychology of computer vision* (pp. 211–277). New York: McGraw-Hill.

Morgan, L. H. (1871). *Systems of consanguinity and affinity of the human family* (Smithsonian Contributions to Knowledge No. 17). Washington, DC: Smithsonian.

Mosenthal, P. B. (1985). Defining the expository discourse continuum. *Poetics, 14,* 387–414.

Mosenthal, P. B., & Na, T. J. (1980). Quality of text recall as a function of children's classroom competence. *Journal of Experimental Child Psychology, 30,* 1–21.

Mulkay, M. J. (1972). *The social process of innovation.* London: Macmillan.

Murray, D. (1972, November). Teach writing as process not product. *The Leaflet of the New England Association of Teachers of English,* pp. 11–14.

Murray, J. D. (1995). Logical connectives and local coherence. In R. F. Lorch, Jr., & E. J. O'Brien (Eds.), *Sources of coherence in reading* (pp. 107–125). Hillsdale, NJ: Erlbaum.

Myers, G. (1985a). The social construction of two biologists' proposals. *Written Communication, 2,* 219–45.

Myers, G. (1985b). Texts as knowledge claims: The social construction of two biology articles. *Social Studies of Science, 15,* 593–630.

Neimeyer, R. A. (1993). An appraisal of constructivist psychotherapies. *Journal of Consulting and Clinical Psychology, 61,* 221–234.

Neimeyer, R. A. (1995). Constructivist psychotherapies: Features, foundations, and future directions. In R. A. Neimeyer & M. J. Mahoney (Eds.), *Constructivism in psychotherapy* (pp. 11–38). Washington, DC: American Psychological Association.

Neisser, U. (1967). *Cognitive psychology.* Englewood Cliffs, NJ: Prentice-Hall.

Nelson, J. (1990). This was an easy assignment: Examining how students interpret academic writing tasks. *Research in the Teaching of English, 24,* 362–396.

Nelson, T. H. (1965). A file structure for the complex, the changing, and the indeterminate. *ACM Proceedings of the 26th National Conference* (pp. 84–100). New York: Association of Computer Marketing.

Newell, A., & Simon, H. A. (1972). *Human problem solving*. Englewood Cliffs, NJ: Prentice-Hall.

Newell, G. E. (1984). Learning from writing in two content areas: A case study/protocol analysis. *Research in the Teaching of English, 18,* 265–287.

Ninio, A., & Bruner, J. (1978). The achievement and antecedents of labeling. *Journal of Child Language, 5,* 1–15.

Nold, E. W., & Davis, B. E. (1980). The discourse matrix. College *Composition and Communication, 31,* 141–152.

Nold, E. W., & Freedman, S. W. (1977). An analysis of readers' responses to essays. *Research in the Teaching of English, 11,* 164–174.

Norris, C. (1987). *Derrida.* Cambridge, MA: Harvard University Press.

Nowell-Smith, P. H. (1977). The constructionist theory of history. *History and Theory: Studies in the Philosophy of History, 16*(4), 1–28.

Nystrand, M. (1986). *The structure of written communication: Studies of reciprocity between writers and readers.* Orlando, FL: Academic Press.

Oates, J. C. (1973). The myth of the solitary artist. *Psychology Today, 6*(12), 74–75.

Ohtsuka, K., & Brewer, W. F. (1992). Discourse organization in the comprehension of temporal order in narrative texts. *Discourse Processes, 15,* 317–336.

Olson, G. M., Duffy, S. A., & Mack, R. L. (1984). Thinking-out-loud as a method for studying real-time comprehension processes. In D. E. Kieras & M. A. Just (Eds.), *New methods in reading comprehension research* (pp. 253–286). Hillsdale, NJ: Erlbaum.

Ort, C.-M. (1989). "Empirical" literary history: Theoretical comments on the concept of historical change in empirical literary science. *Poetics, 18,* 73–84.

Ortony, A. (Ed.). (1979). *Metaphor and thought.* Cambridge: Cambridge University Press.

Otter, A. G. den (1991). Literary criticism as reception data rather than interpretive truth: A case study of *Christabel* criticism. *Poetics, 20,* 363–390.

Palincsar, A. S., & Brown, A. L. (1984). Reciprocal teaching of comprehension-fostering and monitoring activities. *Cognition and Instruction, 1,* 117–175.

Paris, S. G., & Lindauer, B. K. (1976). Constructive aspects of children's comprehension and memory. In R. V. Kail & J. W. Hagen (Eds.), *Perspectives on the development of memory and cognition* (pp. 35–60). Hillsdale, NJ: Erlbaum.

Paris, S. G., Lipson, M. Y., & Wixson, K. K. (1983). Becoming a strategic reader. *Contemporary Educational Psychology, 8,* 293–316.

Pascal, B. (1958). *Pensées* (W. F. Trotter, Trans.). New York: Dutton. (Original work published in French 1670)

Pascual-Leone, J. (1987). Organismic process for neo-Piagetian theories: A dialectical causal account of cognitive development. *International Journal of Psychology, 22,* 531–570.

Paul, I. H. (1959). Studies in remembering: The reproduction of connected and extended verbal material. *Psychological Issues, 1,* Monograph No. 2.

Pea, R. D. (1993). Practices of distributed intelligence and designs for education. In G. Salomon (Ed.), *Distributed cognitions* (pp. 47–87). New York: Cambridge University Press.

Pearson, P. D. (1974). The effects of grammatical complexity on children's comprehension, recall, and conception of certain semantic relations. *Reading Research Quarterly, 10,* 155–192.

Pearson, P. D., Hansen, J., & Gordon, C. (1979). The effects of background knowledge on young children's comprehension of explicit and implicit information. *Journal of Reading Behavior, 11,* 201–210.

Peirce, C. S. (1931–1958). *The collected papers of Charles Sanders Peirce* (Vols. 1–6, C. Hartshorne & P. Weiss, Eds.; Vols. 7–8, M. W. Burks, Ed.). Cambridge, MA: Harvard University Press.

Perfetti, C. A., & Goldman, S. R. (1975). Discourse functions of thematization and topicalization. *Journal of Psycholinguistic Research, 4,* 257–271.

Phelps, L. W. (1985). Dialectics of coherence: Toward an integrative theory. *College English, 47,* 12–29.

Philippe, J. (1897). Sur les transformations de nos images mentales. *Revue Philosophique, 43,* 481–493.

Philips, S. B. (1983). *The invisible culture: Communication in the classroom and community on the Warm Springs Indian Reservation.* White Plains, NY: Longman.

Phillips, D. C. (1995). The good, the bad, and the ugly: The many faces of constructivism. *Educational Researcher, 24*(7), 5–12.

Piaget, J. (1928). *Judgment and reasoning in the child* (M. Warden, Trans.). New York: Harcourt Brace. (Original work published in French 1924)

Piaget, J. (1932). *The language and thought of the child* (M. Gabain, Trans.). New York: Harcourt Brace. (Original work published in French 1923)

Piaget, J. (1954). *The construction of reality in the child* (M. Cook, Trans.). New York: Basic Books. (Original work published in French 1937)

Piaget, J. (1970). *Structuralism* (C. Maschler, Ed. and Trans.). New York: Basic Books.

Piaget, J. (1985). *The equilibration of cognitive structures: The central problem of intellectual development* (T. Brown & K. J. Thampy, Trans.). Chicago: University of Chicago Press. (Original work published 1975)

Piaget, J., & Garcia, R. (1989). *Psychogenesis and the history of science.* New York: Columbia University Press. (Original work published in French 1983)

Piaget, J., & Garcia, R. (1991). *Toward a logic of meanings* (P. M. Davidson & J. Easley, Trans.). Hillsdale, NJ: Erlbaum. (Original work published in French 1987)

Pichert, J. W., & Anderson, R. C. (1977). Taking different perspectives on a story. *Journal of Educational Psychology, 69,* 309–315.

Piovani, P. (1969). Vico without Hegel. In G. Tagliacozzo & H. V. White (Eds.), *Giambattista Vico: An international symposium* (pp. 103–123). Baltimore: Johns Hopkins University Press.

Polanyi, L. (1985). *Telling the American story: A structural and cultural analysis of conversational storytelling.* Norwood, NJ: Ablex.

Polanyi, M. (1958). *Personal knowledge: Towards a post-critical philosophy.* Chicago: University of Chicago Press.

Porter, J. E. (1986). Intertextuality and the discourse community. *Rhetoric Review, 5,* 34–47.

Pratt, M. L. (1977). *Toward a speech act theory of literary response.* Bloomington: Indiana University Press.

Pressley, M., & Afflerbach, P. (1995). *Verbal protocols of reading: The nature of constructively responsive reading.* Hillsdale, NJ: Erlbaum.

Pressley, M., Harris, K. R., & Guthrie, J. T. (Eds.). (1992). *Promoting academic competence and literacy in school.* San Diego, CA: Academic Press.

Pribram, K. H. (1971). *What makes man human* (39th James Arthur Lecture on the Evolution of the Human Brain). New York: American Museum of Natural History.

Prior, P. (1991). Contextualizing writing and response in a graduate seminar. *Written Communication, 8,* 267–310.

Propp, V. (1968). *Morphology of the folktale* (2nd ed.). Austin: University of Texas Press. (Original work published in Russian 1928)

Purves, A., & Rippere, V. (1968). *Elements of writing about a literary work: A study of response to literature.* Urbana, IL: National Council of Teachers of English.

Raphael, T. E., Kirschner, B. W., & Englert, C. S. (1988). Expository writing programs: Making connections between reading and writing. *The Reading Teacher, 41,* 790–795.

Rathbone, R. (1972). *Communicating technical information.* Reading, MA: Addison-Wesley.

Ratteray, O. M. T. (1985). Expanding roles for summarized information. *Written Communication, 2,* 457–472.

Reddy, M. (1979). The conduit metaphor. In A. Ortony (Ed.), *Metaphor and thought* (pp. 284–324). Cambridge: Cambridge University Press.

Reither, J. A., & Vipond, D. (1989). Writing as collaboration. *College English, 51,* 855–867.

Rentel, V. M., & King, M. L. (1983). Present at the beginning. In P. Mosenthal, L. Tamor, & S. Walmsley (Eds.), *Research on writing: Principles and methods* (pp. 134–176). New York: Longman.

Resnick, L. B. (1991). Shared cognition: Thinking as social practice. In L. B. Resnick, J. M. Levine, & S. D. Teasley (Eds.), *Perspectives on socially shared cognitions* (pp. 1–20). Hillsdale, NJ: Erlbaum.

Reynolds, J. F., Mair, D. C., & Fischer, P. (1996). *Writing and reading mental health records: Issues and analysis* (2nd ed.). Hillsdale, NJ: Erlbaum.

Reynolds, R. E., & Anderson, R. C. (1982). Influence of questions on the allocation of attention during reading. *Journal of Educational Psychology, 74,* 623–632.

Richgels, D. J., McGee, L. M., Lomax, R. G., & Sheard, C. (1987). Awareness of four text structures: Effects on recall of expository text. *Reading Research Quarterly, 22,* 177–196.

Riffaterre, M. (1979). Criteria for style analysis. *Word, 15,* 154–174.

Riffaterre, M. (1983). *Text production* (T. Lyons, Trans.). New York: Columbia University Press. (Original work published 1938)

Rivers, W. H. R. (1913). Contact of peoples. In E. C. Quiggan (Ed.), *Essays and studies presented to William Ridgeway on his sixtieth birthday* (pp. 474–492). Cambridge: Cambridge University Press.

Rivers, W. H. R. (1914). *The history of Melanesian society.* Cambridge: Cambridge University Press.

Rivers, W. H. R. (1922). *Instinct and the unconscious: A contribution to a biological theory of the psycho-neuroses* (2nd ed.). Cambridge: Cambridge University Press.

Rivers, W. H. R. (1968). *Kinship and social organisation.* London: Athlone Press. (Original work published 1914 as a set of lectures)

Rivers, W. H. R., & Head, H. (1908). A human experiment in nerve division. *Brain, 31,* 323–450.

Rodeo News Bureau. (1985). Rodeo. In *The new book of knowledge* (Vol. 16, pp. 277–278). Danbury, CT: Grolier.

Rogers, T. (1991). Students as literary critics: The interpretive theories, processes, and experiences of ninth grade students. *Journal of Reading Behavior, 23,* 391–424.

Rohman, D. G., & Wlecke, A. O. (1964). *Pre-writing: The construction and application of models for concept formation in writing* (Cooperative Research Project No. 2174). East Lansing: Michigan State University. (ERIC Document Reproduction Service No. ED 001 273)

Rosenblatt, L. M. (1976). *Literature as exploration* (3rd ed.). New York: Barnes & Noble. (Original work published 1938)

Rosenblatt, L. M. (1978). *The reader, the text, the poem: The transactional theory of the literary work.* Carbondale: Southern Illinois University Press.

Roth, R. G. (1987). The evolving audience: Alternatives to audience accommodation. *College Composition and Communication, 38,* 47–55.

Rothkopf, E. Z., & Billington, M. J. (1979). Goal-guided learning from text: Inferring a descriptive processing model from inspection of times and eye movements. *Journal of Educational Psychology, 71,* 310–327.

Rowe, D. (1987). Literacy learning as an intertextual process. In J. E. Readence & R. S. Baldwin (Eds.), *Research in literacy: Merging perspectives* (36th Yearbook of the National Reading Conference, pp. 101–112). Chicago: National Reading Conference.

Rubin, D. L. (1984). Social cognition and written communication. *Written Communication, 1,* 211–245.

Rubin, D. L. (Ed.). (1995). *Composing social identity in written language.* Hillsdale, NJ: Erlbaum.

Rubin, E. (1921). *Visuall wahrgenommene Figuren.* Copenhagen: Gyldendalske Boghandel.

Ruddell, R. B., & Unrau, N. J. (1994). Reading as meaning construction: The reader, the text, and the teacher. In R. B. Ruddell, M. R. Ruddell, & H. Singer (Eds.), *Theoretical models and processes of reading* (4th ed., pp. 996–1056). Newark, DE: International Reading Association.

Rumelhart, D. E. (1975). Notes on a schema for stories. In D. G. Bobrow & A. Collins (Eds.), *Representation and understanding: Studies in cognitive science* (pp. 211–236). New York: Academic Press.

Rumelhart, D. E. (1977). Toward an interactive model of reading. In S. Dornič (Ed.), *Attention and performance VI* (pp. 573–603). Hillsdale, NJ: Erlbaum.

Rumelhart, D. E. (1980). Schemata: The building blocks of cognition. In R. J. Spiro, B. C. Bruce, & W. F. Brewer (Eds.), *Theoretical issues in reading comprehension* (pp. 33–58). Hillsdale, NJ: Erlbaum.

Rumelhart, D. E., & McClelland, J. (1986). *Parallel distributed processing: Explorations in the microstructure of cognition: Vol. 2. Psychological and biological models.* Cambridge, MA: MIT Press.

Rumelhart, D. E., & Ortony, A. (1977). The representation of knowledge in memory. In R. C. Anderson, R. J. Spiro, & W. E. Montague (Eds.), *Schooling and the acquisition of knowledge* (pp. 99–135). Hillsdale, NJ: Erlbaum.

Rumelhart, D. E., Smolensky, P., McClelland, J. L., & Hinton, G. E. (1986). Schemata and sequential thought processes in PDP models. In J. L. McClelland & D. E. Rumelhart,

Parallel distributed processing: Explorations in the microstructure of cognition (Vol. 2, pp. 7–57). Cambridge, MA: MIT Press.

Sadoski, M., & Paivio, A. (1994). A dual coding view of imagery and verbal processes in reading comprehension. In R. B. Ruddell, M. R. Ruddell, & H. Singer (Eds.), *Theoretical models and processes of reading* (4th ed., pp. 582–601). Newark, DE: International Reading Association.

Sadoski, M., & Quast, L. (1990). Reader response and long-term recall for journalistic text: The roles of imagery, affect, and importance. *Reading Research Quarterly, 25,* 256–272.

Salomon, G. (Ed.). (1993a). *Distributed cognitions.* New York: Cambridge University Press.

Salomon, G. (1993b). No distribution without individuals' cognition: A dynamic interactional view. In G. Salomon (Ed.), *Distributed cognitions* (pp. 111–138). New York: Cambridge University Press.

Saussure, F. de (1983). *Course in general linguistics* (C. Bally & A. Sechehaye, Eds.; R. Harris, Trans.). London: Duckworth. (Original work published in French 1916)

Schallert, D. L. (1976). Improving memory for prose: The relationship between depth of processing and context. *Journal of Verbal Learning and Verbal Behavior, 15,* 621–632.

Schallert, D. L., Lissi, M. R., Reed, J. H., Fowler, L. A., Dodson, M. M., & Benton, R. E. (1995, November). *How coherence is socially constructed in oral and written classroom discussions of reading assignments.* Paper presented at the annual meeting of the National Reading Conference, New Orleans, LA.

Schank, R. C. (1975). The structure of episodes in memory. In D. G. Bobrow & A. Collins (Eds.), *Representation and understanding: Studies in cognitive science* (pp. 237–272). New York: Academic Press.

Schank, R. C., & Abelson, R. P. (1977). *Scripts, plans, goals, and understanding: An inquiry into human knowledge structures.* Hillsdale, NJ: Erlbaum.

Schmalhofer, F., & Glavanov, D. (1986). Three components of understanding a programmer's manual: Verbatim, propositional, and situational representations. *Journal of Memory and Language, 25,* 279–294.

Schmidt, S. J. (1981). Empirical studies of literature: Introductory remarks. *Poetics, 10,* 317–336.

Schmidt, S. J. (1982). *Foundations for the empirical study of literature* (R. de Beaugrande, Ed. and Trans.). Hamburg: Buske.

Schmidt, S. J. (1985). On writing histories of literature. *Poetics, 14,* 279–301.

Schmidt, S. J. (1989). *Die Selbstorganisation des Sozialsystems Literatur im 18. Jahrhundert.* Frankfurt am Main: Suhrkamp.

Schmidt, S. J. (1992). Looking back—looking ahead. *Poetics, 21,* 1–4.

Schnotz, W. (1982). How do different readers learn with different text organizations? In A. Flammer & W. Kintsch (Eds.), *Discourse processing* (pp. 87–97). Amsterdam: North Holland.

Schnotz, W. (1984). Comparative instructional text organization. In H. Mandl, N. L. Stein, & T. Trabasso (Eds.), *Learning and comprehension of text* (pp. 53–74). Hillsdale, NJ: Erlbaum.

Scholes, R. (1985). *Textual power: Literary theory and the teaching of English.* New Haven, CT: Yale University Press.

Searle, D., & Dillon, D. (1980). The message of marking: Teacher written responses to student writing at intermediate grade levels. *Research in the Teaching of English, 14,* 233–242.

Segal, E. M., Duchan, J. F., & Scott, P. J. (1991). The role of interclausal connectives in narrative structuring: Evidence from adults' interpretations of simple stories. *Discourse Processes, 14,* 27–54.

Seifert, C. M., Robertson, S. P., & Black, J. B. (1985). Types of inferences generated during reading. *Journal of Memory and Language, 24,* 45–422.

Shanahan, T. (1993, April). *Starting a conversation: The development of author awareness during reading.* Paper presented at the annual meeting of the American Educational Research Association, Atlanta, GA.

Shanahan, T., & Lomax, R. G. (1986). An analysis and comparison of theoretical models of the reading-writing relationship. *Journal of Educational Psychology, 78,* 116–123.

Shanahan, T., & Lomax, R. G. (1988). A developmental comparison of three theoretical models of the reading-writing relationship. *Research in the Teaching of English, 22,* 196–212.

Shannon, C. E., & Weaver, W. (1949). *The mathematical theory of communication.* Urbana: University of Illinois Press.

Sherwood, R., Kinzer, C., Hasselbring, T., & Bransford, J. D. (1987). Macro-contexts for learning: Initial findings and issues. *Applied Cognitive Psychology, 1,* 93–108.

Shklovsky, V. (1965a). Art as technique. In L. T. Lemon & M. J. Reis (Eds.), *Russian formalist criticism: Four essays* (pp. 3–24). Lincoln: University of Nebraska Press. (Original work published in Russian 1917)

Shklovsky, V. (1965b). Sterne's *Tristram Shandy*: Stylistic commentary. In L. T. Lemon & M. J. Reis (Eds.), *Russian formalist criticism: Four essays* (pp. 25–57). Lincoln: University of Nebraska Press. (Original work published in Russian 1921)

Shotter, J. (1990). The social construction of forgetting and remembering. In D. Middleton & D. Edwards (Eds.), *Collective remembering* (pp. 120–138). London: Sage.

Sidney, P. (1599). *The Countesse of Pembroke's Arcadia.* Edinburgh: Robert Walde-Graue. (Original work published circa 1590)

Simon, H. A. (1989). *Models of thought* (Vol. 2). New Haven, CT: Yale University Press.

Sless, D. (1986). *In search of semiotics.* London: Crook Helm.

Small, H. G. (1978). Citing documents as concept symbols. *Social Studies of Science, 8,* 327–340.

Smith, B. H. (1980). Narrative versions, narrative theories. *Critical Inquiry, 7,* 213–236.

Smith, F. (1971). *Understanding reading.* New York: Holt, Rinehart & Winston.

Smith, J. Z. (1982). *Imagining religion: From Babylon to Jonestown.* Chicago: University of Chicago Press.

Smith, W. L., & Swan, M. B. (1978). Adjusting syntactic structures to varied levels of audience. *Journal of Experimental Education, 46,* 29–34.

Sperling, M. (1990). I want to talk with each of you: Collaboration and the teacher-student writing conference. *Research in the Teaching of English, 24,* 279–321.

Spiro, R. J. (1977). Remembering information from text: The "state of schema" approach. In R. C. Anderson, R. J. Spiro, & W. E. Montague (Eds.), *Schooling and the acquisition of knowledge* (pp. 137–165). Hillsdale, NJ: Erlbaum.

Spiro, R. J. (1980). Constructive processes in prose comprehension and recall. In R. J. Spiro, B. C. Bruce, & W. F. Brewer (Eds.), *Theoretical issues in reading comprehension* (pp. 245–278). Hillsdale, NJ: Erlbaum.

Spiro, R. J., Feltovich, P. J., Jacobson, M. J., & Coulson, R. L. (1995). Cognitive flexibility, constructivism, and hypertext: Random access instruction for advanced knowledge acquisition in ill-structured domains. In L. P. Steffe & J. Gale (Eds.), *Constructivism in education* (pp. 85–107). Hillsdale, NJ: Erlbaum.

Spivey, N. N. (1984). *Discourse synthesis: Constructing texts in reading and writing* [Monograph]. Newark, DE: International Reading Association.

Spivey, N. N. (1987). Construing constructivism: Reading research in the United States. *Poetics, 16,* 169–192.

Spivey, N. N. (1990). Transforming texts: Constructive processes in reading and writing. *Written Communication, 7,* 256–287

Spivey, N. N. (1991). The shaping of meaning: Options in writing the comparison. *Research in the Teaching of English, 25,* 390–418.

Spivey, N. N. (1992). Discourse synthesis: Creating texts from texts. In J. R. Hayes, R. E. Young, M. Matchett, M. McCaffrey, C. A. Cochran, & T. Hajduk (Eds.), *Reading empirical research studies: The rhetoric of research* (pp. 469–512). Hillsdale, NJ: Erlbaum.

Spivey, N. N. (1994). Constructivism. In A. C. Purves (Ed.), *Encyclopedia of English studies and language arts* (pp. 284–286). New York: Scholastic.

Spivey, N. N. (1995). Written discourse: A constructivist perspective. In L. P. Steffe & J. Gale (Eds.), *Constructivism in education* (pp. 313–329). Hillsdale, NJ: Erlbaum.

Spivey, N. N., & Greene, S. (1989, March). Aufgabe *in writing and learning from sources.* Paper presented at the annual meeting of the American Educational Research Association, San Francisco.

Spivey, N. N., & King, J. R. (1989). Readers as writers composing from sources. *Reading Research Quarterly, 24,* 7–26.

Spivey, N. N., & King, J. R. (1994). Readers as writers composing from sources. In R. Ruddell, M. R. Ruddell, & H. Singer (Eds.), *Theoretical models and processes of reading* (4th ed., pp. 668–694). Newark, DE: International Reading Association.

Spivey, N. N., & Mathison, M. A. (1997). *Emergent authorship: Identity and community in disciplinary writing.* Manuscript in preparation.

Steffe, L. P., & Gale, J. (Eds.). (1995). *Constructivism in education.* Hillsdale, NJ: Erlbaum.

Stein, N. L., & Glenn, C. G. (1979). An analysis of story comprehension in elementary school children. In R. O. Freedle (Ed.), *New directions in discourse processing* (pp. 53–120). Norwood, NJ: Ablex.

Sternberg, R. J. (1990). *Metaphors of mind: Conceptions of the nature of intelligence.* New York: Cambridge University Press.

Sterne, L. (1925). *The life and opinions of Tristram Shandy, gentleman.* New York: Liveright. (Original work published 1779)

Stillinger, J. (1991). *Multiple authorship and the myth of solitary genius.* New York: Oxford University Press.

Stotsky, S. (1983). Research on reading/writing relationships: A synthesis and suggested directions. *Language Arts, 60,* 627–642.

Sukenick, R. (1979). *Long talking bad condition blues.* New York: Fiction Collective.

Sulzby, E. (1985). Children's emergent reading of favorite storybooks: A developmental study. *Reading Research Quarterly, 20,* 458–481.

Swift, J. (1766). *Travels into several remote nations of the world: In four parts by Captain Lemuel Gulliver.* London: Printed for P. Turnbull.

Tate, G. H. H. (1982). Armadillo. In *Encyclopedia Americana* (Vol. 2, pp. 328–329). Danbury, CT: Grolier.

Taylor, B. M. (1980). Children's memory for expository text after reading. *Reading Research Quarterly, 15,* 399–411.

Taylor, W. (1984). Metaphors of educational discourse. In W. Taylor (Ed.), *Metaphors of education* (pp. 4–20). London: Heinemann.

Temple, C. A., Nathan, R. G., & Burris, N. A. (1982). *The beginnings of writing.* Boston: Allyn & Bacon.

Thibadeau, R., Just, M. A., & Carpenter, P. A. (1982). A model of the time course and content of reading. *Cognitive Science, 6,* 157–203.

Thibault, P. J. (1991). *Social semiotics as praxis: Text, social meaning making, and Nabokov's Ada.* Minneapolis: University of Minnesota Press.

Thorndyke, P. W. (1977). Cognitive structures in comprehension and memory of narrative discourse. *Cognitive Psychology, 9,* 77–110.

Tierney, R. J., & LaZansky, J. (1980). The rights and responsibilities of readers and writers: A contractual agreement. *Language Arts, 57,* 606–613.

Tierney, R. J., & Pearson, P. D. (1983). Toward a composing model of reading. *Language Arts, 60,* 568–580.

Tierney, R. J., & Shanahan, T. (1991). Research on the reading–writing relationship: Interactions, transactions, and outcomes. In R. Barr, M. L. Kamil, P. Mosenthal, & P. D. Pearson (Eds.), *Handbook of reading research* (Vol. 2, pp. 246–280). New York: Longman.

Todorov, T. (1967). *Littérature et signification.* Paris: Larousse.

Todorov, T. (1969). *Grammaire du Décaméron.* The Hague: Mouton.

Todorov, T. (1990). *Genres in discourse.* Cambridge: Cambridge University Press. (Original work published in French 1978)

Tomashevsky, B. (1965). Thematics. In L. T. Lemon & M. J. Reis (Eds.), *Russian formalist criticism: Four essays* (pp. 61–95). Lincoln: University of Nebraska Press. (Original work published in Russian 1925)

Toole, J. K. (1980). *A confederacy of dunces.* Baton Rouge: Louisiana State University Press.

Trabasso, T., Secco, T., & van den Broek, P. W. (1984). Causal cohesion and story understanding. In H. Mandl, N. L. Stein, & T. Trabasso (Eds.), *Learning and comprehension of text* (pp. 83–111). Hillsdale, NJ: Erlbaum.

Trabasso, T., & Suh, S. (1993). Understanding text: Achieving explanatory coherence through on-line inferences and mental operations in working memory. *Discourse Processes, 16,* 3–34.

Trabasso, T., & van den Broek, P. W. (1985). Causal thinking and the representation of narrative events. *Journal of Memory and Language, 24,* 612–630.

Trimbur, J., & Braun, L. A. (1992). Laboratory life and the determination of authorship. In J. Forman (Ed.), *New visions of collaborative writing* (pp. 19–36). Portsmouth, NH: Boynton/Cook.

Trubetzkoy, N. S. (1933). *Principes de phonologie* (J. Cantineau, Trans.). Paris: Klincksieck.

Turner, A., & Greene, E. (1978). The construction and use of a propositional text base. *JSAS Catalog of Selected Documents in Psychology, 8,* 58(Ms. No. 1713).

Turner, J. C., Hogg, M. A., Oakes, P. J., Reicher, S. D., & Wetherell, M. (1987). *Rediscovering the social group: A self-categorization theory.* Oxford: Blackwell.

Tyler, S. A. (1978). *The said and the unsaid: Mind, meaning, and culture.* New York: Academic Press.

Tyler, S. W., & Voss, J. F. (1982). Attitude and knowledge effects in prose processing. *Journal of Verbal Learning and Verbal Behavior, 21,* 524–538.

Ulichny, P., & Watson-Gegeo, K. A. (1989). Interactions and authority: The dominant interpretive framework in writing conferences. *Discourse Processes, 12,* 309–328.

Vande Kopple, W. J. (1983). Something old, something new: Functional sentence perspective. *Research in the Teaching of English, 17,* 85–99.

Vande Kopple, W. J. (1985). Some explanatory discourse on metadiscourse. *College Composition and Communication, 36,* 82–93.

van den Broek, P. W., Rohleder, L., & Narváez, D. (1993). Cognitive processes in the comprehension of literary texts. In H. van Oostendorp & R. A. Zwaan (Eds.), *Naturalistic text comprehension* (pp. 229–246). Norwood, NJ: Ablex.

van den Broek, P. W., Rohleder, L., & Narváez, D. (1996). Causal inferences in the comprehension of literary texts. In R. J. Kreuz & M. S. MacNealy (Eds.), *Empirical approaches to literature and aesthetics* (pp. 179–200). Norwood, NJ: Ablex.

van Dijk, T. A. (1972). *Some aspects of text grammars.* The Hague: Mouton.

van Dijk, T. A. (1977). Semantic macrostructures and knowledge frames in discourse comprehension. In M. A. Just & P. A. Carpenter (Eds.), *Cognitive processes in comprehension* (pp. 3–32). Hillsdale, NJ: Erlbaum.

van Dijk, T. A. (1979). Relevance assignment in discourse comprehension. *Discourse Processes, 2,* 113–126.

van Dijk, T. A. (1980). *Macrostructures: An interdisciplinary study of global structures in discourse, interaction, and cognition.* Hillsdale, NJ: Erlbaum.

van Dijk, T. A. (1985). Structures of news in the press. In T. A. van Dijk (Ed.), *Discourse and communication: New approaches to the analysis of mass media discourse and communication* (pp. 69–93). Berlin: de Gruyter.

van Dijk, T. A. (1995). On macrostructures, mental models, and other inventions: A brief personal history of the Kintsch-van Dijk theory. In C. A. Weaver, III, S. Mannes, & C. R. Fletcher (Eds.), *Discourse comprehension: Essays in honor of Walter Kintsch* (pp. 383–410). Hillsdale, NJ: Erlbaum.

van Dijk, T. A., & Kintsch, W. (1983). *Strategies of discourse comprehension.* Orlando, FL: Academic Press.

van Rees, C. J. (1983). How a literary work becomes a masterpiece: On the threefold selection practised by literary criticism. *Poetics, 12,* 397–417.

van Rees, C. J. (1987). How reviewers reach consensus on the value of a literary work. *Poetics, 16,* 275–294.

Verdaasdonk, H. (1985). Empirical sociology of literature as a non-textually oriented form of research. *Poetics, 14,* 173–185.

Verdaasdonk, H., & van Rees, K. (1992). The narrow margins of innovation in literary research: Sigfried J. Schmidt's proposals for the empirical study of literature. *Poetics, 21,* 141–152.

Vico, G. (1968). *The new science* (T. G. Bergin & M. H. Fisch, Trans.) (3rd rev. ed.). Ithaca, NY: Cornell University Press. (First edition published in Italian 1725; third revised edition first published 1744)

Vico, G. (1988). *On the most ancient wisdom of the Italians: Unearthed from the origins of the Latin language* (L. M. Palmer, Trans.). Ithaca, NY: Cornell University Press. (Original work published in Italian 1710)

Vipond, D., & Hunt, R. A. (1984). Point-driven understanding: Pragmatic and cognitive dimensions of literary reading. *Poetics, 13,* 261–277.

Voloshinov, V. N. (1986). *Marxism and the philosophy of language* (L. Matejka & L. R. Titunik, Trans.). Cambridge, MA: Harvard University Press. (Original work published in Russian 1929)

von Glaserfeld, E. (1984). An introduction to radical constructivism. In P. Watzlawick (Ed.), *The invented reality: How do we know what we believe we know?* (pp. 17–40). New York: Norton.

Vygotsky, L. S. (1978). *Mind in society: The development of higher psychological processes* (M. Cole, V. John-Steiner, S. Scribner, & E. Souberman, Ed. and Trans.). Cambridge, MA: Harvard University Press.

Vygotsky, L. S. (1986). *Thought and language* (A. Kozulin, Ed. and Trans.). Cambridge, MA: MIT Press.

Wade, S. E., & Adams, R. B. (1990). Effects of importance and interest on recall of biographical text. *Journal of Reading Behavior, 22,* 321–353.

Walker, C. H., & Meyer, B. J. F. (1980). Integrating different kinds of information in text. *Journal of Verbal Learning and Verbal Behavior, 19,* 263–275.

Ward, J. (1918). *Psychological principles.* Cambridge: Cambridge University Press.

Ward, J. (1886). Psychology. In *Encyclopaedia Britannica* (Vol. 20, pp. 45–46). New York: Encyclopaedia Britannica.

Warrilow, D. (1987). Interview with author. *Review of Contemporary Fiction, 7*(2), 95–96.

Watson, J. B. (1916). The place of the conditioned reflex in psychology. *Psychological Review, 20,* 158–177.

Watson, K. A. (1975). Transferable communicative routines: Strategies and group identity in two speech events. *Language in Society, 4,* 53–72.

Watt, H. J. (1905). Experimentelle Beiträge zu einer Theorie des Denkens. *Archiv für die gesamte Psychologie, 4,* 289–436.

Watzlawick, P. (Ed.). (1984). *The invented reality: How do we know what we believe we know?* New York: Norton.

Weaver, C. (1985). Parallels between new paradigms in science and in reading and literary theories: An essay review. *Research in the Teaching of English, 19,* 298–316.

Weinstock, M. (1971). Citation indexes. In *Encyclopedia of library and information science* (Vol. 5, pp. 16–40). New York: Dekker.

Wells, G. (1986). *The meaning makers: Children learning language and using language to learn.* Portsmouth, NH: Heinemann.

Wertsch, J. V. (1985). *Vygotsky and the social formation of mind*. Cambridge, MA: Harvard University Press.

Wertsch, J. V. (1991). *Voices of the mind: A sociocultural approach to mediated action*. Cambridge, MA: Harvard University Press.

Wimsatt, W. K., Jr., & Beardsley, M. C. (1946). The intentional fallacy. *Sewanee Review, 54,* 468–488.

Wineburg, S. S. (1991). On the reading of historical texts: Notes on the breach between school and academy. *American Educational Research Journal, 28,* 495–519.

Wineburg, S. S. (1994). The cognitive representation of historical texts. In G. Leinhardt, I. L. Beck, & C. Stainton (Eds.), *Teaching and learning in history* (pp. 85–135). Hillsdale, NJ: Erlbaum.

Winograd, P. N. (1984). Strategic difficulties in summarizing texts. *Reading Research Quarterly, 19,* 404–425.

Winograd, T. (1977). A framework for understanding discourse. In M. A. Just & P. A. Carpenter (Eds.), *Cognitive processes in comprehension* (pp. 63–88). Hillsdale, NJ: Erlbaum.

Witte, S. P. (1983). Topical structure and revision: An exploratory study. *College Composition and Communication, 34,* 313–314.

Witte, S. P. (1985). Revising, composing theory, and research design. In S. W. Freedman (Ed.), *The acquisition of written language* (pp. 250–284). Norwood, NJ: Ablex.

Witte, S. P. (1987). Pretext and composing. *College Composition and Communication, 38,* 397–425.

Witte, S. P. (1992). Context, text, and intertext: Toward a constructivist semiotic. *Written Communication, 9,* 237–308.

Wittgenstein, L. (1973). *Philosophical investigations* (G. E. M. Anscombe, Trans.). New York: Macmillan. (Original work published 1945–1949)

Wolf, D., & Hicks, D. (1989). The voices within narratives: The development of intertextuality in young children's stories. *Discourse Processes, 12,* 329–351.

Wordsworth, W. (1974). Preface and appendix to *Lyrical Ballads*. *Wordsworth's literary criticism* (W. J. B. Owen, Ed.), (pp. 68–95). London: Routledge. (Original work published 1805)

World Book. (1986). Rodeo. In *World book encyclopedia* (Vol. 16, pp. 397–398). Chicago: Author.

Wundt, W. W. (1900–1920). *Völkerpsychologie* (10 vols.). Leipzig: Englemann.

Wundt, W. W. (1916). *Elements of folk psychology: Outlines of a psychological history of the development of mankind* (E. L. Schaub, Trans.). New York: Macmillan. (Original work published in German 1863)

Youniss, J., & Damon, W. (1992). Social construction in Piaget's theory. In H. Beilin & P. Pufall (Eds.), *Piaget's theory: Prospects and possibilities* (pp. 267–286). Hillsdale, NJ: Erlbaum.

Zangwill, O. L. (1972). *Remembering* revisited. *Quarterly Journal of Experimental Psychology, 24,* 123–138.

Zurburgg, N. (1993). *The parameters of postmodernism*. Carbondale: Southern Illinois University Press.

Zwaan, R. A. (1993). *Aspects of literary comprehension: A cognitive approach*. Amsterdam: John Benjamins.

Name Index

Numbers in italics refer to the pages on which the complete references are listed.

Abelson, R. P., 12, 13, *269*
Abrams, M. H., 5, 215, 239, *244*
Ach, N., 44, *244*
Ackerman, J., 14, 22, 127, 206, *244, 247,*
    254
Adams, R. B., 76, *274*
Afflerbach, P., 69, *244, 267*
Alexander, P. A., 84, 86, *244*
Almasi, J., 90, *244*
Anderson, J. R., 231, 232, 233, *244*
Anderson, R. C., 12, 13, 58, 64, 65, 70,
    76, 84, 85, 135, 193, 239, 240, *244,*
    266, 267
Anderson, T. H., 76, *245*
Anderson, V., 195, *258*
Angenot, M., 112, *244*
Anzai, Y., 232, *245*
Applebee, A. N., 14, 16, 136, 194, 201,
    203, *245, 261*
Appleman, D., 87, *246*
Aristotle, 6, 94
Armbruster, B. B., 76, 159, 196, *245,*
    255
Armstrong, W. E., 48, *245*
Asch, S., 78, *245*
Au, K. H., 90, *245*
Austin, J., 212

Bacon, F., 6
Baird, W., 76, *258*

Bakhtin, M. M., 27, 86, 89, 91, 102, 106,
    112, 117, 208, 209, *245*
Bally, C., 99, *245*
Balzac, H. de, 105
Barclay, J. R., 12, *248*
Barth, J., 94, *245*
Barthes, R., 66, 86, 98, 103, 105, 106, 110,
    111, 112, 129, 135, 216, *245*
Bartlett, F. C., 11, 12, 13, 14, 16, 20,
    22, 27, 28, 29, 30 ff, 56, 58, 60,
    64, 66, 67, 70, 78, 84, 85, 89, 90, 91
    92, 93, 97, 104, 121, 124, 135, 136,
    147, 154, 158, 161, 192, 207, 211,
    221, 222, 234, 235, 236, 238, 241,
    246
Bass, D., 227, *259*
Bazerman, C., 22, 73, 88, *246*
Beach, R., 82, 87, 135, 216, *246*
Beardsley, M. C., 216, *246, 275*
Beaugrande, R. de, 72, 75, 82, *246*
Becher, T., 21, 22, 28, *246*
Beck, I. L., 82, 137, 239, *246*
Beckett, S., 94, *246*
Beezley, D. A., 230, *260*
Benton, R. E., *269*
Bereiter, C., 24, 127, 128, 242, *247*
Berger, J., 94, *247*
Berger, P. L., 21, 26, *247*
Berkenkotter, C., 22, 73, 127, *247*
Bern, H., 79, *247*
Bertus, E. L., 19, *256*

277

Betz, A., 44, *247*
Bickman, L., 233, *247*
Billington, M. J., 85, 179, 193, *267*
Bizzell, P., 217, *247*
Black, J. B., 13, 75, 77, 79, 172, *247, 248,*
    270
Black, M., 2, *247*
Bleich, D., 98, 216, 240, *247*
Bloome, D., 91, *247*
Bloomfield, L., 98, *247*
Bluth, G. J., 76, *264*
Bly, R., 242, *247*
Boas, F., 34, 38, 49, 52, 55, *247*
Boccaccio, G., 59
Boehme, J., 56
Bolter, J. D., 192, *247*
Boring, E. G., 53, *247*
Botkin, P. T., 16, *253*
Bower, G. H., 13, 67, 79, *247, 248*
Bower, T. G. R., 181, *248*
Boyd, R., 2, *248*
Bracewell, R. J., 14, 136, *248*
Brandt, D. M., 76, *264*
Bransford, J. D., 12, 28, 57, 58, 64, 77, 78,
    86, 135, *248, 263, 270*
Braun, L. A., 139, *273*
Bremond, C., 66, 104, *248*
Brewer, W. F., 78, 80, 82, 83, 101, *248, 265*
Bridgeman, B., 136, 179, 194, 199, 224,
    248
Britton, B. K., 75, 77, *248*
Britton, J., 125, 240, *248*
Broadbent, D. E., 53, *248*
Brooks, C., 216, *248*
Brown, A. L., 14, 167, 168, 195, 204, 205,
    239, *249, 265*
Brown, D., 217, *249*
Brown, J. S., 19, 22, 239, *249*
Bruce, B. C., 14, 74, *249*
Bruffee, K. A., 238, *249*
Bruner, J., 1, 2, 7, 12, 15, 16, 19, 28, 78,
    181, *249, 265*
Burgess, A., 240, *248*
Burke, P., 22, *249*
Burnett, R., *252, 254*

Burris, N. A., 127, *272*
Burton, R., 214, *249*
Bush, V., 209, *249*

Cage, J., 94, *249*
Cairney, T., 88, *249*
Calfee, R. C., 72, *249*
Callinicos, A., 236, *249*
Calvino, I., 94, *249*
Carlson, R. A., 127, *250*
Carlson, S. B., 136, 179, 194, 199, 224,
    248
Carpenter, P. A., 232, *272*
Carr, E. H., 236, *249*
Carroll, J. B., 58, *254*
Cary, E., 218, *250*
Cazden, C. B., 90, 133, 134, *250*
Chafe, W. L., 75, *250*
Chambliss, M. J., 72, *249*
Chapman, M., 15, *250*
Charney, D., 127, *250*
Chatman, S., 143, *250*
Chaucer, G., 131
Chen, C., 148, *252*
Chomsky, N., 66, *250*
Cicourel, A. V., 26, *250*
Clark, H. H., 12, 75, *250*
Cobb, P., 24, *250*
Cochran, C. A., 130, 179, 203, *250, 252*
Coe, R., 206, *250*
Colby, B. N., 66, 71, *250*
Cole, M., 15, 52, *250*
Coleridge, S. T., 215, 239, *250*
Collins, A., 14, 19, 157, *249, 250*
Conrad, J., 139
Cooper, C. R., 162, *251*
Corbett, E. P. J., 128, *251*
Coulson, R. L., 210, *271*
Crismore, A., 61–62, *251*
Cronin, B., 134, 218, *251*
Crowhurst, M., 127, 168, 190, 191, *251*
Culler, J., 111, 142, 143, *251*
Cunningham, J. W., 6, *251*
Curtin, C. B., 149, 150, *251*

Dagenais, J., 213, *251*

Daiute, C., 18, *251*

Damon, W., 15, 276

Daneš, F., 75, 102, *251*

Danesi, M., 7, *251*

D'Angelo, F. J., 206, *251*

Danziger, K., 2, *251*

Darwin, C., 20, 31

Davis, B. E., 157, *265*

Dawes, R. M., 62, 71, *251*

Day, J. D., 14, 167, 168, 195, 204, 205, *249*

de Man, P., 111, 113, *251*

Denis, M., 89, *251*

Derrida, J., 86, 98, 106, 110, 111, 113, 114, 135, *251*, *252*

Dillon, D., 144, *270*

DiSibio, M., 12, *252*

Dobson, M., 148, *252*

Dodson, M. M., *269*

Donaldson, M., 16, 180, 181, 182, 183, 187, 190, 209, 210, *252*

Dooling, D. J., 58, 78, *252*

Dorsey, S., 87, *246*

Dos Passos, J., 94

Douglas, M., 51, 52, *252*

Duchan, J. F., 82, *270*

Duffy, S. A., 69, *265*

Duffy, T. M., 77, *252*

Duguid, P., 19, *249*

Dunn, K., 214, *252*

Durkheim, E., 20, 21, 25, 28, 32, 49, 55, 115, *252*

Durst, R. K., 14, 199, 201, 203, *252*

Dyson, A. H., 127, *252*

Eagleton, T., 142, 143

Ebbinghaus, H., 37, 42, 55, 221, *252*

Eco, U., 107, 110, 116, 117, *252*

Ede, L., 128, 137, 138, 141, 145, *252*, *253*

Edge, D. O., 7, 242, *253*

Edwards, D., 18, 54, 90, 91, *264*

Egan-Robertson, A., 91, *247*

Eichenbaum, B., 101, *253*

Ellis, H., 233, *247*

Ellison, R., 192, *253*

Emerson, R. W., 30, 31, *253*

Emig, J., 14, 28, 212, *253*

Englert, C. S., 127, 242, *253*, *267*

Esveldt-Dawson, K., 227, *259*

Faigley, L., 127, 223, *253*

Fechner, G. T., 37

Fekete, J., 29, 96, 97, 121, *253*

Feldman, C. F., 2, *249*

Feltovich, P. J., 210, *271*

Ferriar, J., 215, *253*

Fillmore, C. J., 59, 71, *253*

Firbas, J., 75, 173, 198, *253*

Fischer, P., 230, *267*

Fish, S., 21, 23, 93, 98, 216, 221, *253*

Fitzgerald, J., 6, 126, *251*, *253*

Flavell, J. H., 16, 128, 180, 181, 182, 183, 184, 186, 187, 189, 190, 210, *253*

Fleck, L., 21, 22, 23, 25, 28, 45, 92, 124, *254*

Flower, L., 14, 35, 78, 124, 129, 136, 137, 144, 205, 246, 242, *254*, *256*, *257*

Foster, D., 218, *254*

Foucault, M., 28, 96, 106, 111, 112, 222, *254*

Fowler, L. A., *269*

Franks, J. J., 12, 57, *248*

Frawley, W., 70–71, *254*

Frederiksen, C. H., 12, 14, 58, 62, 63, 71, 84, 155, 179, 193, 206, *248*, *254*

Frederiksen, J. D., 14, *248*

Freedle, R. O., 58, 60, 85, *254*, *264*

Freedman, S. W., 126, 143, 162, *254*, *256*, *265*

French, N. H., 227, *259*

Freud, S., 106

Fry, C. L., 16, *253*

Frye, N., 56, *254*

Fyfe, R., 203, *262*

Gadamer, H.-G., 129, *254*

Galda, L., 126, *255*

Gale, J., 2, 24, 122, *271*
Garcia, R., 8, 15, *266*
Gardner, H., 97, *255*
Garner, R., 76, *255*
Gaudí, A., 212
Gauld, A., 53, 85, 179, *255*
Gee, J., 22, 126, 220, *255*
Geertz, C., 22, *255*
Geisler, C., 78, 130, 136, 137, 148, 179,
    238, *255*, *259*
Gentner, D., 14, 157, *249*, *250*
Gere, A. R., 144, *255*
Gergen, K. J., 4, 19, 23, *255*
Gibson, J. J., 143, *255*
Gilbert, G. N., 23, 124, 134, 196, *255*
Gillingham, M. G., 76, *255*
Glavanov, D., 89, *269*
Glenn, C. G., 58, 67, 71, 79, 81, *271*
Glock, M. D., 77, *262*
Glucksberg, S., 180, 181, 182, 183, 186,
    187, 189, 190, 198, 210, *255*
Glynn, S. M., 75, 77, *248*
Goetz, E. T., 13, 64, 76, 159, *244*, *255*
Goldman, S. R., 75, 81, *255*, *266*
Goldstein, L. J., 19, 236, *255*
Gomulicki, B. R., 36, 60, *255*
Goodman, K. S., 12, 242, *255*
Goodman, M. S., 79, *262*
Goodman, N., 4, 11, 17, 18, 22, 25, 28,
    103, 124, 235, 238, *256*
Goodwin, G. G., 151, 152, *256*
Gordon, C., 78, *266*
Graesser, A. C., 19, 69, 77, 82, 84, *256*,
    264
Graham, K., 90, *256*
Green, G. M., 132, 134, *256*
Green, J. L., 90, *256*
Greene, E., 78, 152, *260*, *273*
Greene, S., 14, 147, 182, 199, 205, *256*,
    271
Greenleaf, C., 126, *256*
Greimas, A. J., 103, 104, 118, *256*
Gretter, M. L., 77, *262*
Grice, H. P., 129
Griffin, S., 229, *256*

Grimes, J. E., 12, 60, 71, 72, 74, 153,
    182, *256*
Gulgoz, S., 77, *248*
Gumperz, J. J., 91, *256*
Guthrie, J. T., 239, *267*

Haas, C., 78, 125, 127, *256*
Haberlandt, K., 77, *264*
Haddon, A. C., 31, 48, 50, 51, 55, 221, *257*
Hajduk, T., *254*
Halász, L., 93, *257*
Halbwachs, M., 20, 25, 26, 49, 50, *257*
Halliday, M. A. K., 18, 74, 75, 91, *257*
Hansen, J., 78, *266*
Hansen, K., 127, 223, *253*
Hare, V. C., 84, *244*
Harris, K. R., 239, *267*
Harris, R., 99, 100, *257*
Harris, Z. S., 98, *257*
Hartman, D. K., 13, 87, 135, *257*
Hartman, G., 111
Hasan, R., 74, 75, 91, *257*
Hasselbring, T., 86, *270*
Haugen, D., *252*
Haviland, S. F., 75, *250*
Hawkes, T., 106, *257*
Haydon, B. R., 18
Hayes, J. R., 14, 35, 124, 125, 129, 242,
    254, *256*, *257*
Head, H., 32, 41, 51, 55, 221, *257*
Heath, S. B., 90, *257*
Hegel, G. W. F., 6, 8, 9, 10, 20, 22, 25, 27,
    45, *257*, *258*
Heidegger, M., 113, 114, 119
Helmholtz, H. von, 37
Hicks, D., 208, *275*
Hidi, S., 76, 195, *258*
Hiebert, E. H., 76, 127, *244*, *253*
Higgins, L., *252*
Hildyard, A., 76, *258*
Hill, C., *252*
Hinton, G. E., 14, *269*
Hodge, R., 118, *258*
Hoey, M., 198, *258*

Hogg, M. A., 221, *258, 273*
Holland, N. N., 98, 119, 216, *258*
Holmes, G., 41, *257*
Honan, W. H., 218, *258*
Horn, D. G., 77, *262*
Horowitz, R., 126, *258*
Hoy, E. A., 180, 181, 182, 183, 187, 190, 198, 210, *258*
Huckin, T. N., 22, 73, 127, *247*
Hughes, M., 190
Hume, D., 6, *258*
Hunt, K., 127, *258*
Hunt, R. A., 81, 82, 141, 142, 143, *258, 274*
Huxley, A., 18, *258*
Hymes, D., 89, *258*
Hynds, S., 16, 82, 216, *246, 258*

Iser, W., 98, *258*

Jacobson, M. J., 210, *271*
Jacoby, R., 54, *258*
Jakobson, R., 102, 103, 106, *259*
Jarvis, P. E., 16, *253*
Jetton, T. L., 86, *244*
Johns, A. M., 195, *259*
Johnson, B., 113, 114, *259*
Johnson, M. K., 57, 58, 78, *248*
Johnson, N. S., 58, 66, 67, 68, 70, 71, 81, *262*
Johnson, R., 60, 70, *259*
Johnson-Laird, P. N., 89, *259*
Jones, R. S., 168, *249*
Joyce, J., 94
Jung, C. G., 50, 55, *259*
Just, M. A., 232, *272*

Kaltman, H., 91, *256*
Kanin, E. J., 230, *259*
Kant, E., 6, 7, 8, 9, 10, 11, 12, 17, 20, 28, 40, 42, 72, 119, *259*

Kantz, M., *254*
Karan, D., 212
Kaufer, D., 130, 148, 242, *259*
Kay, H., 36, *259*
Kazdin, A. E., 227, *259*
Kearsley, G., 148, *259*
Kelly, G. A., 11, 16, 28, 238, *259*
Kennedy, M. L., 202, *259*
Kermode, F., 83, *259*
Kieras, D. E., 77, 196, *259, 260*
King, J. R., 14, 147, 163, 196, 202, *271*
King, M. L., 127, *267*
Kinneavy, J. L., 103, 126, *260*
Kintsch, W., 12, 13, 14, 58, 59, 60, 71, 74, 75, 77, 78, 89, 115, 135, 152, 159, 172, 240, *260, 274*
Kinzer, C., 86, *270*
Kirschner, B. W., 242, *267*
Klusewitz, M. A., 86, *262*
Knapp, P. A., 131, *260*
Koffka, K., 43, *260*
Köhler, W., 43, *260*
Koss, M. P., 230, *260*
Krauss, R. M., 180, 181, 182, 183, 186, 187, 189, 190, 198, 210, *255*
Kress, G., 118, *258*
Kreuz, R. J., 77, *256*
Kristeva, J., 28, 86, 98, 103, 104, 105, 106, 111, 112, 135, 216, *260*
Kristof, A., 93, *260*
Kroll, B. M., 16, 127, 128, 168, 180, 182, 183, 184, 186, 187, 189, 190, 191, 198, 210, *260*
Kucan, L., 239, *246*
Kucer, S., 3, *260*
Kuhn, T., 21, 22, 92, *260*
Kuiken, D., 83, 101, *264*
Kulikowich, J. M., 86, *244*
Külpe, O., 44

Labov, W., 81, 142, *260*
Lacan, J., 106, 111, 112, *261*
Lachman, R., 58, 78, *252*
Laclos, C. de, 104, *261*

Lakoff, G., xiii, *261*
Landow, G. P., 209, *261*
Langer, J. A., 14, 201, 203, *261*
Latour, B., 179, 196, *261*
LaZansky, J., 129, *272*
Leeds-Hurwitz, W., 118, *261*
Leenhardt, J., 23, 56, 93, 239, *261*
Leibniz, G. W. F. von, 42, *261*
Lemke, J., 73, 90, *261*
Leonard, K. E., 230, *260*
Leont'ev, A. N., 18, 89, *261*
Levin, S. R., 7, *261*
Lévi-Strauss, C., 32, 103, 104, 121, *261*
Lévy-Bruhl, L., 20, 22, 32, 49, 55, *261*
Lewis, G., 203, *262*
Lichtenstein, E. H., 80, 83, 101, *248*
Lindauer, B. K., 15, *265*
Lipson, M. Y., 239, *265*
Lissi, M. R., *269*
Lloyd, P., 181, 187, 190, 209, 210, *262*
Loban, W. D., 127, *262*
Lodge, D., 94, 95, *262*
Lomax, R. G., 76, 127, *267, 270*
Longacre, R. E., 155, *262*
Lorch, E. P., 77, 86, *262*
Lorch, R. F., Jr., 77, 86, 196, *262*
Lotze, H., 32, 42, *262*
Luckmann, T., 21, 26, *247*
Ludwig, C., 32
Lunsford, A., 128, 137, 138, 141, 145, *252, 253*
Lyotard, J. F., 94, *262*

MacCurdy, J. T., 48, 51, *262*
Mack, R. L., 69, *265*
Magliano, J. P., 19, *256*
Mahoney, M. J., 4, *262*
Mair, D. C., 230, *267*
Mallon, T., 214, *262*
Mandler, J. M., 58, 66, 67, 68, 70, 71, 79, 81, *262*
Mann, W. C., 72, 74, *262*
Mannheim, K., 20, 21, 26, *262*
Many, J. E., 203, 204, 242, *262*

Maratsos, M. P., 181, 187, 190, 209, 210, *262*
Markus, H., 233, *262*
Márquez, G. G., 212
Marshall, N., 77, *262*
Martin, N., 240, *248*
Marx, K., 8, 18, 20, 101, 105
Mason, A. W., 142, 143
Mathesius, V., 75, 102, *263*
Mathison, M. A., 14, 72, 136, 148, 179, 199, 200, 212, 223, *263, 271*
Mauss, M., 20, *252*
McCaffrey, M., *252*
McClelland, J. L., 14, 232, *263, 269*
McConkie, G., 60, *264*
McCormick, K., 129, *254, 263*
McCutchen, D., 127, 168, *263*
McDougall, W., 32
McGarty, C., 221, *258*
McGee, L. M., 75, 76, *263, 267*
McGinley, W., 124, 204, 209, *263*
McKeown, M. G., 82, 137, 239, *246*
McLeod, A., 240, *248*
McNamara, T. P., 77, *263*
Mead, G. H., 181, 182, 183, 209, 210
Medvedev, P. N., 102, *263*
Meglitsch, P. A., 169, 171, *263*
Mehan, H., 90, 91, *263*
Mehlenbacher, B., *252*
Meltzer, F., 87, 212, *263*
Mendelbaum, M., 70, *263*
Merrell, F., 107, *263*
Merton, R. K., 21, 237, *263*
Meutsch, D., 92, *263*
Meyer, B. J. F., 58, 60, 61, 64, 70, 71, 72, 74, 75, 76, 126, 149, 153, 172, 182, 207, *248, 263, 264, 274*
Miall, D. S., 83, 101, *264*
Michailidis, A., 148, *252*
Middleton, D., 18, 54, 90, 91, *264*
Miller, D. L., 77,., *263*
Miller, J. H., 111
Miller, O., 87, 135, *264*
Millis, K. K., 77, *264*
Milner, E., 227, 234, *264*

Minnis, A. J., 213, *264*
Minsky, M., 12, 13, *264*
Miró, J., 212
Mitchell, E., 203, *262*
Montague, W. E., 64, *244*
Morgan, L. H., 32, *264*
Mosenthal, P. B., 72, 75, 85, 172, *264*
Mulkay, M. J., 23, 35, 124, 218, *255*, *264*
Murray, D., 240, *264*
Murray, J. D., 77, *264*
Myers, C. S., 32, 33, 45, 51, 52, 55
Myers, G., 23, 199, 202, 218, *264*

Na, T. J., 85, *264*
Narváez, D., 80, 83, *273*
Nathan, R. G., 127, *272*
Naus, M., 85, *254*
Neimeyer, R. A., 17, *264*, *265*
Neisser, U., 54, 221, *265*
Nelson, J., 14, 205, *265*
Nelson, T. H., 209, *265*
Neuwirth, C., 148, *259*
Newell, A., 232, 233, *265*
Newell, G. E., 14, 201, *265*
Nietzsche, F., 44, 119, 216
Ninio, A., 19, *265*
Nitsch, K. E., *248*
Nold, E. W., 157, 162, *265*
Norris, C., 113, *265*
Norris, L., *254*
Nowell-Smith, P. H., 19, *265*
Nurius, P., 233, *262*
Nystrand, M., 129, 144, 238, *265*

Oakes, P. J., 221, *273*
Oates, J. C., 217, 218, 234, *265*
O'Connor, M. C., 91, *256*
Ohtsuka, K., 80, 82, 101, *265*
O'Keefe, G., 212
Olson, G. M., 69, *265*
Omanson, R. C., 82, *246*
Oros, C. J., 230, *260*

Ort, C.-M., 92, *265*
Ortony, A., 7, 12, 13, 64, *244*, *265*, *269*
Ostertag, J., 76, *245*
Otter, A. G. den, 92, 239, *265*

Paivio, A., 89, *269*
Palincsar, A., 239, *265*
Paris, S. G., 15, 239, *265*
Parkhill, T., 142, 143
Pascal, B., 146, *265*
Pascual-Leone, J., 15, *266*
Paul, I. H., 53, 82, 154, *266*
Pea, R. D., 19, *266*
Pearson, P. D., 3, 78, 212, *266*, *272*
Peck, W., *254*
Peirce, C. S., 106, 107, 112, 117, *266*
Penland, M. J., 75, *248*
Perfetti, C. A., 75, *266*
Phelps, L. W., 143, *266*
Philippe, J., 39, 221, *266*
Philips, S. B., 90, *266*
Phillips, D. C., 2, 24, *266*
Piaget, J., 8, 11, 14, 15, 16, 18, 19, 20, 28, 35, 51, 96, 97, 116, 121, 128, 168, 180, 181, 182, 183, 186-187, 189, 190, 197, 198, 209, 210, 238, *266*
Piché, G. I., 127, 168, 190, 191, *251*
Pichert, J. W., 13, 85, 193, *244*, *266*
Piovani, P., 8, *266*
Polanyi, L., 81, 142, *267*
Polanyi, M., 4, 21, *267*
Pople, M. T., 82, *246*
Porter, J. E., 21, 123, 217, *267*
Pratt, M. L., 142, *267*
Pressley, M., 69, 239, *267*
Pribram, K. H., 1, *267*
Prior, P., 143, *267*
Propp, V., 66, 71, 102, 104, *267*
Purves, A., 216, *267*

Quast, L., 89, *269*

Racine, J., 105
Rada, R., 148, *252*
Raphael, T. E., 242, *267*
Rathbone, R., 196, *267*
Ratteray, O. M. T., 196, *267*
Rave, J., 35
Reddy, M., 4, 71, *267*
Reed, J. H., *269*
Reicher, S. D., 221, *273*
Reither, J. A., 23, 122, 141, 142, 143, 217, *267*
Rentel, V. M., 127, *267*
Resnick, L. B., 19, *267*
Reynolds, J. F., 230, *267*
Reynolds, R. E., 13, 58, 64, 70, 84, 85, 240, *244*, *267*
Rice, G. E., 76, *264*
Richgels, D. J., 76, 127, *267*
Riffaterre, M., 143, *267*
Rippere, V., 216, *267*
Rivers, W. H. R., 31, 32, 33, 35, 41, 47, 48, 49, 51, 52, 55, 104, 221, *267*, *268*
Robertson, S. P., 77, *270*
Rogers, T., 87, *268*
Rohleder, L., 80, 83, *273*
Rohman, D. G., 5, 124, 239, 240, *268*
Rosen, H., 240, *248*
Rosenblatt, L. M., 5, 82, 143, 216, 240, *268*
Roth, R. G., 129, 130, 134, *268*
Rothkopf, E. Z., 85, 179, 193, *268*
Rowe, D., 88, *268*
Rubin, A. D., 14, *249*
Rubin, D. L., 127, 221, *268*
Rubin, E., 64, *268*
Ruddell, R. B., 86, *268*
Rumelhart, D. E., 13, 14, 64, 66, 71, 102, 232, 242, *263*, *268*, *269*

Sadoski, M., 89, *269*
Salomon, G., 19, 28, 238, *269*
Samuels, S. J., 126, *258*
Sandora, C., 239, *246*

Saussure, F. de, 97, 98, 99, 100, 101, 102, 103, 104, 106, 107, 109, 110, 112, 113, 115, *269*
Scardamalia, M., 127, 128, 242, *247*
Schallert, D. L., 13, 64, 84, 91, *244*, *269*
Schank, R. C., 12, 13, 79, *269*
Schelling, F. W. J. von, 215
Schmalhofer, F., 89, *269*
Schmidt, S. J., 23, 28, 82, 83, 92, 239, *263*, *269*
Schnotz, W., 73, 172, *270*
Scholes, R., 143, *270*
Schwartz, L., 85, *254*
Scott, J. A., 76, *244*
Scott, P. J., 82, *270*
Scribner, S., 15, *250*
Searle, D., 144, *270*
Secco, T., 79, 80, *272*
Sechehaye, A., 99, *245*
Segal, E. M., 82, *270*
Seifert, C. M., 77, *270*
Seligman, C. G., 32
Shakespeare, W., 218
Shanahan, T., 78, 127, *270*, *272*
Shannon, C. E., 4, 102, *270*
Sheard, C., 76, *267*
Sherick, R. B., 227, *259*
Sherwood, R., 86, *270*
Shklovsky, V., 101, 214, *270*
Shotter, J., 54, *270*
Sidney, P., 218, *270*
Siegel, T., 227, *259*
Simon, H. A., 232, *245*, *265*, *270*
Sless, D., 117, *270*
Sloane, S., *252*
Small, H. G., 87, *270*
Smith, B. H., 195, *270*
Smith, E. M., 33
Smith, F., 12, *270*
Smith, S., *252*
Smith, J. Z., 143, *270*
Smith, W. L., 127, *271*
Smolensky, P., 14, *269*
Spencer, H., 31
Sperling, M., 140, 143, *254*, *271*

Spiegel, D. L., 126, *253*

Spiro, R. J., 36, 58, 64, 84, 86, 88, 89, 135, 210, *271*

Spivey, N. N., 12, 14, 69, 73, 132, 134, 146, 149, 152, 163, 169,182, 196, 197, 202, 223, 241, *254, 271*

Steffe, L. P., 2, 24, 122, *271*

Stein, N. L., 58, 67, 71, 79, 81, *271*

Stein, V., *254*

Stephenson, G. M., 53, 85, 179, *255*

Sternberg, R. J., 7, *271*

Sterne, L., 101, 212, 214, 215, 237, *272*

Stevens, R. S., 144, *255*

Stillinger, J., 139, 217, *272*

Stone, O., 212

Stotsky, S., 127, *272*

Suh, S., 79, *273*

Sukenick, R., 94, *272*

Sulzby, E., 127, *272*

Susann, J., 139

Swan, M. B., 127, *271*

Swift, J., 25, *272*

Tate, G. H. H., 150, 151, *272*

Taylor, B. M., 76, *272*

Taylor, J., 212

Taylor, W., 238, *272*

Temple, C. A., 127, *272*

Thibadeau, R., 232, *272*

Thibault, P. J., 118, *272*

Thomas, C., 227, *259*

Thompson, S. A., 72, 74, *262*

Thorndyke, P. W., 58, 67, 71, 82, *272*

Tierney, R. J., 3, 127, 129, 209, *263, 272*

Todorov, T., 103, 104, 116, 117, *272*

Tomashevsky, B., 80, *272*

Toole, J. K., 132, *272*

Trabasso, T., 79, 80, 81, 82, *272, 273*

Trimbur, J., 139, *273*

Trubetzkoy, N. S., 102, *273*

Turner, A., 152, *273*

Turner, J. C., 221, *273*

Turner, M., xiii, *261*

Turner, T. J., 13, *248*

Twain, M., 139

Tyler, S. A., 131, 132, *273*

Tyler, S. W., 89, *273*

Ulichny, P., 141, *273*

Ulloa, A., 148, *252*

Unis, A. S., 227, *259*

Unrau, N. J., 86, *268*

Vande Kopple, W. J., 62, 77, *273*

van den Broek, P. W., 79, 80, 81, 82, 83, *272, 273*

van der Rohe, M., 212

van Dijk, T. A., 12, 13, 58, 60, 66, 76, 77, 84, 89, 108, 109, 115, 116, 152, 158, 159, 195, 202, 204, *260, 273, 274*

van Dusen, L., 77, *248*

van Rees, C. J., 27, 92, *274*

van Rees, K., 92, *274*

Varnhagen, C. K., 81, *255*

Verdaasdonk, H., 92, *274*

Vico, G., 5, 6, 7, 8, 9, 10, 20, 22, 28, 45, 120, 133, 134, *274*

Vipond, D., 23, 81, 82, 122, 141, 142, 143, 159, 217, *258, 260, 267, 274*

Voloshinov, V. N., 91, 102, *274*

von Glaserfeld, E., 4, *274*

Voss, J. F., 89, *273*

Vygotsky, L. S., 18, 19, 20, 89, 92, 238, *274*

Wade, S. E., 76, *274*

Walker, C. H., 207, *274*

Wallace, D., *252, 254*

Wallat, C., 90, *256*

Ward, J., 32, 33, 42, 51, 55, *274*

Warrilow, D., 94, *274*

Watson, J. B., 43, *274*

Watson, K. A., 18, *274*

Watson-Gegeo, K. A., 141, *273*

Watt, H. J., 44, *274*

Watzlawick, P., 4, *275*

Weade, R., 90, *256*

Weaver, C., 143, *275*
Weaver, W., 4, 102, *270*
Weber, E. H., 37
Weiner, N., 47, 51
Weinstock, M., 196, *275*
Wells, G., 126, *275*
Wertsch, J. V., 18, *275*
Wetherell, M., 221, *273*
White, J., 76, *255*
Whorf, B. L., 120
Wilkinson, I. A. G., 76, *244*
Wimsatt, W. K., Jr., 216, *246*, *275*
Wineburg, S. S., 78, 239, *275*
Winograd, P. N., 14, 195, *275*
Winograd, T., 129, *275*
Wishart, J. G., 181, *248*
Witte, S. P., 14, 77, 118, 124, 157, *275*

Wittgenstein, L., 209, 236, *275*
Wixson, K. K., 239, *265*
Wlecke, A. O., 5, 124, 239, 240, *268*
Woehler, C. A., 86, *244*
Wolf, D., 208, *275*
Wordsworth, W., 114, 215, 239, *275*
Worthy, J., 137, 239, *246*
Wright, J. W., 16, *253*
Wundt, W. W., 37, 55, *275*

Yarbrough, J. C., 75, 172, *260*
Youniss, J., 15, 276

Zangwill, O. L., 53, 54, 221, 276
Zurburgg, N., 94, 276
Zwaan, R. A., 85, 89, 179, 276

Subject Index

Academic discourse, 2, 14, 21–23, 35, 36,
70, 72–74, 88, 92, 108, 119, 127,
130–131, 134, 135–136, 137, 139,
141–144, 179–191, 217, 218, 237,
239; *see also* Arguing, Critiquing,
Discourse synthesis, Proposing,
Reporting, Summarizing
Accommodation, 15, 35
Active text notion, 119
Aesthetic response, 82–83
in Rosenblatt's transactional conception,
82, 240
Aesthetic convention, 83
Affect in reading, 82–83, 89; *see also*
Structural affect theory
Affective fallacy, 216
Agent
constructive
collaborative group as, 18–19, 89–92,
123
community, society, or macro social
group as, 19–23, 92–93, 116,
123–124
contrasting conceptions of, among
various constructivists, 2–3, 7,
10, 23–26, 55, 123–124,
239
individual as, 10–18, 26–27, 44,
56–89, 123
in poststructuralism, 111–112
in structuralism, 103–104, 111, 116–117
text as, 112; *see also* Active text notion
Allusion, 87, 134, 220, 232
Apprenticeship, 21, 118
Appropriation

by individuals, 18, 39, 136, 209
by societies, 192–193; *see also* Cultural
change
Architectural metaphor, 5, 96
Arguing, 120, 127, 179, 192–194, 201–202
Argument, 179, 204–205, 227; *see also*
Causal argument
Argument, propositional, 59–60
overlap, 59
Artifacts, as focus of study, 1, 34, 38, 47, 92,
222, 241–242
Assimilation, 15, 18, 35
Associationism, 9, 42–43
Audience, *see also* Author–audience
relationship
adaptation for, 16, 46, 123, 126–128,
131–133
awareness of, 16, 126–128
community members as, 22–23
epistemic effect of, 130
heuristic effect of, 129–130
strategic use of, 131
Author
as accolade, 213
death of, 129, 216–217
deemphasis of, 215–216
disciplinary, 216–218
function, 222
medieval, 213
myth of solitary, 217
readers' inferences about, 78, 129,
133–135, 236–237, 239
Romantic, 215
Author–audience relationship, 26–27, 38,
46, 117–118, 125–133

287

Author–audience relationship *(continued)*
  constructivist conception of, 129
  other conceptions of
    classic rhetorical, 128
    cooperative, 128
    hermeneutic, 128
    poststructuralist, 128
    strong reader, 128
Author-based interpretation, 215–216
Authoring identity
  Bartlett as illustration of, 53–55, 221
  as construct, 27–28, 219–234
  development of, 223–234
Authority, *see also* Transformation
  approach to conduct of studies, 70–71
  of author, 87, 204–205, 213–215
    questioned, 83, 111
  in authoring identity, 143–144, 221–222
  in collaboration, 138–139
  of one voice undermined, 112
  in response, 140–141
  of textbook challenged, 239
Authorship, 22–23, 27–28; *see also*
    Transformation
  disciplinary, 22–23, 215–218
  and discourse synthesis, 179
  issues raised in postmodern literature,
    94–95
  literary, 214–216, 217–218
  medieval conception of, 213
  as originality, 214
  as ownership, 214
  after printing press, 214–215
  and response, 143
  Romantic conception of, 215
Autonomous text or intertext, notion of,
    86, 114, 119, 216

Balancing, *see* Symmetry
Binary opposition, 100–101, 104, 115
Biographical approach to literary studies, 215
Borrowing
  in authorship, 213–215, 241–242
  and cultural change, *see* Cultural change

Breadth/depth ratio, *see* Report; Topical
    chunk

Categories
  of knowledge, 2, 6–7, 8, 9, 11, 20, 21, 72
  in personal construct theory, 16–17, 238
Causal argument, 72–74, 182–185, 188,
    194, 201–202, 207
Causal chain, 79–81
Causal connections, 38–40, 42–43, 67–68,
    75, 77, 79–81, 90, 157, 193
Causal model for story, 79–81
Causal pattern, 72–74, 184; *see also* Causal
    argument, Story
Causality
  philosophical debate regarding, 6
  sociological debate regarding, 49
Center for the Study of Reading, 12, 58, 62
Center for the Study of Writing, 14, 212,
    237
Chronological pattern, 17–18, 72–74, 201
Chunk, *see also* Topical chunk
  of content, 61, 74, 82, 105
  of texts by means of author, 222
Citation, 24, 30, 51, 86–87, 134, 196,
    217–218, 224
Classic studies of discourse comprehension,
    58–69
Co-authorship, 18, 28, 139–140, 141–143,
    144, 214
Co-construction
  in reading, 24, 89–92
  in writing, 137–144
Cognitive complexity, 16
Cognitive constructivism, 3, 6, 11–14
Cognitive flexibility theory, 210
Cognitive-developmental constructivism, 3,
    11, 14–16
Cohesion, 74–75
Collaboration between constructivists and
    structuralists, 115–116
Collaborative constructivism, 3, 18–19
Collaborative writing process, 137–139

Collection pattern, 72–74, 149, 154–158, 165–166, 182–183, 185, 186–187; *see also* Report

Collective cognition, notions of
collective conscience, 20
collective consciousness, 20, 22
collective memory, 20, 26, 49–50
collective mentality, 49–50
collective remembering, 18
collective representation, 20
collective unconscious, 50

Community, *see also* Agent, constructive; Discourse community
critical, 92
interpretive, 21, 221
role of, in structuralism, 99–100, 109–110, 116
scientific, 21

Comparing, 74, 90, 127, 166, 169–178, 186, 187, 189–190, 194, 204, 206–207, 233

Comparison/contrast connections, 60, 158, 189–190, 204

Comparison pattern, 72–74, 172–174, 178, 182–183, 186–187, 197–198; *see also* Report

Composing process, 3, 14, 27; *see also* Co-construction, in writing; Collaborative writing process; Intertextual connections; Organic plant metaphor, Audience, Author–audience relationship
Bartlett's, 50–52
product in, 125
reading as part of, 125, 136–137, 138–139, 144–145; *see also* Discourse synthesis
relative to comprehending, 3, 14
stage or step conception of, 124–125
varying perspectives on, 123–124; *see also* Problem-solving model of composing

Comprehension
agenda of Center for Study of Reading, 12, 62

new views of, during 1970s, 12, 57–58

Conduit metaphor, 4, 71, 237

Connectedness, as feature of discourse, *see* Argument, propositional, overlap; Cohesion; Topical connections, described as topical continuity

Connecting, *see also* Causal connections, Comparison/contrast connections, Inferences, Intertextual connections, Temporal Connections, Topical connections
in reading, 38–41, 47, 56, 59, 69, 71, 76–78, 81–82, 93, 196
in writing, 125, 131, 132, 208–209

Connectivity
as constructivist theme, 1, 7, 8, 12
of social product, 90–92

Consensus approach to conduct of studies, 70

Conservation, *see* Cultural change

Constructionism, 19

Construction metaphor, compared with other metaphors, 2, 4–5, 115–121, 241

Constructive agent, *see* Agent, constructive

Constructiveness, 1–2, 6–9, 35–36, 48, 52, 54–55, 211, 233; *see also* Causal connections, Comparison/contrastive connections, Connecting, Cultural change, Inferences, Intertextual connections, Temporal connections, Topical connections

Constructivism, *see* Cognitive constructivism, Cognitive-developmental constructivism, Collaborative constructivism, Constructionism, Construction metaphor, Critical constructivism, Radical constructivism, Social constructivism

Constructivist predicament, 69–71

Constructivist tradition, 57–71

Contact and cultural change, *see* Cultural change

Context, *see* Macrocontext, Psychosocial
    context, Situational context,
    Sociocultural context
Contextual cues, *see* Cues, contextual
Conventionality, *see* Originality, versus
    conventionality
Conventionalization
    and authorship, 217
    Bartlett as illustration of, 52
    and linguistic development, 126–127,
        223–234
    of social products, 46–48; *see also*
        Cultural change
    and writing for readers, 126–127
Conventions, *see* Aesthetic convention;
        Expository discourse, conventions of;
        Polyvalence convention; Post-
        modernism; Story, conventions of;
        Transformation, of conventions by
        postmodern authors
Copying machine metaphor, 2
Cost/benefit trade-off, *see* Explicitness
Critical constructivism, 4
Critique, 72, 130, 182, 187, 188, 189, 191,
        219; *see also* Topic–comment pattern
Critiquing, 92, 130, 185, 187, 199–201,
        236
Cross-cultural comparison, see also
        Mentalités
    of developmental patterns in learning, 15
    of discourse, 47–48, 78
    of ways of knowing, 47, 48–49
Cues, 12, 57, 118
    contextual, 84–85
    intertextual, 28, 86–88, 159, 191
    textual, 12, 13, 76, 77, 124–126, 129,
        138–144, 146, 168–169, 196, 202,
        203, 208, 211
Cultural change, *see also* Constructiveness;
        Conventionalization; Evolution, social;
        Immigration and innovation
    from borrowing, 35–36, 47
    and conservation, 35–36, 47, 48
    from contact, 35–36, 47–48, 55, 235
    from diffusion, 32, 35–36, 47

Cycles
    of conformity and extension of personal
        constructs, 16
    Vichean, of society's development, 7

Decentering
    as developmental process, 16, 128, 180,
        185; *see also* Egocentrism
    of the subject in structuralism and
        poststructuralism, 86, 103, 107, 111,
        116, 119, 121
Deconstruction, 5, 29, 96, 97, 98, 110, 111,
        113–115, 119, 141–142, 235, 237
Defamiliarization, 82, 101
Device, *see* Literary device
Diachronic study of language, 100, 102,
        103, 104, 116
Dialectical development
    of children's cognition, 15
    of society, 8
Dialogue
    in glossing, 213–214
    among texts, 102
Différence, 100–101, 113, 119
Différance, 113
Diffusion, *see* Cultural change
Disciplines, academic
    as communities, 21, 45, 184
    emergence of, 9–10, 31, 97
    perspectives associated with, 65, 119
    as thought collectives, 21
    as tribes, 21
Disciplinary discourse, *see* Academic
        discourse
Discourse analysis methods, 56, 58–63,
        65–68, 70–75, 78–81, 90, 152–154,
        155–161, 165–168, 171–176,
        182–186, 189–191, 225, 233
Discourse community, 21–23, 45, 92,
        123–124, 142, 217, 220, 242
Discourse knowledge development, 15–16,
        22, 116, 126–128, 165–169
Discourse practices, 25; *see also* Arguing,
        Critquing, Proposing, Reporting,
        Storytelling, Summarizing

Discourse synthesis, 29, 135–136, 146–191, 202, 235–236; *see also* Intertextual connections

Discussion, 90, 91–92

Distributed cognition, 19, 238

Dominant, the,
in functionalist theory of communication, 103
shift of, 103

Durkheimian theory, 20–21

Écriture, 101, 112–113

Effort after meaning, 41, 81, 84, 241

Egocentrism, 16, 180–187

Enlightenment, 5–8

Episteme, 106

Epistemology; *see also* Transformation of epistemology
compared for constructivism and structuralism, 119–120
relative to discourse, 22, 72
as social construct, 7, 238, 241
structuralism as, 107–108

Evaluations, *see* Points of stories

Evolution
biological, 20
social, 8, 31–32, 49–50; *see also* Durkheimian theory, Hegelian theory, *Mentalités*

Explicitness, 61, 77, 131–133, 134–135; *see also* Unsaid

Expository discourse, 60–61, 71–78
conventions of, 71–75

Figure and ground
Center for Study of Reading texts as, 64–65, 85
Gestalt notion of, 43, 64
as nature of selecting in reading, 173
Rubin's goblet/faces drawing as, 64

Foci of constructivism, 2–3, 12, 23–26

Folk story, 34, 38–40, 65—67, 78–82, 102

Folktale, *see* Folk story

Formalism, *see* Russian formalism

Functionalism, *see* Prague School functionalism

Functional sentence perspective, *see* Topical connections, described as topical continuity

Functional theory of communication, 102–103, 106

Gap
in knowledge, 15, 51
between signifier and signified, 112
between text world and *the* world, 94

Gap-filling metaphor, 15, 39–40, 51, 207

General impression scoring, 162

Genre, 22, 72–74, 87, 126, 134, 199, 219, 223–225
Derrida's deconstruction of, 114–115
in postmodern literature, 94
shifts in, over time, 103

Gestalt psychology, *see* Figure and ground; Organization, Gestalist conception of

Ghost story study, *see* "War of the Ghosts, The"

Glossing of texts in manuscript culture, 213–214

Gricean contract, 129

Group, *see* Agent, constructive

Hegelian theory, 8–9, 10, 20, 22, 25

Hermeneutics, 128–129

Heteroglossic character of writing, 27, 112, 208–209

Heuristic function of form, 206–207

Hierarchy of text content, 59–61, 67–68, 74, 153–154, 159, 195, 202

Historicism; *see also Mentalités*
Hegelian, 8
Vichian, 7

Hybrid acts of literacy, 14

Hypertext, 101, 148, *see also* Transformation

Hypertheme, 75, 173, 186, 198

Hypotactic relations, 60, 153–154

Identity, 3, 26; *see also* Authoring identity, Social identity theory
  kit, 220
  of reader, 100
  of sign, 100
  as target of deconstruction, 113
  of text dismissed in poststructuralism, 222; *see also* Intertextuality
Ideology, 83, 110, 111, 112, 113, 119, 121, 143, 216, 237
Imagery, 34, 89, 117
Immigration and innovation, 35
Importance, *see also* Metadiscourse, Points of stories, Relevance, Staging
  indicated by readers' glosses, 213–214
  intertextual, 153–154, 159, 167
  in terms of social consequences, 90–91
  textual, 59–62, 70, 74, 76, 80–81, 124, 126, 131, 167; *see also* Hierarchy of text content
Inferences; *see also* Author, readers' inferences about
  contextual, 62, 83–86, 89, 93, 123, 125, 179, 191, 194, 196, 235
  intertextual, *see* Intertextual connections
  made by researcher, 89–90, 107, 116, 240, 241
  textual, 19, 24, 34, 39, 58, 59, 62, 65, 67, 70, 74, 75, 77–78, 81–82, 83, 85, 86, 88–89, 156, 157, 159–160, 167–168; *see also* Causal connections, Comparison/contrast connections, Temporal connections
Information theory, 4, 97
Ingenium, 6–7
Innovation, *see* Immigration and innovation
Intentional fallacy, 216
Interestingness, 76
Intertextual connections , 119, 135
  in discourse synthesis, 146, 159–161, 167–168, 173–176, 178, 186–187, 189–191, 207–211
  in reading, 82, 85–88, 91, 119
  in writing, 51, 133–137, 191, 193, 196, 203, 226, 228; *see also* Authoring identity

Intertextuality, 31, 86, 91–92, 112, 135, 216
Initiation-response-evaluation pattern of classroom discourse, 90–91
Irrealism, 4
Isomorphic summary, *see* Summary, isomorphic

Joint remembering, 90

Kantian rationality, 6, 8, 9–10, 11, 17, 40
Kinship terms, used to study society, 31, 104
Knowledge, *see also* Categories of knowledge; Discourse knowledge development; Transformation, of knowledge
  as cognitive construct, 2–4,9, 11–14, 15, 16, 238–239; *see also* Kantian rationality; Schema
  connectionist conception of, 13–14, 108
  propositional conception of, 13, 58–59, 88–89
  as constructive material, 5, 12
  disciplinary, 22, 84, 238–239; *see also* Discourse community
  metacognitive, 239
  role of in reading, 12–13, 40, 57–58, 77–78, 81–82
  role of in writing, 135, 136–137, 140, 147, 203–204, 206–207
  situated nature of, 9
  as social construct, 18, 21–22, 89–90, 92, 116, 119–120, 218; *see also* Cultural change, Durkheimian theory, Hegelian theory, Vichean theory
  sociocultural, 83–84
  updating of, 88
Knowledge-telling strategy in writing, 128

Landscape metaphor, 105, 209–210
Langue, 99, 104, 110
Lens of constructivism, 23–26, 89, 92, 235, 239, 242
Levels effect, 76, 159
Literature of exhaustion, 94, *see also* Postmodernism
Literary device, 78, 81, 101–102, 114; *see also* Defamiliarization
   laying bare of, 101
Literary discourse, 23, 80, 92–95, 102, 105, 108, 139, 214–219, 221–222; *see also* Aesthetic response; Authoring identity; Biographical approach to literary studies; New Criticism; Postmodernism; Poststructuralism; Reader response; Russian Formalism; Story grammar, French structuralists'

Macro-aspect, 173–174, 176–178, 198
Macrocontext, 86
Macroproposition, 158, 195, 207
Maelstrom metaphor, applied to structuralist theories, 28, 97, 121
Mathemagenic tasks, 85
Mental product, *see* Product, mental
Mentalités, 20, 22
Metadiscourse, 61, 131, 137
Metaphor, theory as, 2, 7, 235; *see also* Architectural metaphor, Conduit metaphor, Construction metaphor, Copying machine metaphor, Landscape metaphor, Maelstrom metaphor, Organic plant metaphor, Telegraph metaphor, Transmission metaphor, Vichean theory
Metatheory of constructivism, 3
Migrant, *see* Immigration and innovation
Myth, 7, 9, 37, 103–104, 105
Myth of solitary genius, 217

Narrative, 7, 17–18, 40, 78, 82, 90, 94, 105, 201; *see also* Folk story, Story

Network of interrelated texts, 179, 219–220, 222
New Criticism, 92, 98, 215–216, 221–222, 240
News discourse, 108–109
Niche, 220–221, 233–234; *see also* Authoring identity

Organic plant metaphor, 5, 215, 239–240, 241
Organization
   as constructivist theme, 2, 3, 4, 9, 56, 90
   Gestaltist conception of, 43–44
Organizational patterns, 13, 60, 90, 95, 126; *see also* Causal pattern; Chronological pattern; Collection pattern; Comparison pattern; Participation structure; Problem–solution pattern; Response, pattern; Story; Topic-comment pattern
Organizing
   in discourse synthesis, 147, 154–158, 165–166, 172–176, 182–187, 191
   in reading, 13, 40, 47,67, 75–76, 81, 93; *see also* Structural affect theory
   in writing, 124, 127, 136, 193–202, 211
Originality, 3, 55, 214–219, 234
   versus conventionality, 241–242

Paradigm, 21, 22
Paradigmatic relation, 100, 102
Paratactic relation, 60
Parole, 99, 104, 110
Participation structure, 90; *see also* Initiation-response-evaluation pattern in classroom discourse
Pastiche, 94, 219
Personal construct theory, 3, 11, 16–17, 238
Perspective, 1, 4, 17, 19, 21, 25–29, 49, 54–55, 101, 123–124, 136, 144, 219, 227, 235–236; *see also* Historicism

Perspective-taking research, 15–16, 62–65, 85, 127, 180–191, 193, 238
Plagiarism, 214
Points of stories, 80–81, 141–142
Polyvalence convention, 83
Possible selves, 233
Post-Kantian thought, 6
Postmodernism, 93–95, 126, 219, 237, 241
    Tristram Shandy as example of, 101, 214
Poststructuralism, 5, 29, 86, 96–97, 103, 105–106, 107, 108, 110–115, 141–142, 216, 221–222, 235
    compared with constructivism, 118–121
    relative to structuralism, 111; *see also* Structuralism, transformed into poststructuralism
Practices, *see* Arguing, Critiquing, Discourse practices, Proposing, Reporting, Storytelling, Summarizing
Prague School functionalism, 75, 97, 101–103, 115; *see also* Functional theory of communication, Topic–comment pattern
Predictors of quality in writing, 162, 176, 197, 200–201
Problem–solution pattern, 60–61, 72–74, 184–185, 190; *see also* Proposal; Report, research
Problem-solving model of composing, 242
Problem-solving task, 62, 84, 206
Process versus product issue, 239–242
    in study of writing, 240–241
Product
    mental, 1, 13–14, 23, 24–26, 69, 88–89, 123, 125, 240–241
    social, 7, 8, 9, 18–19, 22–23, 24–26, 34, 89–91, 92, 116, 120, 123–124, 192–193, 213
Proposal, 74, 179, 182–185, 188, 191, 199, 207, 224, 233
Proposing, 147, 179, 190, 194, 198–199, 201, 205, 206, 207, 228, 230–231, 236
Proposition, 59–60, 104, 108, 152–153, 194, 203; *see also* Macroproposition

Propositional conception of memory, *see* Knowledge, as cognitive construct
Protocol analysis, *see* Think-aloud research
Psychophysical approach, 31, 32, 33, 37, 51
Psychosocial context, 85

Questioning the author, 239

Radical constructivism, 3, 4
Radical relativism, 4
Rationality, *see* Hegelian theory, Kantian rationality
Reader response, 215–216, 221–222; *see also* Aesthetic response, Affect in reading
    contrasted with New Criticism, 240
Readerly text, 105
Reciprocity in communication, 18, 34
Recursiveness of writing, 124–125
Relevance
    intertextual, 202, 211; *see also* Symmetry, criterion
    rhetorical, 202–203
    textual, 75–76, 195; *see also* Hierarchy of text content, Importance
    to context, 84–85
Remembering studies, 11, 29, 30, 31, 33, 34, 36–50, 223
    opinions about, 52, 53–54
    writing of, 50–52
Report
    organized as comparison, 169–178, 186–187, 190, 197–198
    organized as collection according to author, 186
    organized as collection according to topics, 72, 147, 154–168, 183, 186, 189, 193, 196–197, 224
    breadth/depth ratio for studying, 154–157, 165–166
    research, 22, 60, 72, 74, 87, 134, 224–225

Reporting, 72, 123, 130, 147, 192–193, 194, 196–198, 209, 236

Response, *see also* Reader response
pattern, 72–74, 184, 186, 200; *see also* Problem–solution pattern, Topic–comment pattern
register, 85
statement, 200–201, 240
to writing, 140–144

Rhetorical relations, 60, 72–74; *see also* Causal connections, Comparison/contrast connections, Hypotactic relations, Paratactic relation, Temporal connections, Topical connections

Romanticism, 6, 239–240, 241, 215, 221

Russian formalism, 66, 80, 101–102, 103, 106, 214; *see also* Defamiliarization; Literary device; Temporal duality; Story grammar, Propp's

Russian scandal approach, 47, 51

Scaffolding, 19

Schema, 10, 11, 13, 22, 41–42, 44, 45–46, 49, 54, 55, 64, 66, 97, 108, 221

Science as guilds, 21

Script, 13, 97

Seductive details, 76

Selecting
in discourse synthesis, 158–159, 161, 163, 167, 168, 173–176, 191
in reading, 40, 60–65, 69, 75–76, 81, 84–86, 90, 93
in writing, 136, 137, 193, 202–204, 206, 211, 218; *see also* Authoring identity, Summarizing

Selectivity, as constructivist theme, 3, 56

Semiology, 100

Semiotics, 91, 97, 98, 100, 106–107, 110, 112, 115–118

Shared meaning, 24, 93, 123

Sign, *see also* Identity, of sign
Peirce's conception of, 107
poststructuralism and the, 105, 110–112
semiotics as study of, 107

as signifier and signified, Saussure's conception of, 100–101

Situation model, 88–89

Situational context, 84–86, 211

Social change, *see* Cultural change; Evolution, social

Social cognition, 127

Social constructiveness, *see* Constructiveness, social

Social evolution, *see* Evolution, social

Social identity theory, 221

Social versus cognitive issue, 238–239

Socio-cognitive conceptions of writing, 238

Sociocultural context, 26, 83–84

Sociocultural knowledge, 83–84, 147

Sociology of knowledge, 7, 10, 20, 21, 216

Sociology of literature, 92

Sound pattern, 100; *see also* Sign, as signifier and signified, Saussure's conception

Source-based literary studies, 215

Soviet theories of language and learning, 18–19, 89, 91, 101–102

Staging, 74, 126, 136, 163, 202, 206

Story, 11, 16, 38, 41, 47–48, 65–67, 78–83, 87, 101–102, 104–105, 126–127, 128; *see also* Causal connections, Causal chain, Causal model for story, Folk story, Narrative, Points of stories, Talk story
conventions of, 67, 78–81, 93–95

Story grammar
American researchers', 65–67, 71, 81
French structuralists', 66, 71, 104, 105
Propp's, 66, 71, 102

Storytelling, 11, 34, 38, 46, 80–81, 131; *see also* Points of stories
collaborative, 18
oral compared to written, 78, 81, 141

Structural affect theory, 83, 115

Structuralism, 5, 29, 66, 75, 96–110; *see also* Agent, in structuralism; Post-structuralism; Prague School functionalism; Russian formalism
compared with constructivism, 115–118
French, 103–106

Structuralism *(continued)*
    Lévi-Strauss's, 103–104
    metaphor of, 5
    method of, 109–110
    relative to discourse analysis, 107–109
    relative to semiotics, 106–107
    Saussurean, 97, 98–101
    transformed into poststructuralism, 103,
        106, 110–112
Structure strategy, 75
Summarizing, 135–136, 168, 194–196,
        201, 205, 227, 236
    copy-delete strategy in, 167, 195
    in critiquing, 199–200
    generative nature of, 77–82
    in news discourse, 108–109
Summary
    citation as, 87, 196
    isomorphic, 194–195
    variable type of, 194–196
Symmetry
    balancing to create, 173–176, 204, 206
    and comparison pattern, 171, 173–176
    criterion, 173, 178, 202
Synchronic study of language, 99–100, 102,
        104, 109, 116
Syntagmatic relation, 100, 102

Talk story, 18
Task interpretation, 84, 86, 93, 140,
        166–167, 204–207; *see also* Problem-
        solving task
Tel Quel, see Poststructuralism
Telegraph metaphor, 4
Template
    approach to research, 61, 62, 69–70, 71,
        148–149, 203
    composite, 152, 154
Temporal duality, 80–81
Temporal connections, 67, 72, 75, 80, 157,
        158, 187; *see also* Chronological
        pattern
Text analysis, *see* Discourse analysis methods

Text base, 59–60, 89
Theme, *see* Topic, repeated, in identity
        construction; Topical connections;
        Topic–comment pattern
Think-aloud research, 240
    analysis of protocols in 13, 35, 36, 69
    insights from, 124, 128, 129, 204–205,
        206
Thought collective, 21, 23, 45
Thought style, 21, 23
Tool, language as cultural, 19, 92
Topic, repeated, in identity construction,
        222, 223–234
Topical chunk, 154–159, 162–163,
        165–166, 168, 173, 178, 186,
        196–198, 207–208
Topical connections
    across texts, 196, 207–208
    descibed as topical continuity, 75, 77, 91
    represented as topical chain, 155–157,
        165–166
Topic–comment pattern, 72–74, 185, 186,
        199; *see also* Critique
Transactional theory, *see* Aesthetic response
        to reading, Reader response
Transformation, *see also* Authoring identity;
        Connnecting; Cultural change;
        Discourse synthesis; Organizing;
        Selecting; Structuralism, transformed
        into poststructuralism
    and authority, 208–209
    and authorship, 213–215, 218–219,
        225–233
    of conventions by postmodern authors,
        241
    of epistemology, 8
    in hypertext, 209–210
    of knowledge, 1, 27, 242
    of texts, 3, 12–13, 27, 28
    of worlds, 17, 27, 103
Transmission metaphor, 4–5, 102
Tribe, community as 21, 22

Unsaid, the, 131–133

Verum-factum principle, 6–7
Vichian theory, 6–7, 8, 9, 20, 134
Vygotskian theory, 18–19, 89, 92, 238

"War of the Ghosts, The," 34, 36, 38–42,
    45–46, 47, 66–67, 68, 85
ways of knowing, seeing, understanding, 3,
    5, 7, 8, 9, 10, 17, 20, 22, 48–49, 56,
    64–65, 84, 93, 124, 127, 217, 220,
    238–239

Worldmaking, 4, 11, 17–18, 22, 25, 235,
    238; *see also* Transformation
Writerly text, 105
Writing, *see* Arguing, Composing process,
    Critiquing, Discourse synthesis,
    Proposing, Reporting, Summarizing
Würzburg research, 44, 51

Zeitgeist of reading research, 29, 56